PHIL K

THE WHOLLY VIABLE

AN AUTOBLOGRAPHY

HEROES BOOKS

I would like thank Coleen Berkeley for her transformative work
and chiselling the first huge draft into a workable text.
And thanks too to Nick and Bob,
the finest pair of birthing partners.

First published
in 2013 by

HEROES BOOKS
www.heroesof.com
in association with

Desert Hearts
www.deserthearts.com

© Phil Kay 2013

Typeset and designed by Desert♥Hearts

Printed and bound by
Ashford, Gosport, UK

British Library Cataloguing in Publication Data
A catalogue record for this book is available from the British Library

ISBN 9781908755094 PBK
ISBN 9781908755100 HBK

The Wholly Viable Titles Series

~ Quantity Street ~

Giggle Earth

Fullfilled

THE IDYSSEY

Verbal Dairy

~ Feral Will ~

Faithbook

Sorry I'm late...the orphanage was on fire...

Notworking

Fish n Chip n Pin

"...More Speed Vicar...?..."

Not to Sixty

MERRIMENTAL

KEEPCLEAR

B R E A D S T I C K S are C R U S T S

This book's got a Great Cover

Phil Kay : Incomparable legend of Mirth.

The Atacama Desert: Its Climate, Geology and Peoples.

Phil Kay In Tweed

Phil Kay : Nae Dogs In Boots.

Phil Kay : Wallowing in a Bath of Self Pity.

Napalm 'Jamas

No Pun Intended

Me, Me, Me

BoHo HA HA

The Hymen Manoevre

TICKLEBUTTONS

Phil Kay A Novel Comic

High quality homophonics

Phil Kay A Graphic, Novel, Comic

Notwerking*

The Very First Chapter One

. . . allowing for the best, that's basically it. The handy guiding guide: work out what's best and do the stuff that can allow that . . . get there in time and do well by summoning up what you need. Yesterday it was a v.late arrival cycling at the train and sweeping in to swoop and grab an all-zones travelcard from the see-through plastic-bag bin without even having to get off the bike. Cheers terra-bombers,the laugh's on you because it is far easier to see a nineteen pound note in the bin since them security measures. And hands up who was just cycling back from the shops at the beginning of night in the rain with an umbrella up, a bit wobbly on the pavement and singing and got overtaken by a Volvo that slowed down to gawp and it may well have been your old 740 that was bought for seven hundred and forty . . . just me . . . Anyway, I have just now cleaned this typing keyboard upside-down with fire from a lighter and some keys are stiffer now because the hairy lint funk-and-fuzz particles fused under the heat into a clammy sticky skin of dust-toffee – and all this just moments after shaking the vomit off a bedsheet. 'Twas with an ill-advised whip at the wrong angle and, in a shot, it all flew past my face, drawing that familiar image of entering hyperspace in the films amid an asteroid storm of hurled chunks, in a flat parabola of the perfect starburst . . .

Swings and roundabouts, fortunate and unfortunate, rough with the smooth and even the smooth is rough compared to smoother smooths.

Hopefully this here book will skip up the Kindle like a good gig. And it will not all be frenetic frantic and frenzied.

Start all fractious and gather, then move into real recent things, then link into longer herded stories from the past, then build to a freedom to totally reveal what you most believe as examples, is the aim. Like a rather long gig. Rather like a long gig.

Writing now, write now, I do, with the crispy keyboard of a brand-new second-hand gifted old iMac with a friend's old iTunes store. Heavens below, that is the best thing in the world . . . when it finally works because as a gift all the things that are there are a surprise. The vast music storing machines have never worked for me because the feeling when you get the song on is nullified by the easy access and plethora and the knowledge on it.

The bottom button on the tweed jacket at the moment is a beer bottle top.

They always ask if the glass is half full or half empty . . . it's neither . . . is it not amazing that we can even make glass and distil fluids that affect our vegetable-consciousness in an exciting way? . . . the glass is packed . . .

Just now I got my wee son to jump into his jumper . . . And there are seven bikes in our yard that work and a foldee with rear-wheel issues.

Right, this first chapter had better start immediately, right now, without any further ado . . .

One lastish gig I did was in Chelmsford with a genuinely exciting two hundred and fifty-strong provincial crowd on a Thursday night. With a wide stage and a new town the world's my oyster and the gig has the chance of being the best ever. There are other acts, we muck about in the green room. I drink some strong malt beer from a terrific Mauritian shop round the corner.

Everyone is referencing the Olympics and Westfields and the new 24hr walk-in Aspers Casino that the train goes by on the way here and yet co-in-ci-den-tal-ly I am the only one that actually went there today in my spare hour for research and the crowd are thrilled by my Prada vs John Lewis routine and we sing "where do the skinny wee trees in Westfields come from?" And what of the fartoobig bark chippings surrounding them . . . a threat or just something to aspire to . . . ? A cruel accidental wooden irony. Treeing up the wrong bark . . . In the Casino there was a man playing poker getting his head massaged by a really small wife . . . and then in the fourth floor sports store Olympic merchandise shop with the free view over the whole Olympic . . . the wholympic . . . wholly limping site there the two older, fierce, harsh looking butch women coaches in viable Kazakhstani gym team tracksuits with official accreditation laminates round their necks, and me who's felt the arse on a man-size mascot, me who's woven all these things into the act tonight. It's a loose knit though.

All through I keep calling it "Chelmsfield".

Ah Comedy! Among those who were tickled and laughing there were those who didn't get it, who had the furrowed brow, who are sure it's

"Chelmsford" and think at the very least you ought be able to hold all the words and the getting here and the years of it and hold the name of the town at the same time, and they look daft and can be seen from up onstage . . . and then there are those in the crowd who are laughing at such a silly bad joke and yet get that somewhere there will be someone who's not in on it, who'll keep the eyebrows touching. And you can twist the clown crank. Wheat from the chaff . . . wit from the chav . . .

The intention is to clown with comedy itself and those that get it get that it is a silly double and minus-times-a-minus-is-a-plus. It has to be daft that it is even happening ... , ; ... ... ==-

In the end the greatest revenge is compassion and the greatest joke to play on Comedy is the facts; to just end up telling the truth and amusement and love as laughter can be there.

Quite often I do gigs that simply do not fire, do not take off and just look similar in contents to a good gig or end in near-psychotic meltdown and violence between me and the crowd. When these sad gigs happen there is no worry from me to me, no punitive slaps on my own leg. No, it just feels like a sprinter who has pulled up after sixty metres with a sprung hamstring – people don't boo him for being an absolutely shite sprinter: "Look he's rubbish! He Is Just Not Fast. He's walking in, it's going to take him thirty-five or forty seconds. This guy is the worse sprinter I have EVER SEEN!"

Honestly I have been to all my gigs, have done tons that are like this and so there are thousands of people who absolutely don't get it and think what I do is worthless and me shouty, rude, direct, foul, abusive, bigoted, arrogant. And yesterday's travelcard was in a bin, laden . . . and going for the awful word play joke could be brilliant at another stage.

There were some people at the Edinburgh Festival once who told me they came to see me one year and it was good so they brought their friends next year and the show sucked. They said: "Gosh, that's crazy; let's go again!" So they did and it sucked again. Next year they persuaded them to try one more time and hey presto, yahoo, it was a stunner and they all exhaled and said, "Aaaaah, we get it now . . ." Adored,abhorred,restored. Usually there would be a gap between the comma and the words, not there though.

In essence, for me it is about what way you are good when you are good, what are you up to, what is achieved and what happens when it is going as well as it can. What laughter are you after?

*

This electric typing is mostly concerned with things that happen out at gigs, after them, on the way to them and the days leading up to them or the days afollowing. Yes, a-following, as in a-roving. What started as a typing error becomes a doctrine.

So it's a bit fractious this writing. Yet it often is at the beginning of a gig. Rushing in, spilling over, trying too hard, too many speedy words trying to be too much and so keen.

This first chapter is just diary-moments from the last year of my life with the aim of setting the setting and contextualizing context, the feel and the mood of me, in emotive form and example.

Here's the kind of things that happen around me yet are also what I get up to and get involved with. They make me and are a result of me. Chicken and egg.

And so, each thing, just being in the mix of mixtures that will make up the whole. Like tweed: all different colours that cause an overall hue to the coat. Up close they're all unique strands of naturally colourful material woven together, slightly twisted for strength, resilience and an extra warmth.

And after you will know how I feel.

If I was a country this next bit'd be a tourist map: a City Guide foldee-outee mini-concertinaed map with Key Sites To Visit . . . The rest of the book can serve more as the Ordnance Survey.

My kids' names are Coco Blue, Felix Jay Django, Lion Hazelton and Delilah Butterfly . . . and Alizah Josephine . . .

My network is T-Mobile, well EE, the worst pay-as-you-go deal of all times: a fiver at a time and it costs to get my messages and they keep giving me web and walk that is not possible to use on my oldskool nokia, my dim phone and yet, and yet, all this shit and calls interrupted by "One Minute Remaining", all this and for what, why . . . well there is never a bill . . . no regular allotment of money away.

Simple as that. Never a worry, never a small build-up to a hundred and this or that, no need to have money in the direct debit's hoover-path at a certain time, no!

My pin number is 6789. Yes – try forgetting that after being away on holiday. Once I wrote my pin up high in chalk above my local hole-in-the-wall auto-cash where all could look at it and see it, and totally read it and be helped by it and yet no one needs to know. Like that time I came back to my camper-van housing and it had been stolen and I just calmly kept walking cos nobody can tell I've just lost my home . . .

Parsimonious is a word that has never been typed by me before.

I have written thirty tunes that can meld together for dancing over a two-hour music gig with a Simon on the accordion and an Erika on voice or with a flautist, organist and three percussionists.

I once built a bender structure from hazel and willow, thatched with marsh reed and simple long grass and put a tent up inside it and lived in it on a piece of land beyond the fence of the Buddhists' mansion on a bit of croft-type land that got tidally-wetted a couple of times a year so, though dry and twenty feet back from the brim of the beach and the driftwood baseline, it was in-between and technically Crown Property yet unfrequented by its position; so handy and secluded, off a beaten track, sheltered, remote, outlying, in a state of being sequestered from the state of sequestration by the State . . . A nook: The Croft, a Refugio bothy.

You will not find me mostly a fan of capitals or High Upper Class Casing. You will find me a friend to spelling mistakes that may not always be and the long oral-grammared sentence.

My best friends are Gil, Des, David, Cammy, Doug, Ros, Frankie, Nicola, Stuart, Rose, Dean, LesKirsty, the Clancy, Lucy, Zac, Will, Vixy, Em, Jim, Jim, Lucy, Lorenz, Claude Insect, Douglas Gordon, just kidding, PhilN Geoff, Merlin, Griffin, Amber, . . . and Simon and Ben and Erika and Jasmine . . . and Loulee and Lola and Reggie and Marcel . . . Estuart . . . Chris, Jonny, . . .

Best kid friends are Lilly, Katey, Gloria, Berty, Ruby, Rouridh . . . Leya, Abe, Hebee, Finn, Sorrel, . . .

I make a massive six-cup espresso every morning after there has been at least half a litre of old tea or waters put in me first.

In one of my recent splatter, dabble and splash paintings I used mostly gloss paints gathered from people who lived of our street; from under their stairs in a cupboard all badly stacked and half forgotten.

There was too: coffee, tissue, wool, seeds, petals, stamens, earth, broken teabags, thread, gold lace, eggshell, bodily fluids and sap.

Usually you will see me in Birkenstock sandals from May to October 31st. Often people are amazed and ask are my feet not cold and I remind them of the old Chinese grannies in plastic court-wedges, in skirts, carrying shopping.

By far my favourite author is David Foster Wallace for the details, the details, the details.

Mostly when I smoke marijuana it is from a wee potato pipe with the least amount that works and let the high run its course.

Words that hold two very-different meanings interest me because, really, words are like an intersection of meanings and connotations, a crossroads: "refrain" means to hold back from doing and it also means to repeat a doing.

"Mind" can mean the thing that thinks, or the thought thought, or the concern or neutral memory. "Apocrypha" is the name for the older 14 books of the Bible that were an appendix to the Old Testament and were then removed from the Hebrew canon, while and so "apocryphal" means of questionable authenticity. Well, all is worth questioning and that which has its authenticity questioned is then either validated or authenticized. It may not mean untrue, just doubted as to it being what it says it is. Or maybe it is not saying it is what you are saying it is. *Id est*: it is all self-validated and devised and human choice.

Homonym is the name for words that are spelt the same and mean different things. Like "mean". Mean means different things, hence mean's meanings are a kind of mean, mean meaning.

Once I had my Dad describe his signature over the phone so I could fairly well imitate it on a bogus form for car insurance.

The only magazine for me is Sight & Sound and it gets read cover to cover each month, folded in half up the vertical axis it fits snugly in the tweed's inside pocket and the cover, the lovely cover the new fresh excellent brand-new cover that is so good becomes more and more known and used to and worn down and changes. Not worse. This is mostly because I would not separate out an end to the new period and build my own gallows. Get up each morning for a week and construct an organic friendly fur tree gallows and then slip into a noose for a laugh in the dewy woodsmorn and die by mistake . . . no, no I see it an other way.

*

Usually it is the same clothes on me for about five days then there may occur some rotation and a tee-shirt may stay on.

So hello Dear e-Reader and regular original page-turners . . . I am talking directly to you now how you doing where you from what the most likely way you'd re-tile your bathroom if money were no object?

I prefer the fertile ground for their answer in a way it cannot fail. I'd rather not ask a boring question and then make a daft joke about that. I do it, yet when I'm doing it it is rare an an error and, fuck it, uncondoned. When it's a funny question then even the worst no-fun answer is okay because there is already a different trajectory. One of my favourite words trajectory . . . old lady crossing the five-lane roundabout in Guangzhou and all the cars accounting for it and being led by her steady trajectory.

So yes I am talking to you directly now and this initial chapter's main aim is to focus interest and slip in a few nuggets while making more.

Bite-size canapes.

I'm so happy to be writing this book that I just did a wee run and one of those leaps where as you jump you lean a bit to one side and crick your heels together.

What else . . .?

If I can try and get a nod from very elderly Ethiopian ladies, or Iranians, or Guyanans on the tubular train or ones that run overground.

I have sent only one erotic text to the landline of my dentist in Nairn. The one above the baker and I used to enjoy having a doughnut in the waiting room and heading in there to the man with sugar in my beard.

Last winter me, Coco and Felix ended up stranded for two whole days and no nights in Gatwick waiting to see if our plane could land in Inverness where the engine thawing machine had frozen and we befriended a waitress from Madeira and used the Frankie & Johnnie's restaurant's kids' area's DVD-player to watch films we bought and then exchanged for new ones with the receipt at HMV, waiting for the staff to change to do it again.

Top of the list of Best Ever Things That I Have Seen While Looking-Out-The-Window-And-Not-Looking-At-The-Money-They-Were-Counting-Out-In-Front-Of-Me-In-The-Bank is definitely:

An older lady with the special enormous Club Footwear boot-shoes for balance; and two folks passing on bikes both seeing at the last minute it was someone they knew and doing a delayed hello in perfect imperfect tandem harmony.

Recently I used my Dad's over-65 bus pass in Edinburgh with my collar up, though it was new to me and I didn't realize you have to place the card on the reader like Oyster so I just held it up for them to look at and was called back and then panicked and got off saying it was the wrong bus. This happened again and it was hard to act as me Dad. Acting and me are not good bedfellows. Plus, my collar is always up on the tweed jacket.

Last week my friend Rose gave me a Feb 29th travelcard and we made a pact to laminate it, keep it safe and use it again in four years' time – time scam like the tailor who sewed the nine of hearts into a jacket and was able to pull off a great trick when he coincidentally was at a party with that jacket thirteen years later.

Imagine if things are going awful around you: all these troubles and hassles and the common link is you and, clearly, it's your fine arrangement. Well, so too if there's groovy fun, fascinating dopey imaginative creativity with laughs: It's your thing; man-karma – karmha man, parmaham karma man . . . Hmm it's Parma ham and mango kurma Ma'am . . . And we'll stop there, for some verbal ways that are funny onstage don't sit well upon the page.

Ink sits there and remains: solid, chosen, interpretable, scrutable over time.

Stand-up evaporates and is gone like music and gravy and hate and smoke.

More held at the time, less held in time and showing.

Melina and I have just come back from Pembury health spa hospital . . . sick, no having a baby, and we brought back a whole bunch of their grey stackable cardboard bed potties and lots of blue slightly pre-powdered latex health gloves from a dispenser in our delivery suite. Powder blue gloves and grey hats: it's cabaret outfits so me and the kids who are bigger all wear them and do a bit of song and dance.

Now if you have babies you'll find out that a "show" is an event whereby a bit of deep red blood might appear in the panties of a pregnant lady and it's usually a bad sign, some sign of inner trouble, though not always.

So when they say to you as a couple "and have you had a show . . . ?" of course Melina answers, and it is my business.

So birth is a show-business and there's no business like birth. Me and the kids dance and sing there's no business like show business . . ." Pun intended.

Turns out I closed some speech apostrophes that I had never opened. Keep your eyes peeled also for brackets that are opened and never close . . . hyphens without reason and the odd semi-colon-that!oughtn't to be there. Emoti:con . . .

There will not be too much trivial word play, homophonics, synonymity . . . rather trying to keep it serious word ploy.

My keyboard for typing this up is getting loose and greasy now, lubed up through use and maybe even the remelting of the matter after the hard and fast tough toffee type typing . . . the nutterscotch letter block, . . . the so set butterscotch type caste . . . type set to tight nutcluster knuckle duster . . . at least your keys are looser, Alicia keys . . . cast this keyboard in toffee . . .

The keys are easier now, greasier now, way later after the fourth edit so due to of all the hand-eaten snacks and fingerfeeds: There has been bacon sandwich with beetroot and tomato, with access to a jar of Vitam-R – the Bentley of yeast extracts – and a spoon. And there was a bit of date syrup at the last bit of the bacon's cooking . . . there's been cashews galore, baked seeds, spelt crust in humous, salvaged tomatoes from dave in the woods . . . coffee cider . . . cold beans crunchynut and pancakes, pancakes.

It is hard to avoid competitive sprain wrist-issues when using a mouse with a keyboard on the table in a caravan at the edge of the garden, so one method that works for me is to have the opened-out cardboard shape from a mid-size box and have your mouse on that and have the cardboard hanging over the edge of the table so you can really bounce a bit on primitive padded suspension there. Plus you are free to scribble with pens or scribe notes with any pointed thing in all shapes and sizes and angles on this cardboard as a bonus and do something which is enormously important a feature in my life: writing down these ideas on a big bit of paper keeps them visible and in the realm and cover of the eye's periphery vision gaze . . . the one like the horse seeing an awful good amount of the rough uneven terrain over which he's running. And the fact that they are always around to be seen I feel lets the back brain contemplate them more without obvious requirements in the present. The same thing goes for photographs, everyone does it with family photos and walks down the hall with that holiday and those kids on a beach and all.

Me, well it's done by having a sort of top twenty photos of things I'm into and at the moment it's scavenging the likes of 'UlTravel', the tri-ultimate monthly holiday uber-duber outsized supplement from the Saturday Financial Times, for e.g. and ripping out a picture of people picking tea or a boatplane . . .

Bikes: I have mastered . . . Running, longboards, badminton, ping-pong, rock jumping and river-pool leaping. All completely mastered, totally, fully and by that I mean utterly loved, hurled at as receivers; all pits for my verve, full open fields to receive the crowd of various enthusiasms and the parking of their vans and pitching of their tents. I have only mastered my positivity for things.

Have you tried the thesaurus game where you have to get from one word to its opposite in as few moves as poss . . . ?

Master; accomplish:able: competent: adequate: satisfactory; alright; okay, slack . . . incompetent . . .

Refrain; repeat; reisist.

My Achilles heel is the ankles. So many times twisted and never broke and it's weak now, the left, weaker than the right.

So not so the skiing or shortboard skating, or the high-speed delivery of myself via the gravity pull on one on ices. Rather on a beach with six people in a shape throwing a tennis ball low between us all padded and un-spikey and no major joints at risk. Longboarding, or cycling . . . badmington and trampoline.

Don't want to be a molecule that way, like folks who jump out of a plane, surfing the skies with a board attached to their feet, then parachute onto a snowy off-piste mountainside, then surf the mountain and then fly a jump into a river to shoot the rapids heading underground for Black-Water Rafting.

Black-Water Rafting? I'll tell you: it's like white-water rafting – foaming, heaving herds of stampeding bucking albino bulls – except in a dark cave underground. And there are men in the land of a very new zeal who are actually good guides at this. Meaning you can start this, do a bit, progress, and then start to get experienced at rapids in the dark.

Of course, it's like learning the recorder: a thing you can improve through practice.

In an old jotter in a box is a list I wrote four years ago of the things that Melina and I share, apart her nutty brown beautiful mane of hair that is like as sexy and important as an extra limb.

A love of baking, badminton, hot-tub, wood-burning stoves, whisky, wood, lemons, those photos, camping, Lady Gray, Steiner, picnics, ground almonds and hazelnuts in the spelt pancake mix, 2-CVs, sandalwear, Bill's Café, John Martyn, whisky, late-night adult snacks, you in jeans, Gwendolyn the bodice.

Once I went fluffy-white-cloud rapid jet-boating on the river rapids rapidly off of Montreal with Bill Bailey and his Kris and me false teeth fell loose and I had to bite them to keep them in place as both my hands were busy. Me Mum's dog Jake recently chewed her false teeth. Thats a nice sight, a dog with a mouthful of extra big teeth. All Kris's fags were sodden in the packet in a way only wet fags can be.

These recent paragraphs are like photographs all over the place, and all over the place touching on as many fresh things as possible, for a great way to shop is just to go in and buy all the loveliest things that grab your fancy, go home and you will find a way to eat them well.

Sometimes I will repeat myself and the only thing I can say is . . . (a) oops, and (b) well you've dipped in, read it through and gone back to it so many times . . . are you sure?

It was not wholly viable for me to aim to be completely sure that it is cured of all error and repetition: it's just not a thing that could be, so there's no waste of energy on it. Plus there's definitely a very loose approach to the grammar. Please forgive me in advance. New words made of two old ones joined together, lots of dot dot dots to connect things in the breath of reading. Gaps, inconsistency in spelling and casing. All a great underside to the rug, where the women weavers send their messages. And if this is a price paid for the way I am, then with it there was bought a willingness to proliferate in this text.

I'm drinking tea from a bowl, like most of the planet, to write . . . Oh, and I have just thought: You know when you turn a tea cup around and the bubbles stay in the same place? Well that could be a form of early compass when they have to stay immovable and fixed, floating in the near frictionless environment of tea. Wow did I just invent that?

"Eurethra! Eurethra!" shouted Archimedes when he pissed in the bath.

You can't have too many of them gags though . . . it wouldn't work for me as a reader, it would pull the rug after pulling the leg to pull the wool. It would turn the reality sour, or sour the reality to turn.

At the moment, sewing for me involves a truffle and a lighter. So many little sewings mean I am picking up the needle all the time and putting it down and my man's fingers don't like that and find it very hard to do to pick up a needle from a flat surface so I have just moved a chocolate truffle close enough to pop the needle in and the lighter is so speed up the process: as swift as a scissor or a hand, yet it seals the thread, helping its cauterized end poke through the eye much more easily on a first approach every time. See there's method in me hand-sewn man-ness . . . manners in my meth-ness.

My top Dragons' Den innovation inventions: the AquAlarm – every year over seven hundred thousand litres of of bath water overflows from unattended baths being run by mums who have to use this time to be in other rooms. Now affix AquAlarm to the side of the bath and it will play a programmable tune out loud when the limit is reached. It's great for the environment and single mums with their hands full and people with short memory spans . . . It could also be bought in huge numbers by Councils and supplied to Hospitals, care homes and boarding schools . . . AnyWhere They Use Precious Water.

Or:

TrampoLize: Accessories for Trampolines: Everyone has got a Trampoline. Now you can add bits onto them like Slides and Platforms and Steps Up for kids . . .

The other day I was wicketkeeping over fire. The thin backyard game with Merlin, me and Geoff was pretty cramped and, in fact, we had to bowl through the frame of the swing.

One of the best twenty things about having kids is the kids of your friends and mucking around with them:

The other day at the dump me and the kids just smiled at a guy and he came over and gave us a huge inflatable "2" that he was going to re-cycle; he was floating around unsure which skip to put it in: probably in the inert gases/polyurethane/ribbon skip.

The fabulous reality of writing is that you can choose what to write. You can only choose what to write – so, with that, the fabulous reality is that things keep happening as the book gets written and I want them in.

What would you do, if you were writing instead of reading?

Dear Scroller, I married him.

This reminds me of a time I was thrown out of a nightclub in the best possible way:

Out in a real student-type disco, the C Venue of Chambers Street fame, with two friends, the marvellous Miss Vixy and (the same height as her) Steve, lead singer in Jim Rose's horror-circus-sideshow showband. In there we danced and bought Jack Daniels and Cokes and we all danced till I came back with the third round and they were off kissing on a wide step.

Now a great place to be is suddenly lone and free in a nightclub with three drinks. Downing them and getting in the dance floor is a priority. No one knows you are on your own and you can even wave across the dance floor at anyone you feel could be there. In the middle of it all I found a broom by the edge of the bar and started making moves and dance shapes with the broom getting laughs never heard above the music. Then it seems a natural progression to balance it on my chin and in doing so it is an extra bonus to discover that the distance from my chin to the roof is the same as the length of the broom so I just kind of wedge it up there and look like I am very able and doing a hugely good dancing-balance thing. This is probably when the bouncers first saw me.

They are by my side saying, "What are you up to?"

Now I don't want to be letting down the broom or letting down the folks around who love a sight like this. So I says, "Der. I am doing exactly what it looks like I am doing, which is why you are here." And all this with the broom still on the chin which makes it a Herculean task to do a decent "der" and push the tongue down into the spare soft bit below the lower lip to do the sound.

Down it comes and I'm off, a norm again, just a dance on my own, still with the whole club as a near friend.

Then I see Colm, a lad from a Hebridean island, who is six feet four and so for a laugh I say, "Hey, get on my shoulders!" and he says, "No. Why don't you get on mine?" and he scoops me up and there I am rising up and, I swear to God, accompanied by the Rocky Theme – Risin' Up . . . The Eye Of The Tiger. The whole place goes nuts.

"Look, it's the broom guy. He's great!"

What would you do? ±Would anyone do?? . . . there's no options . . . You'd do comedy Rocky Balboa punching-the-air type stuff wouldn't you? Then, as Colm gets to his full height and a few steps forward, there it is: the mirror-ball for the whole disco and it had to be done – what would you do? – I'm ducking and weaving and punching the mirror-ball.

It's like the Poseidon in there now: the level spirit-level reliable turning orbit of the lights is upset; the ship is wobbling; the disco's listing and the whole room starts to make a new concerned noise. This is probably when the bouncers caught sight of me again:

"Heavens above. I wonder who that can be . . . ? Let us go and have a look, Davey."

I felt a tap on my leg and one of them said, "I think it's time you left now."

"Yep."

It was the loveliest way to be thrown out ever.

. . . Risin' up . . .

Never judge an ebook by a tiny picture of the cover.

To interview someone to find out about them: For me now it would be to ask them what they do these days: breakfast stylings, rituals at the kettle; dressing tempo; walks; routes, ways to alter; la de da . . . That would provide enough spurs on to other questions and would replace posturing and rehearsed views on things.

And the facts, the facts, they are so nutritive. They are the vitamins in text. And, luckily, the genre of Autoblography with an "l" . . . with an "l" of a looseness, "l" for leather and a hell of lithesome lissome nature . . . in fact the "l" doesn't even need to be at the beginning it can be in the middle of supple, nimble, agility that suits this natural simple state. Silvery, slipway slides.

It has been a very Olympic year. We have been buying Brussels sprouts on-the-stalk and keeping the last few sprouts on the top and running around with it held up like the Olympic torch is coming through town.

Plus I have been opening the back door of the old eight-seater estate car with two hands like the clean-and-jerk weightlifter and, the other night in a gig, I threw a lady's handbag to the back of the room with a majestic triple-spin revolutionary hammer throw.

Here, right, this is the reasons for the possible titles.

– Quantity Street – Just such a good phrase to make anyone with a brain chuckle, and then be free to touch on the whole notion that it's not just quality, or in fact that's a word for when it is it is quality, and we want more. The thing about quality is you want a quantity.

Giggle Earth is so fine and strong a phrase, someone has to use it. Sloa, also, olsa, salo . . . Also it is like that the true map is your own . . . mapping is personal, your history define the place and everywhere is a chance for mirth for only the actual material can be a place, and that laughter is an understanding and experiencing that is accessing the brain self like google searches, yet it is instantaneous.

Fullfilled. For in the end that is what we can be. A fool, Phild . . . fully filled and it's just hard finding a way to say that. Joy in people says the artist . . . yes, of course . . .

THE IDYSSEY IS A LONG DRAWN OUT SET OF ADVENTURES AN ODDITY OF AN ODYSSEY.

Verbal Dairy: for that is what it is. It does what it says it does on the can and that could be anything yet it does say a thing you want it to say then say it's going to do it in a way that is well said enough for you on a tin to be happy with and purchase it.

– Feral Will – Come on, like a tops-turv Will Ferrell . . . the international guy clown who has just nailed it, just got it so that everyone loves what he does and yet want him to do it more better and always does it just not too well enough and too much and overdoes the doing not enough. So upside down it's me the unpolished and unexpected. Joy for people.

Faithbook. Not just for christians with a lisp. No, this is because I believe it is a book of beliefs as residue from action. That capitalized 'c' that used to be just above there in christians was hard to get rid of with spell check wrist slapper app in Word . . . so I had to do a small 'c' before it then erase the capital. The way round it seemed to just be sure of my fcapability with the options available on the keys.

Notworking. Doing all that can connect by not aiming to.

Fish n Chip n Pin . . . because life is a total mash-up double cla$h of senses and technology, of the breathing in and the breathing out, of the start and the bit before . . . of the ying and the booty . . . of the talk and the tease . . . of the thing we love and the ability too love. I love fish n chips, the phrase of paradise . . . the batter the fish . . . and then the chips . . . christ. And free brown cauce in Edinburgh. The chip is becoming stolen and heading to meaning more to folks attached to pin than fish . . . and . . . and . . . and the best way to mock that is to take the piss.

"...More Speed Vicar...?..."...was a catchphrase that summed up my teenage conciousness and summed up that things could be summed up, that at the time it occurred to me that I had lived long enough with a certain awareness to then have it solidify as, like, a period in my life...a n era of epoch eon.

Not to Sixty. For that is the title of another book written after driving across america, america . . . which will come out free with the second book that is being written. Not to sixty because the car we drove would not go to sixty.

MERRIMENTAL. I like because it was the name of the show I was devising when I got arrested for climbing inside that display bath on a pedestal outside the bath shop in my local English village . . . merriment is characterized by the 3d actual sound of laughter . . . and a formal word for thinking is mentation.

KEEPCLEAR . . . because there could have been a massive picture on the cover of me lying in the road next to a huge "keepclear" sign painted on the road . . . and there's something in it to . . . not getting anywhere, remaining there that is good . . . and it was right under our noses all the time . . . Plus every time anyone passes it they'll be alerted to remember this book . . . ah, sales . . .

B R E A D S T I C K S are C R U S T S . . . yes they are, yes they are . . . dip em in oils . . .

Great Cover . . . could not put it down. Just the archetypes to be explored. Secret cheat trick: Do judge the cover by the book. For there are all kinds of clues in the cover photos to references on the inside. Just like D. Brown's cod DaVinci and now his inferior infernal one there are secrets in the Tweed jacket . . .

Phil Kay : Incomparable legend of Mirth . . . why bother limping in your dreams . . .

The Atacama Desert: Its Climate, Geology and Peoples. My knowledge is limited, yet I have made a trip to this most remote arid area where there have been some of the most severe weather statistics since measuring things and remembering them began, so it would be the shortest and least informed book in this field. Well somebook has to be. There has to be a last person to board every plane.

Phil Kay In Tweed: Why not it's the truth . . . there I am in the tweed jacket . . . the ultimate . . . the near waterproof, breathing, serviceable garment of local, sustainable, unstainable, natural resource . . . woven from the offcuts for a unique and individual cloth . . . a naturally colourful blend of blends where the threads are twisted to give a stunning toughness and warmth.

Phil Kay : Nae Dogs In Boots . . . There's always a chance an auto biography will be named after its best or most resonant story . . . the one that kind of sums up the essence of the writer's subject or the subject of the writer's essence. Didn't seem to work here.

Phil Kay : Wallowing in a Bath of Self Pity. Lenny Bruce had to contend with court cases that sucked up his conscious time and he went onstage a lot with notes about the charges towards the end of his life. Me too: just received today, 17.06.13 a letter regarding: Section 36 Youth Justice and Criminal Evidence Act 1999 . . . there has been arranged an application for a direction prohibiting me from cross-examining the witness under an s36 of the Youth Justice and Criminal Evidence Act 1999 . . . this seems to be to set up the possibility of me not being allowed to ask questions of those whose words have put me in court. It's the bath shop thing . . . still live . . . will tweet you later, tweet you to a twully gweat supwise . . .

No Pun Intended.

Me, Me, Me or me, me memoir . . . it's the first syllable . . . and how many time does one try and avoid using "I" in this book's lines . . . yet it is about I and me, and me me me and again me. Awful, and there it is.That's why so many sentences start with a verb.

BoHo HA HA is the kind of thing a think tank might come up with a shitstorm braindance . . . a barnside brainstorm . . . a big bunch of men minds might arrive at putting on the table in a long list. Bohemian and humorous being the sub-header.

The Hymen Manoevre. The Heimlich is of course a mechanical yet surprising upward thrust just below the ribcage to expel air and shift lodged object that is causing choking. Not dissimilar to the laugh . . . gasps of air, involuntarily expelled . . . only ever on the on the out-breath, or making the out-breath occur.

WHEN THE LITTLE MAN IS GETTING HIS 'JAMAS ON I ASK HIM SHALL IT BE SIMPLE NORMAL BUTTONS OR TICKLEBUTTONS . . . AND YOU JUST DO THE SUBTLEST HARDLY ANY TICKLE AT ALL AND RESIST AND THAT'S THE LAUGH.

Phil Kay A Novel Comic . . . for everyone loves a good pun.

High Quality Homophonics: Means Good Puns; same pronunciation, yet different meaning . . . Get It! . . . Preferable is homophony: the simple harmonization of one melody by all voices, rather than all different actual parts.

Phil Kay A Graphic, Novel, Comic . . . for everyone accepts a great pun.

Notwerking* is Networthing when it's not worth it to be not networking . . .
. . . intertnetworth King . . . what're you notworth nutjob
on either nets . . . ether net for ever not . . .
nightworking . . . neither networthing or
not networking either . . . nor
neither or either or
. . . no not ever
ethernet
not . . .

A Very First Second Part

So, here we go – The Top Forty Recent Events:

Last gig I did that other night I had a stainless steel food trolley and had a recycling pedal bin on it at one point and pressed them down to fire a Scotch egg at a lady in the front row and ended up using a spare table top as a cubist surfboard and wishing for a wrong number phone call from Picasso. Why can't there be a wrong number from a famous person in my life . . . there's a joke in there somewhere: oh there it is its not that good.

The other day I hoovered up a pen and was able to get it back out again with a whip action and the hoover still on and it reminds me of the time I was in Menemsha Bay, on the island of Martha's Vineyard where they filmed Jaws, and I was waterskiing and fell in, went under, held on and came back up again. The guy on the boat said he'd never seen it before.

The other last-nite's gig was in the Constitution Club above a bingo match game and it was good. So good that the silliness of telling a room full of English people that they are a bit uptight – with examples – had a Polish lady in a red slidy very polyester sportslidy tracksuit slipping off her chair with laughter. "Why are there so many mountains in England . . . because they keep making them out of molehills . . ."

Me, the longboard, at night: My home is in the English countryside in a lovely wee town, right at the edge, within cycling distance from our school, with my love and 4.0 children. We're up at 7:09 and mostly doing porridge and fruit, or toast and sugarless jams. The other day I went longboarding down a beautiful B-road late at night. Drove to where we last lived, drove in and parked in the old driveway with my headlights down a long hill stretch of newly re-smoothed road with the new super surface, superficially rejuvenated. Dark, quiet and fast. Like I like my coffee. The longboard was with me and I had been waiting for this for ages; waiting for the three things to converge: the board, night-time and me. And I zoomed off and was among the dead cats-eyes and getting the speed-wobble and going faster than ever before. Hands up if at this moment you might consider strapping the mobile phone on torch mode to the front. Imagine the catss' eyes' eyes' glowings and a glitterings.

We're in here now.

Don't forget if the stream of water from the tap is too strong going into the kettle spout and you have up-rush gushings then you can just move the spout half out, splitting the stream, if you like.

Recently I saw Dr Brown, a no frown clown comedian. Thought he sounded good, read an inspired review of his antics, dug his poster, saw him, found out he was good, did a gig with him then went out with him and did a few impromptu drumming bits and pieces around Camden with him and Cammy; invited him to stay with us and then took him up the private Mansion House mile-long steep downhill drive and raced him down on my bike as he carved at hugely higher speeds on the longboard, sticking to the tighter thin single-track bends while I zoomed a more curvaceous big zigzag slalom route down, up the grass verges either side, following him trying to use only the grass as brakes.

Just this evening I did one of what I would consider one of my greatest achievements: I am leaving our bedroom upstairs and grabbing up a wee pile of laundry just as I go, swooping, in the movement and at the exact moment I'm making the cluster up, Lilly (9) comes out of her room to put her pants in the armful and puts them up near my face to have a look at, and I manage to refrain and restrain myself from making some "Oh no, yuck, get your pants away"-type remark . . . Had to think fast – one does for family – had to think fast and not say the obvious. Very like being onstage and the mind wants to go straight to the thing we all know could be said and would get a laugh; yet too big a part of this laugh would be us all sharing what anyone could say – gotta think fast – reminds me of the time I got caught putting the money for the Tooth Fairy Union under the pillow (had to think fast – that tale, though, is definitely one of the longer ones and not for this shorter-form beginning) – to have the thought arise as the first obvious p'tang-yang sound you hear as meaning, and then refrain was saying it was better. Because then it was truly unexpected (which I hold close to an essential). Not limited as just being just the smartest way of saying the nodded-to, the already-known in new examples – there'll plenty of time for the making fun of in the regular ways – often the first thought is the most expected and that's very comic, yet it's not always very great comedy. It can't be it, can't go that far. The best it can be is hilarious. That's all. And plus, too ultra, plus deep down it's simply just not the staple accepted truth in me that females' pants smell bad.

A while back I flicked on a light switch with a dish towel. Zip, flash. At the time it was the first time I'd ever tried it so for a while I was thinking about never trying it again and retiring with a 100 average . . . like if Bradman had got three more runs with a hard-on and no box and immediate scones in the pavilion.

Driving through London the other night and concluded my personal and unrecorded "Worst Balcony" survey. Where the overall awfulness of those small inner-city balconies that are so ignored, so abused and so mournful, is scored by still-revealing categories: Un-usability – junk collects that hints at the chance, the space this balcony affords you to be "outside" and yet, how being in a city has robbed the beauty of this, and this just manifests itself in an inverse relation to commit to leaving it, so this exhibits itself in un-gooding the outside you have. A staement of love through the bespoiling of it to match the bespoilling you feel.

Like besmirching the achievements of others to cover one's own

l   a   c   k   .

The scant poignancy of a duvet scrunched up against the glass with painful tiger print. There was one balcony that was a smallish glass-fronted wee semi-circular platform affair on the side of a toppling or slanted sharp new building: It had a bike encased by binbags, lost to the casual check, totally engulfed by stinky bags themselves. It had a crushed clothes-horse on top of another binbag, behind the arch the door would make if opened. This, and how it overlooked a Morrisons car park and a huge grand entrance made it a "Winner", with little to gain save being able to watch an entrance of a major supermarket . . . somewhere there is a research team being paid to watch traffic, monitor lorrys on an underpass,, la la . . . so you just could clear the balcony and turn staring into a PhD: What time do most youths go in . . . richer types . . . those that park far away do they shop longer so to push the fullest of trolleys all around in a parade of glory and double exhibitionist-ness. What are the patterns. Read em and tweet.

. . . place an add for middle-aged models in the foyer AdBoard and have them turn around and audition by binocular, feet up smoking an e-fag.

No tweeting has me ever done. Nor phasebook neither. Even it it is popular in an unrivalled way, facebooking is just a phase. Maybe the selling of of deets will deter some, it will be another thing that replaces it in love.

Three best places to have an e-fag: in surgery . . . in church . . . and in a yoga class. Particularly church if it's up the back and you are a few and they glow like satan's eyes glow and attract the eye of the vicar and then you can stub them out on your own face in an interesting/intimidating way and hold his gaze.

Recently I was making pancakes and had the spelt flour, ground up nuts, molasses and tahini in the bowl and an egg in the hand and I cracked it and felt the need for a well in the flour and, in a moment, I elbowed the flour and created one. Like a samurai in the kitchen. Problem? Whoosh: Solution.

A few men and me are in a music band, a man-band, a bar-jam-band and one of the songs is called "It Was Only Cos I Was Mucking About With My Friends In The Garden As They Left That I Found One Of My Kids' Anoraks Lying Out Here About To Get Wet Overnight".

Our home is a brilliant brick building with a massive garden; the organic veg shop is within a four-minute mountain-bike sprint. There are about ten or eleven spheres in the garden, two of them are regulation-useable as footballs with the boy, kicking it at or near him and going to where I can see he is going to kick it, is what happens a lot. It's pretty obvious as he aims his body to the ball, he toe-pokes it and I am coming onto it at speed calling "I'm open!" It has to be how Barcelona train: no goals and just encouraging the fun through clever movement and creation of space.

Last week I was dribbling two balls at once and carrying the wee man's spade across the garden and I caught myself with the sharp new shiny corner and got a tiny bloody nick on the inner calf.

There are several nicks on my hands from breaking sticks for the seven fires we've had in the garden in the fire-basket recently. The kid loves them and you can light one for like half an hour's fun and then let it go.

Right, the body, the house, toys, possessions:

One cut on my right index-finger came from trying to open the bonnet on the old BMW from under the passenger's foot-well with pliers gripping the wire cos the plastic handle had snapped and they slipped off, the pliers, and I grooved the same slice twice in my hand off the sheared plastic point on the bonnet release handle.

Last week cycling by a stream I spat some gob out that bounced along like in the Damnbusters. Ill enough for the phlegm, and well enough to give it a good "hoich", all the infection mucous thickness and weight works for me.

In Galway latterly for the gig there was a lovely flat one could use and go and be a loon for a while and make a mini-henge out of those wee electric radiators on wheels. Dominating the open-plan kitchen is a massive clock. A no-excuses, two minutes from the gig, massive clock. This big-handed metre and a half diameter motherfucker of a timepiece ensures you are simply not allowed to say you were not sure what time it was. When I get home later I challenge it to a boxing match by putting garage gloves on its hands at ten to three for a right cross.

You can hang on the intercom phone for a while and sing a bit of a song out to folks you hear passing, or just listen for an opportune moment to drop an end to one of their sentences . . . and there is time to go out on the balcony and shout a little revolutionary Spanish. Every revolution in some South American country at some point involves someone shouting to a cheering crowd from a balcony, So, there's no way that shouting Spanish from a balcony could safely be called un-revolutionary or "in no way connected" with revolution. That's the deal just to be still in with the chance of the best.

When you hitchhike what you need is a car to come along – stand by the road, that's where they come and you're in: every one that comes along could then be The One for you . . . Here the gig was awful, stodgy and red-wine slow, I nearly got going shortly before the end.

We got free bottles of rum, all got high afterwards and did the crossword drinking non-stop with the staff until it was five fifteen time to pop home for a fifty-minute nap.

I awake to the sound of a cleaner and the massive clocks got both fists up in a good guard, good gawd, it say five to noon so I'd missed my flight home by four hours at least, six if you count actually getting up and getting there, and it turns out my phone was lost as was my hat and no socks with my sandals. Shit! It was raining too and all that helped, as I skipped around the corner to recover my tracks, was a stylish laird-type in hyper-modern-yet-classically-cut, full-body tweed, as I watched him I aquaplaned in the slipshod flips flop across the ancient paving. Fucking Luck-a-Lily: somehow, miraculously got to find the wife of the promoter, who woke him up and got him out of his bed to run me to the airport at high speed to catch a brand new flight he had paid for and get there to find the Ryan desks closed. Our only option is to drive home slower and with even less chat and have the promoter who watched the gig fail put me up again and then buy a brand new new flight once again. Or 2: ask an older lady at an info desk in that utterly hopeless way you do, with a last beyond-last-resort-nothing-else-to-try, just-have-to, pressureless ask . . . And she asks a name and does it: She just goes over to the printer and brings me the flimsiest boarding pass there has ever been, on squeaky satin fax-paper from the last millennium.

I had a pie and a pint-set that have a chance of remaining unrivalled in this life as the good queue-ing folks boarded. It is a very interesting place to be and a subliminal aim, for me, doing stuff that absolutely heightens tastes, vision and sounds. When you go to the fridge naked, still trickling afterwards, and the things you lift out of there into your mouth or lay on toast are so much more flavour-filled and intense.

There has to be someone who is last to board every flight.

Beautifully, I got off at Gatters and had left the flimsy silk pass on the plane. So, to proceed out and through, I just used the original boarding pass I had printed at home before I left and that I still had; which may or may not be causing consternation as a kind of loophole through the system. They give you a wee barcode to make sure you are the same one came off a flight that gets out the door . . . They'll find that I am still there . . . I never came through, yet I did leave.

Recently my way-ex-partner's boyfriend and me have been recently exchanging marijuanae, plural. That's a great place to be too: to be benefiting from a thing one could easily choose to be turned away from.

Me and the boy have been racing the llamas who live up the road a bit. We whistle them and they come over all curious and bucktoothed.

Just the other day me and the boy were parked by a field to look at horses far away and I remembered the words of a Monty Roberts who said you stand side-on to them to intrigue them and remind them of clustering up with their mum and running back to her warm belly and huddling in for safety. I tried it and these two came padding over and get their noses right here to breathe on our hands.

The boy took it in his stride. Saw it all. Never didn't notice.

*

It occurred to me a while back it is possible that kids kind of think you are magic.

When they see you blowing on to hot food to cool it down they might for a while think you are actually warming it up to be nice and tasty. Plus before they can read they are not too aware of the complexity of written prose so for a while they just think you are improving and making this shit up each night. Remote controls never raise an eyebrow from a kid because they don't know they don't know.

And hitchhiking is the fairy bridge made of unicorn eyelashes that connects the worlds . . . it is the portal, my boy, very portable . . . hitchhiking regularly in Scotland small distances to and from the Town of Forres and back – it is normal, wild then normal again, you are out with kids and what you do regularly becomes the norm and so the lion tamers' kids are yawning at your pet tortoise, or not.

They see it perfectly normal to ask for another person's help with a groovy universal thumb-sign and then later they realize it's not done much. The decent integral human ability to reach out as empathy and accept aid is totes amazeballs.

And I truly think the involuntary leap I just did a while back was a throw back to being an ape-like creature who clapped his feet more often. A while back in the book, and about the same time ago in your reading time was when I did the leap and that's how it must go for writing, right now it's me doing a second edit on a bus. A jump in the air a leap in the imagination a bounceback in time and in the text and in evolutionary terms.

Thank heavens, I missed a shed recently: Lined up the red spongy gym ball for a stonking swipe from the outside of the right foot – "three-toes" they call that kick in Brazil, where, yes, they have names for kicks. The boy mostly toe-pokes yet we have worked on several other kicks: The trap-and-kick, the rear-heel, the soft-push and the modern instep-guider. The one you see in newspapers when a guy has scored with a guided bendy free-kick around a wall.

Well, this three-toes kick is different. It is the kick of my youth, which I spent playing football with a tennis ball and coming in from wet-day games with massive polka damp dots on me jumper. Playing for twenty-five minutes after lunch and picking teams and scoring twenty goals between us and, after school, we played as the cars gathered around us. This kick I set up for sheer power, hoping to catch it right and swerve it in the top, your right corner, and bang it inside the Hula Hoop that hangs on the shed and looks like a target. There are lots of kicks to do around the garden – there is an official eighteen-hole crazy golf game we set up, me and Lilly, where you kick a ball over an obstacle course rather than putting with clubs.

It's called CrazeeBall or FunBall or GolfBall or FoolBall. It can be practised very gently every time one crosses the garden, goes to the bikes, the compost, the shed, the recycling, the caravan, the trampoline, to talk to Myra over the fence, or even just mooch down the municipal paved path to Way at the end of the garden there is a fully functioning mini-sewage plant for the houses on the posh estate behind us. It too is brick and it therefore a built-like-a-brick shit out-house or, at least, it is a brick shit-house, and is therefore hosting the Olympics of symbolism in that it is built like itself.

In 'FoolBall' there's the basketball to go through the legs of the mini-small school chairs we have stuck in the ground from being thrown (another game). So many holes, loops, plant pots, the Fire-Hose – we made a list, I'll find it . . .

There are many kicks: The small semi-deflated tellytubby ball to land on the trampoline and to go up the door we use as a wide ramp up onto the tramp. There's the kick of the tennis ball into a hula hoop.

Anyhoo, I swiped it with the three toes and shot hard and missed the shed which was great because Melina was in there doing intricate jewellery work and could have conceivably got a shock and dropped a diamond. She works out there on bespoken-for hand-created wedding rings and engagement blings. MELINAJEWELLERY.COM

That time in the bay on Martha's Vineyard where my brother saw Jackie O on the water, I fell. I plunged in at high speed and kept a hold on to the thing and the boat kept going and I came back up. Went in, did a bit of ploughing, a bit of being the plough, the ploughman, a man-plough, ploughing straight in, riding the wave, grooving the wave riding the groove, grooving the groove as a needle reads the record . . . groove-rider, wake-star and rose again – Jesus zooming on the water – better than walking – the skimming Saviour, a very directional self-resurrectional.

At the moment the hoover is kept behind a sofa or in the stair cupboard fully plugged in. Then it is easier to just use to master to dominate to rule, it's another form of Heaven is a ready plugged-in hoover, ready to go, no wrestling trouble of the wires and pipe.

A three-minute hoover, which I see as a cross between boxing and fencing – what with the lunges and the accuracy and the footwork – and the sweeping and the brushing and warming and surface tension-loosening/lessening and speedily flattening to smooth the ice of curling.

There is a daftness that nevertheless helps me be cheerful in the regular activity, plus it's well known that women love the smell of a freshly-washed athletic man. I'm sure they also love the smell of recent hoovering.

Confucious say hoovering warms you three times: the effort, the hot filter fan air and the cuddle after.

So then me and the boy who is four point three now and called Lion were jogging across the garden after the pancakes and he had twin trails of snot running down from the nostrils to the mouth and flowing over it even with the licking in and going down to the chin. As we ran I took a stolen serviette out of my pocket and motioned to the boy for a noseblow and he actually offers his nose up to me. A great boy, a fabulous kid, you can still see his rosy cheeks from behind. He gets the snot removed and then I stuffed it in my top pocket and we went through the end of the garden through a hole in the hedge. There we saw the Postie pulling up for he always trots down our lane not reversing. We've seen him a hundred times coming in and leaving. This is the first time we are ready in wait, secretly hiding. And this, lo and behold, as he turns walking into our lane, this is the first day I've seen him come to have a pee into the bush we are hiding behind.

As with the pancake flour or the time I was in Paris with the taxi on my foot or the fairy money moment, as with these, one has to think and act fast. No options as he is approaching and with one hand tensing the trouser and the other fixing to pull the zip down. I gently emerge surely as a new bright thing and say,

"We're here!"

The best poetry is economy that gains. Here there seemed enough to be said, no need to explain anymore or throw a question. I mean, we all have to pee and this little tiny wooded bit just beyond our hedge is perfect.

He did a very natural swift and complete one-eighty without any break in pace. We followed back up and passed him once he'd done the letters and as he passed there was nothing from him, his embarrassment or something had rendered him emotionally un-presenting and I actually raised and eyebrow wanting some kind of "hey ho" interaction-eering or "hello" or "what?"

"It's us from the hedge," I said.

There was no answer.

And the boy? He was not expecting anything and so looked content.

That's what he's like, the boy: amoral or pre-moral, or as I prefer to say, exempt.

Hanging out with him is fabulous and I love living in a world where a tractor with a wonky wheel has every chance of beating a Ferrari in a race. Where moulded lamby is bigger than dragon and can dent the unicorn-horn in a quick battle. Where mythological beings cross-pollinate the fun with "real" one-thirtieth milkmaids, dinosaurs and knights on horseback, gorillas with a bit missing and all hang out with a wizard and a bull with anatomically correct massive balls and a plastic play-whisk and an unspecified superhero who can spin all the way round at the waist. Obviously I love his unconditional love of his daddy, and then with that do then think of good things to do on the way to everywhere. Obvs: adults come and go and are a bit moody and distant sometimers, you never made any of them, and them kids though you are going to be able to enjoy hanging out with them forever, enjoy the truth that connection to them is definitely love.

Once at the train station, we were in the big disabled change-your-baby loo and he finished a wee and I started mine and he went to open the door. My first half of reaction-impulse-kneejerk was to call out in that "No, the door must stay shut. What are you doing?"-type style – then I didn't. In that moment I realized you could birth a morality there, feed it on personal worry and phobias lite, begin the big slide that way . . . and there is a day he'll need to know and he just will know his way through it, so I just stayed quiet as he walked away and loitered with the huge door doing its large sweep to reveal hundreds of folks milling around.

One option: pretend to be blind, pee everywhere, flush poorly and walk out with a limp. Then, of course, it dawns that it is baby-change place too, it's disabled access wider door, ramp and some decent turning circle for a wheelchair serious dimensions in there. We're valid, all okay, viably vindicated and free from the vituperative looks and phrases.

An Option too: walk out proud as possible, whisper that you've saved a hundred million lives many times.

Kids say the funniest things. I knew one, he couldn't say industrial tribunal, he used to say dusty boons.

Surely I'm not the first person to fill up the empty plastic moulded presentation layer from a tin of Christmas biscuit selection with small daft items and take it round to a friends for his birthday.

It's so warm here writing in the caravan with a wee electric fan-heater, though it has this little white safety button – a bright white pygmy thing – a button so that if the heater falls over then this button is no longer pressed by the weight up off the floor of the entire universe being held, pushed supported to be there and hold it down like Newton on a camping mattress . . . up on it. Oh fuck! Now it has fallen over, it cannot WHAT? Set fire to something or what? That can be the only thing. I mean, surely it can't overheat, a heater. Can it? Have we made a heater that can overheat itself? Oops. Anyhow, when it's on a carpet for the reason that then the force up of the earth is baffled by the deep pile of the fibres and can't maintain pressure, you have to reach under and diddle it.

Is it wrong then, to make love in a disabled loo . . . ? Is it just flat-out wrong? If it is wrong even just to be in there. And if it's wrong, then it just is and you may as well use the special handles in there, the ones for to help the disabled do normal mandatory positions, may as well use them for highly athletic erotic positions, athrotic, erothlete . . .May as well use the emergency chord as a kind of teasing garrot So does it follow it's Wrong to use the emergency cord as a kind of sexy garrotte? Once you are wrong, what is your impetus to influence to cease?

You were at the airport and you were sad to leave a love and two guys in wheelchairs were on your side, for love and honour, and they stood by and egged you on and guarded the door and when you came out all the mirrors were steamed and their wheels span. Is it wrought when it feels so right? Can it be wrong?

English cars peep me a bit more than Scottish people: "You are in a car." Peep-Peep. " . . . You pay no road tax and until this delay my life was on schedule . . . ." Peep. "I want to be on a bike and all that doesn't entail . . . ." Peep . . . is what I hear.

Recently I realize that you can buy those huge circular, is it *concave* mirrors they use on bends in the countryside, you can buy these wherever you live and just have them in your life: gardens, hallways, stair-corners or just above the bath for fun.

Same too with white ribbon on your car: Get it on – don't need to be wedding soon – and people just wave and cheer and excuse you certain driving moves, and are cheery and specially sighing, or jealous and ram you, which is very rare. Can you see the smoke from the orphanage, man?

Same too with buying Scout badges: help yourself, there's no law.

Same with children's plasters, they can be used humanely on an adolescent and they will still fit.

And a travel iron, you can get one of those . . . Imagine you are buying one and they want to know where you are going and you hesitate and they refuse and want to see the booking reference and there is a scuffle over it.

Right now, 18.01.13, 15:35pm, it's still the triple backseat for me on the Nationally Expressive bus service from my obscure English village that'll take me to Nottingham, Notts, and right by me they have a teeny weeny toilet brush in the bog and it's great that they believe in us tending to our skidmarks bad enough to need attention in this small space all bustled about by the swaying. As optimistic as hitchhiking at the end of a runway.

Right now, really now 06.03.13, 15:36pm . . . I have just eaten a chocolate truffle picked up by the needle.

Same too with waving at a tower block: No one knows you are just waving at thin air and no one is technically there, that you just feel like a cheery screamed whoop of fun and used this truth; PLUS there might be a guy who can't see that you are aiming vaguely and feels a bit of the goodness of the waved wave. Good feelings are good feelings.

Like my mate's mate who was running on a running-track and thought he was a world record holder and felt a bold pride for three months until he told someone and it turns out it was only a three hundred metre track.

Ballsack lid-snag: There is little worse than sitting on a loo seat you really ought to have fixed ages ago and there is one bolt missing and it keeps sliding off to the side and you are saying to yourself "Oh heavens, I must really fix this" and it slides off to the right and snags your ballsack – ooh! – though not that bad. Worse than when I got a bit of sand in the eye from my own turn-ups doing a bit of amateur yoga . . .

Doing a bit of amateur yoga and getting a bit of sand out of my turn-ups in the eye – can't tell you which feels better of those two sentences.

Usually there is one rhythm that feels simply the best. Sometimes with comedy it is a matter of something bothering you about a joke and you just have to swap words and lose a syllable to help it come out in the single breath and before the concept gets too worked out and the laugh becomes diluted as the idea creeps out ahead of the motherload.

Each comedy delivery and sketch thing or punchline or what have you has a best or better form. So, generally, the better you mask the silliness to come the better you mask the silliness to come.

Not that bad though, the lid snag, as it must have been for that lady whose bungee snapped in newzealand on a big jump. Imagine the range of sounds she must have made.

Before you jump there can be noise of low worried warbly moanings and then the scream of the initial leap and can you figure the woo-hoo she would make, the shape and sound of it as she drops sixty metres, and then it's a wailing of wonder in this expectation of going wildly, as badly, back up again suddenly, and then feeling that not happen yet not really be sure as it is the first time a giant bungee has snapped on you, and your noise now changes to a genuine terror-scream, as much as you are able to summon up from the plummeting diaphragm muscles weak in amniotic zero-G in the belly.

I imagine the sound something a bit like Tarzan being slowly sucked into a jet engine while doing his yell. This sound may not immediately have registered as that different to the experienced guys up top.

She is screaming, as the fall is not truly horror-filled, and then it snaps and it is horror-filled and then the scream is interrupted – the fall broken by a plunge into a shocking cold fast river.

The briefest possible respite from relief that it was water, the friend, then the cold, the physical breathlessness, and the last noise held and released with the last of the breath. And now the noise of that final human outpouring under the water; no more mystery, just the rushing unperturbed cold noisy rush-wash of the river's truth – that it is inanimate and does not care and is always there at night, unseen, like a tree permanently falling, making a massive crashing sound in a forest. And that noise under there, if there was one, might be the privatest thing of all times. And all in this moment the fact that this river might never have been felt. They say one can never step in the same river twice. Well, you are certainly most likely never going to get dunked by fate into the same river twice or fall from a bungee into the same named entity, snaking across the flood plain, delta, a-meandering. Imagine if one of those molecules was one that you had already encountered as rain or mist or from a sneeze on an aeroplane.

Then the final conscious mental agony of this fall, as the crocodiles are seen to approach – yes, the river is populated by crocs – the unconscious acceptance that you are lucky to be alive to die, or at least it is a cat's chance, second death-cheating coming-uppance . . . It's too much to be taken in, fighting for breath to spare for a sigh in this torrent, until a laugh comes as the speed of the river has saved you, taking you away faster than crocs like, yet, even by now the sure saving of your own life realized is, here now not enough wind left to make any more sound.

And then the ultimate last snag as the long trailing bungee cord gets snagged between two boulders, holds you back with some underwater elasticity pulling at you harshly in the current, forcing you under as the crocs reassess. It is the time to undo carabiners for the first time, underwater, against the clock, as excellently as possible.

Worst thing for me, nothing like the bungee in September, was driving to a gig with five hundred millilitres of farm-strength cider in a label-less bottle and getting tipsy and being lost, and then late, and then desperate for a pee and short of time, getting late for the gig, pissing in the bottle and then still being behind time later and having to hold the bottle between the legs and then getting nearer the venue then, at last, coming round the corner and being met by the staff and then taking a drink from the bottle just as I realized and calling out, "It's okay, it's piss."

Better, though, than overtaking the Police by mistake on the inside lane while texting with a seatbelt shut out of the car clanging around banging on the road and undercarriage.

Hot Chip on the iMac playlist. Who are they and which family member liked them? It's great having the wide range of an entire family's music choice.

Hang on, me and the eldest daughter Coco saw them on the third of our three-in-a-row Glastonburys and they were a total blast as we shared that most excellent of all square pies in the feetdeep mudslush with a pint of pear cider.

Once again e-Reader and leaf-turner this is still the fuzzy eclectic eccentric electric shambolic beginning enrapture chapter and exempt from regular criteria demands. It's the first misplaced pieces of pots and coins that are found when a large archaeological site is being discovered; an encouraging pointer to greater tectonic seams lying lower down.

On that wasteland in Glasgow where I parked up and lived once for a few months was the Jag that once I had to sleep in because I came back to my van and there was the very loud sound of the pissed-snore and it felt close – aah! like inside the van – I jumped out and there he was, sleeping underneath the axle, on the ground. It was too hard to be so bunked, double style, so I took the Jag that night. Once, in the van, some ludicrously, feasibly drunk, students tried to tip me over and, as I was banging on the window from inside saying "excuse me!", they failed to see. I had to slide open the sidedoor leaving me a Buster Keaton-space in case it fell and, still in my sleeping-bag, request their restraint in this matter from now on. They actually shouted out, "Watch out, there's a bearded old hippy there . . ."

On a lighter note: Recently I fired some swimming goggles, lying on me back, using only the toes and feet, making use of the thing that was lying around within my reach, the on-back Da Vinci limb-sweep method with three-quarter arc to feel what's there – Dad Men not Mad Men. This makes Lenny's model of Man's abilities-tied-to-this-physical-dimension allegory of full-body physiognomy a tad naked now to me. Without something to come of it, without a reason, without crisps or a screwdriver. And Da Vinci's guy gets nothing: no goblet of wine, or flax; nothing to reach for, so the move is unreal, so no man would ever actually be those dimensions unless he was doing a pose. And where's the truth in that?

Well there is yoga . . . And modelling for art. Yoga like the stretch-of-a-cat or the leg-of-a-crane at dawn . . . oh and standing naked in a small caravan reaching for the thesaurus on the top shelf, then the maple from over by the sink . . .

Damn! What's the First Rule of rhetorical questions? Check you don't catch yourself out and can't answer. And plus too, as well do rhetorical questions have a question mark? No, because they are spoken.

For the body, the circumference, fuck, the aura, for it is like ice on Mars. And love the sweep, the full extent, the personal jurisdiction – be a reacher, not a preacher – come on DJs and bend the other way – it's not enough to stop the buck with art. It does not matter that there may have been ice on Mars.

There was a thing handy to play with the three-year-old boy while I was on my back. On back, like Ong Bac, inventive, physical, dexterous, improvisatory. Well, except mine is actual and un-worked out so I beat the Ong Bak guy.

The goggles flew. They were born to fly.

Plus I have got a little better at fixing the goggles over the years, though these were the new ones. Not the old style that were harder to make smaller and it was always a guess of a kid's head and you had to pull very-ribbed stretchy-tipped ends though, one way then the other, the tight little gate-gap right by the eye-bit and they were fiddly and yet always could go wrong. Have I gone through one? Ripped one? Not them. These were the new kind with the fully-bonded and formed-as-one-up-front-by-the-eye-bit and have all the adjustments and fixing done from a trimmed-down simpler-action to the rear of the head with a quadruple carabiner affair allowing tightening in the desired way, out and back from the back of the head by arms already tuned for power.

Fixed the car with leather and foil last month wrapped around the exhaust to keep the pressure on the pipe flowing, it was like fixing a massive recorder which had an extra hole that needed to be blocked off. It was whistling and fluting terribly . . . Once I fixed an old Volvo with wool by re-tying on the radiator with the colourful strands weaved round and round. It felt part Morgan there, which has an ash chassis, or the old Morris Woody Tourer. It may well be a move in the future toward natural materials.

Did a little bit of hedge-trimming on the trampoline. It was right by the hedge and nothing was too drastic; yet it is a truth, it is something I have done. The scandal is a scandal because it is known. If someone had seen me they might think I was a bit loopy, yet it was just the natural thing to do as I came along the hedge trimming and standing on a plank between ladders, well it just seemed smart and fun to do a little light bouncing, nothing special and yet if someone had driven into our land yard then it would have been a discovery. As it is, I am owning it owning up, owning out this information and so obvs I am not bothered by its implications . . . its clues its indications its pointers to my psyche.

Like I do get quite a soothing foot-massage in sandals from the foot-braille by the platform's edge on many an occasion, with more to follow. Especially good in old thin soul-ated Birkenstocks.

Me and my friend Cameron Sinclair the drummer oiled Frankie-from-the-Darkness's fridge door the other morning with olive oil until, in the silence, there was no squeaking noise to wake folks, no just the wheezes from us two struggling-to-breath as we laugh at trying to be quiet at dawn that had floored us . . . the laughs becoming fiercer as they were trying to be quieter.

Like Harvey Keitel handing out the trolleys at the beginning of that film, I once oiled a lady's carboot with her own olive oil.

Anyway I didn't finish that story . . .

The other day I went to Galway and met a guy I know in the airport lounge with his two sons, whose mum had died in India in childbirth. He was handling them well and I forgot I knew him even after watching him for a while. He looks like me: shortish hair, beard and woollen jacket. We get on well and try to pre-board before the others as a gay family group. They're not into it and so I wave him on, giving one of the boys a kazoo, and he gets to make the whole lounge much, much, much more fun.

We talked, had a laugh, got off the other end and walked through customs. Now I always have a little travel-spliff to smoke and never hide it, just have it in my pocket. As we come through the other side they have got us going left to right following those extendable thing corridors and then at the last moment I see why, because there is a sniffer-dog. Two things: first, I believe all dogs are sniffer-dogs, and second, that most of the folks they catch are caught because they give it away and try to hide something or move in the opposite direction. I was so cool, by mistake, didn't see it as I was still playing the kazoo, then got carried away and leaned down to pat the dog. All flushed in the heart-rush of possibly not getting to the gig (what a hassle) and we are though.

Now it kicks in and I get the wobbles and, as me and Bruce part, I am calling out across the arrivals area, "They need to get a new dog. That one's not very good!"

Bit like that letter I wrote complaining that the breathalyzer machine that did not find me positive me on Oct 11th 2004 was faulty because I had in fact been drinking plenty. Sadly, though, I had no proof.

The exact postcode of my latest breakdown was FK17 5LY. Now, when you break down you have to know where it is on a global satellite list of places. We hung out at the Co-op in Stepps outside Glasgow, filling time with the literature in there with a window wiper not working and the rain huge. It didn't want to stop and the AA were taking an hour and thirty, so as an absolute last resort I opened the bonnet and in eleven seconds found a set of spare fuses along the bottom of the Mercedes 230TE's wee fuse box governing all electrics and we were off. Sorry AA, nothing for you here.

This having to know the postcode is a bit of a hassle if you don't know it and yet it means that, technically, one could be telling a funny anecdote about it and than someone listening could go on Google Earth Images and go down the street and see all you mentioned. Then, if you had exaggerated, you might have no leeway for readjustment.

Through all the technical advances of home computing, the web and laser camera home-applications, the biggest thing seems to be that people can make far, far better "Lost Cat" posters nowadays.

Sometimes I think perhaps they are just showing off. Like there is no real lost cat, just a will to advertise their own graphic skills. Worse even, people are kidnapping cats and then offering services.

The other day I nearly used a bikini top for a bib. It had hung there since summer when it was not required much due to the tricky trick of getting summer warmth, fit car, available time and the beach altogether in the same place. Then as I picked it up off the cupboard handle to slip on the kid for spaghetti it hit me in a chorus: "Resist this Phil as she may go to the beach finally and be heavenly happy, slip it on and then be running in slow motion to the waves and then get a crusty chafing rub from the dried sauce on the inside of the bra cup."

The other day the laundry was conquered: For fifteen minutes there was none to do, we were ahead – fuck you, Humans are Masters of the World – the machine was full and, ha ha the clothes we had gathered to enhance and aid our daily life were, for once, in full check.

Plus, I had left a magazine with the young Twighlight chap in a vest on at the bottom of the basket so that, every time we emptied a load into the machine, my love would have a wee treat. It would have been Beckham in "his" Armani pants if there was no photo of him found at the time when that thought went live.

These days in England I ask for people's travelcard as they come off the train at 6:23pm and I am going to do comedy to others who work in London to afford tickets and we are opposite numbers, going in as they come back. ". . . do you have a travelcard I can keep, going back into London . . . it can't go on its own . . ." It needs a human to keep it going.

Going in for free on their ticket to talk to folks about my life and it can't be too like theirs, and it can't be too far from theirs; it could be that the ones who can talk about it have to weave that consciousness into every day a little. I am of us and yet we are all atypical, so anyone can talk and all details are fine-flavoured with the individual.

"Ah, you're a comedian . . . ," the taxi drivers always say. "Surely mate, fundamentally, comedy's about the transfer of an idea in a fun creative way that involves someone getting/receiving an invisible flying sentinel mystery. And, in the getting of a concept, you can receive as far-out-there an idea as you want because they are already physical, imagined, suggested abstracts in a sweet way: two for one . . . Why limp in a dream . . . ? You can have that mate."

The transference of ideas. That's the secret of comedy. Shut up.

Well, listen to this: This thinking is just me trying to match the totally-mad concept of standing in a room, surrounded by people, weaving a thing that, by definition, has a weight and a form to their eyes yet, secretly, is actually being spun in front of their eyes, like Sherlock running through the circus gathering what he needs to make a disguise as he moves forward to catch up with the person he is chasing who will recognize him so he's Gathering On The Hoof: two for one to achieve an end he already knows; this thinking is very closely linked to the gigs I do and has resulted in way-the-best gigs I have ever seen.

I know, I know, my great gigs are way, way as good as the best gigs I've ever seen. You can be first-equal when you really do the greatest thing you, as a person, can manage in the shape of a comedian.

It says on the back of the Suma organic peanut butter:

Unrealistic Dreamers? We think not, a successful
worker owned & managed co-operative since 1977.

Most nights someone on any given bill will be as good a comic as some have ever seen.

Before gigs I follow my nose, fuck about, try and get just a little first bottle wave pissed, smoke a wee tatty, la-de-da, be outside chatting up the crowd, looking for little human paths around the back of buildings, looking in the props bit, nicking sachets or teaspoons from a kitchen, riding a foldable bike to a museum or folly or tower or the Freeport

Designer Village . . . Can share the bill with ten-minute open spots doing the comedy getting less laughs and yet share style with and be a bridge, a loose ropebridge to Ken Campbell or Spalding Gray and the whole world of theatrical monologue and one man showings.

And the thinking is so closely linked as a cause and as to cause and is being a result and is a result of at the same time that then causes a cause.

"What came first the chicken or the egg?" is a statement not a question. It is a statement of observation turned into a confusion. Where is the dividing line? Ah, what is really being said I feel is: there is a point there must be an egg then a chicken, a point between no universe and some universe . . . and how can we intelligently handle this actual conscious definite concept with our brains which are made of the stuff we are questioining.

Chicken is the egg. Fool's top. Last week I gave a kid a sandwich, he asked for a chicken sandwich and I put egg in it from a kedgeree that was still going and it was hard to define how he might be let down.

You know you're with the right woman when you are standing masturbating in the hall looking at a painting you have just done and she comes out and says: "Do you want some oil for that?" Right with the woman.

Like the neutrinos that travel faster than light: We see scientists loving them, inventing in discovery of the things we already do daily in thought's neurological composition, and do and are aware of in our consciousness: That a thing occurs before it occurs, that we invent and are led by ourselves, that perception is precedent and predatory – of the moment, filling the void – it has no other choice. The chicken is the egg. They are one thing in ever-changing form.

We do make up the universe through neurological process. We are all inseparable as all the string theory finally tied together to tether is to the big empty mansion. We are mostly empty space.

So are all atoms, undefinable as being separate from another. So we may as well move with that held, in order to let go.

Let it go. Go to the beach and go swimming.

The meaning of life is a wordless letting go . . . In words it is a simple phrase.

This year it occurred to me to pick up one of my own shits. I have been shitting all my life and in one moment it occurred to me that I had never picked up and held one of my own shits and yet right at the same time was a stronger concept of the realization that it was occurring to me that it had never before occurred to me. It is an inventing, a creation, an occurrence . . . oh currency.

The moment was wrapped into and with the idea that it was amazing that it had never occurred to me before that it had not occurred to me before and that happened as an awareness of an assessment and an impulse at the same time.

In a way, time is the word for what we have come up with to hold events – like they need it. This proposition is that it is the other way round at the same time: that time is the word we have come up with for the conceptualizing of everything. We use it as a medium and our definition of it is causing trouble round the microscope. How can the universe just be? It can't – quick, let's get a parallel something going that we can know about and teach it. Like he says in Baz's original Strictly Ballroom: "How can we teach the steps if we don't know the steps?" So they restrict and limit and cauterize the invention of steps. What it is because we made it – quick, measure things, invent a standard moveable super egg-timer set of numbers on the world and then we can relax . . .

I can't wait to see Hawk-Eye in football and everyone is happy as it can tell by millimetres when it is over the line, and it will all be cool. Until one day one is just a pixel over and not-seeable and it will come down to this: that measuring gets only more accurate, a guide to the thing it cannot really tell us exactly about the thing. Hawk-Eye will have to become SuperEagleEye . . . then UltimateFalconEyePlusUltra-Max 3000 . . . opening up a fractious fractal opening that in scale is as big as the last branch and a chasm now too.

What does all this mean? This all means I am writing as closely as I can about the thoughts in actions I do as a comedian, around how it is prepared and executed or what scatological shambollocks happened tonight after that afternoon.

What this means is no end in absolutes: just an ongoing list, so that next gig can be the best and that you only need one good idea and that's the next one.

Our consciousness holds time, so why be bothered by a thing you have made up? If you have not budgeted enough for it, budget again.

So I leaned down and picked up the shit and all I want to tell you is that it was a lot less dense than I though it was going to be. All that pressure, all that intimacy all the weight and the compression resulted in THIS?

Then it occurred to me that it was funny that I imagined I was going to get a certain feel of density holding it; that I was wrong in my assumption about my own shite.

So, the meaning of life, in that handy phrase, is "how could it be any other way?"

Don't be confused about what isn't.

Archimedes said that the lessening of the weight of an object in water is equal to the weight of water displaced by the body.

So you weigh yourself then get in a bath that is right full . . . Collect all the water that spills over in a big clear plastic sack and hang that sack from a big spring-weighing device. Both weights will be the same, as water displaced by a body is equal to and balances the original weight of the body in the water. It is "weightless".

That's "floating", in other words. It's a huge "oh yeh, it is, isn't it? well put!" and . . .

"How could it be any other way?" Well you may pee in the bath.

Shit floats.

Put a kid to sleep recently playing the kazoo because, essentially, they do not find them ironic or tongue-n-cheeky to distract them from the beauty and down flutter the heavy lids.

The other day I did the finest gig of my life. Sure, as it happens, it had lots of mad silly laughs – it had the other width too. I was in a room in Limehouse in East London where the young artists have set up and there were five other acts. One did magic, there was slideshow, freestyle rap, the incredible Nanna and her OAP-sychedelic singalong and a cute chubby gay stripper man who whips of his lederhosen suede shorts and braces to end up in a teddy-bear thong.

Last on, I had been standing watching like everyone else. So, although I started with a high-octane incredible little kind of rap song, I did a kind of magic trick in which I asked a lady for her favourite leaf, she said "oak". Handily, I had collected a few oak leaves on the way to the gig and had just taped one to my stomach and I did a full striptease, ending up with just the leaf adjusted to Adam and Eve it where the bear had been. I did all this and there was mayhem and fierce momentum laughing going around the room in waves, like how it is when singing a "round" is sung: People getting to laugh at the fact they are laughing at what they were laughing at, and laugh at their own laughing. Two for one oily morning fridge histrionics time.

Then I settled down a bit and just told the story of my day getting back late from Galway with no phone and how it felt good.

So the gig was a fundamental achievement for me in that it brought in all the reality I could muster in the sense that half the act was literally from the point of view of the audience, a filtering of all we had all seen togevva. Up the back watching, I was kind of un-objectively attached, or actively un-unattached, so it was like one of the crowd just got up when I went up, and that is handy for a crowd to witness every now and then. That I have that space in my act to bring it: magic! Very happy about that. Never have to ask: "What is it I am meant to be saying?"

A little bit of altruistic from that film, Keyser Söze using all the unique words and particular phrasings that are just behind him on the Police noticeboard in the room where he is being interrogated. A little bit that, a little bit charades at Christmas, a little bit near-mental levels of automatic-speak and actions coming all-swift, yet all framed in the lovely proscenium.

I feel pangs for that gig and a pang is when the pain of a pine is thought of as glorious.

The other day I was peeing while drinking from a cider bottle and I was thinking, "Wow, I am just a pipe. In the best way I am just a pipe and organism to support this pipe, a vessel for the things that keep me going. A self-circular and that is okay."

This gig was my high achievement, as good as anything I have ever seen:

The fabulous maddeningly zooboid momentum of Corky and the Juice Pigs, the riffing professorship of Kitson, and the absolute double-clowning of Johnny Vegas, the truest and un-truest of all.

They all were living-genius performers times I saw them.

And Sean Hughes in his terrific sexy pomp, utterly loving life as represented through the actual silly tones.

And Mark Lamarr's intelligence and poise, lighting a fag and asking the crowd questions.

Sadowitz is a genius and Chris Lynam too.

Malcolm Hardee had the best stories because he had the best adventures and knew the most criminals.

I have seen A. Maxwell move in the genius light with quite the most sensationally natural storytelling closeness of a friend that one could ever wish for onstage.

I saw Harry Hill at The Comedy Store one night do the most coveted twenty minutes ever with endless silly loopings and cleverly-daft call-backs and non-sequiturs packed tightly as ten Bensons.

Saw Vic and Bob rework and infuse TV recording with boozy newness, take after take, completely able to write as themselves and just be.

Saw Harland Williams the unknown hick Candafornian goofy surrealist perplex them and win them over every night in Edinburgh.

Saw Eddie Izzard riff a lot within arranged structures in front of two thousand two hundred people at the Playhouse and heard the biggest crowd try to laugh quick so as not to miss stuff. Hey, last time I did the Playhouse for a five-minute slot, 2010, Radio Forth charity do, I left the stage and found the guidedog and made a crap rude joke yet the twenty-three hundred people were forgiving and laughed a bit because at least I was there. In fact reader, you ought to try to get hold of a bootleg recording for that show from an engineer because I told a story that night that had just happened and yet, in an inversion of the dog crap bum joke that worked, the story was so real and good and rushed and gushy and true that they hardly laughed at all. 'Twas a classic: too good a thing to be a good routine.

Now Dr Brown is the best too, he clowns with such beautiful faith there is humour in a positive manifestation of trusting . . . Who'd've thought?

In the July just gone, there I was going into the bogs in J. Sainsbury and there was a Polish lady cleaner in her very early fifties coming out and I'm carrying the small blue guitar under my arm in no case. She's like Ooven Rubaya: "Please play, you play?" So I get it up and start a ditty and I'm singing about what I'm doing, and going, and this place and then she's like "okay, okay that fine!" and told me to stop.

Beautiful. No joke, seriously, no irony, just fab. Women cleaning toilets ought to be able to say what they like to me. Now I am happy that she is over here and commanding her surroundings in the way Europeans can and women do.

Okay back to the cider I am piping out . . . it is cloudy, of unspecified strength and came from a farm where a man I know has an orchard and it was found in the back seat of a car. He is Dutch and tall. He is good friends with my good friend and at some point he told her of an old midnight-blue three series BMW in a field that maybe she could have if her man wanted it. He didn't. Time passed and then I heard from her about it and saw it as one of the loveliest things ever, put a battery in it, drove it home, gave it a quick hoover, re-attached the door trim and under-dash and drove it to a gig in Northumbria.

The promoter had sent me a couple of extra emails that weren't necessary and, after I had spoken to him a few times on the phone, he still typed his mobile number in at the end of these messages. My antenna were tweaked and fuzzed over this precious sign of no trust, a revealer of worry as a dull wizard manifestation. Promoters are often stuck when acts just don't turn up. This must be what it's about: facing up to crap excuses with crap upfront. Anyhow when you've being doing gigs for twenty years you have been turning up, this is the integral chunk you can control: get there in time and summon it up. Quite the reverse, a few times I have not left the town of a gig though . . . only twice have they actually called up to see where I am and in fact I had forgotten. And once recently where they got a call from Melina because I was locked up in Jail. That's another story . . .

At the gig I befriend a Scottish comedienne and get a mildly good reaction from the crowd, yet I can tell I am playing too roughly with the form, disrespecting "I do humour, you laugh". Abusing the trust as I bend to hear a cracking. Although I mean well, there is a guy onstage behind me doing the sound from a schooldesk and the bar staff are posh folk in their fifties. It's too much. My act concerns these details a bit much.

After, I ask if there can be a little cash advance as I have none. Then I ask if they'll follow me to a garage as I am very low on fuel and it's eleven miles to the Esso.

Now it goes. Back at the car park the promoter sees a bike in the back of my car.

Before I had met him at the restaurant and watched them eat fish n chips and had gone for a wee walk around town, stolen in to look at the castle, done a few back lanes and came across a lonesome bicycle. If there is cobweb on the chain, I help myself to a bike, if only to stop it seizing up. This one I rode around and had a feeling for it and still had it in the back of the car when he asked me about it. I told him. Then there was the smoke in my headlamps.

"You've found this car in a field, you have no tax or MOT or insurance and you have openly admitted you are a thief and have stolen this bike. AND THERE IS SMOKE IN YOUR HEADLIGHTS?"

To be fair this is like a huge set of compliments not complaints and I am compliant and nod as it's all facts.

Trouble is, all this he said to me later again on the phone so he can chicken and egg-it and cancel all those lovely gigs in Wales I was about to do for him for decent money, midweek. I'll do most anything to earn eight hundred quid midweek and leave a weekend free.

Anyway before we had parted all was well until at the unmanned Esso, where they only take cards and I had to get him to use his card and I gave him back twenty of his own real paper pounds that he had given as an advance that I was going to use for petrol and then he let me drive off in the wrong direction. Funny thing is I gave him thirty by mistake, the three tenners, and he never mentioned it when I had only put twenty petrol-eum in-eum.

Anyway I sped off to get to Glasgow for the Comedy Festival.

Overnight driving is fab and, after a wee nap, I am on the lovely A1 and pull in for gas at Alnwick just after dawn. Halfway through filling her up the Police car comes in. I stop pumping at eight quid twenty with a cold carwash feeling sweeping from my top of head hairs down to my chest front via the neck's nape hackle. Nevertheless it's worth a try and I pay to leave – then the Policeman comes over and he's like, "What are you doing? You've no tax or MOT. What are you doing?"

"It's such a lovely vehicle and it just ought to be on the road and I'm driving it to my Mum's, near Edinburgh, to park it up and do it up . . ." Not so much a lie as a brand-new truth.

Amazingly, this model was his favourite car too, the old G-reg. He said he used to have one when he was in the TA and he agreed they ought to be kept on the road.

Duty first though, and he let me get my stuff out of it. By this time I had had it two days and had found some lovely red sand from a builder's truck in Bootle that I had used to make a wee Japanese red sand Zen-type dashboard garden. Into it I had pushed mementos and foliage, spare lighter, souvenir knick-knacks and oddities.

"You probably don't want to see her being taken away so I'll give you a lift to the station." He was right and I kissed goodbye to that bike and the sleeping bags and Lilly's tape recorder and the garden.

He dropped me off and then, curiously, called out to me as I left, "I hope you win the gig!" Yes, fucking Jesus, come on. Yahoo! Typical, a Police officer has learnt to think of all work-interaction as a battle to lose. To him it is adversarial, a battle where work is at the front, the coal face, the meeting of the interface of human vs human, the no-lad's land of crimeness.

Really, if your aim is just to tell the story of your recent times then the only way to fail is to not try. So, success is easy. Just stick wiv da deets, da deets, da deets . . .

*

Anyway, hopped the train to Edinburgh sat down real quick with a newspaper and looked settled so when they come round asking for tickets from Alnwick I definitely stay quiet, as I certainly do not have any to show him, and got to Glasgow to visit my friend Gillian and do a show at the Òran Mór venue. An exciting set of nine whiskys came onstage at half-time and I was able to get wasted in front of the crowd and all was going well with the full details of the BMW story singing "smoke . . . in my headlights" to the tune of Smoke on the Water till after the gig I was changing back into the less wet T-shirt and a manager guy says, "Hurry up . . ." Now it seems he is being unfair to an act that has just done an hour and a half gig to a hundred and eighty three folks in his venue with a drinks break and so I gently mock him that he is the one that need to hurry up . . . "Come On Hurry Up you guys clearing away the chairs . . ." He didn't get it and warned me not to be cheeky, too late I said, and so a bouncer threw me out the back, my wrists held together in very strictly bathroom style, opening a pair of fire-doors with my head under his arm and causing it to bleed. THREE years I have done Òran Mór, getting bigger and bigger crowds and it's greater and greater a show, and then this final release.

The breakdown: 180 tickets sold, so 1,800 quid taken, 436 to the venue, 40% of the remaining 1,400 to the festival, that left still about eight hundred quid for a head wound. Fairy nuff. Òran Mór no more for me. In fact this year was the first Glasgow comedy Festival I have missed in all the years. Off the hook now, free to write.

As it happens when I hoovered out the car there was 96p in the back behind the seats so I'll include that . . . fuck you Orange Muff . . . Phil's the winner. As I was outside the back, round the side in the dark alone in the dark, bleeding, away from my T-shirt and dry clothes and the warmth, waiting for my friend there was Kevin Bridges about to go in the big front entrance wearing a Norfolk-style jacket in what looked like cream leather. One out one in. Then Gilsy came out with the tweed and it was great to put it on.

Honestly, I was just zooming a bit after a gig that had held such hysterics that deep in the second half, all eight of the nine whiskys near me gone, I espy one left, way over the other side and orchestrate a great prank prat-fall to land by that last nip and lay there drinking and laughing on the ground . . . je ne suis pas un pipe.

A year and three months ago me and Cameron Sinclair did have the officially best real convulsive-paralytic laughter-dose of all times when he was getting his sexual diseases and AIDS test results over the phone by voice-operated service. They were mishearing and repeating and emotionlessly atonalizing with extreme moments of life-or-death future paths et cetera . . . I fell onto Cameron who was on the pavement outside the Museum of Scotland, Chambers Street, and as he repeats the last choice of Press 2 for AIDS, I am on top of him and our bellies actually laugh into each other. Our hope is that there was a bit of a window open somewhere and our laughter got in and is exhibited there still as a prime example of The Laugh like so much paradigm Tartan or a Shield or the handmade fiddles from thee J. Ferguson in Inverness . . . or . . .

Did I even finish starting all of that Galway story off?? . . . waking up and the massive clock needs another fucking beating as he stands over me like Ali . . . nearly fierce speeds on them beautiful Oirish highway roads which don't have two lanes just an extra bit to go onto if you really need it boys help yourself, go on go on. . . . Oh Ireland, so good . . . gigs all over and mostly the most fun around it all . . . Shit, still owe that tea lady from Father Ted a tenner after she very graciously gave me one in a bar years ago at a festival her husband set up . . .

Now, sometimes I like to write on an atlas when driving and it's large and wide and I'm stoned and in private and it's a long drive and a time to think and you can write fuzzy stuff in the sea off the land, drawing a line to the place where it came to you, its birthplace, and there's room for bad writing and all as you write an almost automatic blind text slowly and with the left hand like my mate Ruby's Dad used to do paintings. Except he did them blind, left-handed and upside-down to give a freedom.

Here is the essence of comedy for me: A Surprise. Tell people you saw an Asian guy across from you on a train and he had two little cans of ginger ale in front of him on his wee table, two catering cans of ginger ale . . . Canada Dry . . . an Asian. There is no joke, it is just what you saw: a unique moment where its constituents are, to me, better than could ever be written. So, subtly, the surprise is that it is not expected – what?! – just simple detail.

This is what Phil Kay has really achieved: Not the improvisational madness and seat-of-pants crazy, messy, brave, denuded, muddy mayhem. Really he is me and he has achieved the sliding in of simple reality to do the job of the Joke. Its job for me is to be a ladder onto the roof for a better view.

Lots of bonkers stuff can get their attention yet in a real show of eighty-eight minutes there has to be a greater place to go: to the facts – and the re-shuffled shifting, the re-sifting, the recall, the rewind and the play. To that point where the crowd have been taken out of the zone where they imagine what to expect – taken out into the wild new prairie where they remember to forget to imagine what to expect. Have you been to many places where you can just run around in the dark or with your eyes shut and have no fear of banging into things . . . ? The mind has.

Some nights it takes nineteen long minutes to get the crowd to see this, sometimes it is more or less instant.

Deep down I believe the joke is actually the recent interloper, when personal news, being enough, was all shot up by big travel and the world wars.

People will start to laugh, one or two – maybe one, maybe most, or a big half that feels like most. The point is some could laugh if it is a thing you say onstage. All can work. And if it is a thing you really did just see on a train and you did not think it was really actually funny in any way, it just had a mighty, mighty weight of the truthful detail about it, then you are their surprise. In the end you are the humour; the vehicle for love as laughs is them jokes.

Like the woman that last other night at the room above bingo with the slidy synthetic tracksuit in hysterics and she's been caught by the bug and she can't stop and I leave the stage and go to her and I approach and she is in the fits and I get closer and just hold the mike to her and then take it away and say she'll probably be done soon and put the mike back and she's doing more and this is a great place to be. We are all laughing at the sound of her laugh, laughing a bit yet keeping it quiet in order to hear a woman laughing; not at any thing any more, just the stomach and diaphragm going for it. The joke is gone, now we're on the roof, watch out it's slippery too . . .

Laughter is a reaction, a muscular thing, and is a sign: liquid, vocal love, a flag-wave of reception. Milking it though, that is the deal: to be able to milky-milk it and still therefore it be more okay . . . Okay-dokay philkay-milkay.

There is an ultimate laugh out there that comedians dare not speak of. Imagine you are doing stand-up in a room of two hundred and ten people with a balcony allowing them all to be in close enough so that if you chose to take a call from your Mum away from the mike and just talked normally enough so as not to give the game away they would all be able to hear what you were saying; a room with everyone laughing really hard at something then the pauses for air and then the high-pitch giggle, then all as one the crowd are hysterically silent together, and in this moment the greatest laugh ever can come when they all draw breath as one in a massive honking intake and its power sucks off your clothes in a vacuum vortex of giant hoover-force. Your clothes fly off, drawn in a fast thump onto the faces of the crowd and the belt buckle on your jeans blinds a reviewer in one eye . . . and you are left there naked and ruffled, teetering for balance and stripped and windblasted on the edge of the stage as the crowd try to compose themselves . . . and falling naked into the crowd to be caught in the arms of . . . well that would be too much.

Weeks later, after massive humility and the five-star review written, the reviewer opens a lovely suede eye-patch you've made for her and delivered by hand . . .

How you deal with it going well is a skill. Like playing football with youngsters just well enough to score and let them score too, using skill to keep the game fantastic. Doing really well with me is an issue for no matter how wild and free and excited and real-story-based and extemporizing from the main drag it gets there is a peripheral, a very feral wish to keep it a good kind of good.

One Chapter Too

Firstly I believe everything is a miracle.

Every table is a chair.

Every year during the Edinburgh Festival for the last decade and a half, my godfamily, the Hunter-Greens have come up to work and be in various guises. First the Parents wore hats and worked the Spiegeltent and managed acts and did promotional activities and their kids were young, then they got older and the kids wanted to see things and they brought out their own sandwiches from the flat of their friend Faith who started the book festival, and they stayed out all day . . . and then they got bigger and the oldest Felix got a Hat and a Job and a Wage and a Hangover and it all ended up last year with Lilly the middle daughter running the door and booking me to do a wee terrible post-Olympics silent toilet roll-gymnastics routine in the middle of the Burlesque discoteque. Anyway never mind all that, every year we go up Arthur's seat with a watermelon and break it open on a boulder and zoom hefty spinning chunks of it down the super slidy grass paths that act as runs. It's a beautiful entry level mystic ritual that just formed itself out of accidental chance. And it makes us all happy to do . . . we leap about in the wind and chase these chunks of fruit down a hill. Large, spinning segments.

That little impish limpy chimp leap there in that there last chapter is a bit of flying.

Well, I'd like to tell you guy? or forward-slash girl, man or woman who are you?? . . . in fact this would be a great application of apps, whereby with a series of clicks ending in one last click that you could get this book in the e-form, dedicated to you and then whenever plus too in the book also there could be your name typed instead of "reader".

So for something like £0.25 you get the book dedicated to you and full of either your christian name n surname and middle names or own nickname or totally private pen-name for yourself or even your pin number which would be a good one so you could always come back from holiday and forget it and remember it is there in a copy of The Wholly Viable . . .

And plus we'll save a lot because the soft technology will save us spending a fortune doing hundreds of print-runs of one for your names, Brenda.

You see that was a guess, you may well not be called Brenda . . . have you seen those signs above the motorway? "Fasten your seat belts" and "Don't Drink And Drive" . . . well, would they not be better off saying "Don't Drink and Drive Davey" as there's a chance that one in fifty people drinking and driving may well be called Davey and then he'll get a real surprise and spit booze all over his dashboard and get it in the heating fans and it'll be blown all around his car and help the Police make a fairer assessment of the situation should they pull him over. Aside from this, technology brings very few new things we need to our lives, just tweaky improvements to what we do already that they tech-firms can muscle in on and get a commission from, no they only really bring new problems. Niche worries. One good application of technology is that nowadays people can print a lot better lost cat posters from home. If you really have to print something and you don't want to go to a printer's as it's too close to your heart, you know that this one you have to do yourself, then this will be very revealing of where you is @. Like the Islamic fundamentalists, if they really were forced to design a poster for a show in the Edinburgh Fringe . . .

Going back a little further: Remembering to my myself, re-minding me that all the messing through and mucking around can end in great gigs – trying only to sacrifice the dull show. Keeping an eye on the natural event and not putting false energy and comic ingredients into this present.

And every chair a table.

What if the love people wanted you to feel for them was defined by certain actions you felt anyway? What if you knew that the love you felt for them must be the one they want because it is the one you feel?

Right now 19.03.13, 13:38pm, on the Linn turntable Miles Davis' Greatest Hits where the sound of his own plural is the sound of his name, and this album I remember laughing at @ school because it seemed so daft and ridiculous that we checked to see if the tape was warped. Mind you there are times that South American peasants were openly laughing at me for disco dancing on my own in a town square high up in the Atacama desert when they were all paired up and in close doing the Desert two-step . . .

So, late June 2011 a little bit of crazy in Sainsbury's car park, totally inSane-esbury – J.sane in J.membrane . . . – leaning on the back of my old car just parked and the family gone inside to acquire and I'm sipping on farm-cider sourced locally of unspecified strength. One of those European guys is pushing the trolley towards me with the stuff to clean cars and a wee high flag like a sharkfin looming among the waves, in the sea of cars, and wearing a horrendous company hi-vis. It must have been on my mind something along the lines of "This ain't right" or "It's all too easy" – which is the feeling of supermarkets for me sometimes: "It's all too easy . . . The drips of rain of the detective's macintosh more noticeable now inside the old deserted nightclub he was led to by the matchbook . . . "It's too easy . . . sump'n ain't right!" he says as the shadows begin to resolve.

And so, as he approached, I suddenly had the urge, just as I did it, without having to move, to spit a mouthful of the cider over my back windscreen and start cleaning it myself with my bare hand.

There'd been a something buzzing around the head all formed like "Hey Brother! I don't think you ought to be doing this job, be able to prey on us and our apathy, swoop round the moment we park as vultures do, with the wee flag approaching, we are helpless and stopped . . . It is a faultless Dragons' Den magic-idea relying on what? Us being predictable and lazy and suggestible. And your relatives are left behind, you miss your cousins and maybe a city is on fire and no, no, no, I am Scottish and do not want it . . . leave my car dirty, we'll take the kids through a carwash for a laugh, pretending the sunroof is stuck open, rather than have you do this for me . . . We are alive, Brother!" All this, as well as the fact that cider vinegar and newspaper cleans windows – there is a Windolene out there with "Contains Cider" on the label. It's sometimes in Windolene, isn't it? There must have been a link to that, as well as I felt encapsulated in the action – very little difference in the time of realizing in mind to the time of realizing it in movement – he wandered past with a plausible high-five hanging in the air between us, a smirk apiece and something better than just a good comfortable £5 business deal or the embarrassed ingnoring he must get.

Something's definitely coming together join-the-dots style: Yesterday I was making pancakes with spelt flour, molasses, tahini and groundnuts and was holding a cracked pair of eggs in each hand, just opened on the side of the bowl, as A. Hepburn did in cook school on VHS the other night, and notice there is no well for the eggs so I just elbowed one in there. Without the thought is how it feels, it's really just without the contemplation in worded thought . . . P'taang! Right in there with the elbow; like a samurai. Job done.

*

Shit Occurs.

What Occurs, Must Come Down.

Early July 2012.

Okay I've said this before, I'll try and say it better: All my life I have been shitting and today it occurred to me that it had never occurred to me to pick one up. They sit there like a seal in a bathtub with nowhere to go and, as it occurred to me that it hadn't occurred to me, I leaned in and picked it up. All that can be said was it was somewhat of a revelation: it was much lighter that expected. All that pressure all that intense intimate involvement feels like it's going to produce an oak-like mahogany-dense item. And all that pressure from you means not what you think.

Anyway, forgot to say when me and the boy are jogging down the end of the garden along the slightly-municipal ribbed-concrete path by the Victorian brick pumphouse and he has snot dribbling down from his two-and-a-half-year-old nose over his lips and onto the chin and he's very Zen-like about it and doesn't seem to notice, like he can have his socks on the wrong feet or his trousers way too high and twisted and it means nothing to him. Looking at him, he is free and a bit like a little mini-Dalai Lama type in that he is without our adult worries and is a bit chubby and doesn't make any of his own meals either. He is a bit rare in that when you go towards him with the hanky to blow his nose he actually doesn't mind, not like a lot of kids who turn their face away as if it's chloroform and they're off to the basement again. No, this wee man actually offers his nose up to me as we are jogging and I take a wee paper tissue out and scoop and wipe and on we go and, sticking it back in the top pocket of my jacket, it takes by chance the exact shape of a dinky Fifties Dapper Dan handkerchief's double-point ridge – the ideal. Exactly like Mad Man Don's – and it jumps out at me that this is better than Mad Men – it's "Dad Men", it's real, it's groovy, it's just as cool and dashing. All they want to do it shag around, look smart and drink at work. Big Deal – just work from home with a supply of serviettes.

Shits happen.

Chapter Free

Every now and then there are trips abroad to work and these are fundamentally the knees of bees and the bollocks of dogs. You get to be abroad, having the eyes to see stuff as any human with the heightened heightened-ness of a new place and a countdown of hours. You are here on this bit of the Earth for a wee while – make use of it, then the best can happen. That is what I try and do most in comedy: keep the possibility of the best occurring. Allow for the wildest thing to take place and that is usually something like: follow le nez, have adventure and be open to telling about it onstage, fresh produce. Produced fresh. Bring it in from a poacher's secret hidden bend of the river and cook it right there on a fire on the bank – the left bank la rive gauche – bring it. Or don't even cook it, sashimi it.

Human crowds are a massive psychic group and they can really love a thing just for being raw and fresh. They can get laughs out, they can enjoy the truly-real and recent.

Hundreds of times I have arrived at a gig with a daft wee story and it is enough because it is authentic, as in the one the other day when I was driving with my arm over the passenger's headrest and I saw another guy doing it and I sped up to get level and let him see and had trouble changing gear with the right hand while driving and so veered toward him a bit; this got his attention and he looked up and over and got a wee flipper wave from my hand bouncing like a flower in the wind of a window . . .

October 2006, Paris: gigs on Sunday, Monday & Tuesday:
Onto Le Metro at eleven on the way to La Grande Arche – the ride is so soft because the trucks ride on wheels with tyres that buffer and bounce. My pink ticket gets me all the way and out at the enormous new municipal square of that grand arch, the great big one: La Grande Arche, so simply named, so enormous, so post-post-modern and, indeed, so big an arch when the achievements it commemorated are not prix de guerre. It is the shadow of a four-dimensional cube represented in three dimensions. The victory is over having no concept. The triumph of idea over emptiness. Arch as gateway. The lifts are huge and I am in a pink jumper. At the top the beautiful restaurant's

professionally-aloof waiters in their nearly-fifties take ages to serve me
as the smiles grow and, after chartreuse and trying to pay for another
age of ages, I just decide to walk out, do a runner. Do the best runner
in recent history: flamboyant, formidable and spontaneous, the big
three of natural not-paying techniques. I have many techniques for,
how I say, being involved in a retail situation, utilizing the service and
yet not interacting through purchase.

The best-ever subtle wander ever. Wanderful – l'urge – then the
shaking leg through to the lifts which take two minutes thirty-five to
come. At this point waiting for the lift it's like a runner to nowhere, a
runner to simply be now here, what a high at this height.

Perhaps ten or eleven times in my life so far I have had limbs shaking
from pure excitement. One was when I cycled through a tunnel by the
river in Glasgow . . .

Les garçons still do not realize, with their styles of vivre, that I have
gone.

The lift does come, I walk in and the doors take their time to un-part
and there is a magic space that a waiter could have filled from the side
for about fifteen municipalité, fraternité, legalité seconds before they
closed again. Ah there's that bit in Chinatown when Nicholson slides
from view in a closing elevator. That is when I looked at the gallery
which briefly appeared to have some very prestigious work up. This
has a fantastic hundred-year-old solid-yet-rickety French-polished
wooden parquet floor with a whole bunch of Van der Rohe Barcelona
chairs all around the place, all worn with beautiful brown leather all
cracked. Technically, it may well have been the world's shortest look
around a gallery, fifteen seconds from in the lift and most of those
seconds on the chairs and the hatching of a plan to come up here, with
the minutes in the lift to change into blue overalls, and with a
requisition order from HQ to replace these goddamn ripped-up old
chairs, and leave with them all. Or, maybe, pink overalls – is that too
much?

The enormous "Place" below the restaurant, in my highly-visible
jumper that they must be looking for by now. Surely they might catch
a glimpse, in both a gay and an un-gay way, of a favourite/not favourite
shade and then boom!, a realization: pow! Some customer relations.

As we all know the cliché: the norm of the aloof older slightly-pissed-
off perma-peeved waiter just looks shallowly deep, as clear as the bells
that they feel you will not be fully appreciating them as a human in this
role (with an umlaut-type thing).

Not so far. I walk across the massive open space in front, still completing the biggest runner and turning to look way up, there's always the possibility of seeing them at the window: Tiny stickmen silently banging on the window.

In the department store called Fnac I buy a CD and say "Pas de la sac" at the check-out and that gets me no bag, so, as I am leaving, a huge department-store security guard comes up to lay a hand on my shoulder. Le receipt calms his mind, his body follows and he and his laden belt move away.

Fnac does not stand for anything anymore. It simply is the name – pas de l'acronym. Forever no alternative concept other than its intrinsic self . . . Fnac, fnac, say it a few times and it sounds as if you have a cleft palate and yet there is no way that they can be trying to appeal to a market that precise. As a very remote possibility it was founded by someone with cleft palate, to breed physical empathy in others through secretly leading them into that realm of affliction. Wow.

The only unlikely aspect of this is that simply this would be common knowledge by now.

On the Le Metro again I notice a black woman crocheting or neatly "finger-knitting" – knitting with wool that is coming from a ball in one of her jacket pockets and as she crochets she passes it onto the pocket on the other side as a thicker. Wow. Once you've got that you can make hats and clothes, bed blankets and tea-cosies, waistcoats. One could pick loose the thread of the garment you are wearing and pull it loose and weave it off your body into another garment, "pre-cycling", to turn one garment into another while still wearing it.

All of life's needs are being met, it occurs to me: natural fibres making a thing she needs for cheap and done by hand, occupying time that might otherwise been temps perdu: lost, "bored" or harder or a waste.

You can stand in the middle of these softer trains and see where the front is going for they seem to take a more curvy nature than the Tube and you can sort-of-surf in the middle, bestride the carriage up by the doors, a bouncy wheel for each foot gauging the trajectory for fun – like a dog I used to know that would sit with her head between the front seats, watching the road and leaning. And we would watch her watching the road and she would lean into the bends as they came, her black, black eyes twitching slightly and tongue out, never really looking at us. Doubsche was her name which is Gaelic for black vomit.

On another urge I jump off at a station that has a bar on the platform. This is definitely a form of Heaven, a nifty bar right here in your trip, right in your way, an actual bar on totally your route. There is a universal attention-getting whistle and, turning around, it's for me the whistle that is for everyone is always for you and there is a man, back a bit, holding my CD out to me among the pips of the door closing. Imagine if he jumped out for me and then the doors closed behind him? I could never just leave him – we would have had to have had a drink at the bar.

At the bar a grand Algerian auntie serves me. Her feet have flattened her leathery flip-flops so much they are beautifully thin between her and the ground, to be the least shoe possible to qualify as shoe. Some of her foot creeps around and obscures the thinnest leather soul and is in contact with the ground it seems. We somehow talk about kids because I see a toy on the counter and wonder if the kid is here. The waiters in the Grande Arche are a long way away up above ground.

A train comes back along and I leap on. This is a blue train and my pink jumper and pink ticket are ineligible, although I do not know this yet. I jumped off the pink train and, after the talking, jumped on a blue-ticket train so that, when the train gets to Champs-Élysées and I want to leave and ascend to the top of a huge single one-way escalator, I find that a blue ticket is the only kind acceptable here. There it is, I am trapped and, half-turning, the brain comes to see the wall of perspex, designed to keep us in, runs close to the top of the escalator's moving black shiny-rubber handrail. I find myself just about to move because into my head pops a line from a Jim Jarmusch film: "The way of the Samurai is one of swiftness." Somewhere in the first syllable of the last word I am moving toward the handrail and skip up onto it, leap to get a foot on the top of the perspex security-wall and am flying over the top of it with a moving black liquid-liquorice boost from the escalator handrail, to see that it is considerably further down on the other side than it was up on this one – je me pleux – I rain me down, very luckily, right into a gap among the commuters below. It is a reasonably good landing like from the Commonwealth Games and I do a little arms-up flourish and then immediately assimilate in, with wringing in my ankles and the CD tucked down the back of my trousers – legal, illegal, l'illicity in an inner city. So, coming back up onto the Champs-Élysées and passing a long quiet queue of Japanese ladies waiting to pass a bouncer to enter the Versace store that was already opened, it seemed the natural thing to do, to walk the white line up the middle of the six lane road and cross all the lanes of the roundabout and strole pas drole all the way to the eternal flame (so far), under a real Arc de Triomphe.

*

Tonight, just now, cycling to the Co-op, holding my mobile phone down low on "torch" as a light for the car overtaking me to see, and I lean over and change gears on the right handlebar with my left hand. It's easier now, easier than in a car. That took a lot of practice in my mid-twenties on wasteground or spare moments around a dog in Kelvingrove Park. It is a great way to win money from cycle couriers all gathered around the steps of a good hangout place with guys who are happy to highly test their own highly tested high testosterone levels: to bet they cannot ride a figure of eight with the left hand on the right handlebar.

That took a while. Learning to throw well with the left hand has taken seven years so far having all started on Findhorn beach with an inexhaustable selection of the pebbles required. In fact learning it felt long and hard and would take years to let go properly – about maybe as long as it would to throw every stone and so move the whole beach back a bit. The arm moves in the same way as the right arm yet it just doesn't have the ten-thousand-times thing about it. The muscles resist through their ally the brain and it just feels like it feels un natural. Triumph. And in fact it may never end, you never finish something like this it is just abandoned for longer periods. Oh, and the tea bag trick: while making kettles boil, you hold tea bag and cup in the same hand with a sly grip and then toss the cup up in a simple somersault and while it's on its way toss the tea bag and then when you've caught the cup nicely after its air turn you catch the tea bag now in the palmed cup . . . Oh, and the spinning of the VHS cassette holder, the joining of three rizlas in a slick lick of glue-on-glue-off manoeuvre that is very quick, the rotating of the pen around the thumb in a three-sixty swizzle . . . I've got hundreds . . . what are yours? . . . The little sub-party piece little personal doodle doos that you do do . . .

I wipe my arse by getting about ten sheets and forming them into a curved capital "N" by laying one half over the other. Then I do that again close but not straight over itself so I get a kind of mobius-width and wipe holding from behind with the paper now gathered slightly to be pinched and held between the middle two fingers of my flat hand. With the mobius method you at least get an infinite wiping surface.

Sneezes are rare: maybe two point five a month.

One large, strong beer or farm-strength cider a night, five hundred millilitres of strong English ale while I'm cooking is good. If I'm gigging, then unlimited drinks of unspecified arrangements . . . two Guinness then a whisky then a half of ale then another whisky . This is what I do.

There is no underwear in my life: just too much to be doing to be having to lay boxers on a radiator to dry, ugly things, no fucking way. I won't do it. Like some DJs don't dance.

There is a pair of lost-property socks at the moment in my life: smart-wool socks. Hey! What's a smart-wool sock? Well it's one where specially-different weaves are chosen for different parts of the sock: Ribbed and ridged on the ankle to allow more double-more material à la corde du roi and so give more support all around the small to grand arch of the foot and then the reinforced heel's double lateral forestep pattern. Truly a trailblazer in foot-specific loomwork.

They came from my good goddaughter Jelly and they have their explanatory term woven onto them. So rare to see descriptive words on footwear.

Our garden is sunny from nine a.m. till about seven and all day the sun's light passes over a perfect creosote shed, with many round objects hanging on it. A trampoline, a caravan, eleven to thirteen spheres, eight bikes, Midi the rabbit and some guinea pigs.

No bikes here were bought by me except the little blue ridgeback that I bought for Felix my first boy for ninety-nine quid nine years ago and just got back recently from his Mum in Scotland where he lives. The rest of the bikes are gathered or found abandoned and done up: rescued from the Co-op one night after a three a.m. lift home from Milton Jones, you know, the Christian Comic, or found in the woods, or reconditioned after being nicked by someone and left at the train station unlocked.

Now Lion, the most recent boy-son with the will to blow his nose, is waiting to get big enough to get the blue one under him. Recently, in a voiceover job, I checked the stationery cupboard and got some WD-40 with the straw still attached. It was like finding a retro searched-for thing that collectors search for. So that old bike is ready and oiled.

Once I gigged in Chile then Colchester the next night . . . once Warsaw then Chelmsford . . .

Last week I gigged in Swansea and Singapore. Frosties then Caviar.

Going to Singapore was another dream job. Fly over there, land, spend day, gig, eat and come back. Like bungee-jumping round the world and leaving your soul for a bit in the lag of the elastic drag-back across the planet, bit of the old pan-planet drag-lag, which I've had before going to China for five days or over to Australia for five nights once. Barely out of the bungee grip of ultra-modern movement and back again, leaving a wee bit of your psyche's anchor and steadiness adrift to come back and find you.

At one point on this Air Singpore flight there were two stewardess-hostesses serving me screwdrivers in rotation, one from each aisle offering me them boozes in the sky even just before they were needed. I watched four movies back-to-back. Starting with Moneyball – Brad Pitt is producing and he'll act how he wants and take a kind of shared back-seat, like a bench all are on, and, though it does work well at being a picture in the style of the thing it is depicting, and, at one point, he is crying and I am crying and I was up all last nite, healing it a bit and killing it again with Alice and her Knut and then I got on the Overground (sic, yet it's me) and fell asleep and went past my connecting station with the dark-blue Heathrow line, headeded (sick) back, fell asleep again and missed the connecting station again, and then, after two hours, was further away from Heathrow than when I started.

So the fact I am on the plane is all lucky-ducky emotional stuff. Plus, especially, as I was going to sneak some grass in, sellotaped into my hair in a cellophane wrap wrapped within other hair already cut off in a wee tight reggae-nodule, yet it was all done last night, all smoked so there is this final muslin ultra-gossamer coating of innocence over me like the insect spray from helicopters sprayed over Illinois and three Scottish young travellers camping out who don't know about it. For, bless, I am flying legal for the first time in years and it's great.

Then Sunset Boulevard came on and it's up close the screen and this film's huge moments and very modern moments . . . Then Erin Brokovich just for the harmony of the beautiful womanly J. Roberts' harmlessly-radiating a harmonic trashiness with that of the character she is playing.

Then The Whistleblower which carries a bit more weight than it is able to and, yet again, that is true of the character and anyone who would take on traffickers of women. It's too heavy for any one of us.

Then Braveheart and it's all hair and arse and spikes and love, love, love. He ends up sexy with Sophie Morceau. It's mad, not visceral, more vicarious. And when the captain switches off the in-flight entertainment in order to land, there's me and my face right up, inches from the empty screen; up close, ready for my close-up. Me with more tears. Here in the sky with my own reflection filling the small screen, Now I am the movie. Not crying for any reason or reasonable thing and loving the feeling of it flowing.

They came around with landing-cards and in the box of nationality I wrote Scottish and a tear fell from my cheek down into the writing.

Land at seven thirty in the morning, yet really the previous night's morning, after beef chili noodle supper breakfast, and am met by the best Scotsman Scott you could ever meet here who is arranging the gig. They have got me a bike and yet cycling is semi-illegal, and easy to get a twenty lashes of a lashing for, when you are mouthy with the Gurkhas – the most immodest of all Himalayan Buddh-ish geezers. To me it is preferable the straightforward up-front mean anti-humanity of the Dalai Lama and his Buddhist henchmen buddies. At least you know where you are with them: their threat is all smiley. La la, fucking Californian gigs, if they can get them, and at least a chance of peace. Ever since I was hitchhiking and a Buddhist in a maroon van passed me there has been an open window in their mansion to climb in, just to see them shit. Here, though, these Nepalese Tibetan anti-Tyrolean nightmares are armed and distinguishable from kind young-looking youths all smiling in the temples. At least the monks are still pretending to be not-normal human lusting animals, so they are mostly peaceful. These guys are openly using big sticks.

The bike for me did not get used much because of the lashings of punishments on offer, and we drank all night, ending up with me using a Lufthansa pilot's identification card for 30% discount smoothing down my hair with booze to resemble him not. And at the bar while chatting up the brand manager for Jägermeister in Asia . . . thinking "How can I get a sponsored tour here from the Asiameister?" . . . and then getting a tiny nick from a swinging shop sign that could practically have been the end of me as I timed it wrong and got caught in an ill-timed high in this peninsula's nightime's ocean breezes.

Anyway, back in Ingerland the garden is used by me and Lilly and Lion (4.3), Delilah (2.2) and Melina. Details of the various kickings, runs, fires and games and tarps and brambles to follow:

Tonight for a snack there was cheese on toast with a dod of rosehip jam.

It's two thousand and twelve and every gig could be the best one ever although that was also the case in two thousand and six when I used a giant potato-masher from the kitchens, heated up over a couple of candles, to brand the ass of a heckler. That's another story . . . well, actually that is the story.

Chapter Fore

Cycling is a destination. I love going there.

Glasgow, 2005.

Cycling just a little way the wrong way up a one-way street and I see two Policemen approaching. A bit like with bears, it is best not to act like prey and so, instead of being a bit meek and getting off, which is still a bit of a gamble because the crime has already occurred, this time I gently aimed myself between them, slowly making them move apart. There are, though, many options here: One could just get off and give them the sheepish nod-of-understanding, culpability and rehabilitisation and then get back on as soon as they are passed. You can even just raise your leg slowly to perform a very long dismount as they pass, the leg looking to take you off and into the lands of "okay" and then, wow, with deft timing, bring the leg back without it ever touching the ground. That is real fitness to do the acquiescent dismount, the finely weighted ride of deference, the Japanese water-balanced slow zen leg-float of implied complicity.

Slipping between them with the lube of bravura, one of them spoke to me: "You must be French to cycle this way up the street!" – which I thought was fantastic.

That was it a beautiful moment, much more inspiring than a caution, a bit of judicial sarcasm, the long sharp forked-tongue of the law. So, here I was: I had to think of something, had to find humorous words, had to be witty and encapsulate it all too. This was it – all the sixteen years of being a comedian came into play now, my Bruce-Lee-in-an-alley-challenged-by-hoods-moment. If I can't pull this off, what am I here, now? What's it all about if it isn't about really being in life? Gigs are a part of life, thinking never stops, better come up with something Phil! Miraculously I could feel my brain coming to it – that feel of the short gestation, the mind in "find" mode. I began to open my mouth, trusting, and before the last spoke of the rear wheel had passed by the last bit of Policeman, I said in French "Pardon?" Found it.

It had everything: it was French, it went with what he had said, it turned his wit into a possible truth ("Fuck's wrong with your leg? Oh, it's a false one!"), it exonerated me, it sounded like "hard on", and it meant that he was back-footed and went "Whit?" – which is Scottish for

"Pardon?" The circle of life. By this time I was into fourth gear and moving at a slightly higher mean velocity away from him – a slightly meaner high velocity and was enough gone . . . Which reminds me . . .

My favourite street in Glasgow was called Park Drive: "Well, make up your mind, which is it to be?" I always said out loud, driving passed it. I walked the narrow back alleys for years. I lined up all the chucked-out Christmas trees in January in a back alley to be like an organic carwash. Had graffiti done across the motorway on a building's side so that my daughter could see for her birthday. Lost teeth, studied for a year and a day, at university just one day in the second year, to pick up the eight hundred quid grant.

There was an owned house with massive open-plan space and a dog and kids born.

Once, after I left an actual wife, I lived in a caravan parked right by the beautiful big Kelvingrove Park. Stepping out of it was like having the biggest garden ever. These whole city acres of green with trees, was mine to enjoy. I stayed nine nights in it either side of a Glastonbury. Where I parked it by the park was for years a free place for cars, no markings at all. Then when I got back from Down South they had installed all the meters and stuff and had actually painted the allotted parking spaces around my caravan. The whole street marked up in sync with my road home. One day I came back with a friend to check on it and it was all smouldering, all burned out. All I really missed was the Tweed Jacket lost. I gathered some smoky blistered photographs and an old black Rosenthal German porcelain plate I had had for nine homes since I was a kid. I put them all in the boot of my car and closed it down on the plate breaking it gently.

This is the second time my possessions had been severely trimmed. Staying in a camper-van on some west-end free land right in the heart of the West End and I had lost the keys. One day I came back to where it was and it wasn't. I just kept walking – there is not much checking to do, its not a phone, it has not been mislaid; it's your fucking home. Gone, they've taken my home. At this moment it's best to just keep walking – it is very hard for anyone to tell you have just lost a vehicle, you could be checking on a wee bird or a bit of unusual litter, your keen interest in the world. Certainly I become a lot less homed that night so it was lucky I met tall BrianTV guy who took me to a bar and then ran in to that future wife.

August 21st 2004, 2:34pm, Assembly Rooms, Edinburgh.

Went to see Phil Nichol do some acting in a play and, just as the lights went down, had answered my phone by mistake trying to shut it down and ended up agreeing to buy that five hundred pound Scorpio estate car from a mate just because it was the quickest way to get her off the line.

October 2004, sunny.

The Jag exploded on the way back from Oban last night. I drove a friend up in it rather than another car because it was an automatic and that left a hand free to stroke her weary head. It was amazing it had started at all. It was a pillar-less coupe – it flew. It was a peerless coupe. In the morning I noticed there were twin leaks from the two fuel tanks dripping onto the twin exhausts. As much as I love symmetry this was a worry. I tried the special fixative putty that requires dry, clean surfaces and forced it into wet viscous rust-bumpy slaky metal cracks and thought, "Fuck it, if it came all the way here it could be okay, I'll just drive quickly to keep blowing the fire out." It is a curious feeling to be checking rear-view mirror for flames as you drive . . . Funnily enough I had put no water in a leaky radiator and, with all that checking for smoke and fire behind, it actually exploded up front: the big end's big end and I abandoned it in a garage in Inverary. Sorry. She was a lovely car. BUY 15S. I remember filling her up for the first time in London, lying over the boot, mid-forecourt, a nozzle from each pump, two at once, putting fifty-four quids worth in and actually feeling the car go down a bit on its suspension with the weight of it all.

That one was one of three that broke down on the first drive. It was not sparking well on all of its plugs and that distracted me. So that going cross-country to Norwich to see K.Ogg, and we ran out of petrol – me and the two tanks in the middle of nowhere and, freewheeling in neutral around the corner, there was a garage and we just drew up nicely next to the pump.

"Shit! Those engines are quiet."

"Can you have a look at the plugs?"

"We had that Danny La Rue the comedian here last year. Fixed his Jag."

"This makes it a brace."

"Eh?"

". . ."

The other car – that didn't get driven to Scotland this or that time with the stroking of the nurse's head who incidently had had an actual electric shock from a cock, an al fresco popstar blowjob, when he touched an electric fence – was the Citroen XM estate that had to be parked on a hill for a rolling start and there were none there that time when I left it outside T In The Park for three hours with the engine running, returned and drove a hundred miles north of the Highlands through Aviemore listening to my brother's band The Darkness's first album for the first time zooming o'er glen roads after a big bonus line of coke from a friend in the counterfeit-laminate trade.

It's amazing when you run back just as the traffic warden is writing the ticket and all the apologies sometimes works and they stop the processing of the ticket. Well it struck me it doesn't have to be your own car. This you could do whenever you see it happening. I have done it twice; once on the road in Glasgow and once when I called down from a balcony on the Dumbledaws flats behind the new Parliament building in Edinburgh as I saw two traffic wardens circling a car way below.— calling down: ". . . sorry mate-ate-ate . . . I'll be down in a minute . . . thaaaanx . . ."

Right now 11.03.13, 15:12pm, have just made a chili and cabbage rice soup with wasabi-salt, roasted seeds, broken oatcakes and old breadcrusts thrust in to soften.

Rovers burn more easily than Jags: Bumped into Wendy my old friend in Safeway Byres Road Glasgow and gave her a lift up the road and we parked to say goodbye by the old green wooden post office at Kirklee on the Great Western Road. Just then the oily petrol-fume smells finally made sense and she burst into flames. Me and Wendy and Urph the dog got out rather pretty smart-quick and then had plenty of time to watch the flames gather themselves, sending out a billowing black storm under the hood and then really go for it.

The folks in the flammable depot were sweating: some of the stamps lost their adhesive power. The fire brigade, or at least part of it, came and soaked it. I had bought eggs and they had turned into a huge omelette on the dashboard. A wee walkman was turned into coal yet the now smoke-damaged J. Joplin Pearl album remained playable. And her voice was a lot more husky now not just from the fags but a good car fire.

We lived around the corner. That's where I read Trainspotting and had a house that formed part of the wall of the Botanic Gardens, came back from six months in Australia with a baby girl Coco and amazingly over the next while had five Turner Prize winners come visit . . .

Starling, Deller, Gordon, Boyce, Wright, Lambie. We had the Rover 3.5 P4 coupe then. And the first three-wheeled pram with inflatable tyres for jogging with. We just parambulated.

The dog was called Urph so it would sound like we were barking when we called her and on one walk she got hit, at like six miles an hour, by a rich boy on his first-ever drive in a new gift-car straight after passing his test with his Mum. Urph shat herself – all the poo from right up to the stomach came out and I realized the meaning of the term "the smell of fear". Just emptied she was, expunged.

The Rover that burned was a Vanden Plas with an onboard seventies computer that sat like two shoeboxes right along the top of the dash and offered "Estimated Time of Arrival" which, after a brief computation period, was always revealed to be whatever time it was now . . . Rover Zen, you are there already. Oh yes: The Journey is The Destination.

"Dad, Dad . . . are we there yet?" "Yes."

My boy Felix will occasionally press his knees into my back on a journey, like a cheap massage seat, and ask "Are we there yet?"

"Good point," I always reply, ". . . see what you mean. Thanks, feel that way too."

In the car park of the big Marriot-or-equivalent down by the Clyde River one night I got the urge to carve something in the wooden dashboard of the Rover and the security guards came out. It took me five words to calm them. No cheek, just the gentle pheromones of truth out here by the water . . . it is my car I have no proof and yes it is an odd hour to do this and no I am not a resident yet I spent the morning with Bill and Kris and a big white cockatoo in the foyer . . . were you on then? No . . .

Once or twice I cooked flapjacks in the engine while driving, and fish-and-mushrooms, together in foil. It was in the massive old Volvo740 turbo estate that we bought for 740 pounds that time.

I came back from Ireland with DavidMacsavage and we taught those teenagers how to juggle on a stormy ferry, drove for thirteen hours to get back before my first night at the Edinburgh Festival two thousand and five. My agent met me as I ran in (on time technically) with twenty-two minutes till Showtime and said, "Where have you been?"

I began listing all the countries I could remember from leaving home and slightly with a sore throat. She seemed not able to be light-hearted and yet, ten minutes into my show, engine-baked flapjack ready to share with the crowd, foil-wrapped warm in my pocket – talking about the best way to teach girls juggling on a ferry is with feet apart and tissue that floats slowly – then here she comes in and hands me a nice big double port to ease the vocals. It was my sixteenth festival at her venue, the Gilded Balloon; she is Karen. Port goes well with flapjack from the VolvOven.

I've seen Karen's house expanded, seen her daughter grow, seen her as a pink champagne-drinking host backstage at her venue at three in the morning when it was absolutely the latest and liveliest place to be; where every wild comic drank and went onstage in the ultimate shaped room at the ultimate shaped hour – Smith, Hardee, Evans, Kay, Frost, Izzard, Hughes, Bailey, Brand, Reeves, Mortimer, Cognito, Miwurdz, Golden, Hegley, Eclair, Evans, Thomson, Coogan . . . the list is ending – seen her as a grandmother; seen her upset and seen her upsetting; seen her sign 64 staff-cheques on a Friday. She used to come to a lot of my gigs. Once my false teeth flew out from the stage and were lost at the Carnegie Hall in Dunfermline and at half-time Karen went all along the rows until eventually she found them in somebody's hood – fairly thorough that. Lucky she did it: would have been a strange un-comfort in the rain to lift up your hood and have my ceramic scraping on your scalp, some kind of squirrelly revenge . . . partial vampire nibble . . . whats it called when someone votes for you as you are abroad . . . ??

The Carnegie Hall Dunfermline – the Original – the Scottish steel-man, first billionaire to build America's buildings, Dark Side of the Moon for the Richest Man Charts, invented Billionairedom. We all, at my school, went to school with great-grandson Joss. He walked in late to lunch, often with a hand in between his jacket buttons like Napoleon: too wealthy and too distinguished even at seventeen to have both arms dangling.

If I was an ornithologist there would be memory with me of important early formatives with the birds most probably . . . With being a comedian 'tis different because everyone is funny and enjoys the jokes, we is all it, and friends are funny, they are funnyness personified and laughs are the currency of this trip . . . – so, however: one of my First Great Jokes:

At school playing touch-rugby, as training for speed in real rugby, my boot is scraped off my foot by Chris Parks' boot in an awful accidental dredging down the tender stretch of my heel's Achilles tendon. Always a gentle vulnerable bit of any body. I lay on the ground making the particular noise one does for this exact kind of partial-agony pain that is not serious, is without actual injury, is keenly big at the time so that it will passed and gone sooner. The noise is an anguished sound gnawing at the spot and maybe helps the pain go quicker. The Sports Bachelor teacher coach came with already-enough-of-this-school and asked what was wrong with me now? In only a second I saw and heard the blanket of fed-up-ness wrapped around him and answered, "I've got earache. What does it look like?" – maybe hoping the pain would be seen as an excuse for my supreme wit. Alas no, he pushed me a little bit down a grassy banking. As I was leaving he sent me more-off.

My mother broke her ankle, a bit pissed in the car park there in Dunfermline. Then later, to kind of prove it wasn't that bad, she sort of hopped on it, put all her weight on it and winced. I winced.

The Carnegie Hall, where I proved I was not a healer when this kid of seventeen made me sit holding his hand during the interval, sitting on the front of the stage to help his fingers move again.

That was the second gig there and the balcony was in use. By the fourth time I was there, there weren't enough folk to need the balcony. Just a boiled-down hardcore of supporters, who usually number about seventy-eight. Often this is the best gig as you can start straight away deeper in, and, in the overcoming by not mentioning the smaller-ness, there is a grandness to the show. When it goes weller than well, all of us are camouflaged from the surrounding by what we see and what is going on verbally.

I am not a great fan of the interval and often in one of the shows that's just me it is only the crowd who has them, not me, I just stay on. It can be a nice rhythm-change to let the lights up a bit, set a few folks free and then just carry on, a bit more relaxed.

Sometimes comedy with me, and for me, is killed by the expectation: Doing what is expected is not that great. If doing what people do not expect you to do is what people expect you to do, then you kind of have to go very wild, or do what they expect which is not what they expect at all. Often the best thing is to do what you yourself did not expect and let them witness that. Do what you would like to do – don't forget I have been to every one of my gigs – if a few suffer because I am a bit out-there then so be it. What I will not do is sacrifice the possibility of this being the best show ever. Sometimes they can't be because natural downs in me will become apparent to the big psychic ouija-cluster that is a crowd; and sometimes the opposite: it cannot fail because all you are really doing with everything is revelation: revealing what you are inside and, if you are optimistic; in love with life, in the middle of a chain of wonders, slightly stoned and up for the moment with a confident bank of lovely tales to sing and tell with four great one-liners, then that is what they will see. I always feel that, beyond laughter, people want to see you do what you most want to. That's what it is for me at the Circus, the Poetry night, the Cabaret my friends . . . Burlesque seems to be to be solely concerned with pweople doing exactly what they most want to and have trained at and for.

Hands up, anyone who has tried to kick hash on the floor through customs, or used their iPad regularly as a drinks tray or a ping-pong bat or for rabbit-herding . . . ?

September 2011.
The three best things to occur recently: hedge-trimming on a trampoline. What started as simply a useful raised, wide strong platform between ladders developed into an actual visual sketch with some bouncing . . . I'm on it that I'm on it, fully aware that an humorous situation is evident; aware also that any bouncing with a chainsaw-like item with the engine on has capacity to interest and engage and can lead then to a smile which is, in entertainment environments, often automatically upgraded to a laugh because of the aura of the context and all.

So a little light-trimming with bouncing occurs because, though I will not set out to do things that are oddly-funny, it seems they are not ruled out. It just seems to be a matter of timing and how much time is spent in the planning.

I did once drive past a sign in the Highlands which, as I approached, it appeared to say "Hotel ZOOM" and I thought "What a magic name for a hotel, what a concept: in you come, zoom-zoom, here's your room, dinners, now let's go swimming, see you, bye! A whole weekend-break done in forty minutes . . . Then I realized it was actually "Hotel 200m" as the car passed the sign at the entrance.

So I tell the crowd this and then tell them that it wasn't "zoom" and tell them all the thoughts I had in real-time in those ten seconds AND that I had thought of them when I was inside it happening: how I would tell them the Zoom-Hotel-concept and the first joke, and thought that, even while being told about that, that it would still be funny to hear that they were considered right there and then – first-press laughs, then laughs that come after in a re-telling of the situation of thought about the source of that laugh.

Come on, it is extra double-good to be a comedian. To be allowed to get laughs doing the joke, then telling about the setting of the arrival of the joke, and then laughs from the crowd as they hear about what I thought they would probably be laughing at . . . Which reminds me . . .

Okay here's a bigger story.
August 2010.
Late one night early in the first week of the Edinburgh Festival and my borrowed maroon bike is taking me down Chambers Street towards the Jazz Bar. The most lovely and fabulous venue to go down under the pavement and dance in; where you know there is a high possibility of the musicians playing onstage being able to respond to what you and the room are doing. You could do a big shimmy and the drummer might go "fruup-ching" and then half the whole room might do a big spin. Many bands give off the vibe that they are just doing what they are doing and they worked it out before you came along. Fair enough, that's a gig and most people face the same way toward the band. Wedding bands, dance outfits, groovy glam-skiffle and shifty rhythm blues-combos in a town hall – they are the ones for me where people are not standing to watch, they are dancing. In fact this is the band I want to be in: glam-skiffle, sandshoe funky blues combo, in fact this is the band I have. Anyway, here they often have a fabulous jam-band of high calibre. Arriving at the door I am all excited yet am not allowed in as I have been banned for slapping the manager's face in a street altercation last year. It had completely slipped my mind.

And it wasn't really a slap.

We were in there four of us dancing away all wild and enthusiastic. Coming out for a fag then going in, dancing for a while, buying drinks, coming outside again, then inside again and, at the bar we get four triple-Bundaburg rums with ginger beer and a piece of lime. About to sip – "No, let's have a fag," says Tim and so, outside, we can feel them on the bar waiting for us like the best four drinks of all time, the Mount Rushmore of rums. Sadly, outside the manager sees that a friend we are bringing in has a bottle of wine in his bag and he decided then to tell us we are all a bit wild and can't go back in and we're all "No, no, no" and "We've got four marvellous rums in there . . . Please . . ." and no dice, it's not happening.

"Please, please. Can't you hear the rums calling us? "Come back, come back. Ees lonely weethout you guys . . . myself, Hugo Chávez, Castro and that guy from Ecuador await you . . .'"

You know you are not getting back in if the manager says quite straightly, "No I cannot hear the rums calling."

"You guys are about to lose it . . . ," he adds. So then I say, "What? Lose it like this?" and do a big pantomime-slap that comes to a halt near his face . . . Everyone winces and breathes in.

So the faux-slap slipped my mind this night and they send me on my way. Fair enough, it's one thirty-five. I'll get home and have a nice early night and push off on the Raleigh Cameo lady's bike – it has three gears: Easiest, Twelfth and Through-Molasses – turning up the hill toward the Festival Theatre at the end of the street, I'm up out of the saddle gathering momentum when there catches my eye one of the best scenes ever: A Police car has pulled over a quad bike. There's nothing more un-arty than the quad bike with its hooning barely sur-legal status, powering around Edinburgh Streets. You see them on motorways looking unstable, like a guy riding a coffee table or an ape on a boulder.

It always interests me when the Police cars whiz by with sirens, on their way to something. How you would have to do a very-visible really-bad thing to alter their path . . . Something massive to make them pull over and sirenize you with the blue Christmas-disco lights. So that means there's quite a lot of space for fucking about – standing by the road with your tongue out hardly matters in this context. So, as I come past, peddling through the molasses in the quiet orange glow of the streetlights, I say out-loudly, "Ooh, look, a Police Man!"

Slowly and surely everyone just turns towards me the variety of disbeliefs is widescreen. The Policeman with the notebook out gives me a stern look that says "watch it now!" and on my face the look of "well, come on . . ." Though, what's he going to do? Leave them and come after me? Leave the suspects who have done something clearly naughty and late-nighty? . . . What would he say in court? "Then I was forced to leave the drug-delivery men we have been following for months because the cyclist went 'ooh' and slightly-mocked me?"

One of the quaddies, holding a helmet, smiles and says, "Look, Christ on a bike!" Not everyone laughs – just me and the two boys . . . Never mind. Christ on a bike, that's funny. Imagine Christ on a quad bike methinks: zooming around all over the place getting a whole lot more conversions done, off-roading to the souls in remote places. Although it was all off-road in them days, as there were no roads – shit, it occurs to me that's what humans have done: redefined the world as being all off a road. This is not fair . . . yet hey this is the wrong time for to fully address this concept . . . later . . .

So I am pulled by bike-power slowly out of this scene, still with all eyes helping and feeling a little hilariously fabulous at the whole affair when I slide up next to another Police car that was parked just a bit further on, watching. Left wheels high up on the high ancient Edinburgh kerb with their hundred-year-old height, eleven inches of granite to keep back the olden days river of filth excrement and offal with what looked like more-senior Policemen doing some observation and having a sandwich. The one on the driver's seat with a thick elbow wanting fries and a shake leans out a bit and says, "Where are the lights on your bike?"

Now I'm not that keen on lights, preferring to skulk about in the shadows, ride pavements, sleek aboot and go slow yet much faster than a walk. Getting around swiftly-er than on foot is the major object; first equal with not-pounding a hard surface all day which, combined with a couple of hours onstage, can make bones ache – and with the right kind of swiftness you can actually be in three bars at the same time. There are no lights on my bike and often taxi drivers and people shout out "Where are your lights?" and I shout back "How can you even see me to ask?" whereupon they all go "Ah yes, I see your point Phil you have illuminated me\us opened my/our eyes to the fact that I/we was/were blind to before and/or now can see that I/we was/were aware of/seeing you all the time and molehill to mountaineering it . . ." and that is the end of that . . .

There was a backwards slash there did you see before the forward ones Brenda?

This time though, I didn't want to piss about, I wanted to just let it all slide. So I don't answer him – no witty answers or "Of which lights do you speak?" and make him define the imaginary and stray into you-are-paid-to-protect-and-serve-not-fanny-about-rhetorically territory – Just keep going slowly in the hope he'll just thinks "What a cheek . . . Well I never . . . In all my days . . ." et cetera and just let it go. Be drawn back to his corned beef and beetroot forgiving my ignorant ignoring.

Also, at that exact moment, I caught sight of the Palmyra kebab-joint and suddenly required food myself: Suddenly, although I'm in something here, the primal feeling for meats and crunch sweeps over all.

Ploughing on fifty metres to the meats, the going very tough waist-high in syrup in twentieth and not really getting away very fast and, for a minute, there is a stillness I begin to think that "hey! They're no coming . . ."

Then the sound of the Volvo estate starting up, the hydraulics kicking in and she starts to rise up off the kerb . . . pulling off, down and out, starting the big cruel circle of a U-turnaround, coming after me. As the Police car does in Psycho, when she pulls over with the stolen money, and the way Samuel Jackson's car goes around in a crane shot to the wasteland to shoot his mate in the boot or trunk. Or the beginning of that film Nostalgia that Tarkovsky made in Italy where the Beetle drives into shot then through it, disappears soundwise then re-enters with its noise first again the conciousness then the screen this time closer and in the classical mist . . . not now, no time . . .

. . . Salivating now slightly and at least with a positive mission, I draw up on the bike outside the Palmyra and spin the pedal, stepping off the bike in one smoovement and it magically just stands up there supported against the kerb by the pedal. Feeling a bit like Bond now on a mission with the Cops on my tail now in my periphery yet getting ignored . . . They arrive and One of Them draws down a window as they pull up and says, "There are no lights on your bike." At least and at last: a pure, truthful entity of a phrase. Excited, I simply say, "Well then, surely you must act."

I keep thinking it's not that big a deal and surely they will just move on.

So on I go, up the stairs and take my money out my pocket and realize there is only twenty-four pence, not twenty pounds twenty-four pence, and this is when my life truly turns into Mission Implausible Too – I'm after a snack, I have no money and the Police are on my tail – yet onward and up, because that's where the kebabs are; it doesn't matter how much money you have if you're not in the shop, so up I go and at the top of the stairs is Jim Jefferies, the huge Australian comedian, standing there all tall, just like his poster and wearing the same shirt, with a young exotic lass clinging onto him, her arm and a leg around him with rave-frayed miniscule denim cut-offs with fingermarks still visible from yesterday morning's fake tan application. There he is kebab in hand and I say, "Money, Jim, have you some money?" It's very responsive and kind of him, he hands me four quid. This is the moment the first Policeman arrives in the very bright shop and says, "I'd like a word with you."

Now Jim thinks this is just an arrest for begging or general vagrancy and tells the Cop to "Go easy, it's alright, he knows me" and I say "Jim, don't worry, it's alright He knows Me too . . . There's a back story . . ." as they escort me out to the Volvo . . . They really do want a word with me, or perhaps several maybe even entire sentences . . .

My hands are on the top of their car and they ask me if there is anything in my pockets that could injure them and my response is to say, "Dunno. You'll have to read all the notebook." Because now here we are: I am facing away from the kebabs yet I am in it now; there is no way to avoid Police contact yet all I can think about is how to get this going my way again so a kebab can be got – meat is hot in my mind. Having said that, witty answers are perhaps a way to pass on the info that you are not a mad violent-offender with other things to hide . . . There are my worldly possessions: four and a bit quid and a pink notebook.

Then they ask my name and tell me I'll have to show them some ID . . . A clever ploy in case I am planning to tell them a duff name.

"I'm afraid I have no ID so there's no point in telling you my name."

They consult each other and one says, almost pleading, "Well, just tell me your real name then."

Poor guys, they had issued the clear instructions presuming I would have ID and have now placed themselves in a tricky mode/place/realm/position/caffuddle/conundrum/catch 22. They are out here on the front line, upholding justice yet justice is a massive big wet pillow-sized bar of soap and hard to hold and giving none of the comforts of a pillow . . . The lawmakers are at home with brandy in the correct glass their feet up by the real fire and these guys who hold it have to try and make us humans and our actions fit previously-devised form . . . Not easy.

"I have no ID so I could just tell you any name . . . I could tell you my name is Mickey Zzezzr."

"Right, how do you spell that?"

It just came out without me thinking, the brain obviously said you cannot hesitate spelling your own name, so I said, "Zee, zee, e, zee, zee, r" like auto-babble.

"No, that's not my name. I'm just making a point. If there's no proof then what's the point in me saying my name? If you guys are not going to take my word for it, how does it benefit me?"

"Right, that's it! I'm booking you for Obstruction."

"Guys, guys . . . Come on, this is just silly."

"Well, where are the lights on your bike?"

The soap-bar is slipping out of their grip.

One of them says, "Well, what do you want us to do?"

"Just . . . let . . . it . . . go," I say.

There is a big fat empty few seconds while their eyelids flutter, a fall into a precipice beginning a kind of tantric-pause in the crime fighting

. . . just fading into the fall from the hubris an outside loop in a monoplane . . .

"No, that's it We're going to book you for Obstruction."

There are stages in any apparent conflict when you just have to accept what the other is saying, accept its energy and stop trying to stop it, use its force like karate. So I just got down on my hands and knees and started crawling away from them . . . Not fast, not trying to evade them, not a getaway-crawl, just an absolutely normal speed trying somehow to represent an opposite to what problem they say I am, and embody a lack of whatever bad force might be obstructing them . . . And I did not look back. If the moral can exist then it is for me a top tip . . . If you ever have to crawl from the Police, don't look back, whatever you do don't look back at them, don't be the fluffy squirrel to the bear who really doesn't want to eat you.

I crawled past Jim, who was standing watching with the exotic lass, jaws doing less chewing, past them and up the stairs into the kebab shop, rising up, onto my feet and up to the counter and ordered a mixed grill kebab. The vendor announces a simple refrain with now a huge semi-spiritual significance, "Do you want that in a pitta or in a wrap?"

"I just beat the wrap" is what I could have said.

That's when being a comedian is great: you can tell a crowd what you might have said and get a laugh and then tell them what you did say and get a little more.

I don't want your pity/pitta. (Delete as appropriate.)

It tasted great and Jim came back and got another one and the wee lass – is she from the Caribbean or Stirling?

In fact, it tastes more than great and, as we step out of the shop she says, "Why don't you come back to our place?"

I tell her, "It's okay. I'm not a vagrant, honestly, thanks there is a house I can go to."

"No, no . . . Come back tae oors." Not the Caribbean, then. "It'll be good for you."

So, it is at that exact moment, as we three steps out onto the top of the steps, that I realize this is an holy kebab, summoned up from on my knees-not-praying; a spiritual holy kebab – believed in, charmed into existence that I always had faith in – and that I'm knocking back a threesome and the Polis has parked my bike safe up on the kerb on a stand I never noticed the bike had . . .

There's a stand . . . ? Surely they never fitted it as well.

What were they doing while I was crawling away. . . ? Now, that is some CCTV footage I would like to see. All around is the threat of see see tv cameras seeing our badness before it's done . . . the cameras showing us a wee movie not committed yet of the illegal so we don't do it. Well what about great acts of goodness, the cameras must get them too?

Later I was thrown out of my own venue three times one year at the Edinburgh Festival, twice by the security and once by myself. This is the nineteenth year I had come back to the Gilded Balloon to perform with a poster. This night I nipped up the front steps to the security men at about three a.m., bobbing around town on my unlocked bike spending time among the three regular haunts and was just breezing in when I was told, "No, we're not open." I immediately said, "Ah yes, well, we are open. It is the festival till four every evening and perhaps I'll be passing my poster on the way round by the pillar . . . nudge nudge . . . Nineteen summers is many." Naught is working to turn them.

It seems silly to fight it yet if I could just get to my picture on the poster. A distraction is needed. They turn toward each other unconvinced of being convinced and I point over there saying, "Look at those hinges!" They look and I nip in quickly imagining I can get around to the pillar in time. They are hot on my heels as we approach the part of the wall that has my poster and it is not there, it has been replaced by a lady in Y-fronts who plays her own twin brother in her show. It doesn't take long for bouncers to peel Phil off a pillar. Particularly with their training and soon I am out the front door and definitely now have to complete negotiation from off the bottom step, below the bottom wrung on the ladder of in.

I am keen that the river of truth is nonetheless flowing in my direction and come up a step and know they must be engaged with and must engage the man they have just thrown out.

Happy still, I somehow manage to just listen in on their conversation and at one point laugh at something my man has said, so that he turns to me and says, "You're awright. In ye go."

Trying to work out the headline I summarize to: "Banished Comic Let Back Into His Venue Of Two Decades By Letting Bouncer See That He Actually Found Him Funny." "Bouncer Amuses Banished Comic Back Into Own Venue."

This is rare. I mean to nash in then be caught and thrown out then let in again. It never happens . . . It indicates to me that they knew all along and just could not go along with a U-turn or in the chase they passed my poster in a relocated position and subliminally re-cognized.

The next evening event was better: Thirty of us hovered around backstage at Phil Nichols' show, all unclothed and ready to make a scheduled entrance at the finale of this show when Phil himself ends a huge story with a re-enactment of how he came to be running naked down the street in Amsterdam to face up to some skinheads after he finally could not take hiding any more, dug deep and got inspired by a group of French who resisted fighting the Russian army by stripping off naked and offering no threat. People met in hushed, joshing clothes-shed tones and latecomers, like us, undressed so as not to be rude and all milled around watching PhilN approach the finale. We could all see the crowd too, watching unawares, watching them as they are un-aware and like a mini piece of theatre in reverse, the emotional calm before the responsive storm, thinking all they would get would be Phil's nudity, just three genitalia, one set of meat and veg, when in fact there is a massive feast of many more meats and veg and fannies. I had bumped into two Welsh women who had been at my gig and come with me to this, knowing what was happening, one of them called Ratchel said one of the best phrases ever said to me in a Welsh accent: "Phil I'm menstruating do you mind if I keep my pants on . . . ?" Of course, I say for this impromptu striptease on a mass scale onstage for the first time ever as an unrehearsed un-repeatable debut performance as final curtain call finale encore finale to end all nude impromptu mass nude encore finales, yes keep your pants on.

It went well, so well that everyone milling about was relaxed with themselves and them bodies and no one really wanted it to end, and I actually saw a guy pulling up his trousers than just pulling them down again in the same movement. It's post-erotic, pre-primal, very Scandinavian family, hot-tub sauna scenario-feel. V. chilled.

What shall we do, let's do more bare work is the nude consensus, so about twenty five of us go on to a cabaret club called Spank where they do compere comic compere comic, musical act, lady comic compere go go go and at the end we all run on naked and surprise a new crowd again and jump about and spank each other. It's all very exciting and a young man so full of fun he throws a half jug of beer over near me.

Anyhow this goes well, we're all backstage again crammed in the wee backroom with the sixteen-year-old American commune sister with her multiple scarring scars on her arms all free to be and another comedian and Anna, and staff from the Forest Café and and and . . .

And then the Castle . . . We stormed the Castle naked.

Standing backstage with Foster's reward-beer we were unwilling again to get dressed and were all waiting for the phrase I suddenly came up with: "Let's storm the Castle!"

We undressed up the top of the Royal Mile by the Witchery restaurant – favourite hangout of business diners, lovers and politicians; finest-of-fine posh – dropping all our clothes outside the low pavement-level window to the low sub-pavement-level room and, sprinting up to the two Royal Highland Fusileers that guard the entrance to the parade-ground performance-space of the military Tattoo – guard it from little cubicles with a phone. As we pass giggling and jiggling they see all that they are bred to defend people from: naked revealing revelers, the crazy enemy, armed to the teeth with just teeth. Immediately one highly confusileer is on the phone. We inhabit the great big Tattoo-gig-space, running in to the open where they do the military displays, all the tarty gun-twirling and the highly distasteful races with artillery. Ricky Gervais too. So it is ours now and we milky-white flesh it – a threat, a multiple threat. We're jogging swiftly right up to the front doors of the Castle that they are hurrying and locking, and I remember this is not the first, or even second, castle I have stormed, and "I think we can get it . . ." I say as my hands try to prise it open. We could be in and nick some crowns and be out in a minute. The wee soldier through the perfect comedy wee hatch-door in the door, pops his head out and protected by a wrought-iron grill square says we must go or he will "call the Police" . . . The Army call the Police, that don't seem right the Army calling the Police – then what if they can't come? Who're ye gonnna call? Ghostbusters??

At that point the Castle is ours anyway, ours in many ways: It is the place where we are now and it is un-ownable anyway and, if we are the people of the Crown, and it is Edinburgh's and Scotland's capital's citadel, the last line of inner defence for the population to recede in to defeat the siege, and plus as well now anyway ken nowadays it's for hire so it's ours again anyway, if we book it.

Things change: a fusil is a lightweight musket. The Fusileer no longer has that. More he is a seventeen-year-old choosing this career over the dole.

Jogging back down we got accompanied by a superior in a nightglo highViz waistcoat and told to get out and "We are on our way out . . . that is what we are doing . . . yes sir . . . ," we said, and ran together.

Back at the clothing-pile we answered a big question among the diners and got back into our clothing with big cheerful success on our faces. Down the road and it was a lovely end to stroll in my venue unbarred, even after all the very recent stuff that just happened. Like now there really is a reason to be refused entry yet it is not known. The bouncers can only ever have limited knowledge of who they are doubting. Either they see something or they assume. Base a universal truth on simply what relates to you. And it works. They are employed to do it and that is why I never have a problem with bouncers: just love them and you are more likely to get in. Always my urge is to dance inside venues, not be having conflict outside.

The metaphorical weight in this for me is that people can only oppose that which touches them really. Or are most-opposed to things that do touch them – England hates France, France fights Spain fights Portugal. To me it is not real as these words, not real-hate, it is just physical actions and they happen where they are possible . . . Across the excessively aggressive boundary . . .

So, in we stroll, like mobsters all-massaged, get Guinnesses and head outside to relate the story to groups we pass to join. With three of my recently-naked pals I bump into one of the Walsh brothers who coincidentally happens to perform nude in a nude comedy cabaret show. They don't know each other and I clown out loud about what we have been up to and say to him how he would never be brave enough to do that, just take off his clothes. He smiles and nods and undresses and I join him again. Thirty seconds naked with drinks and then shoof them back on up again. A minute later a young frizzy-haired bouncer called Abraham arrives to throw us out and we are like "Well, we have our clothes on now." It is a bit daft to throw us out for being naked when we are not any more – you are just bringing the image back stronger. "It's over," I say. "We will not do it again and we'll be good. Or we could strip again to justify it . . . if you want."

That's not enough, it has been done. We were naked and that's it. Then as he tries to hoof us-two out, a few friends rally close and we link arms and there is solidarity between us all, we give each other support and strength and we are still sipping our drinks as we are being ejected like one big twenty-legged thing even as more bouncers come and we are moved as a big group. Then resistance gets like to an even match – the force they are putting on us would mean we have to be violent to balance it out. So we capitulate and let ourselves be escorted away. At that point outside in the smoking bit we were already outside, so instead they had to just throw us more outside than before . . . Force fool exit.

Outside, me and the American and a very vocal lady defender of our cause are thrown outer quite quickly and, with that momentum, I realize we could keep going past the main entrance and find a way back in, in round the back I know through the kitchen. Jogging, again just as excited, we head around the back and, without having to stop, find the door I glimpsed from the inside once and zip in through the out door and whiz by the kitchens down in the bowels . . . Incredibly, amazingly, we are only metres inside, giggling and moving swiftly to the bottom of the stairs to go up and in, when we see Abraham spotting us . . . he is in the basement too. Wow! No Way, Wow, Way! So we rush up the stairs with him chasing us with us running to throw ourselves out before he does and into the main hall and out the exit, rushing past two other bouncers who had just thrown us out. Double double-takes. We are a bit giddy and just stand out the front of the steps a bit floaty. Turns out in the meany-meantime that the day-manager, my friend Richard, has heard about it and is able to be out the front here talking to the head bar-manager. The two aspects – the entertainment and the booze sales – they are talking for a while, I get a nod and they talk some more and then I edge up a step or two and ask if it is the right time for me to talk to the bar-manager, Richard ushers me in and very swiftly he tells me it must not happen again and I say, "Of course it will not. It was a complete one-off event." Then he has softened and he says we can go back in yet only to the upstairs StarBar, where we will not be seen. He says it will look strange if they are seen to relent and let us back in.

Bravely I say "No!", that we will not have any stipulations put upon us and, quite the contrary, it will be the most amazing thing for your image that you are able to hear our words, reappraise, reaffirm the close link to the wild world of performing artists that keep this venue with a function, relent and let us back in . . . So he does. A minute later the Guinnesses are revived and we are back out to the smoking sub-basement balcony and people are cheering our return triumphant, back from the dead like Lazarus on waterskis coming out the ocean again after a fall . . .

Every night Macsavage and I would pop in and watch a bit of ReggieWatts show and there was a group of NewYork dancers and one night two of them and me went up the mountain called Arthur's Seat and we fell into the heather laughing at the fact that we had no summit – it just kept getting bigger in fabulous reveals. With her friend, the dancer sat on a wee rise smoking and I rolled down the hill a bit to get a laugh and rolled a bit more to go out of sight and I flew off a wee cliff of about fifteen feet and continued rotating a bit through the sky and fell to a lucky, lucky landing between the two large boulder rocks that were actually there. All this was out of sight of them two and so, when I came back after a minute or so clutching my side, it just looked like the obvious joke you would do to allude to an injury. Alas.

Then we all came together and looked over its edge at the wee cliff and were in fits because: My God, I was lucky.

Could have considered my kids when I was mucking around and fell: what if they can have a disabled dad? Well, that's okay; you can still be a great dad in a wheelchair. It's all about creativity and energetic excitement levels which cannot have some of their manifestations – I would not want to change a certain thing in an attempt to change the overall me, There will just be continuing me and that will result in more situations like this – or, maybe, only a few more – and result in lots of good situations.

Choosing the spur-of-the-moment exciting option is a groovy thing and in itself is not bad. That state of mind is as rewarding as the feeling of safety I feel.

That whole thing about "if I had taken that left road that night everything would have been different" is all bollocks. We have already taken a hundred lefts. This now is what would happen if we took the other way. And anyway, when does it stop? Just cos three minutes after you took that left-instead-of-right you had the crash . . . Well is "it" reset then and you have no longer to be under "its" influence?

I did that: I drove back in an uninsured car and took a spur-of-the moment left instead of right. The right had no really-bad corners so driving it was relaxing knowing there was never a time you were helplessly catapulted slingshot-fashion onto the other side of the road without really trying. Thing was, if ever this was a week not to take a spirited left in an uninsured lover's vehicle then this was the week.

2006 while sharing a flat with this big-Edinbruvva and there are cameras everywhere and all is being recorded and all going out live on nine hundred thousand channels and is all 'vailable to everyone, all the time.

It is called consciousness.

I come back and there is a note:

Sorry, I took one of your beers
It looked so good.

It was my note. It is still here.

I took a beer . . . hope that's okay . . . there were four others . . . I
just presumed
I've left a bit; whose-ever's it was

Know it's not a big deal. I didn't have to leave some note anyway.
Just an offering.
So I took one borrowed one; well, technically, you could say I lifted
one.
There we are: I've said it – stole one.
Is this what you want?
Are you happy now?
Whoever you are
Hiding behind invisibility.
Who are you anyway? I mean it.
So I took one. BIG fuckin' DEAL
It's not as if I have not been keeping an eye out to the things you
have taken so, although I have noticed you have taken nothing.
That's just not normal.
Obviously we all do it and all want to do it so you're no better, you
are worse for two-facedly hiding it.
Your theft is more nasty as it surrounds us with imminence.
Evil thief!
It's just a little bit of your own medicine
You hypocrite, fuck you. Whoever it is.
Why do you feel the need to hide?
Why are you so fucked up?
I don't even know who I am dealing with
Fuck you all then. It is probably a case of all you versus me. So
fucking what, I couldn't give a shit about any of you. Phil, you are
lazy and all thin, pretending to be all neat by tidying all the time.
You'd be cleaning up as I was cookin', you fuck; if I ever dared to
around you.
So just to be clear: Fuck you all to death. I am leaving.

My note . . .I had been doodling and got carried away for a laugh and written it up this note for fun and then left it on the kitchen table of this shared, rented accommodation, and it got a bit of accidental Atonment treatment and got read.

I thought I had luckily retrieved this note before its discovery. In fact it had been read and could hardly be believed and was left, a dimension shattered. Weeks later it came out when they told me they had all read it and only one didn't get it. That was my fictional fantasy note. Fun to write and my only foray into this kind of daft revenge-ance fuelled piece of writing.

I did though come across a real note left by the Australasian who had sneaked into our house, the one with the nine strong Bad Boys percussion group and lived with us until someone realized no one knew her; and stole a small bedside lamp.

Dear guys remember me? Jane the . . . Kiwi . . . yeh. Well, I remember leaving on the worst of terms.

I would like to say that I am so sorry for all I did and I hope that there is a way for you to forgive and forget so that if I ever came by it would be fine, okay, easy and happy.

I have been hanging out at this place where they are all into this New Age stuff and it is all about facing up to what you have to admit was you and your past and get on with a new path.

Essentially: To forgive.

I hope to achieve this one day and hope you and all the others who I apparently wronged will one day let me off the hook.

I meant well and all that behaviour was really part of a disorder I am in the process of shedding.

I realize I have "to let it all go as being anyone else's fault" and "just see it as the constituents of past parts of my life". Not giving it the power myself of being worried by it bringing it to life . . .

I have to say you guys didn't make it easy.

Jane

Hang on, a few pages ago Brenda we were still in a subset of Three Things Good That Happened Recently . . .

So hang on go back fourteen pages and we were doing the best three recent happenings:

One: The unbalanced, aware it looks and is, slightly insane hedge-trimming and, in places, shaving.

Two: A few days earlier, overtaking a man in a car with his left arm over the empty passenger seat all casual with the hand sloping downwards, with me in exactly the same position. Or, rather, finally, at last seeing someone doing the same thing as I do all the time and can't imagine why everyone doesn't. Although it does look a bit pushy airport-taxi-guy, it is purely for posture and helps me body feel straight and relaxed . . . Especially without gears, in an automatic car

Especially in a lucky, lucky car: one that got stolen for a week and then came back. And came back improved.

No one could believe it. There it was in the purgatory of a salvage yard waiting for collection after ten days and no apparent troubles.

Sure, the boys had taken her from festival-parking in a field and sure, they would have driven her madly around fields and farmyards, raced her down lanes and laughed loudly as they couldn't believe the keys were left in the coin trough between the seats.

When I drove it it felt better, swifter, lighter on its wheels, smoother and because of all the Police fingerprinting, all shiny and glittery with a super-fine silver fairy-wingtip dust all over the dashboard. I put my own fingerprints all over it and enjoyed the silversmithery, the luster, the gleam, the nighttime magical stealth matt sheen. Driving along she is shimmering and aglow, leaner almost, and it turns out the boys had switched a small button to "sport-mode" down by the gearstick. It silently just read "S" not "E" and so it was true, she was quicker. They could have broken her they could have maimed her and shamed her, yet they could not.

See if this is a more exciting extrapolation. Before it was an extended reference now it is allowed more of its own place even though it's a small one:

So I'm overtaking this guy and he too has the arm up around the empty passenger seat. I feel lucky to even have a car to be up leaning on a spare seat, with petrol enough and somewhere to be going; he too has it up hugging no one yet everything, hugging the world, scooping up all in the one-armed wonder that is The Mileage. It's a thrill to see him so I speed up a bit then let him come back taking-over me to get his attention and maybe even give him a wave from the similar hand. We are in his periphery, me and the redeemed Merc, speeding up to get attention yet it seems he wants to kind-of ignore us even though he is aware of us and is speeding up so we can't come up next to him. It all feels a bit dangerous to do the things of road rage even though there is none, it's more road joy that I have. Road rave.

Reminds me of the time a guy and his family overtook me and they were watching Ben Hur on the old DVD headrests. I was only in the Mini Clubman yet sped up to keep up to watch a bit. If only it had been the chariot race scene and Dad speeds up and I do and he veers over to ram me with all that racing affecting his mood mode and the drama and Tony Curtis's oysters and Gore Vidal shortening all the leather tunics . . .

Off the trampoline and with the hedge-trimmers or cutters on the ground and I'm raking up the non-variegated with a stiff brush and being happy that no catastrophe happened by falling into the hedge and trimming myself unconscious and bleeding inside a hedge – who's going to look for you there? La de da, just ruminating, I bang my elbow's funny bone, up in the soft tender fuzzy bit, on a stiff-brushed backstroke and it sets my hand on fire. Lilly comes out, I'm near a hedge trimmer in pain, she puts two and two twogether.

Mind The Time. June the nine 2009.

It is only a nature that can be nurtured.

The Chicken is still the egg, all one emergent process. Why bother inventing the possibility of a riddle then being confused by it? No reason, apart from man seems to be addicted to it. Getting a theory together then penalizing the world for not fitting it. Using more knowledge to get less.

One moment is the next. You cannot separate a chicken from when it was an egg. Yet we have the words; and the words for beginning and start, and they cause trouble.

That the fact we can exist is the only miracle so that's why I feel it's all a miracle.

The using of our minds to then compromise the universe and its forms into following our formats: wrong, seems daft. We are made of the stuff we are quizzing. We are using the atoms in our brains to look at the atoms. What it is comprised of, we look at it with. There is only so far we can go. An atomic endpoint. We are the thing we study: "This party is crap . . ." You are the party. The best is "Fucking Traffic . . ." Usually you are traffic when you're saying this . . . aiee have a good time and help make the party great.

Pure quantum mechanics now has fully brought awareness to the truth that by witnessing something you affect it. There is nothing that can fully just be observed. The way this is now best illustrated is through the scientific effect that by seeing the tiniest particles there must be light on them and the light affects their position – so one can never actually say where anything is. By positioning it and locating it you reposition it and relocate it. So one could reiterate and redefine a thing over and over in new micro moments, smallest interval quarktime halfspecks . . . and hey: what is what it is?

The best words I read about it recently are the scientists' name for the natural occurrences in nature without a pattern yet bits of pattern: quasi-periodic . . . Poor nature it seems to be missing something. Either that or rthe whole history of the universe is the first half of a pattern never to be repeated.

This is handy on a large scale when you think about an audience – as a performer you are one of them, we are us – and your mood can be infectious. Often going on after an act has done well is considered hard. Silly really, as from the audience's point of view there was an act that did well he was great, wonder what the next will do, he he . . . There is no bad atmosphere in a room you are not part of, so you can then more easily access the energy to be the change, be one who does well going on whenever. There is always the chance the gig will be the best ever. There have been lots of gigs the-best-ever. Every time I head off there's the thought that this gig tonite could be another. And the most one can do is to let the possibility of this exist: allow for the best-ever-gig to be possible this night.

There have been at least four or five best ever gigs for me in the last year: the compering at Goldsmiths . . . the recent fifty minutes at Uckfield cinema . . . that one at Limehouse. The secret aim is to make the best a new best.

In finding your route to the positive you will essentially define the physic of the universe well enough. We exist to be excited.

There is so much thought about this measuring of the world. Even so many theories about time's possible consistency. Even here in this book there are different time zones.

A while ago, like an hour and a bit for me in this time, a bit less for you who are just reading this, unless you stopped reading for a while or overnight or a long weekend, I was editing this book on the bus to Notts and am pleased to report that either people shat and left shite on the bowl and cleaned it off or they never shat on the bowl. We'll never know, although it would be simple to check. Go to office, get list, email everyone.

Chapter Thrive

Right now, 12.03.13, 11:27a.m. Wow, I have just hitchhiked from here at Brockhurst the mansion to East Grinstead, gone to the bank and come back and my coffee is still warm.

I love hitchhiking and there is always excellent details and so a story to tell about whoever picks you up. Telling people about it can really Work.

Almost recently I had two sisters pick me up when I was accidentally hitching at a bus-stop at Wytch Cross for twenty mins and the moment I realized it was a bus-stop and leaned in to read the timetable on the post and put my thumb down, that is when they turned up in a gold Passat and pass me then turn back and do a tricky three-point and reverse in the exit to the Ford dealership, let me in then let me try the Nescafé espresso in a can they have.

Anyhoo it reminds me of getting a lift from a lady friend another time when I didn't even have me thumb up.

There is that beautiful moment with hitching where one starts, where you are in the middle of nowhere and just a guy – who is he? what's he doing? – and then the thumb goes up to commit to going for it, to asking for help. Tom Robbins is bound to have covered flying around this magic act, fuzzing and sticking to the sides, the manifestation of will and want and good.

Ethereal whisps of anthroposophy.

Hitchhiking is so exciting because each car that comes along could be the One. You see them first at a distance where they just are at that point the thing you want: a car. It's chocked full of chance and good feeling often I am screaming a little bit as they come. Not too much; you have to ventriloquize a bit as they find it hard to pick someone up who looks like they are shouting at themselves. It's a bit tantric to hold all that excitement and urge to wave and appeal more all in check, waiting for the amber indicator of love to flick on for you, for the human urge to help others .

So this time I was hitchhiking from Forres to Tain to buy a car. I wanted to arrive needing a car, not turn up with a mate and have an out, an excuse not to buy; a lot of people buying shoes are wearing shoes: "I'm afraid you've had enough madam." There is six hundred and fifty quid in the inside pocket of the tweed and here we go. Just at the edge of out of town and with the last stroll up to the road I am about to raise the fist and thumb when I hear my name called and it's my friend Nessa, the undercover aristocrat, in a wee Nova. I've got a lift and it's before the actual hitchhiking has even begun. What an omen, oh yeh that's right I don't believe in omens, just events. It gets better because in the back I am next to Nessa's daughter who is about to go on her first ever drive as she's just passed her test. To Inverness. In the front is Granny, dad's mum. She is smoking roll-ups that last for ages and leaning over to exhale out the window.

Nessa asks what I'm up to and I tell her about picking this car from the wanted ads, a maroon Passat diesel estate, and she says it is her favourite car. Instead of browsing through the whole list of cars – Mondeo, mondeo, mondeo, Laguna, laguna, laguna, Bravo, brava, bravo – I just thought of the car I most wanted and went to it and found one in Tain.

By now Granny is amazing and is telling me she never learnt to swim: "There was nae need." Can't argue with that. "Never went in the water because I'd never learned to swim, never learned to swim because I never went in the water."

She leans over to exhale and I pull her seatbelt tight a bit to help her exhale and she gets it, doing a wee laugh and cough.

Nessa is dropped off and daughter gets into the driver's seat, Granny is shotgun, and a large bearded man is trying not to fill her rear-view mirror too much on this her Maiden Voyage. Wow.

It is smashing and they drop me at the roundabout just north of Inverness as they scoop back round the ring road. What a start.

In the lay-by it starts to drizzle and that is the Hitcher's Friend as it makes people act on their feelings for you more, if they have a reason framing it to hang on the goodwill. Every car could be the One, yet as they pass there are lots not being it. Some cannot stop: young women or solo mums drive past me – lovely car, on you go. Some cannot because they are off to work and why should they stop because they have to drive to work to get the money to keep this car on the road that they need for work. Some are middle-aged men in coats in cars and you can avoid mocking them in their staid ways and lack of balls anymore. One man goes by in a Jaguar diesel and it ain't right – he looks at me like I am responsible for his shrivelling from big generous semi-warrior type to this uptight safety freak model of humanity.

Then the Mondeo Zetec that was at speed, brakes and pulls in and I jog up to the front door and open it to see a wee four-year-old girl in the front seat inadequately strapped in who was not visible above the doorframe of the car, so I get in the back and there are lots of single yoghurts moving around the seat. We zoom off and stay fast and what's the story? Well, Sinead is with her Dad today who works for the council who provide lunches at the schools around this area and in their charter remit-promise they have to provide a pudding with the meal and this is yoghurt and sometimes they run out here and there and this is where they call Gil. In short, he is an emergency yoghurt deliverer man to schools in the North East.

"Help yourself," he says.

Blackcurrant and a few peaches, one raspberry and the rest are all summer fruits or fruits of the forest. Aye aye, that's what they always are: aye, some are fruits, some are not. So I open one and am drink-licking it out into my mouth and I notice that guy in the Jag; we are overtaking him so I give him a big lactose smile with the white joker lines around my mouth form the yoghurt pot. With no Sinead visible it must look like I have a chauffeur. He does a rare triple-take which has to angle itself forward, not an easy manoeuvre when it requires the very flexibility that seems to be missing yet informs its very incredulity.

You can't have your cake and eat it and throw up and then take my cake.

Well you can, yet no one wants that, and having your cake and eating it is a finite arrangement.

He asked me what the story is and, when I've told him, he says, "Och, may as well just run you up to Tain." Probably he said this because by now I was leaning well forward wedged in between the front seats getting on well with Sinead. Kids this young just want to be told silly things and not really be asked all the seven questions adults always want to put on to them. We're older, we're forty and we can say interesting things about the animals and we don't have to ask "What's that?" as we point at a cow. Fuck, it was a cow yesterday, has it changed? Jeesus why's he doing this? Is it a trick question? . . . Go away adult . . .

He says help yourself so I do and it is a raspberry I choose from among the Fruits of the Forest and other euphemistic flavours. At school we always fought for rasp then strawb then peach then blackcurrant then, only then, the lesser fruits. Yeh: fruits of the forest could be squirrel shit. Now I ate and was extra happy at the magical silliness combined with nutrients and then too, overtaking more cars that definitely had had a chance to pick me up yet hadn't.

Gil is bonkers, it's twenty-one miles to Tain – that's forty-two out of your way man, I say, and practically have to force the wheel after he has ignored his own Dingwall turn-off and pulled right heading up the coast.

Anyroad he does pull over from the right-hand lane into a lay-by; over the other side of the road. A car peeps us . . . My motto is: If you've time enough to peep, you've time enough to be cool.

S'probably one of the Westminster Council Parking Fine phone call-centre workers that were told they could keep their jobs if they moved here.

Some of Scotland's best bits you just have to grow up around to get.

They speed off and I can see a wee hand of Sinead visible just in the window waving.

So now I phone my love, she says, "I'll put you on the insurance for the Toyota, come back." So I agree and start hitching back now with the flick of a turn – all the omens-portentous, good-luckness and flowing script of this day I turn my back on and start hitching back the other way; whereby the Jag man we'd overtaken back there comes by me one more time. This time there is no double-take, he just gazes at me with the look of a man that knows he could not answer the question he cannot even work out to ask. He literally has not the expression available to suit this situation. To be quizzical of something one at least has to set the parameters. Something along the lines of: what is it that that man has been up to that he can be done with by now to be heading back from in this fashion and could I have been part of it?

It is very enjoyable and worth it, could have been missed if I had had a scowl or turned from him in the proud miff.

Minutes later a battered small-time Fiat Brava estate comes by and stops, with a futon base on the roof. The guy is a huge, wide entrepreneur whose leg goes right over to lean on the gearstick and who had lent this frame to his ex-girlfriend for her new apartment for her bed, for her to sleep in and of course, you never know, sleep with someone. He was expressing how it was cool, it was all part of it, he was progressive and it seemed to make sense that there was an overlap on the Venn of People Who Pick Hitchers Up and People Who Are Nice Enough and Groovy and Open and Sexually Unjealous Enough to Lend a Bed for Shagging On Then Take It Back and Go and Pick It UP.

"Do you like music?" he asks

"All the time."

"Listen to this then." And he speeds up to about sixty-five and the futon base starts to hum loudly. It's doing a kind of drill-wave. Then he says, "Try this," and goes up to seventy-five and it starts to make a two-tone japans techno-prisoners dance pulse and has a kind of beat and we open the sound-roof to hear it better. Bravo, fiat.

The six fifty in the tweed is now spare and, in telling him what I'm up to, I say, "Drop me at the massive retail park at Borders by the View cinema and I can go in and buy all those films I said I would buy when there was spare money." Spare money: there's no such thing because it always has somewhere to go and all. Well, here now it is free to go to Borders. I love the View as a name, it's so Scottish . . . "Come in View these films and leave . . . go, buy snacks, view and exit . . . nae waste, nae analysis . . . just View Them . . ."

I come out with a Buñuel box set; two copies of Mulholland Drive, Inland Empire. Five Easy Pieces and 2046, the sequels to In The Mood For Love . . . There's -The Apartment, Black Cat, White Cat, Stalker, Dig! the Documentary, . . . An Actor's Revenge, Life Is A Miracle, Superman II . . . and many more. So, when I start to hitchhike the one last leg, millions of cars go by with a single eyebrow glare at my hundreds-of-quids-worth's here in two bulging pink plastic bags and no bulge in the tweed no more. Of course, how can they miss what they never knew was there?

Then I got a lift from Jez. He stopped in a massive tear-shaped Honda civil like – all disappearing vista dashboard and can-holders with dietary Coca-Cola – pleasant exchanges of this and that, then he asked about my day and I am "Well, wow! What a day" . . . The lift, a thumb not-up, maiden voyage and dry-land-smokey gran . . . the drizzle, the tantra, the yoghurts, Sinead and the Jag and a musical futon . . . Trying to keep it not too amazing.

Then there is a pause and he says: "Well . . . once I hitchhiked a Jet." . . . Shit! Now, it is fun to tell a story and be the one doing it, yet we all want the next better story whoever holds it.

"Right . . . ," he goes; he was courting a wee lass in the Navy when he was in the Air Force – for all the Services get to mingle up here in Scotland – and they were then just married three months when, lo and behold, before the love-making had settled down to regular levels when they were in primo vera green spring newdays, she gets stationed on a submarine for two years, to Africa and back.

His mind was boggling. "Fucking Africa, I thought they had no water," he says. "I thought the enemy were supposed to be the ones who took your women. Aiee!" and what have you . . . So, one night he's a mess in the mess moping about and mopping his table with his elbows and complaining to a friend who listens and says, "Well man, I'm flying to bloody Nigeria on Saturday, get to the end of the runway, bring your own jumpsuit and I'll give you a lift." Ya dancer! Get to the end of the runway, and bring your own helmet . . . very high ho. The trick is, as they pass the control tower the pilots have to recite a declaration, some kind of disclaimer along the lines along the lines of "I have no known entourage or live rounds in their possession, Sir" and, at that time, it would be true – yet get to the end of the runway and it's all's fair in love and war; and in love, in war. And all's fare in love and war. And all is fair in the wars of love. Love in the war is all fair. All war's fair love.

Come the day there he is, in a slightly-too-small jumpsuit waiting and Jez's not sure which Tornado jet is his so he is speculatively hitching his thumb at all the other ones as they go by. It must have got a wild reaction from some of the pilots who must have really been amazed at his optimism – Foxtrot Charlie Bravo Zebra Hotel . . . I'm leaving the Forces. Look at that guy . . . Such belief . . . Making a mockery of the whole thing . . . Soon as I get back I'm taking some charlie, learning to foxtrot and buying a zebra for my hotel . . . and, eventually: ninth plane and it's his mate. Now the best thing about the cutbacks in the Tornados in the RAF is that there are still two seats yet just one human operator when there used to be two: navigator and pilot. Now the one man does both jobs like the bus drivers who also do the tour-talk. This means when you hitchhike a Tornado first you don't need your own ladder they have one on the side and secondly you are going to be right there at the front in the pole position taking all them Gs and: "Can you imagine, I'm smiling?" he says. "Cos I'm going to surprise her." And, he said, "It gets better!" It happened like in a film: he landed at Lagos, got a supply-truck and was waiting for her when the Sub smoothed into the harbour. "And here it came, Phil," he said, "the Moment!" He was standing there as her Sub floated to the pier, tied up and the top hole opens and out they come and he's waiting and waiting and she comes out, takes her cap off and shakes her hair lose, eyes blinking in the rebirth-to-light and "it happened" he said, that she looked up and about and right at him and he was a total non-expected-thing and he says he saw her regard him standing there, just as a man, as a geezer in a too-tight flightsuit sweaty in all the right places and he said he felt her eyes liking him as a man and then turn away – glance no more, turn her head. He said he felt soaring, like he was the object of ravenous adulterous desire as well as the object of loyalty. Best of Both Worlds: the stud and the companion.

Thanks man. My legs were shaky on getting out, giddy. Joy with people.

*   *   *   *   *   *   *   *   *   *   ***

Imagine what is might be like being an out of work actor and going to auditions and it's not going well, you keep turning up and they don't want you yet you can hardly know why because they don't tell you there and then, so you are never sure of what can be improved and you know there is a kind of shelf-life to you and your hotness, and too many failed auditions spreads the word. Your agent answers calls less and less quickly and feigns less and less until you feel like you are a nuisance. It's debilitating and, even if you get the job, you still have to wait for them to tell you when to act. You are going off your craft and vocation, losing it for it yet still going along and sitting among the others. The love-life starts to suffer because how can you offer loving kindness and fun for others when you are having this bad a time? Partners sense this and become unavailable, don't want to be around you. One day you are parked in the car hiding from the world way out the back of a garden-centre eating a guilty fast-meal that has steamed up the windows and you see her: a woman so lovely you have to stare and follow and hope she works here regularly and find her schedule and start to hang around steaming up the windows with your breath and wanting her and one day, trying to get her in the back of a van, and it goes horribly wrong and you have to kill her.

Next call from your agent is about a job and it's to play the murderer in a Crimewatch reconstruction, of your own murder. Wow, you are torn: It would be tempting fate and kharmically very cruel to play the role, and yet you know this piece so very well – you're the perfect for it, you know it inside out. You're an actor for Christ sake. Gosh, what to do? In the end you believe in the integrity of the trade and art of acting and you take the role and you shine on set. You are able to help the director and Police with setting it all up with a suggestion that the killer might have watched from a secluded part of the car park unseen. and you are very popular. People stop you on the street, "Hey, it's Him!" and your blood freezes; then they say, "That actor off the telly who resembles a killer!" and you relax. Off the hook in full view. Doing a Savile.

It weighs on you though, the guilt without a name and you start to feel not so good, bad enough to commit more murders in order to get more acting and consultancy work on Crimewatch.

Imagine that, it would be terrible . . . Imagine if that was your idea for a grisly crime thriller you would write for money. Feeling dreadful yet well reimbursed. Imagine if being this writer who then writes a script about being a writer of grisly crime books who then is hunted by someone whose murder was not solved by Crimewatch . . .

August 2011.

Crawling away from the Police is some CCTV footage I would like to see.

There is some more footage I would also love to subpoena: It all starts with a box I found when we are moving house that had not been unpacked since the last move. In the box was a nice wee tweed hat, so wow I've found a hat, a hat that I did not know I had, a hat that was found that was not yet known to be lost, 'twas though, lost and found and now known not to have been known that it was unknown, Schrödinger's hat: if someone had take it I would not know and I would not know that I did not know. Lost its lostness in a certain way, already gone from the mind, lost and found. So it's straight on the head I wear it out to London and I lose it – lost and found and found and lost. Lost properly. This affects me. Next week I'm cycling down from the top of Lewes town in East Sussex, a classic English town built around a castle, the whole town gets younger as it all spirals round the hill and way down through a one-way system and all spills out into a Waitrose – ah Waitrose, a bit posher; the only supermarket with a place to tie up your horse outside. I am cycling one bike and bringing another along, just holding it by the handlebars like a cowboy with an extra pack-horse, or a colt learning the ropes. Zooming freewheel down the main street. There are three second-hand shops that I've gots to know quite well from the outside, well enough to be able to cycle by them slowly and be able to tell if there is anything really new and worth a look in; a drive-by stockcheck. It's drizzling and, looking for a hat, I see a new wool one on the polystyrene long-necked lady display-head in the men's section of British Heart . . . In and out and it feels good on my head . . .

I don't pay and don't have a plan to bring it back. Its just it is raining and I've spent years buying stuff from charity shops, so no I don't feel bad at this realistic, necessity moment. I need help and am a wholly viable beneficiary of charity. The wooly valid. Now off, round the last three bends of one-way medieval-width hairpins and I come to the last right-hander, with cars coming from the opposite direction to join the stream. Coming right towards me is a glorious, blonde, big-haired woman in her forties driving an open-topped convertible car with the roof down and a massive double-mattress bending back and bouncing up in the movement. She must be on her way to the dump. Either that or she is just feeling permanently turned on and very sexy, in one of her primes and highly available and well equipped. Our eyes meet, to form one huge eye, as different as two road-users could be, and join the stream in the lanes right next to each other heading down the hill side by side. Then my young colt starts to play up, leaping his handlebars up out of a pothole and in an error-choice I pull on the front brake a bit sharpish and the front wheel then, is flipped and is now, in the same instant, pointing back. No curve, no delay, just floop, jammed in a second, which throws me straight over the handlebars. Somehow my brain is in a hyper-present manic glory setting and turns me round in mid-air, somehow I do enough to incredibly be flying backwards and now bumping, skidding down the road with my legs straight uphill, coming to a halt and banging my head on the road. Only the slight cushioning of the new tweed was enough for me to feel nothing and have the cranium intact. The lady in the cabriolet stops suddenly next to me and the mattress boings all the way forward and back, a giant albino tongue licking the air.

"Are you alright?"

"Let's make love in the road" would have been the ultimate response and, judging by the local paper's lack of news items that don't concern Travellers or the Restored Clock, I think we would have made the front page if we'd lost ourselves to each other and made healing filter-lane love on the mattress: blood from my wound sealing the picture . . .

"Yes, all fine, thanks."

And she drives off.

In fact my ankle had had to come through a straight line, scraping past the gear cog and, bang, past the frame as it turned, so there was a sliced-injury down there somewhere. Preferring not to look under the trouser, I give it a compression hold for a few minutes. In the first seconds I remember sighing into words, "Oh no, what am I going to do now?"

Then it dawned on me: just keep going down the road. It was not that bad an injury and it was fun to realize my first reaction was just emotion turned into words – they could have been other words. There's blood in me sandals as I stand at the free bike-maintenance guys on the precinct. They fix bikes for free and I give them a large bar of chocolate and they give me some back. We all eat chocolate.

Back at the house I think, "Right, this is it! I am going to name this cap, protect it, do all that I can to keep it and sabotage the sabotage." Inside, on the label, in biro I wrote "Cap Sized . . . If lost, return to philk8@hotmail.com"

Next evening at a birthday party for my man Will, who is thirty, I arrive at just the right time, when you can hear the beat as you come down Breakspeare Road and, opening up the letterbox, you see the place full, like a portable widescreen party-movie; the place full of folks leaning on the hallway walls and chatting. Most of the good work has been done by those who get there early when the crisps are still filling the bowls and there has not been the magical breakthrough-zone where suddenly everyone is pissed and feels everyone else is too. It had some great moments and I certainly love any party with ping-pong played through a net of fire and slidey-dancing on a wet conservatory floor. The booze ran out at about half two, then yahoo we found another litre of vodka in a cupboard, hurrah! Then it ran out again and we were forced to drink some half-bottles of Inheritance dessert wine – sweet and very strong, wrong wine. All terrific and I leave for an early bus-stop round the corner. When I get to it, it is the finest and most interesting bus-stop one could ever hope for at this hour: it is completely filled with young women, all fourteen or fifteen, all beautiful, all mouthy and laughing, all black and all completely oblivious to me. They'd been out junior-clubbing, they are all sober it seems, and they are all friends. Me: I am a forty-two-year-old guy in tweed almost camouflaged and surplus to their evening.

Then suddenly Will comes running over the road from the party calling my name. We meet in the middle of the road and he gives me my mobile I'd left there. We have a big man-hug then he's off. All the girls witness this and suddenly they're all enlivened. They're whooping: "What was that all about? . . . Hey man, who was that?"

"It's my friend. He was giving me my phone."

"Aha, your phone . . . Yeh . . . Can I borrow it?" one of them says.

They all whoop and laugh and slap their legs at this dawn impertinence.

"Yes," I say.

Even more whooping and expressions of unbleevabel-ness. The young lass takes my phone and, as she makes a kwikkawl, the others all gather round me and ask me what is up and then one asks me about my jacket. They get the history as well as the explanation of the fibres and weaving process, the door to door collecting, the use of colour, the individual nature, the way that natural material is twisted for a rough warmth.

This is an old second-hand Harris Tweed jacket I found in a charity shop in Harrogate. It was amazing that day: As I drove into Harrogate I saw an odd sizeable stone rotunda alone in the green park expanses on entry to the town, and was interested in what on Earth would be going on and, slowing down, there was a sign saying it was a Tailor. I stop and pop in, expecting three sewing-machine ladies with a bit of chat all marooned here in a park on the outskirts of town. It wasn't, though, it was run by a thirty-year-old slightly-gay Italian man and I had to quickly think of something and told him about my tweed jacket that was a bit tight. He said, "Well, bring it in", and told me about how, when he turns the heating up, water drips down the wall. It was later that day when the actual new, present tweed jacket was found, so I did come back wearing this beautiful old, old style, rough, ugly, gorgeous cloth. Standing there in the stubby circular alterations tower I did up the buttons and he walked round me touch-tapping both my shoulders and stood in front of me. "Ees perfect."

So back to the bus-stop, back to the girls: Turns out they like a bit of history and the phone comes back and the laughs are here; then I go off to the all-night garage to get change and ask if they want anything. Twelve young women, sun just up, and all they can say is "Ten Bensons Silver and a can of Tizer" amongst them all . . . "Okay dokay . . ."

So I'm still in the queue and the bus comes, and they all start shouting my name and it's so swift and I'm running to the bus and they actually stand in the entrance keeping the doors open for me and taking the wrath of the driver who is a bit perplexed behind his bullet-proof perspex, all protected yet easier to ignore too.

We all hop up the stairs and hang out at the back. After a few minutes the novelty of me has worn off yet there were a few exchanges of fun and seat-movings and, in the end that is some CCTV footage I would like to see.

In fact it would be worth slashing a seat just to get to see it in court; see if a judge would look favourably on me when I got them to show the footage from the beginning: the doors being held, the run up the stairs, the dancing in the aisle . . . the cross-generational cultural bridges . . . You could slow the footage down and re-edit and get it released, like a director's cut . . . the defemdant's cut.

As it happens I fall asleep, go to the end of the line then get back on, fall asleep again then wake up where I got on nearly and finally stagger off the bus at ten twenty without the woollen cap.

Three days later I get an email from Auriel, who has the hat, and meet her at my next gig with the hat, where she gets off with the sound man. Happy ending.

*

Further stories in this book include:

Travelling without a passport, just using flyers from my show . . . Alan Davies; the turf of Montreal and naked on a rooftop in eleven minutes and how to be shit twice on QI . . . a three-hour gig in Dublin, drinking half a bottle of Jameson's and losing my trousers twice . . . being admonished by the Police in my bath for having the front door open . . . taking my daughter to Glastonbury with nothing save an umbrella . . . and how Lost Property is just Left Luggage for free.

Top Ten Meltdown Mad Gigs – Disasters, Riots and Audience Uprisings.

Oh, and buying machetes in a Venezuelan supermarket . . . posing as a drug-lord for Russian billionaires in Ecuador . . . accidentally firing fireworks at a five-a-side football match . . . getting my balls out on Australian TV when a man squashes my ping-pong ball that I had made a game with over the panel show's table when he asked "What are you going to do now?" . . . getting a hat back, like a crown, at a gig in Brighton, that I had given away exactly a year before . . . oh and prisons, crack-kidnapping, draughts with refugees, the three-month marriage, and the most exciting of the near-death experiences . . .

From 1989 to 2005 Glasgow was my well-loved hometown. The Glasgow Film Theatre and the Art School, The Variety Bar and The Third Eye Centre all close to the listed duplex I owned in G3. The dog-walking, the child-rearing, the money gigs on Channel 4 and the first whisky TV adverts ever, for which I got seventy-five grand for writing and being in, I think in nineteen ninety two.

After the first great loss of all me possessions, all I really missed was the Tweed Mark-One, the first one to be really spot on: Harris Tweed no 3051063, found after a phone call tip-off, of the jacket's whereabouts in a chazza in Nairn, from Willie, the utterly positive plumber, a parent at the Moray Steiner School – the best and cheapest Steiner in Britain and the one with Tilda Swinton coming up through the trees in the snow at the same time that she is coming up through the trees in the snow in the cinema as the Snow Queen in Narnia.

You can play a numbers bet-off game with the number on the Harris Tweed label inside the jacket like Altman has Elliott Gould do with his friend in TheLongGoodbye using the numbers on the dollar bill.

In London this last three years I have found that asking men "Are you keeping that?" is a good way to get their shirt. There were three in a row for me that way and then I told the story at a gig and a woman in the crowd perked up: hey, it was me her boyfriend had met in a club at Waterloo Arches who he gave his shirt to . . .

What are the chances of that?

Well, there are two million men it could be. They are either in or out at an entertainment that one in four million then have a girlfriend come to a gig. Four million times five hundred times five hundred. So, about one in 4,000 million. Either that or one in two: you meet them tonight or you don't.

Gathered from the grave Kelvingrove caravan-carnage: some smoky blistered photographs and an old black Rosenthal German porcelain plate I had had for sixteen houses since I was a kid. I put them all in the boot of my car and closed it on the plate, breaking it gently. This was the second time my possessions had been severely trimmed. About two years before I was staying in a camper-van on some free land right in the heart of the West End and I had lost the keys. One day I came back to where it was and it wasn't. I just kept walking; there is not much checking you need to do when you are sure a vehicle was where it was. At this moment you can just keep walking it is very hard for anyone to tell you have just lost a vehicle, you could be checking on a wee bird or a bit of unusual litter, your keen interest in the world. Certainly I become a lot less homed that night so it was lucky I met tall Brian the TV camera guy-guy who took me to a bar and then ran into that wife I mentioned. Misled? No, segue. Interim? Nae such thing. Another planet, nope. Afterlife, sorry. Another moment, move along now. Spare money, rare. "When I'm settled in", best of luck.

Sometimes you just find the money you need for rent yet when I could avoid it I would. There was the thought that we ought to all leave Glasgow, myself, Diane and the Kids Coco and Felix, in 2006 and, I guess, by living in a van, then a flat of my brother's that was getting done up, I was trying to let that be easier.

Chapter Number

E equals mc squared.

E is ecstasy, the human love of stuff, the unquantifiable weighty near-infinite matter of human enjoyment, interest and elevation.

M is the mass of stuff, the condensing of the weight of belief into substance, ritual; the repeatable mass, the matter for concern. Things substantial, regainable and quantifiable; so experiencing of belief as a commodity within a place.

C is to see, the ability to witness the universe, process it as experience. And also "see" squared: the other seeing done by the observer, self and the you; the intuition of the "seer", the ability to get deep understandings that are irrefutable and untouchable, highly lateral; a human gift.

E equals mc squared: ecstasy = belief times the visions.

Love weighs heavy as the universe.

Enjoyment equals matters times conception.

Happiness is being conscious of things.

i.e. it is good to be alive and love is knowledge.

At the chemist they don't want people failing to get their meds by not having ID and proof of status so they have to allow all prescriptions to be filled without a check. It is just the move to make. If one cannot be sure of all, one has to ask nothing of all. When you have a party at your flat there can be no list as friends bring their friends.

Under certain conditions checking is not viable, so the beautiful other of not worrying can be the context, not ned to define a position on the matter. A given.

This is messy yet keep reading it:

Quantum physics is where it is at, though it has only shown us that we can never absolutely say where any electron actually is. It is not traceable and when it is pinpointed it is not there. When it is looked at it is affected, moved. The philosophy, the molecular intuition, is a way to truth: we have an input into that which exists.

Light is a wave and yet a particle stream when you are looking.

If one cannot name and be sure and one cannot plot the position of any atom for real or name the edge of anything, then . . . then one is free never to feel the need to define any position . . . So, one can live life like animals, just relating to experience.

Now, hold on Phil – there are bridges to build, measurements to make and medicines to isolate, and iPads to standardize.

Well, the point for me is that they are not required for a great life. They are fine-tuning. They did not get us here and, in fact, we did not get here to need them.

The tree falls in the forest and kills two philosophers arguing who never heard it.

Yet they were on to something. The thing is though, to let this be not an un-understanding. We have to exist to even be alerted. There are two states: the thing exists and we know of it, and also that we know we cannot know how it does.

April 2004.

"Sorry I am late, the orphanage was on fire!" – great title for a book – it's what I said to a theatre manager that one distant last night when I was late for a gig in order to allow him to be instantly kind and forgive me sharpish; and it reflects the central philosophy that all can only be well if you are saying so. That context is up to you and context allows all to be fine. The trousers you borrow after the earthquake are always nice enough; using a wok for pancakes at a stranger's house works just great; cutting my finger while slicing beetroot was painless because the red juice hid the blood. Our brains are amazing. All the tide of witty negativity is done and washed up and light is the new black.

Why do you always wear colours, Phil? Because colourful is how I feel on the inside.

Tell the kids the crusts are like juicy breadsticks and give 'em a wee bowl of olive oil.

Lay out lunch snacks just before they announce they are hungry and place them on corners of tables in their path. My friend Simon Munnery tells his many girlchilds that cabbage is princess's food. They devour it giggling as the real meal is being cooked. Much as he is the finest mind and best comedian of the world, a fiercely inventive new forms fylmy, talky, annual general meeting man, songsmith, poet, bookwriter – that cabbage thing with the kids is as good as it gets as an achievement

All I have known is that people have said that this relentless positivity is silly and yet this book has revealed its aim: That is, to be a list of the uses of this reality and lay out that twenty years of jokes, gigs and telling the stories of how it is possible, are not theory, they are practice.

I never practice the guitar, I practise it. Or is it the other way around spelt? That flour, how is it spelt. The band of musicians, when we play we don't rehearse it is an event.

There is only one big fat Now . . . The other night I rekindled my friendship with Gary Lightbody from the world's second biggest band by playing table tennis with him through the night at the George Hotel bar after a festival at Inveraray Castle on two wobbly thin restaurant tables with menus as the net, one time diving and hauling myself over the table to grab him around the waist to congratulate him on a fabulous shot and breaking my bat. Improvised some songs with my guitar and one day may open for the band in a lovely Los Angeles venue. Yes that was the night me and Phil Nichol and his lady friend had a platonic hot tub and I changed into a completely clean white outfit of spare clothes from my bag for the ping-pong, ten in the morning, knocked over a huge vase and dented the rim yet found a pair of top-of-the-range Oakley sunnies and when I hitchhiked I was picked up by an optometrist who was able to name the frame number of these Oakleys and tell me about the titanium they were made from. We went up the back road from Inveraray up to catch the A85 tae Oban.

All artists are just marvellous people making things. That is what we all are and there's usually just then the level to how well they are done. I shall try to avoid strange humorous accents to say the things I really want to say – will not have a shield or a medium to say that there is a best, always. Whatever the situation, it is an opportunity and you can see the best of it and this leads somehow this attitude of there being less-awful situations that need this coping.

Almost always on my mind are the last couple of gigs. If they were wobbly then there is an urge to do the next, which could be the best-ever type and, if they were of the best kind, then there is a feeling of being on a roll. If I am on a roll there is the urge to do the next one which, again, could be the best-ever. A really good show can be because I just told where I was at that point in my life and that cannot easily be told again later.

I have been to a publisher and talked to a managing editor. Luckily there were chairs with loose leather backs that could retain the indentation of your spine on them as a soft fading reminder of anima.

Pointing this out and not sitting down yet helped me quickly launch into first-time, on-the-spot compressed précis of something not-yet-existing. Imagining what it is going to be, inventing it each time you are seriously asked to talk about what it is, describe it, magic it into being. It being there in you as your life yet to say it, to put it into words, is why there is Stories – the Stories of the Bedouin, the Eskimo, the Clans of Scotland, the folks of Stirling near Tillicoultry. She never heard what happened when I was waiting in the foyer: That a man came in and sat waiting with me and I told him they would not at all be interested in his book. Didn't think twice, didn't think once, just said it as it occurred to me. His was a crop-circle trilogy and I was justified to warn him this was Canongate and he needed to be in another dimension of publishing.

Mind you, last year at Outsider, the best tasting restaurant in Edinburgh, with the comfiest booths and the most flamboyant owner, we had the best lock-in with all these fancy folks and her, Romola of The Hour and J. Byng who runs Canongate. For auld times' sake I made a wee pipe out of a lightbulb box and we smoked it up. About a month later backstage at a festival I notice an old friend of mine is playing fiddle with Mogwai and I'm trying to somehow attract his attention when Romola walks by and I say hey hello it's me, the lightbulb box guy . . . and nothing lights up over her head in recognition.

This is an Autoblography: When can that be finished? When can that be done? When is chess solved? Never, never, never . . . So, it is just handed in at some point then there is a bound entity of actual achieved length.

SO, bear that in mind: that the bit just after this bit was going to be that which was read first.

Fuck the preface! Who reads them? Who's going to put that into context? Naeb'dy.

Happily, I have recently done gigs as good as any that I have ever done; or more that it was what I really want to do.

At one point recently I threw a guitar at some wonderful man in the front row, as he caught it I said, "He's got it. Don't give him time to make mistakes. This is where he is best." This is a solid belief of mine: That we are incredibly able beings, all of us, who have believably amazing brains that can all do all of what can be seen to be done by some. All the stuff James Bond does is done by about eleven stunt men yet there it is, it is being done and that is why it appeals unreasonably, yet it is feasible, worth dreaming about, within our human abilities. We can draw like the autistic kid, we can remember all Mozart tunes by loving them – play them again and they are familiar.

Then there was the strange noise that happened in the room at this gig with the flying guitar: In a pause, like a strong creak and we all heard it and then, every now and then in the gig, I would ask us all to remember that noise then, later, remember remembering it and what we thought it once was thought to be, and it was all communal and invented there and . . . Enough, Enough, enough, plenty, ample sufficiency, my runny-cup over-spilleth, abundance. Always there can be masses, plentiful muchness in a room full of people. Already there are as many universes as folks.

Then there was the photographer I upset by refusing to pose for a photo with my hands up near my face where they always want them so it looks good – that you are not enough – and he had gone off grumpy and so missed the jumper-explanation as to why it was folded up to keep cool air on my belly. That was done for the crowd that resulted in the story of how I bought the jumper in a small town called Sale and it is a school jumper and only if you are from that small town would you recognize it and think I was a bit mad. He missed too then the American accents I asked the crowd to all do in their heads; the story of the trip over; the rally of love with the handwritten map . . . Love is: changing gear with the right hand . . . Gigs, gigs, gigs – they all have a story, they all then can be the next story to tell.

More recent gigs have included: standing on a table with my head in the seventies lampshade being astro-naughty; another lady falling off her foldable chair at the 99 Club with laughter and it collapsed and she's in a heap with me standing over her like Ali over Liston, resisting one last joke . . . also getting a permanent marker from the crowd and then encouraging a lady without much smiles to smile and then take off the coat that was hugging her safe to come up onstage all reluctant and put a wee apostrophe before the "s" in "Philips" on a huge widescreen TV attached to the wall right behind me to make it mine; getting five men as a boy band up onstage to strip to the waist and dance to a song me and the crowd made up; improvising a song about chlamydia in the Footsbarn Tent in Victoria Park at Maxwells Full-Mooner night – nothing rhyme wit chlamydia . . . .

The best of the best of all time was at Koko in London where I hosted a big sponsored night and ended up drinking Drambuie from a drawer, wrapped in a tartan rug as Scottish superhero cape, it didn't get good until interval: 700 people off for a drink, a hundred or so left in their seats and a couple begin to get close and kiss and I spot them and say, "Hey, please close your eyes and kiss for twenty seconds . . . We'll all count," and into the mike I count loud and down towards one and they are kissing and the room begins to focus. I start to get closer and closer to them, climbing off the stage and quietly over the rows of chairs, counting out loudly until I am right there at seven, six . . . they hear the whole room count . . . people have returned and are leaning over balconies watching it . . . five, four . . . smiling in the kiss . . . I am right up close and my trousers start to fall down . . . one . . .

They open their eyes with me joining in, cheek to their cheeks, the last bit of intimate space, with all my manhood held tight safely in the pouch of my T-shirt and hand.

Yes, that was all a preface.

Call it that though and folks will avoid it like . . . a prologue.

One Chapter December 31st

I say I say I say, how warm is a draughty old barn that you come across in a storm?

Incredibly warm. Very sheltering.

Shelta, however is the secret language based on Gaelic with the consonants systematically changed used by the Romany travellers to hide within. This became a groovy plan so during the war there was a version in English called "Uv-a-Guv" with the same concept to hide from occupying forces. Eventually it became the "E . . . after double-U . . ." song of Worzel Gummage.

From a lollipop stick, this: How can birds fly? – Because they have hollow bones. Get it? Their bones are lighter for flight.

In order to cycle along a thick white line in the park more easily, look further ahead . . . look about four or five metres ahead as opposed to just where the front of the wheel is. You can be carried to your gaze, by your gaze.

Here now is a recent last-detail adventure to have happened so far, up till now, at this point. Of a certain kind though: Finding details of in terest in a situation I am held in as opposed to an adventure of unstoppable, ongoing nose-following wonder; like canoeing down a long South American river with a bag of nuts, raisins and chocolate.

Coming off a very easy jet up from Stansted to GLW, my car is cleverly parked one free bus-ride away beyond Enterprise Rental in Long-Stay Number Nine for one night in order to get a flat battery so that, when I turn the key, it only sends the milometer and rev needles dancing up high in some fabulous accelerating mockery while we go nowhere. The beautiful deluxe Ford car I bought while accidentally answering the phone in that play, is parked on inclined, giant-gravel off Row B which has the smoothest possible concrete so, if she could be pushed back, there could be a lovely gentle start down the long row which could certainly look like normal driving.

At the time, and now, these things are important: How it is not too far distant, the two things: Evolving as a species to be one being that owns a car and is sitting in it moving down the road with no actual battery-power, or the one who is moving down the smooth car park road with battery power. It is just finding the angle to allow this closeness. No need to feel daft.

A lovely long row of rear white-lightless boots – you know nobody is about to be backing-out-from because there is no one here save me and the man that came out on the free bus. The gravel is the biggest, Man, like Rubik's cubes, perhaps the only surface possible to repel any effort at the purchase necessary for the feet to give it a push out. There have been lots of times the car I am with is pushed out by me alone from a dip into a roll.

I go past the option of starting it myself and see that the other two options are: A nice quick jumpstart from another driver hailed as they exit this arrowed soft-maze; or: The man whose job it is to help folks who, statistically, must surely leave the odd overhead on and, we're all human, or a glove-compartment glowing, and because it's long-stay, it's long enough; so they must they must account for this even-chance-happenstance eventuality . . . (is how I say it when I sing it) . . . (and there is a lot of singing.) . . . (primarily, to get better at all parts of it – the invention and the throat's tonal control – there are always those stories of the girls singing since they were in gospel kindergarten and I have to catch up with the hours).

The man in Customer Services says that because they are understaffed he can help me in just over an hour at two-ten at his shift's-end. Really it is lucky the flight was delayed because it has shortened this time for me. So for this hour, life offers a chance to try other stuff. My membership is breakdown-related, not general RAC or AA, so would take no less than an hour, I imagine, and would count as one of the four times allowed and so hey, next door is another cheaper independent car park company that folks can book a place at online, turn up and park, ride and save. "Flying Scot", lovely name, it sounds of speed and old days and traditional reliability, of myth and good and it is just the most ludicrously simple true definition of what many of the parkers are going to be shortly after. They know when they are coming, they budget with a finite finance and it can work. Still, with all the fences it still feels like Jurassic Parking: humans trying to control the future around expected states that will please them. The woman tries to help and offers a recharge pack at her head office down at the thingy. I guess she means terminal so when the free bus comes around I jump at this lead. The bus sweeps the bus-stops that people are actually standing at dotted around the large lot. They are scooped in and luxury first-classers and un-easy budgeteers alike mix in the unsaid soup.

Back at the thingy I see no Portakabin-headquarters and so leap a fence and ask at the multi-storey who are also tender-staffed to be unable to send someone off with me to help.

"And you would be uneasy for me to go away with your charger?" I foolishly ask him to agree with and he does.

Free bus back to home-park there are potential helpers and I have only forty-nine minutes until definite help. SO, only forty-nine minutes to find a more-super solution. There is a feeling in me to not be too upset yet, to turn it all upside-down. It is a laugh. I am not late yet for the promised lift-giving a hundred and seventy miles north I have to do later on this New Year's Eve-evening. So far, so tricky, though not that bad.

It is windy and wet and the couple get off the bus at Enterprise Rental and the man left has no jump-leads.

It is windy and wet and I hover with my collar up. Enterprising, mental.

After a minute or two a car comes towards the entrance and finds perhaps that it is not the certain cheap parking he is looking for and does a U-turn.

The wind blows me back to the car where I sit in the passenger's side and realize a beautiful thing: My life right now is troubled and it is going to be alright. That is one way of putting it yet there seems to be no actual end to the point when it is sorted and then life continues on. So, happily, my life is alright. This is tied to the hope that no one comes and parks next to me because that would make it very hard to get jumpstarted because the Ford would then be boxed-in; followed by the dull flash that if someone did come in and park here they could be the one that jumpstarts me. Just press the button, down the window and make a friendly New-Year-ish request. Here in the rain in the wind in the coldish car in a now wet tweed with the possibility that it is worse than a flat that I might have to leave the car parked for price and come back later – let friends down, miss them get solo-travelling, Aha, all that, and yet in there right here there was a best-that-could-be. Clouds, lining – true. Dictatorial nature of clichés means they sound like kharmic orders you have to follow. Based in brilliance, though.

Trouble and alright. Plus, in the passenger seat-I-would-never-have-usually-been-in, is how it can be seen: there on the ground, a Curly Wurly wrapper.

"Did I eat all the Curly Wurly?" This out loud. For a laugh I half-ate lots of bars before giving the kids a Cadbury Selection at Christmas and maybe there would be half a Curly Wurly to chew on, all car-cold hard toffee going soft inside my warm smile eventually. Alas, yahoo, no.

Plus, no plus – see, plus just means "and" whereas minus has to have something more to be taken away from.

A couple came and parked their Peugeot two spaces away diagonally. Prepared, I pressed the window button and the key in the ignition is not at the position for power. Even if it was, would there be power? Was a concept never touched to the lip of my mind then.

Close with a whiff of cigar. Opening the door, I loiter while they are still chatting then in the gap where they both stop talking I walk in having made myself noticeable with gentle physical movements and ask about jump-leads. None with them and they leave with wheelie-bags, turning around after twenty yards to return to their vehicle swiftly yet without any body-clue intimating that they have suddenly remembered leads, more like something else forgotten and remembered-that-it-was-forgotten-in-a-moment and yes, he extends the arm and locks the car from about three metres away. No doubt the company probably says it can be done from ten metres or more yet you would probably want to see the things go down to make sure, if there was a old-wet-jacket-wearing man sitting in a car with time to kill and steal in a lonely long-distance car park.

Back in the Ford I feel the tweed gets warmer as well as heavier when a little wet. How handy that natural fibres do the best thing. It pelts down on the pelt.

I need a pee and do it near the car. Not really worried about being caught because anyone to catch me would have to be another candidate for helping me.

Same with talking to myself. There is a great freedom in a place where one is almost sure there is no one to hear or see. Top of a mountain or car park nine. SO I make use of it and talk loudly and openly, articulately, all about whatever. There is very little one can ever speak out loud that cannot be said onstage.

There's definitely a song coming: "New Year in the Long Stay . . . The longest stay I've ever had . . . Away from love, no party had . . ." & cetera.

Next it occurs that there is still a better place and that is in the Customer Services warmth where, maybe, a personal saviour could come by the silver-lined waiting room.

Surely clouds are all made all of silver lining. The goodness starts when you consider it goodness.

Surely light at the end of the tunnel is light in the tunnel: to be seen it is reaching you.

In there I place a "Full Valet Service" pamphlet on my lap thinking it would be fun to feel how far am I from this amazing service: One could arrive back to a car that was running, waiting, warmed up, with painted and shining tyres, oil-changed, interior trim-trimmed, externally polished and obviously washed and vacuumed, the tyre-pressure checked, with the boot space taken care of too . . . Also there is the chance that someone, upon entering this space, may immediately see me as a Valet-customer and feel more inclined to help me because, in a moment, they have confidenced me in their own mind into a rich man with a car worth Valetting . . . Who knows? That was my received groovy off-chance.

A lovely family car joins in our scene and out smartly is Dad and in, saying hello to me without the pamphlet being clocked.

"Have you called the man?" he says, pointing at the summoning buzzer. Good question by him, it covers "Are you waiting to be served?", it moves to getting what he and his family need as quick as possible, for now he knows he is next.

"On you go, he is here." With an arm raised he brings out papers required to confirm the pre-booking deal, I say that it is jump-leads that would be best and then add that I don't want him to have them because he's got kids, they are wantin' to move . . . Twenty-four minutes now . . . So.

"Sorry we don't have any."

"Good."

"Best of luck!"

"And to you."

What would be the advantage of pre-booking then, if you still have to come to the car park, drop it pick it up and then come in here in person and verify the deal with paperwork? What if you lost that? Could you prove you were the you they had a deal with without paperwork? Probably with another form . . . In that case why have the paperwork if the other way works? . . . Must be a reason.

Right now it seems the reason is to remind me never to worry if paperwork is lost cos it seems it is not really ever needed, it is only your presence that is essential.

Next a lovely mother and son came in who had pre-booked on the internet and could not find the particular car park they were meant to be at. The son was tall and said they had booked it with Flying Scot on the internet. They had been told to come here and now my man was telling them they had to go back as it was definitely not here they had the deal with.

They had booked the park on the internet and it was not going well. All that to save a few quid and it was jeopardizing their actual trip. Stopping them from actually being flying Scots.

Didn't hear exactly what his Mum said, he said, ". . . if I was older I would be driving." Which sounded like, "If I was older I would be away from you, my mother, not here with you. Free, roaming; a warrior out in the world."

Then Mum says, "We had better hurry or we are going to miss the flight."

"No we're not. Will you stop saying that, you're doing my nut in."

An amazing piece of Scottish language: "nut" is head. the approximation of the feeling of compression up there in the consciousness and head that comes from processing the nonsensical realistic pessimisms of Mum – thinking about missing the skiing, the fun, the booze, the sneaking away from Mum, the party, the girls, the icy warm lips, the freedoms, was to be not thought about.

Sitting there I laughed out loud and, as he was turning to go to the door, it was entirely possible that he would lash out at me. His eyes met mine to see if it was going that way. His Mum's eyes were finding out too. They left and I helped with the door in the wind . . . Twelve minutes.

So far I have had water and shelter, a promise of help, glimmers of swifter aid, interesting incidents, time to write and have escaped violent injury. It's going as well as a good holiday. More than this, I have not been let down. Seems to me that if one has a car it can break down and such, yet that is not out of line with an expectation. Harder it is to be these folks who have pre-booked and can't even find where they have to be when they could just leave a car and walk away in this giant area designed for that exact purpose. What would the fine be for leaving a car here? Perhaps the same as just parking.

A beautiful woman in her late thirties came with ideal freckled décolletage and side slashes in her festive dress and a husband to carry the two biggest wheelie-trunks ever, laughing as he looked for the paperwork they did not have handy inside them. He was unzipping in an upright position – it must have been too much to lay them down and go through it, emotionally too much like actually unpacking again. The bags stood there like a nice travel-Stonehenge set and he did some very opposite work to the ritualistic druid activities usually carried out: he sought forms. Still he was smiling and when I asked if there was any jump-leads in there he did laugh and say there was everythin' else. His actual car was a private-hire cab. She was still laughing as she told her kid in the loo, "I'm coming in, Sandy." She had it all: free ways, the wherewithal to allow time to find paperwork, someone to carry her bags and her own personal private-taxi without a meter running. Wow! A flying Scot.

My man in behind the glass is looking up. Just then, wondering how to spark up a conversation through the glass, he starts talking about checking the battery in the transponder.

"Thanks very much. Yeh, I never thought about checking that . . ."

". . . Aye, on the new bus . . ." He wasn't even talking to me. Now, though, I am up and on my feet facing him. Handy that this overheard is in the realm of my needs so, it's good to stay . . . When he finishes his phone call . . . What was he looking up at?

"What have you there? TV or security screens?"

It is security and I imagine him watching me talk loudly to myself and writing on a notebook in the passenger seat and then looking for the car key lost when I had not been anywhere and putting a Curly Wurly wrapper on my finger, loitering, singing and peeing.

Surely he must have felt close to me by now.

It seemed right to tell him about the couple who'd come back to lock their car and how, if they hadn't and if anything had gone, I would definitely have been a suspect, Yeh? With the most-ever footage of, and my registration plate. And probably still here, unable to leave the scene of the crime. The getaway car fucked.

He got it.

The van arrives with the man with the leads and the man tells me he is Colin. The wind helps me open the door for him.

"Thank you."

"That's alright, Colin."

He takes me in the van to my car and as he huddles the vehicle in I see for the first time it says "OPTIMO" on my tyre's rim. It is successful. Colin starts me up to smoothly cruise around to the pay-slot with the radio on already and, my parking ticket now over the grace period and in excess. Five eighty they want over the eleven pounds for two days already paid. It had only been six and a half hours of the twenty-four I was allowed for five twenty after the initial five eighty for the first day. SO it would have been possible to not pay before I returned to my car and to have another seventeen and a half more hours for sixty pence cheaper than this hour-and-ten. Reversing, the ticket is still in the machine and, in parking, I switch off the engine and go into the office inform them of the lost ticket and am told it's okay, they'll let me off as they were with me all the way. Super . . . and . . .

"Hello, foolishly I switched it off too early. Colin, please could you start me one more time."

He is not openly grumpy and it is all part of his job and we all have slips. This time he knows to come in real close for the leads to stretch to this side where the battery is, without a re-huddle, so it is much quicker and bingo, the barrier goes up for free. Optimo escapio.

Looking further down the white line, the essence of the future, the bit we can see of the shape of things to come, works as a kind of optimism and steadies your balance for a freer and more efficient trip. Everyone knows they use the cobra's venom as the antidote. Everyone knows that tight-rope walkers never look at their feet.

All this had happened on the thirty-first of December and so all the missing fun, to maybe miss, was big real Hogmania parties being set up and put together by people I know and don't know, an actual party for me to go to while all this time spent in the car park with the options.

At my Mum's, a bit later, she has been keeping a secret lunch warm for me for hours. We drink wine from a chateau and, after being asked, she tells me what she would like to be done with her body after she dies. This seems like a marvellous thing to happen, especially as Radio Three was packed with Beethoven's music, apparently built on torment, in the fine drive over from the airport, which I presume and assume and expect to be long enough to charge the battery fully. Who else of my friends may have listened to the radio at the same time as me?

My new years ambition this year is to go to a carwash with the klids and oh no, terrible the sun-roof will not open and ha ha there's umbrellas in the back and we open one for the kids in two thousand and fourteen.

Free Chapter

Driving always felt good, like the time me and Des took a long wrong turn and went on to the as yet un-opened M77 down towards Prestwick Airport. We had to resemble laughing surveyors without helmets as we went a bit slower along the very quiet road passing construction guys doing finishing touches. We waved regally for definite at some point. Like sneaking in cinemas when you already have a ticket; like using the momentum of confidence . . . like moving . . . like liking. Amazingly this was a road that I had lived at the camp which protested the building of this needless bypass and was there the day after the politician ill-advisedly threatened some protesters with a shovel. Protest it, then they build it. March against the war, then they wage it. I am the missing link.

There is a fabulous natural element to events that spurs me on and, when it comes down to it, that makes me feel that any event can be retold in a way that will make it interesting. It could be a life, it could be a day. Why do things get reminded to ourselves by ourselves? I think it is because, when they happened, they summed up and continued a pattern of the world as it was felt to be. The Great Chinese Wall: thin yet continued enough to be seen. They sum up what the world is to you. They make the world. What is the world other than which people see it to be? Naught. What is it other than what it is to you? Well, what it is to everyone yet this still has to be processed for you by you. I like to hear anyone's story.

In the grandest terms: when a person tells their story they define their universe.

And how did the protesters get to the protest site? By road presumably, though not through countryside they disliked.

Things that interest me arouse my interest in my own interest. Just last decade I went to Donegal in the North of Ireland. I take no euros and, after meeting Mikey the only Cuban Brother to know all three of my five brothers, land at Belfast, help in jump-starting the cab at the airport, would you believe?, and, lending the driver the parking-fee in pounds not euros, for that's all I have. My kind of guy, and who am I to have any issue with all this? Phil. So I am walking to the gig that night with no available local currency. This is very fine and happens a lot; often do it; hand-to-mouth; timing it that way means you spend less and then, if you don't get cash, then you have a few more days where your outlays are superbly curtailed.

Things then happen. Have to . . . I have done busking to get cash, I have done busking not-to-get cash, this time I was happy without. Passed an old pub called The Cottage Inn and, remembering that it had all the exciting instruments of saddlery and farm activity hung on the wall, and though there might be an actual funny-thing there to then talk about onstage fairly soon – the recent and true is always an aim for me. The recent and true does not have to be that funny to be delivered strongly and well and be something to hear. I have found crowds are quite psychic and generally pick up on all the pheromones and tiny hair-raisings-of-truth on their ears and napes. They can be amazed and smiling at this well before jokes are required. To this pub there are two doors. I look in one and four regulars at the bar on stools look my way. I take the other door to the lounge side and enjoy a quick observe of the mounted brass then back out again.

There are the four faces again on leaving, now with the quizzical aura laminated. Out on the street with their eyebrows on my mind, I turn back in. This is it: the instant relating to what you feel. What comedy performance gives me, both onstage and in the hours surrounding is: a reason to act entirely on whim. I knew I wanted to explain. I knew then I was going to go back in there and, as I open the door, there are The Four and they this time have the extra something of "isn't that that joker who just . . . ?"

"Hi there, I . . ." Eight eyes at me. "You know how it is sometimes a little thing happens and it is a little mystery – what happened there? what was he up to? Well, I thought I would just like to explain . . ." Just say what the exact thing they are considering. "I am a comedian over from Scotland with no euros so I can't buy a drink and I remembered this pub and I am just on my way to do a gig and I wondered if they still had all the field-utensilry and mystery brasses on the walls here and I saw your faces and I thought it could be fun to have a tiny mystery explained fairly soon after it just occurred . . . Although I know if you don't believe me it will definitely seem like a plea for money."

Three looked at me, one asked where I was on, and she seemed to simply be hearing what I said, believed it and I told her what time it was and got her name for the guest list and in departing our smile was stretched in a parting.

Believe me, I know it's not a funny story – not really, though it did just occur and when I told it a half hour later to a big, mostly empty, theatre they were absolutely sure it was not that funny. Certainly funny was missing by then as it was the topical recent-ness that was big for me – a starting point – funny was required. It was me though, I lost the faith in it, though. I am sure that if I had waited until it was appropriate and it had come out as a relating, quirky cerebral-link – perhaps as a cross-reference to Dead Ringers, made by Cronenburg, where Jeremy Irons' cruel gynecologist's twin brother makes his own gold instruments (because I saw Cronenburg's Crash just then) – yeh, perhaps that would have given it a life. The belief from me would have been the electricity to move the limbs of laughter, the lube to slip it all in.

Just laying out for them was too much. They just kept thinking: Is this true? Where's the punchline?

The thing with this story is that it was about that moment just outside the bar when I had just left and was carrying their quizzicals with me. There was an understanding, I wanted to communicate that to them. I have a lust I won't let go. I knew what I was going to do. Which reminds me . . .

Reminds me of standing looking over the eleven lanes of traffic at the Arc de Triomphe roundabout. I knew what I was going to do, knew that I was going to do what had just occurred to me, knew that what was about to occur was what had just come to me. What was coming occurred.

Knowing what is funny is bullshit-mad and old-timer safety-talk. No one knows.

Knowing what you think is fabulous and energizing and to be done is great and very possible . . . knowing what you might want to say, a definite plausibility. By the time I wrote "field utensilry" you and I know what I am on about and a laugh can be a bridge to this understanding and a flag expressing this shared understanding. Nobody actually has to suffer. Suffering is two-way, like all things, and not so set. What it does though in comedy is give a very definite thing we all are aware of: a certain definitive identity, paradigm time, and then the humour can all be got because of that. We take it for granted the Irish are stupid in the joke to then be creative with examples, not re-establish it each time. Women are this, Americans are that, bosoms, drunk folks, checkout girls, it just gets subtler and subtler. Or in alternative comedy it jazzes away and twists and replaces the given with a new-given given . . . Then you can just start doing long-enough gigs so that you and your attitude are the thing that then becomes the given . . . You call back to yourself and become the parade of paradigm; you get to relate to your movements, quirks, twisty wordings, clothes, mood, place in the room ideas as a limitless possible subject matter hypothetical set list.

Even the Policeman who came over to me just before I was about to step into le swirling vortex at the Arc de Triomphe here in Paris said, "The underpass ees over there." Even he does not need to suffer. He was just doing his job. Plus beautifully, grammatically he was not actually telling me not to do what I knew I was about to do. Plus, I had just walked right up the middle of the huge wide Avenue des Champs-Élysées, Elysian Fields, on the thick white line separating the four lanes, so I was full of adrenaline, achievement and already a soupçon of triumph. The cars on either side are not allowed on this particular bit, it is the thick central line they cannot cross. Imagine No Line. It is the border that is not land. It is the space marked that is the thickest nothing. It is like the point in math that has no length yet all hinges on it. A massive fat hinterslice having the balls to be as thick as any line. They are all fractal and have a start side a not not the line and then they have the middle bit of the line that is not the beginning and than they have the other side that ain't the middle and yet is not the thingspace beyond the line. Humans have made impossible lines in the world where they try to be a divider, simply a denoter, yet they are a place themselves and here is one fat fatherfucker, massive enough for me to reside in. Land of the Hawk-Eye, the atom is mostly nothing. Bonus.

Zipping up the middle slowly the eyes have it, in a moment as they pass: le concept.

The pavement was good for a while, passing that strange obvious sight of Japanese ladies queuing to get in to the Louis Vuitton shop, for the Sale, because the bouncers were not letting them in. Doorstaff at an all-night garage in Aviemore once, and now they queue here to 'ave more. This was like a nightclub and worse: imagine looking in the windows and seeing everyone kissing and dancing, drinking and touching. Well there is that nightclub in Barcelona where the men's toilet becomes see-through one-way glass allowing everyone to see in. They were staring in the windows watching the handbags get caressed and possessed, put into bigger bags, and the very still most minimalist, ultra subtle, nuanced conga dance of the next queue they will be in to-the-till in full flow.

This was the time I was in Paris and a bunch of us had been trying to hail a cab for ages, looking for the yellow light, then we got one then inside that one we saw another one and all hailed that from within because we all got it at the same time – the urge. The understanding. The laugh. So yeh once and for all for a laugh we all got out and in the Stepping Out and Down to get into the other one, the cab drifted and ran over onto my foot, the wheel moved up on to my steel toe cap boot and just sat there, balanced atop it. I called out in French the most appropriate word I could muster, "Reversez. Reversez, s'il vous plaît!" then I just pulled the foot out of the boot. And stepped back. Leaving it there under the wheel, hopping back it was a sweet little image that Renault just jacked-up-a-little on my footwear, me bouncing and it all very comically obvious what had happened.

So: there are eleven lanes – onze – and I step in as there seems to be a congestion-pause, because of priorité à droite, to allow cars on. The outer lanes are faster and I need this gap which helps me as does the realization, from crossing roads in China, that if you just go for it drivers will see your trajectory, will see your path and can work theirs around it. That though is an Eastern thing a bit and here in t'West we face the wrath of upset, angered, annoyed drivers who may well speed up to put you in danger to teach you a lesson by showing you how close you were to danger. Unnaturally bring upon the horror to show you the horror you could be bringing upon yourself.

Faces above steering wheels look at me five lanes deep and there is a "yes" from behind motorcyclist's visor via a gathering of more eyebrow and a bus-load of tourists actually see me wave their driver on, moving them on through somewhere like about lane seven or eight, like I am in control – the traffic attendant without the white gloves and podium. The last two lanes are easy to cross because they are right in the middle and slower, centre of the centrifuge. I step through and between the last bumpers and wide eyes up on to the high paved island, higher than an Edinburgh kerb with the triumphant arch and the eternal flame to the known and unknown dead soldiers. At this moment it occurred to me that these low symbolic chains they have around the memorials do not actually keep you back, they do not stop you – it is you who keeps you back stops you. I just kept going, stepped up and over, continued my magnificent walk up the avenue, walked over to the eternal flame and warmed my hands.

Later, in the gig, we have entertainments extra extra to go to and it seemed perfectly humorous to ponder on having had some chicken fillets with me and popped them on the grate over the eternal flame and brushing a wee bit honouring, commemorative, highly respectful seasoning and oil on, before the gens d'armes got there from the underpass . . . running away, salad leaves, greasy fingers, Cop trouble.

In fact they have an office right here under the Arc and one just pops his head out and says "Enough!" as I approach eternal fire.

September 20th 2008.

This is the month I saw a Bounty bar rapper on the ground all stomped on crushed and folded over so it read "cunty". All my life I've been folding photos in newspapers over to make them daft, Beckham legs look much better shorter and moving the nose down to the lips or chin up to the nose makes everyone look gurnier . . . the Queen on notes works well . . . And Here It Was.

Writing right now 13.03.13, 10:29 a.m., I'm using a large piece of lining paper to keep notes on, the cheapest ever supply of gnarly, rough, absorbant paper by the ten-metre roll on offer at two ninety-nine, and its roughness helps the ink on beautifully. There's three quarters of a metre of it to my right hand under the dark soft matte of dull grippy rubber from the back of a table tennis bat that is my mouse mat. The mouse has gone and got a lazy lazer eye or got something in his lazer eye, whichever is funnier, and as the editing and the correlating, additions and abstract subtractions are going on I'm writing on it little lists of reminders, things to check I have done and check that I mustn't repeat and speeling to check, spelinig to cheek, the cheeky speel to spell . . . as well as also thesaurus synonym requests, oddities, designs, film ideas and new hand-drawn fonts. Now there is a large rounded-square beer-mat shape I have drawn to be the place where I put the coffee bowl or the tea's jar or the HenryWestons vintage. The coffee cups have left a ring on the absorbant blotting paper and then another and a few more looking like a shitty peacock tail spiral, an expanding 3D kids' concertina tunnel from the garden. In the end it looks like this is how they might have come up with the 0()Olympic logo or the Audi one when they sat around with beers and chat and beer wrings appear as they place pints down on the table.

That is what happened one yesteryear: went to do a kids' show and an adult evening show in most beautiful Deeside. Truly is a unique chance to entertain the kids and then their parents at night, and do some stuff only they can get in the kids' show and some childish shit in the adult show and then in-jokes that only certain adults who were at their kids' show will get, and yet that the ones that weren't at the kids' show will not be realizing that they are not getting.

The thing about Schrödinger's cat is that it is a theoretical model to help comprehend a theory about conscious reality through the model of a hypothetical box that to open it will kill the cat inside, and so it cannot be opened to ever see if the cat is alive. Studying and observing it will kill it so we can never know so we have to admit it is one or the other, both and yet there is a third that really we cannot be sure without checking so it is also an unknown to. It appears to me this model from Schrödinger, who did a lot of other stuff in Ireland!, is/was just a lens to see the truth through: material is waiting to be energy. Furanose is a kind of sugar made of a ring of four carbon atoms and a single oxygen atom. Splendid.

And comedy, comedy can evaporate on studying and observing because truly it is not a thing, it is a description of an event. Laughter is a thing. It can be present, alive or not present and yet still be not the true indicator of funnyness felt. Folks laugh to indicate and they smile loudly sometimes when they love it rather than laugh out loudly and drown out the next funny thing. So it's both and neither; that is, it cannot really be known to us, it is at its truest without our focused attention.

In between shows, I have four hours to kill and maim, and was about to drive to Aberdeen, and what? Catch a look at a city I've seen an awful lot. Aah, the all-night bakery for butteries, the park with the life-changing sachet of ketchup, the first of my three great handstands-to-go-very-wrong. Last time I rented my bike out for a pound-a-go to the drunk and excited outside the kebab shop scooped cobbled gauntlet of Bell Street and got given wine and a cravat by new friends . . . This is a basic secret, open with me: That I really do feel up for interactive fun most of the time, the way I see people up-for-it at well-past-midnight with boozes flowing in their bloodstreams . . . Obelix of the Last Tube.

Actually the last last time before that one in Aberdeen I went into the Christian Army late-night "rescue" lorry-bus . . . cups of teas and granulated white sugars for people having whiteys and who are too pissed to walk at their weakest and maybe the best time to pounce on them and prey on their infirmity and vulnerability is here. Nice choice. Circle the wateringholes you bonecrushing hyenas. This is simulacra: the imitation of a thing that never was. People just help others they don't park up and provide aid with an excuse and a logo. It's hilariously topsy-turvy piousness, so I go in and take the piss, my secret aim to rile them and turn them into the uptight right-wing enforcers I believe they are, in as few minutes as possible, a chess match in life, in the least moves and also more like a bull fight, a bullshit fight, because I start off being straight and the whole reason I am doing it is that I believe they are daft and cause trouble worldwide with the imitation of caring and the opposite of mothering and the false veneration of the father with false pretend secretly gay men being unholy holy fathers when it's all a miracle and childbirth of every pope came from fucking. And the Dalai Llama self pleasures. Why deny all the anima to live in ministry. Defense naturally. Oh let us be free of following the hiding, fear and defensive ways.

Study the good and then do it is not the best. You alter it and distort it and then are eminating a mass of non existentialism. Good is not a thing it is a description of an event. Do you believe in good? You cannot be good only called good. Whatever you are you are all that is called good already. You are the wholly viable, the ample, the permissible, the permission, the holy feasible, the most practical and practicable. In the qualifying is the trouble. Who decides the criteria? The Ballroom Dancing Association . . . the Catholic Conference . . . the Scottish Matriculation Board . . . that's who.

Just slip that in like an entire shelf-help book, religious text, prophet livingstone seagull, fucking secret fucking la la llama book of the dead silly. A simple earnest complete truth for me that if everyone believed they were enough for everything already that all they are being asked to do to be healed they already are doing to even agree then hey presto no guidelines would be needed for law of a man-made god text, and the best way to do this is raise kids by taking them seriously. You then would have to take apart your religion, dismantle its obstructions to fun by listening to your children and taking every sound they say as a viable utterance to relate to. So that's the science understood through the science of myself.

So, I'm in the christian pick-up truck-bus – nothing like a massive childcatcher scenario from Chittychitty, no this is me sitting down pointy-chinned and sniffing them out getting cheap instant coffee then starting to test their patients as I complain, not being compliant to raise a little disgruntle, a nibble on the line and then I'm in saying straight away that this ain't right and all the time poking it for one reason that there will be one of these eleven volunteers that is a bit shaky on all this, sees that in the practice a Jesus Army is a fucked-up phrase, wake up and smell the instant coffee blown up the nose to having to enforce belief as an adjective that has been turned into a noun. Aiee it is not a thing. Generally among this many – and this is the first and only time so far I have done this – generally you are safe from physical attack no matter what you say, so I refuse to leave, get a little excited at it, look individuals in the eye to see if there is my tiring bull: one intelligent lass who feels this is counter to the lovely good she had in her heart. Basically they say they are going to call the Cops and then they do and the ultimate golden poker hand winner is to leave there with three young lasses before the Cops come, four hearts . . . then it's to leave with one, then a male, then just more biscuits, get them miffed and leave before the Cops come way then down to the lowest A Pair the lowly of only just getting out as the Police come, and get questioned and allowed to walk away once I were not cheeky to them.

So here now, all's right with me aiming for Aberdeen and realize that I am not going to go and come back. I turn into Crathes Castle – tall flat-sided stair turrets poking, small windows, highly topiarized gardens. As I come up the drive I see a lovely view of the castle up through a small dark garden-gate and that's for me. I park in the car park neither paying nor displaying except attention and keenness, and ruminate on how castles are for the victors, are a sign of military might, and are really there for the invading – they're asking for it and saying they can take it. Their power-hinted-at was enough to scare others away and then they could relax build gardens, enjoy. I wish to invade so I park and cycle the white foldable dear down to that gate. Park and climb. There is a padlock and a small gap above; the first foot slots in there then the other will go right on top to the horizontal gate top bar between vertical spikes that are a pointy row six inches above it. Slotting the heels in carefully since I fell once in this position in Largs because the toe went in first and wedged in even before its widest flat pad middle, so when I stepped forward the foot stayed in between the top spikes and I fell forward and hung by my foot for a while, the ankle wedged at a highly unlikely angle, which stings doesn't it and only possible because of the terrible sprains I had loosened it up with that time jumping out of the bushes aged eighteen in front of a car with Simon Pegg in when I used to know him as a slim and bandana wearing student. He used to have a beaming smile now he does beaming, smiling. In Largs we were filming a disastrous TV show on an open-topped bus that had a massive papier-maché copy of my big face on the front and all improvised banter from me over a microphone about shit that we could see and we'd drive to a wildlife park and I'd make fun . . . it was awful, my mouth just speaking and speaking like

channelling the pointless nonsense easy ass-burgers slight loony part
of the brain comedy. Hyphens between all them words. Something i've
done a fair bit off over the years though not for a long long time and
something that is painfully obvious too and not the chosen form.

Me and the tweed are in the castle grounds now, the foot don't wedge
in there with the heel over and back in way more than halfway out
twards the direction you are going. And a good landing with no
polystyrene white cups popped on the spike, take a stroll, enjoy the
gardens, leave the maze for later. Head to the small windowlights, scale
another wall and then, between the large garden illuminators, big bright
and actually warm square searching flak boxes and apon the wall I see
my huge shadow walking faster than me and big getting bigger then
smaller like it's getting away from me round the corner, and it is,
around the massive mostly-windowless walls of this castle's sides and
re-pointed defensives. It amazes me because the irony is thick and
palpable like trying to do a fast walking strop in the shallow-end of a
pool. Out the back, which is the new front, the new kind of inhabitants
always do it – leave the front door all sealed and perfect and unused
except weddings and conferences and they go right in through the back
door all down to earth and realistic to the eight-oven Aga kitchen
control centre, and the way to control the Hunter wellies and the dogs
is tried and tested three generations deep, and the excellent crockery,
high jars, larders and massive photoboards have hung their little
histories out to dry in this warmth from the enamel range which has
slowly toasted the photos a faded sepia brown on the lifted-up corners.
Well out the back was parked a bright red thirties sporty-roadster and
a huge new Audi Q7 space-bus, fifty four grand, silver giant double tear-
shaped shape of course, massive wheels that need a hug with post-
Cayenne improvements. Of course Porsche bought Volkswagen. The
smaller percentage of those people wealthy enough and inclined to buy
a posh Porsche mount up from all over lots of countries to give so much
strength to this small German car company that it can buy the people's
Volkswagen making entire state-backed nation's national company. So
they probably share parts like Maserati and Ferrari and you and for a
while Ford owned Aston Martin. I really loved a lot of my cars, what
about the old blue ROVER P4, the matt chrome fittings, full width sub-
dash leather shelf, beautiful thin power steering-wheel, the white
ceramic trumpets under the bumper for the stereophonic horn, do that
one in a garage and adore the effect, yes, and rear reading lights and the
SLIGHTLY lighter aluminium boot. What a car, saw it in a film by Wim
Wenders perhaps called The End of Violence and had to have one.

Anyroad, you could get thirty of them for the price of this big suede office jacuzzi tank. There they sat encapsulating it all.

These were the real castles, unassailable, nine seats between them. The big one with the walls was now invaded every day from nine thirty till Santa's grotto closed at five. Invaded every day easily, by bus parties of Italians and non-military Spanish here for the tapestries and the paintings though leaving without them. I stand by the sportscar, the electric security lights come on to keep the hoards back a few metres and a black-coated man nips out and opens the door to the sportster.

"Where you off to?" I ask.

"Stonehaven."

"Ah, a mere fourteen miles." This I leave hanging like a highwayman in a cage, no, like a man in the air when he's leapt offstage and the crowd are about to part and not catch him yet, just before that and suddenly it occurred to feel the urge to follow it with a "That's exactly where I need to go . . ." I fail to utter this and consider how, for a moment, I had claimed the castle and gardens and nearly The Car.

Felt a bit sad at this and then guided myself through a conversation with a French lady who had been at the kids' show earlier, doing far-sillier giant shadows with her daughter now, up to the café. About to walk in, a man with a ponytail warned me not to walk into the small electric vertically retracting, could it lift you up for fun like a partial beaming up from Scotty metal strut designed to go down just for to let in the delivery vans and keep out the hoards like a low memorial chain. When it goes up each time, that's a time when you could flip a hired Smart car over onto its side like a beetle and we'd all make the cute noise and flip it back over, wee thing. It's marvellous, the upside-down shift of the castlefolk: warning me of small obstacles that dropped to allow the delivery of food when, of course, castle defences kept armies out, who then just simply stopped supplies coming in and just waited in the form of a siege until there was no more food and the people inside died or came out, weak and feeble, to fight rather badly or surrender-strongly. Now we go to the castle at opening hours and go straight to the café. They can't stop us, unless it's closed. Who needs a moat when there is a closed sign. We sit and have a snack or full meal inside like it's the café inside the Trojan horse, it's magic like the café is the Trojan horse within the castle, yeh, and the done-up castle itself is an intruder into the memory of all those who died in battle in the castle's heyday of the fighting era. They wouldn't hide the spikes with the heads on and they would drench you in a non-vegetable oil at an uncomfortable temperature. It used to be siege, famine and anguish, now it's chease and ham sandwich.

SO here now entering in and approaching the café-stand, running the gauntlet of gifts that are never truly needed by anyone for purposes known to no one, I am making a coffee-smelling face and, looking up, catch a younger member of till-staff making the same face back at me – filling her own day with fun and amusement, making fun of/with the custom provider is my instant gladwell feeling; summing up to oneself what just occurred in the mind.

On my mind was end-of-the-day ca$hFrEE old-five-to-five filter and now, I had blackmail on my side: "How dare you make the face and what if the manager hears of this? Ha-ha!" et cetera, et cetera and in the next ten minutes I am surrounded by more giggles than I have ever seen in a gig. The young woman who made the face stayed and sorted her scones while I made fun with an avalanche of sandwiches waiting to happen on the overstocked fridge-shelf that was like the crazy arcade overhanging coin-game and tried to get a smile from the younger staff who came out of one kitchen swing door and in the other like a massive Swiss clock-type affair behind the counter. The friendly manageress offered me a cheese scone and, when she was away, me and the others were sneaking me a raisin one and got caught. "Tantamount to theft" became our mini-mantra, and ". . . less than my job's worth".

The even more-manager who warned me of the magic rising bollards comes to a sliding door and calls across the room, talking to the manager next to us. I talk to my face-girl: "Hey, he commands immediate attention; he does not come over and wait by us for a small gap in conversation to step-in with his requests; he is so powerful and charismatic, yet am I staff??" She is doubled up at what seems to be the simplest observation and which must have gathered something on the way about his personality as manager. He then closes the door he was talking from and it turns out, as he walks to gifts, that it was not a ponytail – it was a knot in the back of his large apron.

"Hey, it is not a ponytail, although it must have resembled one to many shoppers."

I left then, as the lights began to go off, with a steaming paper carry-out, a forgiven fruit one, wrapped in serviette, in pocket . . . The spoils of mirth. Scone Palace.

Actually I was at school with Georgina and James Murray, the earl of Mansfield he was, and they lived in the real Scone Palace just outside the original Perth and the site, the seat where they used to crown all the Kings of Scotland, which of course was where the Stone of Destiny was fated to be stolen from in 1296 by Edward to be taken to Westminster and used to crown all English monarchs since. Except when it's nicked back again, or might not even be the real one. Of course many say that it is just a replica stone, and the real one was hid in Dunsinane dot dot dot. Many also say the real one could never be real, not stone can give magical righteous endowments. Many even say royalty itself is a myth that controls and sells a lot o' bunting that is made in factories that are unsafe . . . and the Duke of Argyll was challenged to a fight for his land by a poacher . . .

The big deal with me was to recognize natural ways around the non-mirth. The castle is part of a new movement that has come from an upset world and yet paying-and-displaying two hundred metres from the battlements seems dreary; snapping photos of torture-dungeons and the paintings of Anglo-dandies and second sons gifted entitlements who pillaged on incredibly efficient scales seems to be a garage forecourt-flowers way to accept our bloody history. Like: this is what humans do, we come to visit our incredible past even though it is highly questionable. Visit it uber-ficially: not to really see it and amend where this might occur in our own actual lives happening now. No, just visit enough to let it continue.

All the brutish reality of castle and land-ownership and slavery. All acceptable because of the distance of time fermented to tradition. And yet now here is another castle to see . . . I did not pay. I did not display. I walked the tiny maze freely and supped my full-fat pillages, nibbled my own scone of destiny, thought of my love who has gone today, for to Australia, and climb back out of the grounds with the white cup gripped between my teeth, finish off, bite and drive the polystyrene swiftly and easily over a spike on the top of the gate.

A nod to the heads. Django Unplugged.

Now I wage a little unknown war and the victory is mine. Reclaimant, like the coastline croft, like the crofters grandson the architect coming back. The dead vessel impaled. Like a wee white pygmy skull of weatherdried bone or a wee white trumpet blast of tone we own this place. So that's Edinburgh, Stirling, Crathes, Scone, the Spences' one, Cleish Castle and Burleigh castle, by Kinross – you go in and get the key yourself, an ancient old massive one you could cut yourself with a saw and move in.

It was only when my love was away that this book got started. Best to go to war with an army of the lovesick. Numb to pain. Flag bearers for the pain.

March them overnight on licquorice. That's what the Romans did; to rehydrate.

'MementoS' – the mint you'll remember.

By the way I am thrilled to see PrimalScream the band getting the word "light" into the title of an album. Back in the day they were willing to scare a puppy.

Something much happened before the gig after Craithes: Three things which I happened to see around the town of Banchory and all of which the crowd really dug because they had seen them themselves. Imagine the fun at turning up at a town, cycling around it for a while seeing things, remembering them and then speaking them out to see what happens in the telling. The first was seeing a guitar in the window of the Scottish Hydro-electric power shop on the High Street. I sang about how some shops have to extend their ranges at Christmas to compete with this and bicycles in a chemist's window, or those strange displays in amusement-arcade windows, and loitered singing on the idea of the guitar amp perhaps being powered by standing playing it by a waterfall with a little dynamo travel-sized waterwheel attached.

There was a sign for a shop called "It's Curtains For You". I am in love with a shop with a totally-raw full-frontal completely-exposed pun of a title that is-not-a-hairdresser's and so superb. Also it was not strained, it was still a straightforward description: It is curtains for you, it is . . . There are curtains here and they are available for you to purchase . . . Lovely.

Amazingly, they had a poorly-fitted blind in their own window. Yes it hung loose and unparallel, as if there'd been a saloon brawl in there; too much gaps, looking as only a broken blind can. The Crowd appreciated the irony of this juxtaposition in window-display-excellence I re-illuminated for them and, like Derren Brown, I know that they know that I feel they must have seen it and been aware of it, enjoyed the periphery-centricity. They just had had no crowd for it to be relevant and relate it to, perhaps.

And then was heard a lady singing in the beauty salon opposite while hoovering alone. I stood outside and aurally peeped for the same thing anyone peeps for: intimate moments of personal action, uncluttered by concerns of anyone else's eyes.

This was regular work. This was paths of hoover-line that had been honed down like Pac-Man. This was someone living. This was like those shortcut paths I found in St Johns in Newfoundland. This is gold. Gold cos I love it – nothing is guaranteed, yet if you love it then it has a chance of being the best thing.

Like a nunchuck's elbow or a sail. A harnessing of the energy that allows the power. No thing will definitely be funny. No thing can be absolutely hilarious for all, if it is not loved.

The crowd knew this salon, knew the curtain shop they may even have seen the Hungry Hippos in the window of the charity shop that was going to get snapped up like itself soon.

This was kind of other opposite to Letterkenny and the utensils: where none of it seemed to be what the crowd wanted or rather maybe were even aware of. Here a couple got it, then others got that there was something to get and then got what that was, bypassing actual experience. In fact there are not really any opposites for me. Even like hot and cold: they are not opposites, just points on the scale.

Both times it was what I wanted; just better done here and with some extra funny elements. I will continue to take my bike where I can and gather this way. If nothing else, it at least is clear to the crowd that this is fresh. You shop at a market just gathering fresh items and take them home and see how they can be combined. Above all they are fresh. The crowd gets to be there as you cook.

Oh Edinburgh. Twenty-four Festivals in a row. That's a lot of Fringe. Shit dat mo fringe than hair. The absolute genesis and evolution of me as a man and as a comedian.

For my first solo hour-show at the 1991 Edinburgh, aged twenty, Festival, I had first-class seating where I made the front-row old cinema seats covered with fun faux-fur and they received manicures, massages and cooked pop-tarts from a toaster close enough for them to toast their toes toasty by. That was the year I had a phone connected up to the venue switchboard, all miked-up, in my gig and every now and then took a call and was perplexingly vague or strangely off-hand as I talked to customers doing the obvious: have you thought of buying for Phil Kay not Alan Davies . . . or popping them on hold and humming bad Greensleeves . . .

The show that year began with lots of energy and all my props in a tartan granny-shopping-trolley to the sound of a great song by Grand Funk on a cassette I had bought with Al and Morag as we crossed the American Midwest by car a month before. And the show built around jokes got from that trip, based around real locations so it was easy to remember and it finished with a massive overlong, never ending Iwillalwaysloveyou Whitney Houston tribute song, highly sung, self-twisted nipples for the highest notes, to finale finally, eventually. The best bits were the giant outsize DIY drill and two-foot-high Boots lipstick begged from their shopwindow displays for my "Oh Fuck, Honey, I've Shrunk" section. In the trolley was a thigh-master. I'd halfway-in notice a watch on the wrist of a first-class passenger then later notice it was a bit loose and then I'd bring out my drill to do the tiny tiny screw. With the lipstick I'd threaten the world's largest dog willy.

I had this great joke I would do every night: Holding a newspaper I would say, "Oh, I saw something really funny in the newspaper today – where is it, where is it?" scanning through the page I would then happily find it and turn the paper around to reveal some quite badly pre-soiled underpants I had sellotaped in there. It was a prop, it was reliable; I had it to fall back on, spring up from, whatever. One night I did this and Bob Mortimer was in the crowd. He liked this joke and then got me to do warm-up for his and Vic's big new Smell Of show for the BBC.

This was all great. Fly down to London, see friends, do gig, get two hundred and twenty-five quid. Once I did it though, I was working so hard that my two upper false teeth on a plate fell out and smashed on the studio floor.

Continue warming up, get told to stop, fill in for twenty while they re-shoot; rebuild, stop whenever they say, start again, think of things to continue with, don't get too good. Warm them up, keep them simmering. Fluffer and rodeo clown – the hardest aspect was just standing there waiting for the call, waiting for the action to stop and hear them shout my name . . . Then I would have to just start there and then at that second.

In gigs normally you just come on once, this simple, big, one-off moment where there is the fuzz of intersection: Offstage, waiting – not a comedian – then Onstage – actually being a comedian.

It is one of the best bits: starting a show, playing with the whole concept of good focused beginnings; big hellos; being seen for the first time, setting off on a trajectory. Sometimes I like to commentate on the crowd coming in, spying on them from behind the curtain; sometimes I come in with them from the bar; sometimes I am late and run on and they are all waiting; sometimes I just run on all normal from the wings and just keep going off the other side; really, there are endless possibilities.

Warm-up means you have to keep starting and you can't really make the space totally yours and play with the concept. You are there to do a job for them. A bit like Juantorena the pacemaker ... remember those guys in the Olympics doing the hard fast laps for Coe and Ovett to help them get close and then they would graciously step aside and the real deep, brilliant talent would soar on? Well, Juantorena from Cuba started fast, set the pace, led the race in nearly knee-high white socks and a natural afro and then ... then just kept going, kept setting the pace all the way to the finish and won gold.

Warm-up was great for exactly one year work-wise and London-town-wise and going to after-show-parties-wise and yet to continue would have been un-wise.

Back into the green room once, doing warm-up for The Smell Of Reeves And Mortimer because even though Jim didn't dig my act at the Shaw Theatre when I got all excited and shite and climbed over the seats and confronted Arthur Mullard in row twenty, did a painfull interaction and retreated. Phail.

My false teeth fell out and smashed on the hard studio floor and there was no alternative save to carry on without them big front, useful guys. So fanks a lot bouncer, without the power of "F" and hardly much of the management and executives even smiled at me or met the eyes just above the mouth. There was a big monitor with all the action and sound from the studio to keep folks happy with their booze and food, so they'd seen it, all my trouble and the teeth in my hand, and the image of Charlie Higson, uninvolved like a writer in his shed, nobody able to relate to me and my goodwork. So I felt embarrassed for them, a bit like I am for people who drive past me glaring when I am hitchhiking – sure they want to want to give a lift. Did lots of warm-up work doing Sean's Show, Don't Forget Your Toothbrush ... and that huge ch.4 flop Saturday Zoo where I would warm the crowd up for three minutes before the live-recording and then two ad breaks, down to the last second. Eight minutes work, three hundred and sixty-seven quid. Friends of mine said they sometimes could see me running off as the swooping cameras swooped around coming back to the show as they do. Massive show packed with all the modern greats like Paul Calf, Thomson doing Bernard Righton, Roland Rivron on Jonathan Ross and the big American Guests. Like a big pie with pheasant, beef, quail and kidney, everything was the best yet they went together not-well. Like a bad sentence of good words, just too much destined to doom ... much too destined just to doom ... destined to doom just much ...

All these shows were for Channel 4 and an executive called Seamus

Cassidy kept seeing me do warm-up, came to see a few shows, pushed me to centre shows around themes and then commissioned a series of these for Channel 4 . . . Warm-up, swarm-up . . . Thanks to those pants in the newspapers.

Once they really wanted me to do another warm-up and I said, "Only if you buy me two tickets to America." They did. Me and Diane absolutely flew with Virgin and drove to Vegas and back in a Taurus and handsomely came back well endowed with a routine involving all the things in the free in-flight pack: socks, sleep-mask, miniature toothpaste . . . Yeh, yeh, drove to Vegas and back, 6,993 miles with my love; won a hundred and twenty bucks in quarters; slept in the Caesar's car park; got moved on at seven a.m. . . . Never went to get married; was falling asleep at the wheel behind plastic-mirrored shades, awoke to see a golf course being birthed and sprinkled, a complete green island in the desert . . . Lived off the quarters in a bucket, paying for everything in handfuls.

One night I was in a motel pool just floating; me in the pool, cheap beer in the me. As I lay still, I began to turn. It then occurred to me that I was not turning, maybe I was staying still and the world was turning. It's me who is the needle in this compass. The fluid movement of me in the fluid on this world in the air of space. This crept into my act, this realization as of a shire horse into a classroom that you could put yourself in places and thoughts will come and these are the fuel. That the bigger and better they are, the bigger and better they are.

At first the horse was just ambling and unadorned yet still an impressive animal in the classroom. Yet soon he started to get adorned . . . Lovely livery and harness and brass buckles. In Arizona I let Diane drive the automatic Ford and she'd never learnt to drive and it was great, the sound of a high-pitched giggled scream combined with fraraap, the tyres in the loose chipping gravel at the edge of the road, sounding like a diamonds in a blender.

Back in Britain they got me on The Stand-Up Show. I said I'd only do it if they got an airline seat to do the whole routine as it had occurred to me on the plane: A bit pissed and waking up at all hours of different time-zones and giggling, imagining I was a giant with the socks pulled forward over my shoes for massive feet, the tiny toothpaste and miniature of whisky for feeling like a pissed giant wanting to do his teeth. There was something about the aisle being the aisle of a church, a flying love-cathedral in the sky.

At this time I did a bit with the crowd, saying, "I can't go on to the next joke until the last laugh has finished", and I would just let a tiny titter keep me, and then another, and then get laughs trying to not get laughs, and then appear annoyed with the fact, and then, finally, be annoyingly perplexed and pissed-off as they tittered on. Sometimes there were like two people left giggling, trying to hide it and, over the other side, a few folks genuinely pissed-off that this was happening. I did this the other night – it is such a form of language, a suitable unique thing, it does not seem like an old repeated joke thing, more like it would be a shame for the people who've not seen it to miss out; and plus too that if they have seen it and are miffed they will be silent and that's fine if their miff is vocal then humdinger danger it's cool too.

That, and jumping onto the crowd with a surfboard, then standing up and surfing over the wave of the crowd's hands on a big live benefit-gig TV show set me in the minds of folks for a while.

That gig was directed by Geoff Posner, who I just saw the other night sneaking into a gig with Robin Williams who was going to do a loose celebrity-fifteen-minute stand-up slot at a small regular London club as prep for a bigscale televisual charity do at a large Theatre. The theory is you see how it goes in order to feel better, and having learned what works. Well that is silly. As they arrived I did it, I did – I ran over going "I don't believe it I don't believe it it is it is it's . . . Geoff Posner . . ."

Williams was on . . . He was on it, was going well. Suddenly there were twenty bar staff from all around the building in behind the bar, excitement at just having him in the room – and he was not that good. He stalled he called for a Coke, he talked of being sober, there was a pause, someone shouted, "Sing a song!" and it was definitely then I ought to have run up with my wee guitar and played an easy riff for him to sing along to because I'd done well with that just before in my slot. Could've made the papers.

Travelling was always the thing though. We all travel and write, it is just to what extent. Notes for yourself as you go in a wee pad, or packed little postcards for best friends. Ask yourself who are the five who get, who must get, postcards? Imagine if almost everyone's qualifying for that. For me, getting to go to America, travel, have occurrences occur and spotting the details, then coming back, making a living from telling of this, feels as good now as it did then and still feels the best it could be. Fresh eyes, fresh experience vending – I'm in the retell business . . . Re:Tale . . .

Most of the travelling has been to work and then there can be points where you are abroad telling of another adventure you had while travelling and then making new ones there too. It is best to keep distracted from this thought too much, or there can be comedic-feedback referential-meltdown possibilities: "I am a comedian doing things strangely in order to . . ." Don't even say it. Keep distracted, inventive and as yourself. Storm castles . . . Rescue wasps from trains . . . appropriate Golfing Trolleys . . . Notice, return.

September 2007.

I have to go to Plymouth by railed transport and am forced to board the train with no ticket. I willingly do this. Invention is the son of this necessity. And not like the old days when I would board a train with no ticket on purpose; them days it was with skipping in mind. You had no ticket because you had not bought one. You got on knowing it was wrong and prepared, self-drafted into the dodge. Now this day I have technically bought one though I have no proof.

I have bought one and I do not have one. Superbly crafted is this niche where technological advancements have invented a new space where we can now be disappointed. We are the little inefficiency in the system. Us actually having a/the ticket is possibly a thing that can be bypassed in this, the getting-of-a-ticket-for-travel event.

My lovely ticket was bought over the internet to be more easy – it isn't – it was bought, I have a ticket. What I have purchased is a little pair of nothings. I don't actually have it, or have one, though I have bought one. I own a ticket, the seat has been paid for. I have purchased a ticket. Well, no I have not really done that either . . . I have been involved in a transaction concerned with exchange of numbers and words circling in on the possibility of travelling. The ticket itself is proof of purchase, yet you can't travel with only that proved. One must have proof of ticket in the form of ticket. Yet the ticket is only one proof, the best portable one, of purchase. Without the ticket I had purchase and yet no purchase.

So I board the train.

It is tricky because there are overlaps, lawyer-truths loitering about. I did yes, my very learned gentleman, indeed intend to travel without being in possession of a ticket. Though the rule of "being in possession of" is just the best way to ensure the Railways get their money; so if that is still the case surely the little intermediary-law can be bypassed . . . ? Having no ticket does not mean no transaction has occurred . . . you could also have a ticket, yet not have paid.

I feel good, I feel fine. Money has been spent. I decide to risk it. It was necessity, still a necessity that bore this course because I had not the money with me for another acquisition of an authorized token: an emergency ticket. Well, perhaps, though not enough to eat for the next two days as well. Or rather that money would be gone and more would have to be called in. I had a hundred and twenty Scottish sterlings and a gold card already maximumly maximized outright. I know it is a first thought and first thoughts often have to be left and first thoughts often get returned to. Sometimes the initial thought is eighty-two percent of all you will ever discover about a thing. And sometimes as bathos, a humble acknowledged checkmate, looked at over and over. The first thought here is "Go for it without a ticket." Imagine maybe meeting someone who believes, or maybe a way of phoning to check a travel-company postal address or whatever . . . Either way, I was a bit thick because people must surely try this all the time. Surely, don't they? If they don't they ought to; there could be an enormous amount of folk one day who all together have not received their tickets; there could be a postal strike, a flood, locusts.

There was little in them past yestergone days to happen to the ticket between purchase and the ticket being passed under the unfrosted glass of separation. So this is a new place.

The Railway is safe, although I am intending to travel without actually being in possession of a ticket, moneys are safely lodged in her accounts.

I get on. It is the 10:26 to Plymouth, England. Sadly, before the train leaves it is already late. It is delayed ahead of schedule and says it up on the big departures board. Out of the corner of my eye-based peripheral mind I read it as "beloved" not delayed . . . a platform for love, deliverance, carriage, sliding into the tunnels . . . and . . . you do not have to change . . .

So by the time the train is due to leave it is already late. Its lateness is pre-booked, destined. Ahead of schedule it is already behind-in-advance before it leaves. They predict fairly accurately that a point way ahead in time will be considerably later – predestined-destiny delayed destination at the station – perhaps it can make up the time before it leaves and leave ahead of its delay and arrive behind time yet still a bit ahead of the now-scheduled lateness.

The space in this quizzical concept is that a delay can be made up in time: a delay does not mean it is actually late yet.

This was helpful because sometimes I have to see that there is not a problem until there is a problem.

What if the train leaves now early, incorporating the delay that, although scheduled, has not had a chance to occur yet, and spread the delay out over a mathematics-type formula of a graded-curve with velocity . . . Leave ahead of the behind time, though before the scheduled delayed time, and be on time most of all the way down . . .

What if the prophesized delay does not materialize? The snow and sheep and leaves are cleared from the line and then the railway might feel it ought to stick to its own forecast-delay in order not to look double-stupid.

What if the delay is known about long enough in advance to just change the arrival time; which we, the passengers and clients, hardly have control of anyways? What then if the delay was just part of the expected arrival time, ironed in rolled out smoothed away instead of announced? Now and Zen: The art of Railway timetabling.

Just as I arrive at the station one of the things I go over is this idea that trains are often late aren't they? It happens, shit. Doesn't it? Twice. . . Same guy wrote Forrest Gump and Benjamin Button screenplays.

When I see it is delayed already again, now I am at least let off the wondering if it will be delayed, which often feels some way like the badness of being late anyway – "The Worry" in another form . . . Or the same form from another angle – "Oh God, can I still make it? Will I, could I, shall I phone? . . . Oh God . . . Come on, come on."

Once a definite delay is administered there it is: the cure to worrying if you will be late. You know you are. No need for repeated thought without possible action.

News of the delay gives fresh hope to passengers, for this scheduled-lateness gives a more-reliable arrival time.

"So what if you are going to be delayed, darling, give me a ring!"

"Mama, this is it! The delay has already been woven in, they know how long it is, isn't it heavenly? It is like, my sweet one, being able to fly down the tracks to you ahead of time . . . Allowing our fantasy to be fixed and sure and to rely on. Can it not be said, my one, that folks hold off from promising to themselves and dreaming hard and fantasizing of the moment because so much can go wrong? Well, I fall at the feet of the Railway operator for allowing us to fly in our minds toward each other and touch fingers at a point equidistant between us over the sleepers and iron."

I look up at the departures board and again now see it as both the huge word "Delayed" and "Beloved", and, even though there is no point, I advance toward the platforms without delay or a hitch or postponement . . . My arrival is destined and that destiny alters when WHY Smiths calls me in for newsprint. It's the features I love, the Film&Music in Friday's Guardenin' and oo Charlie Booker and the wee booklet on Sat . . . and the new review in the Observer.

In a way the delay already was woven into the fact that I did not expect a train not to be delayed so there is nothing to then be let down. "Let the events come to meet you, Phil" is the announcement over my personal tannoy, and the whole affair of life is not intended t'annoy. It is v. v. hard to annoy or upset me and certainly no one has ever betrayed me. And it's not just the events, it's more that my head don't believe anyone has a state approaching contract with me. There have been three large arranger managers working for me, and we've never had to have a written ting.

"Beloved" is like delayed. This machinery has a certain state denoted here: thought of, considered, cherished . . . Have you ever heard an announcement that the track is closed for "Sensual Maintenance"?

Let's play the thesaurus game again, once more? Get from a word to its opposite contradictory converse reverse meaning, its antonym, in as few moves as possible

Beloved –favourite-chosen-wanted-longed for- waited on-anticipated-arriving-delayed.

The words are words and tricksters yet they also follow the meaning like a pack of dogs. Biting at its heels, ready and able to tear it to shreds and hugely affect its form, yet very accurately showing exactly where it is.

Legal and amoral; cherished and at odds; inside to betray; trying and denying; pissed-off yet pleading; sad and angry; madly sane; chalky and cheesy; I am both unique snowflake driftwood guy cast up on an island through no fault of his own and a person in the world. Alone, yet not lonely, lonesome yet never alone. Surviving . . . Going with the flaw, and Flowing with the go . . .

Luckily, being a comedian, my life is something that can be talked about, so this is okay. Trouble is fuel, yum yum . . . like a movie, it enjoys it and requires it like man you need Man City.

At this point there has at least not been a delay on the invention of the trains or on my being born. For, if there was, it would be no concern of mine so it is real easy to allow this to be just great:

"There is a delay at the airport."

"What, for coffee and cakes?"

"No. The aeroplane has not been invented yet."

"So why the fuck do they have an airport?"

"Sales. Got to be ready; they've got to land somewhere. How d'you invent the first phone? Who you gonna call?

"Ghostbust—"

"They haven't been invented . . ."

"It's a case of the bell and the wring . . . which came first . . . Alexander Graham Bell or Marconi . . . or Bose in Calcutta . . . ??"

". . . ??!!"

All that not in brackets. completely

Was he Scottish? Bell?

We got roads, Tar-Macadam, we got the TV Yogie Baird . . . we got the rainproof jacket of canvas and rubber, the Macintosh . . . we did vulcanize rubber for the Tyre to drive on the road in the wet making a call.

The ticket-inspector comes by doing a fly-by, not collecting yet, and, as he passes I mention to his moving shoulder that I have no ticket, ask him about it, be open and forthcoming, all upfront and get them all laid out on the table. He responds firmly that I shall have to buy another: An emergency-travel ticket-replacement voucher slip.

We don't really have time to go into it as he is away.

In the quiet coach and things are about to get exciting . . .

The lady in front of me through the seat-gap's V is reading and available to be studied a little in her reflection and if you want the untroubling small inspection through the V by leaning forward, as I have every right to do, and just looking at someone's ear and hand a bit, a mini macro-stalk without having to go anywhere. And there's only the smallest chance of the train coming to a swift halt and thrusting you forward to get wedged in shame and tightly held like a padded munch screamface. Edvard Munch. Seriously though, if you really want to stare at and study women without upsetting them, try it at the estate agent's where they are used to looming forms with a cute head movement, where you can gaze between adverts and then, if they look up, one just averts one's eyes to the property . . . and, while you're at it, may as well stand in the millionaire mansion section . . .

Suddenly she is all the way into the two screechy screams she lets out and is lashing out at a wasp up against her window with her magazine now automatically barrelled as weaponry, sacrificing width and coverage for a power I'm not sure she needs . . .

Wasp may have been passing through and now he was in a barrage of his airspace and finding it hard to proceed, up against the window, running in circles, fuzzy-skimming and banging-like and walking now up high. Surely he must be wondering in some way at the land flying by. Even if he didn't see it as countryside, only as colour-tone received through his many eyes, though surely this would still be an amazing new effect being experienced.

It is such a shame that this newness, of witnessing the countryside move past faster than any of the ancestral experience that had guidance over his genes and eye-type development, left him as bemused as an insect can possibly, feasibly, be. Plus all this while under attack.

I stood up and looked more-or-less straight at the wasp. It was cowering now somehow, up and backing away from where the loud noise came from, into my seat's own personal window-zone – like the lawns of shared-neighbours that get mowed up to a mystical, definite, line and the semis that are painted to a halfway estimated place (no one can ever really say exactly, for certain, that's exactly where that halfway point is and so just do an unspoken more-or-less, good enough, emotional approximation). So it was, that now this would be my territory of glazing, mine to clean if we had to share it.

Stood up swiftly now and, without a jar or tiny net, I reached up, took my modern brushed-velour zipper-top down from the overhead stow and balled it up around each hand a bit and pushed it against the wasp who was into a walking-the-circle thing now and caught up no doubt in the absence of usual sensual, directional dance internal compass, "smells" and stimuli and with visual mystery stretching his or her or its optics. I caught him like a crumb in a cloth, or in fact like a wasp in a jumper. It's deffo one of those-o where the thing is as good and sure as any metaphor could hope to be.

The velour is a light/heavy liquid material and I have to use some instinctual knowledge to gather not too fiercely and in-so saving, kill the wasp. It's easy as this has been a treasured top, cherished worn, repaired by a pink strip on the arm, beloved, then lost, betrayed and then BOUGHT BACK from Save The Children at the end of our road. Its weight and uses are known to me. Also, I can't really check to see if he's okay in there because to check the wasp is okay may let him loose – Schrödinger's wasp: he may be dead; he maybe might be dead; he may be fine. Held to be released; prisoner and exalted one.

I have him inside moving away and absolutely could not hear the hum of his buzz inside the top. A wasp in my jumper, I nod to the lady as she looks up at me, the saviour and protector of her self, not her actions, and back away, aiming myself slowly, reversing the boat of me cautiously out of this zone.

I have the idea to go back to the shop where the shop-guy was and the last known direction of the conductor.

There is a shop on board this new Virgin train. I am riding one for the first time. There is no trolley. There is a shop. Here in this crazy consumerist culture we are not safe even on a moving train from being able to go down the shops. Cleverly, it is not open very often. Well, not that it is closed ever. I mean you can walk right up to it to the guy who is standing behind it touching stock and he will say it is not open. He who is there now in the shop with nowhere to go, who looks unlikely to leap from a moving train; he who could easily serve me seeing as how I am now here with him. We're between openings and closings and bridges and tunnels. Most often they are shut till they are open when a staff come on. The shop is on and it is off.

So the shop you are lucky enough to be walking towards, backwards up the train carrying you fast-forwards, and backwards, altering your own relativistic universal speed and propelling energy into the train kinetically and so adding to the speed of the train; also, the shop you are "moving towards" is already closed – it is possible that it could be closed as you start walking away from it and open by the time you arrive at your seat? Or closed when you start to walk "towards" it and open by the "time" you get there? . . . It is all possible . . . Perhaps if Einstein determined the opening times I could leap to another train and it would just be opening.

And if the train is delayed, does it open relatively early?

The shop itself is very small and sells four CDs and two books and a set of travel-draughts – Maeve Binchy and Martin Amis, Texas and Pink Floyd. I am not open to these.

In a previous year hencepast I once bought the miniature travel draughts set and played an enormous Balkan refugee-type. It was his first game. It was the board's first game. The first time I had played in ages. The first time I had played a game with a man I had never talked to. The first time I had bypassed the talking – fairly stutteringly, the cul-de-sac of where from? Where go now? Good and much rain? And family? To get to the intimacy of combat.

He watched me harvest with pops the little magnetic discs off their plastic retainer vine, and set them up on this alternate pattern gently-magnetized. He watched me nibble off the little bits of plastic that got left on the draughts. He watched me do all the blacks, all the whites and he watched me push the board out a bit between us and look up at him. He shook his head slowly to decline with his eyebrows brought together as punctuation, as his phrase from the international body language lexicon for not wishing to play futile child's game while homeless in exile . . .

Nevertheless I pushed a white disc diagonally forward. He was ready and he shook his head again a bit to decline again. I shook off his shake and moved for him, using the international sign of the scrunched-up nose for "nevertheless, you shall see I am not one to be put off while we are marooned here on this train . . . thrown together . . . life is life my friend . . ." et cetera ad lib – offering strangers chocolate – and he said, "Okay." . . . He moved . . . We moved together . . . Another move each, then I took one of his. He raised an eyebrow. I looked at him, I said, "There it is . . . Welcome to the competitive world of draughts . . ." . . . ". . . land of the ruthless, punitive, hinges of forced takes, tactic, strategy and geography . . . black against white . . . kings, sacrifices and defeat . . ." . . . did this metaphorical combat zone wring any bells to his mystery situation and recent past upheavals?

I swear I have never done a triple-jump before and I got two in this game here. Whoosh, tip-tip-tip – he had to learn. It is the best way. I won the first game. We started on a second. People look at us either astounded at my arrogance or lack of empathy and understanding, hasn't he suffered enough; they could be amused at my luck, thinking me an earnest wanker or a lovely man. Somany options. Even if you don't like what's happening you can surely like it when I play the yes/no game with my kids as they brush their teeth, asking them questions to get the nodding and shaking of their heads to help the brushing.

You can dislike me, you can't dislove me.

He is more animated now. Handsome, huge in black-market Versace leather. I did not know where he was from or going or how big were his family and if they survived or if he liked rain. I know how he picked this up and how he was clever enough not to get upset at losing. He got really into it and I think came relatively close to actually taking off his impressive jacket. A few midway-moves into the second game and his stop came . . . At one point I was travelling backwards, jumping forwards and backwards with a queen.

We say goodbye. As he walks away I see the huge design of a winged graphic dragon on his jacket's rear.

At the shop I arrive, pushing door-buttons with exposed elbows.

The buttons are large with Braille-type grips and are cleverly woven into the design of the door so they are part of the casing of the glass, integral within the component nature of door, in some way fusing the concept of a door with its magical blooming into gateway. Like it is really Stark Trek entrances the designers are after: opening, space, threshold of beyond . . . Swish, nothing . . . All gone . . . enter entranced. This door is heralder of its own disappearance. Load of bollocks: the previous thing worked fine. The incredible invented nothingness free for you to walk into. The deliverer of future-space . . . This door is an inversion. It's a thrashold, not a portal – an unsportal. That is why, when an electric door breaks down, it is slightly-more spiritually perplexing. What has really failed has been the designer's ulterior pride. When this door fails, it is a wall; a wall with a tease-bearing structure . . . unjust joist. This should not be available to fail. A door would suffice, be good enough. No one would have a journey underwhelm them if all the doors worked when they were pushed to the side by hand.

The toilets are insane.

They are fewer now and have a large elliptical door. It operates on the wheel-base of a wheelchair. It caters for all. You simply press one of three buttons to enter and it shakes along the orbit path until fully open, before it can return once more like a comet.

The first one I pushed there was an older old lady hurriedly adjusting upwards a longish kilt skirt – she had shut and not locked. I had to stand and wait for the door to fully open before watching it start moving closed again, it had to dodder like her all the way, couldn't change its mind and I am there in the grimacing threshold trying to be cover for her and yet irresistibly concerning her and, if anyone else came along, doing enough to get grabbed and shaken.

"What'chew doin' there . . . What's goin' on here then?" The reason for this is that the buttons on the inside are four. They are piled one above the other coming down the wall. Three have a purpose. One, marked Door is just the denoter, introducer of the style; it does nothing except look exactly like the others that do. The other three are: Close, Open and Lock. There is a button to close from in here and one to lock. Some people might like to come in, shut and shit and not-lock; so it's a technological alibi, so you could just sit there with your pants down, waiting, thrilled, shitting yourself yet covered because you're on the bog. These weird strange modern conveniences provide the platform for unusually-bonkers eventualities mostly because they do not, strictly speaking, evolve because they are not sorting out a problem; they are not being a solution to a trouble or an inefficiency . . . They are a concept-led exciting new innovation to hasten an independent sale.

This is nothing though, nothing compared to the sink!

When in there, I had a plenty 'nough time to inspect it, just doing the things one normally would. The sink has a sign which catches the eye. It is not really a sink, like on-its-own beneath a window in a train of yesteryear, you know, with taps – it is a hollowed space in the flowing moulding that coats the whole room. It is beneath an overhang that houses mirror and perhaps towelling supplies. Either way, there are no taps. I have guessed that there may be automatic sensor taps – I have guessed because they are around the place now these things, these sensors, taking the annoying whim and inconveniences of the human out of the system where not completely required. Thing is: if someone removes things, then there has to be a new thing that was a little-less-completely-necessary to do that is now the most-unnecessary part of the process. And these are often very enjoyable things.

Plus, the attractive little sign says: "Do not place any items in the sink. Taps come on automatically." How disconcerting for humanity that a sink should be so fucked-up that it has to warn people that what is designed to be a sink is now like some kind of trap. And the people that put this sign up must be the designers and so they must be lamenting their own madness as it continues; that they knew the design-fault and perhaps never had time or money to change it . . . Time though, to write this sign and commission it also in Braille. Yes, it is in Braille. The blind folk, who have not yet discovered that the taps are not there, are being warned of their non-existence: "Things you will never see, which you do not know yet that are already invisible will become doubly-invisible to you the moment we suggest their existence." Mind you, the moment we suggest their existence there must be a few of you who were once-sighted and remember the image of a tap and therefore we give you a picture of something then tell you, "You do not have it to see, even if you were sighted. And you are not. You are blind." That's if they found the Braille first. That's if, in looking for the Braille, they didn't run their hands under the sensor beam and bring on relatively hot water shockingly onto their bare flesh suddenly.

Fine, I see the Braille, fine, I have "seen" sensor taps. What about the old lady in the kilt-skirt? She has been made stupid by the train, she does not know why the taps are missing. She does not try entering her hands under there in the air on the off-chance that they have been automated, that the tap has been removed from the handwash experience. She may tentatively go in there to the cantilever overhang cave and have a feel around tapping and get a short burst on the back of her wrist. It is hard for any of us to guess at what it is we don't know

– the wash of faith under there. Like: Your faith shall cleanse you . . . Hands of faith wash . . . Place your unclean hands into the void; trust and you will be cleansed . . . She only is scared off by the unveiled brailled threat. Or she might think, "Stupid me, they were right. I should never have come away. They are right, I am too old and too stupid . . . All so fangled . . ." Either way, she's not over the moon as she might be with good old brass fittings and a coathook. These loopholes are unnoticed by the designers of this new-fangled bathroom. Only if they are looked for . . . If they are not looked-for they are not only un-noticed they are not possibly noticed . . . In fact they are so blaringly obvious they are all that spurts into your face when you see a new tap-less sink: What about the humans' main objective here? Overlook Hotel. The Dulling.

The Venn overlap larger than which is not-overlapped.

Imagine her there, the much older lady, thinking, "Where are they? Where are the taps? . . . Am I going mad?"

A method or thing that leaves your Gran right out of it, is a recent, indecent advance and a hard one for the youth to want to bridge.

The toilet-seat is held up by a magnet, which is great. There is a warning to draw your attention to this . . . Why a warning? Is the magnet going to fuck up your watch, your Blackberry or just your mind as you wonder, sitting there, if gallstones are moveable or whether the minerals in your turds are going to be filtered out . . . It is just a retro-cuperative legal thing again? That whatever might happen cannot be their fault then. That must be it.

A way of holding up the seat is a great idea. Great if you push it up against the flat of the wall where the magnet is encased.

Released back out into the mis-carriage of justice, you will see that on all the seats there are no reservation-dockets that used to stand up in the grove at the top of the chair. You went along reading, studying to make sure that you never sat in, Christ for-fend, a reserved seat. As you walked along you could check them because they were where the hand went to keep balance. The human is so annoying.

Or you liked them because you could move them around and steal someone's facing-place and give them an aisle seat going backwards.

You could read them and marvel at exotic trips – Warrington from Crewe, Stoke to Birmingham, Carlisle to Peterborough – and you could bathe in the realization that you were used to getting on a train at the beginning and though it is not always the train's beginning, it is always your beginning. These reservation cards became playing cards if you could let a nine-year-old son gather any up the train's carriages that are not needed, giving him a super task for the thirteen-hour journey from East Grinstead to Forres, and it works.

Now there were no wee bits of paper. Now there were overhead scrollers in dark scroller-red. Bats' eyes in the dark, lit slits flitting across the cave mouth. They are lit thin fuzzy red in murky depth, moving, like the first digital watches. If you were to look up and check to see if the stiff little dockets had been replaced by an overhead scroller then you would see it. Damn travellers!

So I am coming back down the train to the shop where the conductor is, with the wasp enclosed within my bundled zip-up top, waiting. I say, "Hi, do any of the windows on this train open?"

The conductor asked why. I said, "Because I wish to release a wasp."

The shopkeeper then said, "Kill it, kill it! Flush it down the toilet." This had surprising metre and the accidental quality of a chant.

I said I would like to flush it away, it is just that the toilets flush by sensor when you stand up so I would have to go through a whole mime with the wasp and pretend to sit and somehow get the wasp in there. And what if the wasp gets out of the bowl area, senses my betrayal with his own sensors and then: there is the arse of his betrayer. Plus it would have some of that old Shakeyspeare tragic extra: "Oh ye, that saved me, kills me now, making that which was so sweet extra bitter now because of the juxtaposition thing."

"I wish it to live. How long is it to the next station?"

The conductor looked at the top I have scrunched up and may or may not have unconsciously been motioning to listen for a buzz or hum.

He looked then to the book he was holding, licked his finger, frisked the pages by and found it was nineteen minutes.

There were no windows that would open because this thing, this train, is a sealed unit. Pressure is maintained. When they pull into a station and open the doors suddenly pressure drops people can blink again, their eyelids un-flip and their clothes fall loose. The doors sit open breathing an hydraulic masked-Darth breath . . . seething.

"Nineteen minutes."

"How long can I keep a wasp alive in this top?"

He had no book for that so I turned to leave. Then I said, "Hi, remember me? I am the one without the ticket."

"You'll have to buy another one: an emergency ticket."

Magically it occurs to me to use all the things at my disposal: "Please let me travel freely or I shall release the wasp . . . Loose in the train. I'll take her to the quiet zone or even first class, club class. Maybe someone will be in there, maybe Richard Branson, and he will get bitten or stung and he might have an allergy or a toxic-shock reaction and die, and the Railways will not be safe then, his enormous personality absent from the brand and concept, will see shares plummet, confidence plummet and a selling-off of the larger enterprises, relinquishing control to another company who are forced to axe jobs. Perhaps yours . . . Let me have authority based on you believing me that, here, I am subject to a postal delay."

It was just the post. That was what denied me. My mind reeled at the thought of the letter on a mail-train and the huge crushing sink of an irony. Post train delayed . . . Both our trains lying idle on the tracks next to each other. Let me just break in to the mail train over there . . . Imagine being caught there breaking in . . . "What the heh?"

"Oh, it's okay, I am getting a ticket."

The conductor and the shopkeeper both look at me and do not give much.

At that moment before any help is not-offered I realize at that point I kind of have the train hostage with a wasp in a jacket. Then I realize that no one has seen or heard the wasp and so I am holding the whole train hostage with . . . possibly no-wasp.

The conductor states his position finally about the emergency ticket which costs hundred and twenty.

This is big news in my life as that it is exactly all of the all that I have with me.

Retreating, retreading back down the train, still going well forward down the aisle with the wasp clutched still in – it's a marriage now. Get to my seat and stow the whole little bundle up in the overhead, next to the acoustic box of my uncased guitar, I still heard not a whimper or fuzz.

There I was, still giving in to fear. I could have let him loose with a few words to perhaps leave him alone and about him not wanting to sting anyone and all. Sitting down at my book to read, my French novel is separative, Atomised de Michel Houellebecq; wellbackward. Hellbent back vent. Le livre n'est pas libre.

Sixty seconds later I glance across, because the eyes have it: detected motion; and look-see the wasp sitting on the edge of the aisle-seat looking dazed. He is like Houdini. How did he get down here? Is there another wasp in on the illusion? It had to have been the slowest fall or the quickest of climbs down. The wasp was a marvel and he stood leaning forward trying to get his wings going. They were a bit shuffled-skuffed, a badly buffeted buffer pair who took the compression badly and not going together, I'd crumpled him in cruel-to-be-kind smothering and they were a bit fucked until, until suddenly they weren't. He'd been taken cruelly sweet from his glamorous speedy window of magic where he passed the world at eighty-five, bundled into the dark, held there then abandoned. He forgave me by simply being able to fly away. No wink, no nod, no thanks, no bitter tears. Just as soon as the wings work, he is away. He was offered a snack and declined.

Flying with HH at eighty-one miles an hour again, this time though up to the long stripped god-light going down the centre of the carriage.

I read and am comforted by his freedom as he buzzes about in accelerated swoops and sideways shimmies.

Twelve minutes later we are at Lockerbie station. I sit up and out of my chair-seat and once again move to take H into the soft oppression of his old prison. My fists within the cloth sliding along the brightness after him. The lady that has seen me take the wasp the first time can just about extend herself to understand that the wasp or another one is the object of my ardor. Many of the other commuters will have no idea and be amused, confused, reduced to crinkle-forehead as they wonder at the strange motions of this man to clean those long light fittings with his jumperhaps maybe. Maybe I'm one of those clean-o-philes, has to have dust away from here.

Right now its not for me to worry about how I look . . . because there is saving going on.

Actually almost anything can look ridiculous at one time. I know for sure that it is only rarely we question ourselves. Mostly we let the concern of others into chain-form and wear them. Loose or tight, that's your choice. I know for sure when I sit on the steps of some remote flat in the middle of everywhere that, if they are the steps of a friend, I feel fine, and vindicable. There is reason.

I gathered H again and all the strange looks and made a one-way visit to the door for him.

We pull in at the platform, the hydraulics open the great doors with a massive "pssht" and normal pressure is resumed in the train. My shoulders drop and my ears pop.

There I grip the top at the edges and do a nice little release throw that lets enough air in there to carry young Stephen out and he flies away for half a second before falling wretched in a small watched-arc to the platform.

Not sure . . . Picking him up outside these doors, the fear in him to sting and the hydraulic pressure too . . . I could be left outside with no luggage, certainly no ticket and no proof I had even been on that train and just me and a wasp on my finger.

"Hi, Stationmaster Wilson . . . Hi, hello, me and Harry here got shut off the train . . . No I have no proof of purchase . . . Hell, I have no proof of travel."

"Prove it."

"Does this wasp look local to you?"

So, now I watch this wasp valiantly come back towards the train. He could have stayed on the platform and done the wing-thing, saved his energy. No, though, he is making one last bid. Excruciating: wasp-walks look like a desperate crawl.

I have never seen a wasp miss a train before.

We psssht-off and pull hugely away. He is moved off to the side, playing till the final whistle. I began to imagine him as a reincarnated relative trying to reach someone .

Back en route, delays allow more shopping-time at the shop.

The conductor comes around into my reading and I say once again that I have bought a ticket and have no proof. We go quickly into the you-must-get-an-emergency-replacement-ticket, or "fine" as I call it, and we take the positioning of draughts and I ask to talk to a supervisor. He says "he is" I say "then you let me travel-on freely" "hundred and twenty quid for emergency ticket" I say "I cannot afford that" he says he'll have to phone the Police I say "let me speak to someone above you" he says again "there is no one" I say "then you have the authority" . . . What we don't want to happen still hasn't happened: we don't want people to travel for free and the Railways be in trouble, and this continues not-to-happen through me: "Do what you have to do."

Pulling into Carlisle station I go to offer something and the guard is on the phone, I don't want to disturb him.

Shit, oops! Turns out he was calling the Police and I see one of them running to meet the train . . . Good way to win a bet, I think: "I bet you a fifty there is someone to meet me here."

Quickly I come out to the hydraulics to meet him and as he comes on I say, "Hello, I have changed my mind I do want to pay. I was messing around."

The Policing-man cannot be too concerned with this and makes the start of the move to put his hand apon my shoulder and guide me out. I realize the seriousness of this. Once a hand at the long arm of the law is apon thee, you cannot move at all except to resist it. Even a shrug or hiccups or a sigh can be seen as the gateway to useful force force.

I step back a little, evading gently the hand. I then move into the carriage and hold up the magical one hundred and twenty pounds which is coincidentally all I have and is starting to look like a decent loss to protect the three hundred and fifty I hope to get apon completion in Plymouth.

I announce out loud twice, "I wish to buy a ticket. Please let me purchase a ticket."

Now the obviously crazy guy is quite rightfully being taken away. It is no coincidence that this wild light-duster is also without a ticket. Of course I feel it, as the agency that bought it for me didn't order it ahead of schedule enough and that I care for animals.

He gets hold of me and leads me off the train. The conductor now I pass and appeal again. The Policeman stands me on the platform and wishes clearly to lead me away further. I do not want to go really and leave my luggage. The transport Policeman wants me to accompany him. I do not want to yet and so I go limp, which I remember is recognized the world over as a non-aggressive action. I am low and the Policeman is left with no option but to give me a kind of wedgy as he tries to lift me up. A small crowd is being born into platform life and the guard comes out with my six-string guitar and the astounding debut from the French author and motions them towards me. I am limp so the Policeman has to take them. This is amusing as a sight. Now I am sitting on the platform and the guard is standing between the jaws impassive as I call out, "Please let me on this train . . . Please, I love this train . . . Please."

And as the crowd is joined at the windows by my fellow passengers . . . "Please . . ." There's only one thing left: "What about the wasp?"

The Policeman gets me up, the doors shut. I walk with him as he carries my guitar. Are we a nightclub act? Nearly.

A tiny push sees me into the transport Police-station and I am sitting in a room. I start to play the guitar to fill the time. Again, they will not break me.

He returns, PC 12787, and says, "Will you stop playing that guitar?"

I consider it a rhetorical musing and reply, "I surely will." And continue playing . . . He tells me to stop now.

At the desk we do the name-thing, the ID, I have the full-looking gold card and a hundred and twenty quid.

"And you refused to buy a ticket?"

"Did you hear me plead with him to give me one?"

He asks my address. I tell him. He asks if I have any proof I live there. I say cheekily he should phone them up and ask them. He does.

"What proof have you that is the same address as the one I am giving you as where I live?"

He cannot answer that one.

Lucy answers and he says to her who he is and I hear the tiny unmistakeables of small-receiver voice across the interrogation table – does she know me and do I live there?

I call out, "Don't tell him anything!"

"Is he alright?" I can hear her ask.

"Yes he is fine."

Then Lucy must have asked to have a word with me because beautifully he hands the phone over to me. She says, "Are you alright?" I say, "It's all fun and I'll have something to talk about tonight."

And it is only two thirds done, the adventure.

Because I love her deeply this is extra magical and touching and like a last condemned-man's call.

He asks for the phone back I give him the "in-a-minute" motion and get a few extra seconds.

The Policeman knows that I am trying to get to Plymouth.

He walks me to the ticket booth and he is holding on to me slightly. We stand together in the queue. At the desk he asks for a ticket and the price of a full bought return is more than I have. We try the credit card and it is maximumed out.

"A single to the next town please," I say.

"No, you need to buy one all the way."

"Am I in custody now?" I say and he asks me to leave the Railway station. I say I am and am backing away. He tells me to leave the Railway station and I am backing away a bit swifter now as I meet three musician friends of mine from Edinburgh, one has a double bass.

"Hey Phil, what are you up to?"

"No matter what I'm leaving the station."

"Do not talk to this man or you could be liable for arrest."

Whooly liable.

Seriously he says this, so they accompany me in the good sense out of the station. I tell them the story and we consider a clever decoy ploy and then I say not to worry.

I bid 'em farewell and get a cab to the next town, Penrith.

In the cab on the motorway I get a call from the flat that my tickets have arrived. "Hoorah!" I say to Zac that I will phone in a while to give him a number and could he go to that shop on the next block, the one where the artful sub-manager wears a longish coat-suit to work, and fax it to me at a number I'll give him in, about thirty-five quid, later.

In Penrith I enter the stationmaster's office and explain and he says it will do and I walk to a lovely music shop, where I need to buy a new string anyway. To find it, I pop into a pub with farmers in it at their elevenses-lunch pints. One of them calls out for a tune and I say what kind and one shouts "Cherry-menthol" so I sing a wee song about breathing more easily sucking on a lozenger, the taste of cherries and Iranian auteur moviemaking . . . "cherry menthol Tunes aren't cheap . . . they cost an arm an' a leggy . . . Abbas Kiarostami's legacy . . ."

They are clapping when I leave. At the town's music shop I explain what's going to happen and shortly we all receive the fax.

I return to the station and the stationmaster, using his christian name, show him the floppy grainy, weakass, blurry, unsubstantial, ninety-nine-pixel photocopy facsimilacrum of the ticket itself, which in fact could easily have been given to someone else and he takes out a wee docket and signs and dates it. It reads "Travel Authority".

Of course we could be faxing a ticket already in the memory of the machine and the actual hardcopy already given to someone else, for it is just that a ticket you hold, not proof of the ownership derived from the person who payed. And that would only be the, wait for it: name on the card.

He hands it to me and I go and sit in the sunshine and have half a pint waiting for my train, seeing people I certainly was able to know that I would never have seen had there not been this debacle. Mind you, I had to be here to see the ones I would never have seen. So I would never have been able to see the people I would never have seen unless I saw them to know. If I had never seen them I could never be sure I hadn't seen them. Perhaps I would have . . . ahem.

And debacle's other main meaning man is "a sudden break of river ice in the spring thaw causing a violent rush of flow water and ice".

Crisis means "time of important events" . . . or "the moment when in a disease the patient either gets worse or better".

I just flew to London and back and, because of the Twin Towers, you can't take too much makeup these days. No nail clippers either because of the threat. Get the captain in a toehold: "To the East Midlands or he gets clipped right back to the red bit . . ." Like bolting the stable doors years after the glue made from the horse that bolted has dried up and cracked on the model airplane it stuck together, lying in a box unnoticed in an attic – if you really want to be a terrorist and get away with it there is always that golf course with fairways right by the runways at Bristol "International", though anyway that's another story.

With all the measures the terrorristas will still want to travel whether they can clip their nails or not – there are always loopholes. The fantastical time I went through Inverness airport with an excess of whisky fluids in a flask.

It was not hidden, just borne within the tweed. There to be found, unashamed, proud and distilled.

"Whats this we have here?"

"That is well over a hundred and fifty millilitres of Bunnahabhain single malt whisky . . ."

And then we had the moment where there right there, there was heard one of the finest municipal phrases ever uttered by an authority figure, air-law-man, and or uniformed officer of the Queen's sheriffrry: "Well I'm afraid you're just going to have tae drink it."

He said it with a tiny shudder of well that'll show you.

I'll have tae drink it . . . oh no, it can't be . . . I was going to drink it anyway so this is great news. So: "Have you a glass?" I have to ask . . .

"Yes," he says and turns around to get me a thin polyester scrunch cup and, just for a minute there, it feels like we are in a bar, a bad Theme Bar . . . Customs 'n' Excise House . . . come on drink up before you go anywhere . . . all drinks in 150ml measure . . . see-through bag??

For a while it was like this was my airport, like I'm a Russian oligarch who has just bought it: "What you mean I cannot drink here, I buy fucking airport and now drink where I please . . ." They tell me to stay here till it's finished and I drag it out like a two-mile-an-hour Police chase and lean on the Police lectern and eye up the other passengers, a few of whom are definitely like "who's this guy and where's my complimentary boozechoice . . . ?"

There's something exquisite about being ordered to drink over a hundred millilitres of contraband by a customs official right here in front of them. A few of them took a sniff and tell me to down it in one. Indeed this was close to being the least atmospheric theme bar of all time. All this and I had my wee bit of grass safely in the sock. Which reminds me: once I came back from the Shetlands and at the airport with my jeans wet from the spray at the beach only a hundred metres from check-in and there was the Orkneys squash team. We got chatting and, for a laugh, I carried a spare racquet through customs pretending to be one of them and in the queue forgot I had not shifted my wee stash of hash to the sock, so right there, mucking about four back from the X-ray machine, in full view of all customs folk eyeing you up who are trained how to eye you up, holding an item someone else had asked me to carry for them I made safe the wee baggie into the sock. Not one to complain of course, yet this however does make you wonder about the competence of the staff . . . Safety of the Nation?

The flask could have been made from fifty pairs of nail clippers . . .

Once I managed to travel without a passport in the midst of all the heightened panic. It was during August's Festival in Edinburgh and I had no passport or new driver's cards. I went to the airport in my tweed suit and flip-flops absolutely positive I had no bomb and posed nae threat, simply with leaflets from my Edinburgh show: a picture of me, the ticket price and a few quotes. They made a call at the desk and it was okay and whenever I was asked for ID I handed a leaflet out from the stack I had. For a moment I must have looked like either the most obsessive self-publicist or just naively optimistic, leafleting for a show on in a town I was leaving. As I handed the orange EasyJet staff the leaflets at these different moments I realized when they looked at me funny that there was indeed no appropriate reaction to this interaction . . . And therefore no inappropriate one. I like this. It feels like a sidestepping to unconventionalism which is the true norm. Conventionalism is a new-fangled interloper for us free beings.

Fortunately and amazingly enough as I wandered off the plane at Gatwick I was subject to a random stop-and-search by the Police with machine-guns because locals had been cottoned on and were living the loophole, getting their kicks here, hanging out ion the special lay-over armchairs, and coming by bus and looking dirty and obvious and eventually treating it like a regular venue and coming here to shoplift. They asked me where I had come from and asked for some ID. Handing them a leaflet they were urged to come to the show. Lots of eyebrow action, especially for the observant who would notice among the dates and concession prices that I was in fact on tonight. Other men came with machine-guns and at one point totally and hopelessly surrounded by six of them I decided to make a call as the Police made theirs. I can see him waiting to talk to me as I tell my friend I might be delayed somewhat. At this point it might have looked very interesting to the casually observant observer: me in tweeds and flip-flops surrounded by armed men, making a call with one of them clearly waiting for me to finish to speak to me. There is a chance, however small, that one of the passengers who passed me while I was drinking my whisky at

Inverness might have seen me here too and could only imagine I was definitely hundred percent an oligarch who can drink at airports and here he was on the phone with his own escort . . . sockless.

Turns out, amazingly enough, that I actually was wanted for arrest due to unpaid Police-fines in Glasgow and technically they could take me to custody now, however he informs me that it was a bit of a palaver to keep me and transport me back to Glasgow, he must tell me though that if I am stopped in Glasgow before I have paid it off I will be arrested. They disperse and I am free to go.

There's a part of me that wants to point out that he used "palaver" wrongly or rather he's wrong to use "palaver" – it implies he has choice and that really only applies to an informal situation's fuss and nuisance. Really he is an officer of the law and its not about personal bother, trouble or irritation. If it's wrong it's wrong and he must act accordingly.

Of course such is life and we are all human after all and we have every right to accept the frailties of men in these kind of roles. Look at ZeroDarkThirty. Of course this whole scandal stroke dead obvious thing with the Police sexist against their own WPCs and racist against their own PCs and beating up off-duty black firemen who've come to help and selling victims as well as Sienna Miller's phone number to the press then getting politicians to endorse hiding it for protection from it yet linking in with getting decent press and the lady with the red hair's horse rides and texts with Dave and John Terry and Thierry Henry, Rio vs A. Cole, the HSBC bank laundering world drug money and the Barclays fixing rates and the RBS still giving bonuses and sponsoring the Rugby and the christian judge giving a woman six years for a termination and a British soldier giving birth in secret, and Minis are massive and all this while England still play Afghanistan at cricket . . .

So all I call out as they walk away is: "Turns out these random checks are worth it after all."

"Confucius Say: 'When you travel you are finding adventure.'" Can't remember who said that. Tom said: "When you plan revenge, dig two graves."

Twelfth Chapter

Being away in a new land and finding adventure and working: marvellous. First time I was employed in Montreal at their Just For Laughs Comedy Festival I went like everyone to stay in the Delta Hotel with all the comedians and, more importantly, the agents from the Americas and Britain. I remember making the crowd at Club Soda laugh and the agents not. I remember taking my trousers down here on this continent and people not being able to see beyond it. I remember walking into Andy Kindler's "State of the Industry" top-notch lecture a bit late. He was the highlight, the unsigned unsignable comic. Still playing the country clubs, still too clever to ever really work for Hollywood, still defying it by being close enough to see it. Being what every comic loves and considers the bravest: honest. Expressing honest opinions about stuff is the ultimate revered on-pedestal ability – which is why Bill Hicks is so workshop-worshipped. People want to adore the thing they secretly love most in themselves: that your actual ideas about things are what you want to get across; finding things to actually say that others can share. I remember coming into that room and Andy Kindler stopping his speech which is only attended by industry and comics, seeing me and saying: "Here's Phil Kay, he only shows his ass."

Unfortunately I never came up with a lovely Zen-like sort of forgiving un-comeback in the moment.

Remember sitting at a table a few days later with Sean Hughes and having Denis Leary stand over us flicking his cigar fairly accurately towards the ashtray in the middle of our table. He nicked the Bill Hicks stuff about Ringo and he's never looked back.

I once overheard Dave Chappelle in Ireland at the Kilkenny Festival reviewing my gig to someone – "No, he was not that great. I had heard so much about him, he just wasn't . . ." Then he saw me and he stopped dead in his tracks. He had seen a show that was not good, I had not summoned up the magic in a festival environment. There's the rub: one can really have a laugh at a festival yet not always in the gigs. They are very formal. Here we are with the bestest acts in a row and they will be worthy. Then it can fail. By the end I was the only guy left in the programme doing an hour-long show, it was all just three or four acts and a compere. So Chapelle would be spot-on and would be wondering what all the fuss was about – this great comic who just didn't have it. SO easily I can lose it when what it is is love made evident for a room; and sometimes, I don't love the room. It's wrong and I'm unjustified, yet that's love.

Chappelle, though, he told a good story about Bill Hicks: about him feeling ill and hung-over on the US-countryside tour and suddenly having to be sick at breakfast, all the way in at the wall-seat in a booth in some diner with three others and so, because he can't get out, just letting up enough sick to fill up a small fruit-juice glass. "Control man, he had such control."

That was Ireland, Kilkenny, the long-running comedy festival. When it began they had extra concept and money to bring across big stars, lured with golf and greenery and heritage links and the causes. First year: Bill Murray; second year: Norm-From-Cheers. All around the place that's all you heard "Norm from Cheers, Norm-From-Cheers. Have you seen Norm-From-Cheers?" . . . When I finally ran into him on the last night he was with the festival director and, excellently, I bounded up and said: "Are you David Hasselhoff?" Sadly this able improviser stepped back and didn't run with it. He sat on it. Squashed it. It died. The director of the festival shook his head and said, "No Phil."

Year after year I got into trouble in Kilkenny, year after year, for thirteen years I did it until I fucked up too big. In the end I had fallen out of love with her as a festival and didn't want to be there and took the fifteen hundred euros – who doesn't want fifteen hundred euros the first weekend in June with free flights and hotel away and tokens and Tynans on the bridge? And the crowds? It got so big, so quick, on that Bank Holiday weekend until the pavements couldn't cope no more; the crowds had bought David McSavage to the streets and there was finally a stabbing on a football field among the thirty-five thousand people who would arrive . . . Johnny Vegas, and the crate of Lucozade, hurling a TV in a hotel window.

Montreal is not like Kilkenny, it is an industry-based thing where everyone is coming to show their best eleven minutes and get a deal. I never quite got this and the only deal I was ever even talked to about was playing Billy Connolly's son in a situation-based comedy which I managed to talk them out of even considering me any further for. Most comics are considered good enough, they must be, by being selected to be here by the all-seeing all-knowing Bruce Hills. He literally knows what folks want and helps shape that by giving it them.

Unbelievably, on the first day you all arrive and are all welcomed like funny-kings because we are all there and could all be the big next thing. For me this was shattered because I accidentally got incredibly drunk on the booze and the jet-lag with Scottish blues legend Big George and came to, out of a truly epic alcoholic blackout, in the heart of the Celebrity Marquee holding a birthday cake that was very definitely not mine. I think this moment is the first one I remember because it was so acute because it was the cake of the host of the whole French side of the festival and people had to act then. I can still feel the cream on my face. I was banned from the tent. De-celebrated, . . . not welcome: Le Marquee de Sad. Jus Pour Tears.

Thankfully this didn't stop me having fun. I remember being way up the mountain with Alan Davies and others and taking my trousers down while they all looked at the view through the large binoculars they have there so they could swing round when I shouted from a bit away and they could get a right good magnified eyeful. The best bit was us all peeling up a wee square of turf and using it to sit on and slide for miles way back down the mountain on the slidy metal handrails that went down for miles by the endless steps. The great Jesus of Montreal is protected from us international hoons by a fence covered in anti-climb goo. Like a real slow thick never-drying Pembury enamel gravy-paint, it is incredibly effective at stopping you start to climb if you know what it is. If you are a bit wasted and don't know that it is there to keep you from climbing you just think it is a very effective enabler; extremely tacky and grippy that in fact you'll have to wash quite hard for ages to get off later, so you don't bother. That was the year someone took out a gun at an Alan Davies gig . . .

I remember being tutted at breakfast this dawn's morning with Alan Davies and a wild San Franciscan stand-up who supported Sam Kinneson and her husband from Blackpool, tutted at by the table where Norm Macdonald was being signed up over pancakes to be the next host of Saturday Night Live. It was a little bit Zelig, a little bit Gump, to be at a time in history yet on a pissed-up all-nite-bender trip, making our pancakes the craziest beautiful good tasting of all times rather than background support for their meet. More Zelig moments of Gump buttons:

There was the moment in Edinburgh one night when Ricky Grover decked Ian Cognito after two warnings, the finest neatest tiny little professional boxers upper cut to just flop cogs into a heap.

Malcolm Hardee's boat sinking on his fiftieth. Julian Clary and the "fisting Norman Lamont" clanger most bold at the British Comedy Awards . . . and the Spike Milligan dissing Prince Charles . . .

Johnny Vegas' late-night full spoken rendition of American Pie at Late'n'Live, that had a magical, unnamable poetic power.

This is where theory is allowed to finally be seen as true example: That it's always best, for me, to be living so your pancakes taste as good as possible; it balances so easily with "Asshole, get on and get sensible and wise up and knuckle down, step up and think on; stop spouting money."

One night us lot all had a party in my room; we took the huge ashtray-hedgehog from by the lift doors in the foyer, where everyone puts out their fags in sand, and stood it in the corner of the room for free smokes all night. There was adequate music and revelry where Jimeoin had to destroy some film negatives and in the morning I found a lovely note of complaint from a neighbouring agent next floor down: "This Comedy Festival isn't just all about fun you know . . . This is business. It is an Industry."

I was not very good at Montreal apart from digging the whole beautiful city and loving Biddle's Jazz & Ribs and wearing a T-shirt that said "Delta" on it and digging a hole for myself. I was actually rather not right for it. I recall Ben Elton buying me a whisky before I went onstage and then reading an interview by him saying the trouble with young comics seems to be they come on with no jokes these days. Thing is, I went on to talk about how my wee daughter, who was actually for real in true life, after all the eighteen months we've had her, starting to walk now, while I'm over here and how I had just found out by phone and had asked her Mum if she could suppress this, inhibit her, hold her back, discourage it, put obstacles in her way, generally put her off it till I got back. I was trying to formulate a routine in front of their very North American eyes. It had truth, pathos and, I felt, a touching comic element of dis-evolving like the Russian gymnasts and their delayed womanhood and general development inhibited by cruel coaches and their DDR-eadful eastern beta blockers communist steroids that was perhaps not right for the late-night Danger Zone at Club Soda.

Some people arrange more safety. They require it. This makes them very successful often. This makes them though raise their own bar of what defines safety until, like Uncle Ben, they end up writing a West End musical with the Lloyd-Webber, sealing their safety.

I don't really believe in a best-eleven-minutes and it was all finally cemented when we jammed all the lifts in the hotel between floors. Apparently one lift was packed with executives, two of which had run to catch that lift and the doors had been held for them.

Me and Mike Wilmot and some curly-haired fiend had decided to head up to my room for a smoke and then return. We did not manage to resist pressing the Alarm STOP button. It could not be un-pressed. Luckily we had beers in our hands and the four of us had partly-written "Shafted", the first sit-com set in a lift, by the time the fire brigade came to prise open the doors with tools fifty big minutes later. Our fault; not our fault. I think we actually said we were not ready to come out yet "could they give us five?" when they held hands down to get us up from between floors.

I did get asked back, got another bite at the cherry. Bruce had me do an hour show, in the same space the year following Bill Hicks, who had been seen by Seamus Cassidy and brought over to become understood in Britain. Trouble is it was a second bite at a Maraschino, marinated to become composed of other matter entirely. Not really a cherry at all, just virtually a cherry, only-just virtually a shadow of its former husked and hollowed and petrified and cast in a mould of its own image, simulated and made by total infusion by sugars.

Morag, Al and me passed a sign in America: "Petrified Forest." Dull, stiff, deadend trees turned to stone, fully mineralized, the water comes into them over the centuries, fills up every cell then evaporates and leaves its image in stone when finally the vegetable matter has gone too.

One thing did work though. The whole festival is called Juste Pour Rire – Just For Laughs. I did a TV bit in a venue with this logo up on the wall, I was able to take the letter "J" off and turn it around to make a nice big lower case: "ɾust For Laughs" – Hey don't you love oxidation? – I say I say I say, what do you get if you leave your metal exposed to water? – Half of them stared; all of me loved it.

I just happened to walk through the back of a famous gig Boothby Graffoe did that had the Americans in fits, fits they could not work out. The agents were all there and the Disney ones, the biggest, had to have whatever-it-was he had. Even the waitresses stood still jaws open trying to laugh enough. They gave money and, years later, it all came out that his agents had flown over a few times to seal a deal-that-never-was and it came down to everyone having to do a massive benefit for Boothby to pay back the agents twelve grand because – well, because.

Oh, and one other event. At that time in my life I was on the eleven-minute-challenge. There was not much one couldn't do in eleven minutes if mind was put to it. At a party one night at The Delta where Sue Virtue was picking up matchboxes off the floor with her teeth while doing the splits, we all saw a lovely rooftop garden on the posh office block next door. Me and Phil Nichol said we could be dancing naked there in eleven minutes.

We set off down to street level, ran around to the entrance and with only rudimentary French I managed to wangle us in to the foyer to speak to the security guard – "Maintenant, je va à l'aeroport mais j'ai oublié mon passaport dans le jardin!" – and pointing up to the sky and stroking our laminates we were in. Coming out the lift we began a small easy mime of looking around and checking, a few flights up across the road our balcony was empty no one was watching. We stood there accomplished and they had forgotten and given up on us. Perhaps we were early – it was only nine minutes. Still miming, Phil and I are looking at each other when we hear a cheer and they are there now, so, quickly, we start to take our trousers down and end up being herded off the roof by the security guard partially-unclothed. In the short journey he had seemed too nice to do the whole thing to. Anyway it was the thought and the effort and the magical carrying-through of the initial inclination-spark that counts.

Not quite the full Monty-Real.

Twelve years after Montreal I bump into a suave and older Andy Kindler in Killkenny out of his hemisphere and looking keen and open so I take him into the back of the kitchen's corridor and manage to get him stoned while he kept looking at me saying he kind of remembered me so I reminded him exactly why in a calm way.

Life is the taste of many bites of cherries from a selection of lovely bowls.

There is always a best in a situation, you know there's usually someone to fancy in a room of people.

Also, one last thing: you know Dom Irrera who played the Limousine Chauffeur in The Big Lebowski, New York (well, Philadelphia . . . .) caustic comic. Well, he was in love with a waitress that everyone had had their eye on and somehow everyone was amazed when they got together. Sean Hughes made some wisecrack about the mismatch and so Dom left a message on his hotel phone: "You mess with me, I mess with you . . . maybe some guys I know . . . summ'tin might happen to your legs . . ." I think that was the night me and Bill Bailey's wife Kris wrote on a message on Sean's forehead . . . Anyway, have I mentioned that already?

*

Cherry Biting: Second Go AT IT:

Here, so, I'm am out with two of my real stepbrothers in London's Soho Town, Tim and Francis, at the opening of The Lab Bar for cocktails on Old Compton Street that although my friend Ian is an investor in we have only one invite and I am smiling up at the man of door and rope to ask please to go in sir and fetch my Ian out to verify, qualify and identify. He say yes. Back-in-a-minute, I mouth as well as say, looking back, going in.

Inside I push past the thin-clothed Londoners all talking like Clangers in the media and get to the top of some stairs that de-escalate in a movie-wide Hollywood-half spiral presentation-type fashion down and out, like Lewes' roads down to the big basement below where certainly it is all at. Caprice is juggling citrus fruits near the bar. Tipping slowly over the edge like John Wayne's foot at the end of The Searchers and slowly beginning the sweep around and down and looking for Ian there I see Noel Gallagher, in the prime PR-corner, some of his group sitting and him and some standing. As I am seeing him he sees me and immediately goes, "Ay . . . You. I love you." The whole part of this corner of the place goes quiet by about six percent.

It was voiced in an accent which made it sound like something that was my fault.

Accepting and going with it, he comes up the stairs to meet me completely shiny with a rich man's clean hair and clothes and shoes and neat hands and the nails with a Mancunian manicure.

I am smiling and he says, "Ay loove dat thing you do ay-bout Alanis Morrisette."

Now that wasn't me, that was Ed Byrne who looks like I used to.

So had noelG mistaken me for a comic cos I looked like him or had he just mistaken me for another human who was a comic or had a third option happened where maybe he'd seen me once long ago with more hair and his subconscious transposed my head onto Ed's speaking voiced-material? The latter methinks; so now I am left with the possibility that he thinks I am just any old guy that looks like the comedian or he has in fact seen us both and unfortunately sort of melted us together like a merger but left my name off the new sign.

I prefer that it is a little bit like a lateral quiz: a man is mistaken for a comedian . . . and he is one et cetera . . .

Just as he finishes saying what he's saying I tell him that it is not me in a way that will not look like I am to any onlookers.

He dealt with it well leaned over the banister's sweep and got me a vodka cocktail and said he could get me anything cos he was the fuckin' Mayor of London.

Then I say I have to go and try and get my brothers in, can you help? . . . a brother asking a brother for brother help . . . bi-bingo, and he's pulling me up the stairs and helping out massive as, back out to the rope we go and he is verifying and identifying saying out loudly that he knows my brothers and they are with him and the last my brothers saw of me was an unconvinced mouthing and here I am returning with a Gallagher, and all of us brothers.

That was more exciting than the first time I had already actually met Noel when I came out of a lift on the hotel floor he had rented all-of . . . Or the time we drove thirteen hours to see them in Brighton after Annie Nightingale had asked me in Miami to come to their gig, on our way over to film a documentary about a total solar eclipse in Chile and, when we got there, Bobby Gillespie was all upset and tried to hurt my puppy . . . or the plastic bottle-throwing riot at Loch Lomond I didn't start (allegedly) . . .

Sixth Chapter

@ the first gig of mine ever, after only my fourth ever minutes of showtime I got offered a televisual opportunity with the Scottish comedy collective The Funny Farm on their STV show from its host Stu Who and this actually happened and plus together with, you've got to see it on your tube, they got Bill Hicks on this wee Scottish show and he kind of does some old tropes and gets that they are not really getting him as always at straight comedy gigs and he kind of leaves a bit early. There would normally be brackets there Brenda, not today. After which me and friends then went upstairs to see an incredible floppy-haired Sean Hughes do a gig – "Me Mum called: 'Sean, we found your bed, it was on top of your porn mags.'" Then ten minutes in he flicks his head forward and some hidden sunglasses drop forward smartly into position on his nose . . . hidden in his sizeable, alternative, indie womanizing fringe.

The second gig I did was the final of So You Think You're Funny? and, after that, my friend Morag took me by the arm – "Come and see these guys." They were Corky and The Juice Pigs. I did not know comedy, or anything, could be that wild and good and inventive and full-force and it was relieving to see a trio as one: Phil Nichol, Greg Hamilton and Sean Cullen. They did by far the most outrageous and mesmerizing shows I have ever seen: All the screaming and lewd genius as well as the diaphanous clouds of sheer improvisatory magic. Watch them strip down to their piggy-nosed golden underwear and really treat a front row man to something new.

The third gig I did was six minutes on the BBC's Edinburgh Nights with Brand, Hegley, Smith and Steel. John Hegley complimented me and said that he liked my act. Comedians are rarely doing this and it was a beautiful thing to do from a beautiful man who I have seen be a beautiful dad. Plus what he does is unlike anyone else for his act is essential and integral to him and the closest to something I cannot imagine failing to go down well because he would have had to have failed to project that self.

After that first eruption I got one gig a month here and there and one every month and a bit at the Funny Farm's headquarters, The Comic

Club at Blackfriars Pub, merchant city, Glasgow. Clare ran it without a pun in the title and she had that brilliant sincerity to love it and know that she was helping us all and you could sense she was just into it. One day I asked to be the regular host she said yes. What a break, and it was me that asked for it. There were twelve in the Funny Farm collective, Fred MacAulay who is incomparable on Breakfast Radio Scotland and was always well organized. Then there was Estuart McDonald the genius writer of the Endill Swift children's books set entirely in a school that was on an island. He used twenty-seven Bic biros to write the book and had kept them all. First Funny Farm meeting I went to his Volkswagen Beetle had broken doon and we pushed it, laughing because the engine is in the back and it was pleasant and warm to push . . . Now he lives in Barceloneta in a tiny apartment and does devised theatre pieces in schools all around Spain. He used to do an act without his stutter just going through the alphabet doing sounds and jokes – fun-etics I just called it. How do you spell phonetic? Just as it soundz. There was Gordon and Philip and the two Davids and there was Stu Who? The kind of leader of it and compere of the TV show that Kim Kinnie from London's Comedy Store was commissioned to make. Another neat, rigid producer assembling a mix tape for his love: the commissioning editors in telly. Yet we are not tracks, we are humans. Blah blah, like a scared parent you all have to do well so they do well, and then if you don't you've threatened their success, so therefore they try and ensure you do well by . . . attempting to edit your work in advance. Like hellbound jongleurs, yes they never came with you and lived and help form the words, no just listened to it in a dead cold rehearsal place from behind a desk and then vainly tried to believe that you might use their slick tyres in the wet.

Once in Montreux we were doing a big gig for American TV co-production heaven . . . At the huge rehearsals me and Ardal O'Hanlon and Hattie Hayridge were told, "Okay gimme your best three minutes!" I stood there talking in the afternoon as they dressed the set about the workmen's bumcracks being like an oceanless border between Switzerland and France and a tiny pong in the mountain crevass crevice . . . The American producer stared and immediately replaced me with Ardal as the host.

Back at STV's The Funny Farm, we all got slots in a steep raked studio circular stage with the Humph Family band.

I remember running on to compere, way back at The Comic Club in Glasgow, thinking, "What will I be on about tonight?" and between then and the mike I slipped and hurt my thigh on the side of the stage so

I was able to do a Bruise-Update throughout the night. It is like a loving relationship you and the crowd, especially if you are compering, because they like a spontaneous reality very much. It certainly is not that funny a joke – a spreading swell of red to purple on your leg – yet taking it as the thing, running with the bruise and sharing it in-time and being relaxed to let all else go is certainly something that laughing can occur around. Fabulously it works even more pointedly in reverse: There are times, doing what you are certain is fantastic stuff, it is just that laughter is not occurring and I have definitely had to stop lots of times and admit this and get out an old story, ask a question, sing a song, shift away. Like love in relationships: nothing can actually be taken for granted, there is always the best space when the heads are free to go off on one, so then it can start to build. And compering is like certain loving relationships: it works because you are on and off a few times and it works because you are about to leave at any time. It is amazing because it does not have to be maintained. You decide how long you stay. This is great for some folks, why some are much better than others at compering and why some are much better as comperes than full-spot comics. And, perhaps too, why the best compere is not better than the best act doing v. well; though sometimes they are way the best thing that night . . .

Mostly I have worked to live in a way so as to make the run at the stage begin much earlier than in the day and so allow myself not to have to injure my leg to have a thing to be on about. I keep my eyes, ears and my mind open. Blotting-paper memory brain-style. I keep my nostrils flared . . . Lo, you never know when an old familiar smell will remind you of an old gardener at your house and the early summers of Borg and McEnroe and then you might see racquets and you might end up onstage in Perth Theatre playing a rather talented guy without a net and inventing non-competitive Scottish sur-Real Tennis and having all those personal references with you that in the end you can be achieving naturalaly what some folks have to rehearse to achieve. Clowning is at its best when it is free, when you don't try and think of jokes, you are the joke. Gary Lightbody wrote sixteen songs in three days for the Reindeer collective . . . Vic and Bob used to have a new hour every week . . . And nowadays there is twenty-four hour improv shows and all. People are living it like Neo in the Matrix: not fighting it, above it.

I once had two very different hour-long shows in a night in East Sussex Arts Club 2002 where those that enjoyed it could stay on for free and definitely became friends forever . . . a few years ago at Edinburgh I did four shows in the evening after a kids' show in the day.

. . . and there was a time when I used to do the hundred-and-eight-seater East Kilbride Arts Centre for fifty minutes then just change the crowd and press on, so it was billed as two shows . . . though for me it was just a bit like a break and fresh paper, or Annabel Chong swapping the men in her gang bang or tyres in the race. NO this has gone too far. There was a good show to integrated minds then instead of no more showing there was a whole new group got the chance to see a show too where I was already fully warmed up. Quite an experiment, and it was only considered because it could allow the best thing ever to happen: a warmly oiled hyper-loose massage of a show from a keen guy earning doubles.

Perth Theatre is big like lots of theatres and they have usually got remarkable objects lying around or even props and one time they had an enormous outsize roll of bubble wrap, enough to have the whole marvellous front row onstage at the end and wrap them up pretending that I store them chilled and post them on to the next gig of the tour.

In fact I never tour or I always tour. There is no end.

Some comedians have posters and a finite context. Me – I simply have shows coming up. Sometimes I have had a poster. Oft' years for example there'd be a truly-keen agent fix up seven gigs covering three months, yet there were other gigs in-between the ones on the list on the poster though.

One of them was in St Andrews. It announced a ten thirty start on my own poster and as I drove the three-hour drive, I got a call at ten to eight asking where I was/was I? Strikingly, the gig was meant to start at eight. I was flattered that they would wait until only ten minutes to go before calling with a hundred and eighty people, sipping unawares in the plush bar, none-the-wiser.

"You're on in ten minutes . . ."

". . . begging to differ, for I am hundred miles away, Sir."

Suddenly it occurred to me that there was not much to do apart from increase my average speed and maintain vigilance. Worry does not actually increase miles per hour or estimated time of arrival much, in fact the constriction of worry often slows the limbs and leads to errrorrs. See, too many r's there as I was rushing. I asked the theatre manager to try and think of it not as a two-hour wait and delay and somehow convey to the crowd that they were lucky that yes the gig was on tonight, Saturday night with all the winds, and It Would Occur. Sorry I am late a tree had fallen on the road. Making my mind not to be apologizing about it in advance and merely waited until eight as I drove, then kept a note of everything that happened in the car and all the details about the drive I could.

Colin kept phoning me, kept asking when I would be there, I kept saying that yes, I was driving very well and finally I drove into St Andrews and told him I would be there in seven minutes and when I was just round the corner. So in the end I got there early, parked softly diagonal, walked in, and just went straight onstage so that humorously I am able to berate them for being late.

Some folks got it. They had the facility to not take it personally, to have faith in their choice. I told them all about the choices I had made and not to worry, I was being funny from eight o'clock onwards, the gig had begun, I was on form; it was just that they were not witnessing it. When a tree falls in the forest and no one is there, there is still vibration flying through the air that could be received and felt. I told them about how I cut minutes off the journey after I had added lots on by going the wrong way as well as ending up driving through Milnathort, the village I was born in, and passing The Lindens, the house I was born in, and waving up at the window, the spare room, the room I was born in and having a real quickdrive-by re-birth moment – It is alright, everything is okay, you can get to the gig and it will be fine – I was re-re-birthed; reminded because I already knew this. I talked for two hours about all this and in this vein and those that could not settle eventually left and a couple who were clearly not that comfortable with it all chose to leave midway through my fabulous routine about "Thank Heavens That Pope Died", with it all turning into a Horse Race with Black Pope at a hundred to one, overtaken by Nazi Pope the rank outsider at five hundred to one, pipping John Paul the Second, who has just fallen at the last.

I thought it was a tremendously successful gig because we all got a big dose of reality. We were not all comfortable. In the end what you have can be enough. Some tell of arranging to meet an Aboriginal at 3pm and they come a few days late at three because that's how they work and in truth things usually get better when we have to wait?, yeh . . . tantra . . . baking . . . the release of the new GHIJK Rowling book . . .

Of course it is possible to write about all the gigs getting done while this autoblography is being written/typed.

The beautiful administrators at the Byre Theatre St Andrews venue wrote me a great letter saying: "Without even the courtesy of liaising with our technical staff he walked straight onto the stage and started his act regardless of the fact that a sizeable proportion of the audience who had waited nearly two hours for him were either in the process of finding their seats or were still in the foyer." . . . Two hours late and I went on too soon. Beat that.

Cleverly I had regarded this as in fact the best way to begin so that those who had found their seats would not have to wait any longer and how else could I berate the folks coming in after me for being not on time. Der! Forgetting the fact that I was late, the whole idea of how I might like to start before people are in, as I do a lot, was never considered. Neither is the idea that "the act", like life, is just whatever it is. Nobody "missed" anything once it began. In a way in life no one misses anything because you never had a list before of what was going to compromise life, to then be able to check having a thing missing. In the end they held back pounds stroke penalized me three hundred and ninety-seven pounds fifty-two pence; which, if you work it out, may well be as low as fifty-one pence a month over an average life of sixty-five years. Let's hope I live longer than average and that will be lessening every day.

Once someone thinks you don't care, it usually take some magic to convince them otherwise. And it is always worth it. Either that or they need to see the show to understand. Or or.

The last gig I did in a library at night? Well you may ask, hmm let me see the absolute best gig I ever did in a library . . . late at night you say . . . definitely the one that was part of a council campaign in East Renfrewshire to get new folks in. I mentioned that I was writing a book to the crowd. It was like emotional feedback, when the sound from a speaker gets re-amplified back into itself by itself – when output informs the input informs the output, can't work at the same time, too close up. This was fine though. Books are about optimism. You believe someone will get what you offer in ink. I just kept going on about how it was lovely to be able to be noisy and drink wine in a library. Yes. They. Had. A Bar. In This. Library. Shh. Then there were some dodgy folks who had heard there was a gig and bar here last night might come in expecting booze every day: "The new Catherine Cookson and a gin & tonic please . . . When do I have to return this Guinness? . . . Hello, I ordered a Piña Colada two weeks ago, is it in yet?"

Cleverly, I won the raffle afterwards in the library in an undisputed piece of sheer luck as I was also drawing the names out of a bag. I sang a country song about Cowboys in the Libray-ree . . . who enjoy a Try-Logee . . . Ah Ties up my horse and head for the Reference Section . . . the li'l ol' canyon of knowledge . . .

Somehow it makes sense that writing down the jokes one spoke about literature in a library are not that funny on paper. Was that a tautology?

"We met way down in Reference . . . Can I look you up tomorra?"

"Yesterday I was weeding in the garden. It was a gweat book."

(Beneficially, that gig is available on a DVD: "Giffnock Library".)

'Twas funny as it happened.

As part of the campaign they magically had very lateral thinking merchandising, you I kid not: There were winter car window scrapers reminding folks to go to libraries. They said it could not be done. It is a quiet right-brain moment, one is occupied and attentive on simply scraping and there is the "Look Libraries" logo there to fill the empty void to and fro Smart!

That day had been spent with my brother Chris and his family and I was reminded to tell everyone about the time we went down the Orinoco River in kayaks. Before the trip we had bought all our provisions from a Venezuelan hypermarket including machetes. We tried them out in the shop, stood there in the aisle swishing them to and fro in Spanish, definitely resembling an armed gang in action, resisted robbing the place because we were armed and put them on the conveyor at the check-out and bought them. They had a barcode like every other item and they beeped like beans or bread. I forgot to take my sticker off and way up the jungle my friend Brendon sees it and says: "Take that barcode off your machete; the natives will be able to tell we are amateurs . . ." All a bit risky as they have highly armed guards by the ram-raid-proof front door with semi-automatic weapons. Resisting asking them where the geggs are is a huge achievment.

At this gig still in East Renfrewshirea man and his wife told me that they had seen me years ago at the Comic Club where I used to come on and say "Ladies and Gentlemen I would like you to know I cannot stand" and then I would fall over. There was always the chance you would be hitting the ground to no laughs. It was an all-in here's my bet, here I am, are you coming?

Even in my beginning was this invitation.

First thing I did in comedy was enter the So You Think You're Funny? competition. KarenKoren started it – and kickstarted them all – I had just come back from Spain and wrote down some jokes on the entrance form. I was going to put out ten pairs of shoes and invent a character for each of them then start wearing one of each pair and mixing them up and it was all pretend and I never had it wrote and Karen got me in because she and thee Steph Harris thought it sounded so bad it had to be worth a look.

The very first heat was the first stand-up gig I had ever seen. It occurred to me, nervously pacing around the green room with the other seven entrants, that I did not know if I was going to hold the mike or leave it on the stand. This is still an issue today.

My first joke, my first laugh: "Good evening ladies and gentlemen. Now, before I start . . . I usually pace around the dressing room all nervous . . ."

It hung in the air until Lynn Ferguson, an Alexander Sister, fabulous friendly comedian, the Scottish one in Aardman's Chicken Run – one of the judges – laughed and this inspired the rest of the ten folks to imagine there must be something funny there and they had a look back for it. "My Mum's idea of a good square meal was toast . . . They say that Bruce Forsyth doesn't have all his own hair. Well it is his, I saw him buy it. He owns it, legally, it is all his own . . ."

All my first jokes were from notebooks gathered over the last couple of years as I was eighteen and nineteen, working in a restaurant and living in Edinburgh for my gap-year. The best bit though was the true bits all about hitchhiking down across the south of France and not getting lifts and how different things mean different things in different countries: Standing by the road in Spain with your thumb up means "Drive past me . . . Lovely car, yeh, drive past me . . . Great!"

Basically it is all the same to this day. One-liners and condensed-concept two-liners, sequiturs and non-sequiturs, thoughtful proposals that I have mostly written down somewhere combined with long open storytelling about what has happened that day, that week, that year, this life.

This two thousand and sixth year I went to Melbourne for the International Comedy Festival to do my Kids' Show. It is called Gimme Your Left Shoe and all the kids do this, putting their left shoe into a shoe-sledge which I am dragging around by rope from a bicycle which they have to chase a bit and don't all get the shoes that a few of them choose to throw at the sledge. Then they invent a skit with me and my many, many props laid out on the floor in order to win it back and not hop home. The right shoe to give me is the left one; the one you should be left with is the right one. The left is the right one to give; if you are left with the left that's not right. Give me the right one, that's left one – over and over, I complicatedly mantra this and keep and eye on the kids and commentate on them. I did three shows a day in the incredible

Umbrella Revolution big top: forty minutes firing elastic bands, wearing plastic ponchos, singing songs, playing pancake tennis, getting dads to skateboard, peeling fruit blindfolded, water-pistol portraiture, catching air in a net, sneaking-up on me wearing a flipper and a ski-boot . . .

My love Melina flew over there with me and we lived in the glorious Penthouse with the free rum and the mirrors and the sinks and the closets and the curtains and the mirrors. We went down the coast to stay in the town next to Separation Creek. We found that Bundaberg Ginger Beer ring-pulls fitted her wedding finger and my pinkie. I declared my willingness to adore her for the next decade on a beach and then ran into the water naked calling out "Going to show this Ocean who's boss . . . !" whereupon I was immediately smashed and grabbed by a deep fast wave that churned me in a spin-cycle against all the toughest sharp shale so that all I could do was cross my hands over my nipples and chest and wait to be spat out again after a good sandblasting. We had a double-upgraded gold car and drove the Great Ocean Road. Made the best pancakes ever and caught real waves on a board.

One night we went to Dimitri Martin's show and the man who stage-managed the venue sneaked us in late through the back, under the scaffold of the grandstand, so we came out of nowhere at the back into the very full venue and were walking down the aisle together with Dimitri already on, looking for seats. He spied us and said a "hey" then a "hello". There were some seats reserved. There we sat and our wine still chilled, cool. Then the staff came and told us to move, removed us. "Those seats were reserved for . . ."

"What? For latecomers and that's us," I say, "so we're going back in." When we went back in, despite their problem with it, and Dimitri was handily explaining who I was. I'm sure he was saying "Phil Kay . . . Something always happens to him" with just a touch of the feeling those who love maths too much can have. Just another v. smart guy who wants to be an actor. Why are there no positive mysteries he asks . . . well we tend not to question that which pleases us.

Next day I saw him in an elevator with a young lady. He never said a word: I can only imagine he never knew her name. Or he was a. – not on for me, or b. – still a.

After my love left I had five bikes in my possession in sixteen days. The first one belonged to my old friend Sara who I had first met when she did a gig in the backroom of the Esplanade Hotel with the legendary Anthony Morgan where the crowd came in and they basically just served everyone a drink and monologued and duologued, took the piss, kept the change and were barkeeps with much personality. She had had this spare bike since, then, nine years ago and so, after an evening drinking an expensive one-off luxury bottle of super luxurious Grey Goose vodka that she was paid for with some screenwriting work, I rode off on it without having to promise to take good care of it. Racing along back into town from St Kilda along well-lit Melbourne avenues – all the best bits of America yet still right-hand drive. Over the bridge I caught sight of my big top venue's bar alive with some kind of action. I leaned the bike against the fence and hurled myself in to dance with all the staff. I married Gus, floated an indestructible twenty in the tip bowl and had several Polaroids taken of me and Natalie and Sara and Emily with a huge two-litre bottle of Grey Goose vodka. Ha! After two hours it is two a.m., we leave, I go to the fence and it's gone. Nine years she loved it and I only managed to keep it half an hour. "Take care," she never said. And there they were: the Polaroids of me doing exactly not that with the ridiculous inflated oversized gauche Goose.

Then I look down the riverside and there are some young late-night kids up to no good with bikes. It must be there, it must be them oh no. Yahoo! I whistle and shout "Bike, you guys!" or something that may well mean something to them. Indeed, they had a recently-nicked bike though not Sara's. As they came close I said "Oh, sorry, though you had my bike . . ." and then they offered me the one they had anyway for twenty. Excellently, I was now skint of notes and so Gus decided to lend me a wet twenty out of the tip jar. Ha-ha. So there I was, with wheels again; I was without a bike for almost four minutes.

I told this story the next night at a late-night comedy club not very well and, as can happen, the crowd just thought of it as rather poor material. Only getting a man out of the crowd to act as a superhero with a red tablecloth tucked into a man's Superman T-shirt balancing on a table got any real reaction, I think. Later that was the night things got so advanced that me and Glenn Wool did a striptease onstage with the DJ at the festival club and nobody really batted an eyelid, then we befriended a woman who had a Shetland pony that had been in the movies and I got given a tube of cracked-heel cream by a drunken lady.

This bike number two sat outside my hotel unlocked for a few days. It only had one definite gear, though if you did pull the actual gear wire as it went along the frame it would go up one gear. That would be fine for a while and then under hard pedalling it would slip down again.

I used to ride it thinking how it was great to have pressure-sensitive automatic gear-shift, drive-by-wire technology for such a bargain price.

If you don't lock your bike outside an Australian-managed apartments the benefits are enormous: you can just walk out of the lift out the hotel, step straight on and off you go, no painful time-destroying unlocking, bending over, averting your eyes from the world. If it is still there unlocked you get a little thrill because your optimism this side of the hemisphere combined with the value of the cycle and the way it came seem to be reflected in this trust-invested instant calmer karma cycle. If it is gone, as it was after four days, then you walk out of the lift, see this walk out of the hotel and just keep walking as always.

On a free tram over to St Kilda, the groovy area down by the beach in Melbourne with the story that it was named after a boat that rescued a highly-charged woman from a beach in Scotland's Hebrides, the boat having changed its name to her name – and entered a v. big Salvation Army Opp.-Shop – they call them not Charity but Opportunity Shops – too right, I found a big racer that needed air. I asked the guy if he though it might hold air in them there tyres and he said just to take it for free and see. It did. I rode it home.

My hotel was the Medina Grand. My love's name: Melina. When she was there it was a gentle written reminder everywhere of her and I scored out a few curly bits of the "d" to make "Me lina Grand" here and there in the privacy of lifts. When she left these fabulous scratchings served as tiny drops of lemon on the tongue of love, a reminding of her in a sheer way, even though she was never out of my mind.

I bought lots of new crockery and moved the furniture around. One day the manager complained to me. He said he had been in and seen four things which upset him:

One, First there was tape on the walls.

Also, There was a burned match on the carpet.

There was a sheet tied to the balcony, all too visible from the street.

The room had only been cleaned twice in nineteen days and there was pen written on the wall.

And oh yes, he says where was the television?

Addressing these one by one: "The tape on the walls is Scotch Tape, Sir, especially formulated to come off walls without taking any off it with it." "The match was well out before it hit the carpet, it fell near the bin in one of my regular tidy-ups." "The sheet was tied to the balcony to stop it flying away while it was drying, Sir." "Surely you cannot order me to clean a room, surely it is a service the hotel offers." He informed me this was not a hotel, this was serviced apartments; subtle difference. Thing is: when they come in the things that look like shit are often my treasured items. Momentous Memento-bits of paper and reminder things went missing and I had had to chase a maid for a list of songs written on the inside of some cardboard. Sensibly, incredibly every bin on the floor was numbered so splendidly she was able to take me au-pairside into the back stairwell storeroom to locate it and, well she located it.

This was all on the phone. I had to bluff the last one because there was pen on the wall. I told him it was pencil and moved a poster for Anthony Morgan over where it was and said it was already gone. He came for an inspection. Of course it was not just this, it was the personalized crockery and furniture re-stylings, maybe the art and their big TV that I put in the cupboard or the huge bird–of-paradise flowers I had borrowed from the corporate function lounge on floor ten. Crappy bikes parked right outside? Last straws? It might have been letting an English lass from the café have a key to my rooms so she could use the toilet and laundry facilities and have a few quiet nights away from her hostel hassles. Or maybe he saw me busking. Perhaps it was the balloons or the ping-pong racquets and ball that sat innocently on the big glass coffee-table.

You treat this place like a bloody hotel, when it's serviced apartments.

I tried to come up with a complaint; though was just compliant.

"Perhaps you could watch out when wiping the toaster not to turn the setting down next time please, because my toast was up unexpectedly early and I wasn't ready and then when finally going over there it was a bit stiff and had to be retoasted and was hard to get right . . . that . . . one . . . slice . . ."

It is just when they get a wee inkling that they feel you are a bit scruffy; it is hard for them to love you in their serviced apartments. Thing is though, it is like gigs where you appear shit, it is best not to run from the bear. Don't act like prey. Carry on about your business and the grizzly will not bother.

Day four and the happy-crappy automatic bicycle went. Automatic because the gears were so stiff I had to pull the actual gear wire to change up, and then under pressure it would change itself down. The racer from the huge Opp.-Shop lasted three days until it developed an enormous blister of inner tube, redefining "protruding" coming right through a hole so that every time it went round past the brake it made me wince with pain as if it was a bad swelling blister on wee Jake my Mum's dog's mouth. It eventually popped with a highly audible pop going across the bridge by my venue and I abandoned it right there and then just stepping off and walking away freely and to some in-passing trams mysteriously. In fact this always feels like to me that dog leaving its owner when his last match is wet and fails in the Yukon in that short story by Tobias Wolff, easy, and trammed-it to George's. My friend, the essential oiler and marketer of high-end exclusive meditation incense. He leant me a scooter. It's not right a grown man scootering, unsymmetrical footering, so just had to meet my friend Neil in a bar then I would take it back.

Neil has BasedOnATrueStory.com and tailors trips for Bruce Springstein in Africa and the like. He comes with two friends and the four of us find the only spot where you cannot see a TV with Australian Big Brother on in the bar – it is all the more sad here because Australia is so happy and fabulous. I laid a ten-dollar note on the pool table and came back and this drunk hoon comes over and tells me not to leave it there as it might get nicked. Telling him not to worry seemed a little odd. We all drank our different colour Coopers from bottles then glancing over the tenner was gone. I had this impulse to do something unusual so I took off my top and went over there slowly all bare-chested and ominous and, as I got there, I saw the tenner was there; it just wasn't very obvious. From where we were. So I smiled and came back.

Then we want to play doubles but a Northern Irish guy with a leg in plaster says we have to play Winner-Stays-On and is adamant, so I nick the pool ball and he chases me round the table without crutches now and is threatening me. Or has he been healed through anger. We tell the owner he is being violentish and turns out it's his best mate and we have to leave.

"You're going out that window," he had said, so enigmatically, unleashing the full accent on appropriate aggression.

Next day George said I could have the Merida thousand-buck super-light bike if I used a lock. Loving moments of abandoning principles I said "Certainly!" however I get there late, missing George and have to get a builder to help+lend me a ladder to get up to the balcony. This is groovy area to live and it is still Junkie Town-on-Sea and they never asked and I pass the neighbour's window on the way down and watched them watching a man carrying a bike down a ladder without sirens at all starting to sound in the distance, then I can flick my focus to see my own reflection and watch me watching them watch me and watch me being watched at the same time. It was like Derren Brown in reverse in practice: there was no con. Like nipping in the cinema when you have a ticket, seeing if you can zip past three staff with a cellphone to your ear, eyes to the ground or a bucket of just the free water and ice resembling lemonade for two.

By now the receptionists at these serviced apartments were intrigued as to the variety of pedalled transport.

Sadly badly later however I was asked to leave the hotel shortly after having been fired from the adult gigs that I had been booked to do. A small tour of towns within a few hours' drive of Melbourne. Booked for these to weigh up the scales on this superb opportunity to do a smallish kids' show that can never really make money.

These adult touring-the-country-towns-extensively gigs went unbelievably well for one night, better for a second then I was relieved of my duties after one of the most exciting nights of my life.

I went in a van to the first gig with three other comedians. We got on well and the show was completed by two more acts who came in their own cars. The compere and the Headliner with the eyeliner. In the dressing room I asked why he had eyeliner on, he said that it was because they said he had "no eyes on TV".

"If they said you needed an extra leg, would you have one added?" is my fully foolhardy reply. There is of course no answer to that as it is not really a question requiring one. It was a statement as a great many questions are.

So, the second night: We four arrived in a small town called Sale at dusk and, while everyone nipped into the motel, I zoomed over to the modern-architected theatre. There was a bit of a soundcheck and coffee. I asked the soundmen if they could help me find some pot and they said it would be hard in this town. I headed out of the venue and there was a bicycle unlocked by the front door. Backing back in I found out it was owned by a kid who works in the kitchen. In Australia they call the kitchen porter the Dishpig. I was in the kitchen getting permission to borrow for tickets when the café manager came over and, with a keen sarky eyebrow asked, "Is this door going to be open all day?"

Turned to him: "Yes it is." Turned away and we just carried on talking. Then turning back our eyes met. He looked challenged.

I offered, "Sorry, was that a rhetorical order?" His eyes smiled and the change was amazing, he laughed and left. No ponytail, no managerial imperial.

The Dishpig grants me free use and so I took the bike, cycled the town, went to the baker's, met the baker's mother who sold me the last pastry of the day and told me she has also to cook his dinner. Then the three young men I needed to meet. They recognized the bike, circled in and one good answer kept me from getting kicked off the bike: "Dishpig." The word made them smile and saved me. They went off with my trust and forty bucks to meet me later. They came and I had a huge coffee and shared spoils with the soundman. A beautiful young front-of-house manager adjusted her stocking and I saw a tiger tattooed high on her thigh. The boys wanted to see the gig yet it was sold out, I said they could watch it backstage with me. "No, hang on, why not come onstage?" I thought. We could do a wee skit about The Youth of Sale, the future: The Century of Sale. They were kind of used to taking the piss and not meaning what they say, and people not meaning what they said to them, that it took me ages to convince them. I did. Then I sat outside and busked for change and cigarettes out the front of the venue. It was then one of the other acts Eddy Perfect, the majestic singer, realized it was me he had seen busking to sing about him in Melbourne the week before. And I remembered him and what was sung about him. What are the chances of that? Well . . . there's eight hundred thousand guys in Melbourne . . .

The show started. I was on after the break. I was loitering backstage by the end of the interval. I meet the boys at the backstage. The Dishpig had recognized them as the ones who bashed him up a bit last week. They were late teens in T-shirts, talented tough and in a small town. I gathered some fallen leaves, had my ping-pong bat and ball in my pocket and these three youths and we all stood in the wings waiting for the compere to finish his "break-up-sex" routine. Interestingly I could not wait and bounced my ping-pong ball onto the back of the stage. I got on there, got a laugh holding my bat, got the ball on the bounce and then was off before he turned round to see what was there. The word timing, the concept timing, was invented for this kind of accidental magic. He had felt good laughter, liked it swelled up, then realized it was not usual, there must be something behind, he turns, I'm not there and the beautiful big random receiver psychic group that is the crowd had seen it all, understanding it all as one. Then, after a suitable gap I did it again, though this time a lot quicker with some acting of pissed-off-ness at the imaginary player I am playing who has hit it here . . . Meanwhile he is trying to finish the routine before introducing me. He goes on, I am out of order, hitting the ball across the back of the stage and trying to get all the way across. This time he kind of runs at me with a look in his eye like he didn't know what else to do.

I had a wonderful time talking about the local bakery and everything always being cheaper in Sale. Then I played ping-pong with the biggest guy in the front row, then I drew out local leaves from inside my zipper top and threw them all up to float down and around. Sang a tune as they floated down, described the Tiger Tattoo and brought on the youths: Presenting: The Future of Sale.

After the gig everyone went for a meal. I stayed and tried to help sell comedy road-show merchandisements and getting a free drink from Simon and the chef out the side on the decking where one could smoke. For some reason they made me accept a terribly long boat-shaped corn on the cob dish. The last thing I need is to return with crockery that is actually superior to my own.

Rendezvousing for a night of karaoke that people are dancing to means the rums in my body have something to do. Tanya, who is the comic on right after the interval in our show, is singing. We all dance to her and a couple of young folks are actually snogging. Then Eddy gets up, belts out the unbelievable Frankie Goes To New York New York, if I can make it there et al. . . and has us all cheering with his neatly-inserted local references at the end. He wins the prize that night for greatest-ever performance. If they find out he's a pro and that he hustled them they'll rip out his tongue like they broke Fast Eddie Felson's fingers: "You're goddamned classically trained at the Western Australia School of Music and Drama, you son of a bitch."

Professionally oblivious to the fact that I am already in the compere and headliner, driver and tour-manager's awfully bad books, I try and get everyone back to the venue with Simon the manager's promise of free boozing. Just me then and three other folks, none of thee acts. There's nothing like it: free access to all the wide range of liquors and liqueurs.

Simon pours the Grand Marnier I have been waiting for all my life – half pint of it in a huge brandy flute with much ice – and I test the photographic memory of a woman by telling her Jimeoin's phone number which is all oh sevens and ones.

Back at the motel I am hanging out wandering around at the back of three a.m. and there's voices raised to hear, and wandering around to hear a big troubled discussion in room twelve. Three men are talking upset, talking about someone who has pissed them off. Oh heavens, it's the compere, the headliner and the driver – it's me, it's me they are bitching about. Yes! Stunning, a rare and valuable moment. I can't resist and sit on their wee stoop and have a listen for a while. They seem a bit out of it and agreeing with each other and the mean returning circles and the not very nice nature of it. Thing is, it was fascinating because they were not wrong. You cannot be "wrong" about these things, about how someone is to you. It just gets wobbly when you try and get others to agree. It took all my calm restraint not to just knock on the door as my shirt was already undone and shout "Where's my tenner?" or something equally baffling to them, Then I heard the best thing ever. One of them said:

"He's definitely ill or something. I think he's got Down's Syndrome."

I'm sure he meant Asperger's or Autism or Bi-polarity, or, as the doctors I went surfing with suggested: "Borderline hypo-mania." I really ought to have lightly tapped on the door at that point and gone in gently to work it through with them. Surely it couldn't really have deep down been about me.

A young man comes around the motel balcony so I up and leave, back to my room.

Then I'm in bed with a drink and I hear high heels coming all the way round the concrete balcony, echo-cho-choing down the steps, around the smoother cement of the forecourt round the pool along the ground floor louder and louder with almost every step closer now surely yes to right outside and into my open doorway. It's the woman with the photographic memory . . . She has rememorized my room number too, 4, and in she comes. We drank and laughed a lot. Turns out that the young man who left a wee while ago had been in her room with her and the husband for some very adult voyeur activity which apparently she wasn't into and now with him gone and the husband was asleep she was free to be here.

And I definitely did not swap my newer boots with any of the fantastic worn-in Blundstone workboots left outside rooms like working class invisible entity sentinel sentry boots ready for their internal soul-stink to disperse yet resembling posh hotel shoes waiting for a shine overnight without the slightest worry of anyone actually wanting them and walking off with them or in them.

She left an earring there and I posted it to her later pressed into a bar of soap for safety, together also she could also make a mould of it, if in fact the other one was lost.

Next morning in the van I had to admit to the driver I had been listening at the door, overhearing. He didn't check the rear-view that much anymore on this leg of the drive.

Eddie's prize from the karaoke was a Ned Kelly stubby holder that I have with me now and Tanya gave me a parcel of leaves in wrapping paper, posted to my Medina Grand Serviced-Apartments and forwarded to me by the bearded receptionist who was always friendly.

There was a café on the ground floor through past reception, linked by a door and also just its own place. It was run by a couple, co-owners, and one day he was in the staff toilet locked in, fighting with her and so I banged on the door until he left. Then he loitered outside and phoned in, ordering the other staff not to serve me from across the street. Revenge was a drink served chilled.

A lot of people had been asked to my cocktail party at my serviced apartments since way before me having then been subsequentially asked to leave. There were even invites printed and a recurring image of ping-pong, dancing by the mirrors, smoking over the balcony and bar-work in my mind. Lots of folks asked were not known to me, just met and clicked with. So they couldn't be traced, it couldn't be cancelled. Show must go on, so luckily my friend Tony lent me his flatbed truck to transport Spike Moriarty and his double bass and we used that as the bar and just parked next door to the Medina outside an office block. There was lots of ice and lychees, pink grapefruit juice and lots of vodka. One of the doctors brought a stool. For me. Have your stools moved? There was violin and guitar with bass with the Opp.-Shopped thirty plastic cups and glasses and we had the bench of a bus-stop and tried to look like we were waiting for one. It was absolutely great: seventeen people that I had met meeting each other and a band. No comedians came though even though Stephen K. Amos said he would after the night before when I managed to get him to take a pair of hedge-trimmers off me as if they were a pipe when I passed them to him in that way around the barbecue and he laughed all the way to a choking. Spike's brother was dating Susan Provan, head of the festival, yet he was the one who would eventually have a kid with her called Madeleine.

Then all of a sudden three Police cars came out of nowhere, all sirens wa-wa, and come in driving real fast to park around us at hard diagonals making up half of a star shape. They definitely had our attention. We all looked. It was like magic without the movement of any articles. Their lights now flashing in silence, acting as super disco lights for our party. No Cops got out, then, in an even swifter move they as suddenly just backed up in curves and drove away. It's a whistle. We all hooted and felt that our relaxed vibe had just magicked them away, stood and gazed t'ward the grizzly . . . we were that old Scottish drunk who fell through the ceiling of Waverley Station, fell from bridge height and was so pissed none of his bones got broke. Superbly the story was a mystery till later when it turns out there was a huge boxing match on that night where a fighter of Aboriginal origins had beaten another whiter man without these apparent origins so obvious and so this was causing tension-based amateur fights all over town outside bars without any betting on them to break out. They thought we were one of them and it only took them eleven or twelve seconds to see our bohemian-based infringements were not sufficient to have to be dealt with – not with one big maul two blocks away and anyway look all our glasses were mostly pretend party Martini shapes and plastic toothbrush tumblers, stubby holders and coloured picnic stackables. The only night of the year when we had cover, when our misdemeanor is miniature in comparison – like sticking your tongue out at a passing Policed car, not enough to warrant anything. They came, they saw we were not nearly violent enough, and they left. I'll see your street party and raise you unorganized fighting. Just try having a decent fight and glassing my face with an Opp.-Shop luminous beaker. It was a danger zone, Chief Inspector, there were lychees everywhere, some of my men could have slipped on one . . .

Next day I left Melbourne for the seventh time.

First time first day I was ever in Australia was landing in Canberra. 1992. That show with the toaster had been seen by Joe Dolce who was mates with Robin Williams in New York yet now lived in Australia with Shaddap You Face as his golden albatross. A way more interesting musical man than that, he brought a promoter back with him to see me again and hey, bingo, life-long friend and with him the whole Hunter-Green family. Got off a plane got met by Douglas Hunter and David Bates, went to an extremely liberal B&B with a Rainbow flag flying in the garden and was about to lie down and be sucked onto a seismic tectonic nap-hole, a black molasses pit swim-out-of-time quicksand for the brain, pothole of the abysmal abyss of lag . . . Gotto gotto got to go to, just got to . . . must keep moving, so when Doug and David asked if I would like to go to a gig outside at the National Art Gallery that evening . . . Same as heading for the pillow in Santiago and instead going out for Gin con Gin at the Halloween fancy dress in the hangar by the airport . . . went out.

Taking my head away from the pillow, away from resting it for the beheading by the guillotine, and instead heading out was the best idea, otherwise I would never have met the christian bikers, "God's Squad", who later took me down the really, really Great Ocean Road from

Melbourne down to the Twelve Apostles at Apollo Bay on their motorbikes. When you feel sea-spray on your face and hear it fizzling on the exhaust pipe taking corners in the sun, drooling on the pillow and being jet-lag's bitch seems less enticing.

In Canberra I had one of those fantastic moments of thunder-striking belief: I saw a group called Prick Harness performing and while they were still on, phoned Karen and got them a midnight-show slot at the Gilded Balloon, there and then, letting her hear my belief as much as their act in the outbackground; holding up the receiver like the phone-call Marvin makes to his cousin Chuck in Back To The Future.

They came over, four of them, and were too artistic and too intelligently different to do well at that time and receded back into art-endeavour, except for Mick who is now Mikelangelo with The Black Sea Gentlemen who have stormed the last few years at The Famous Speigeltent in Edinburgh run by David, who had met me off the plane that first morning.

The other moment of spellbinding thunder-strike was when I was in a kebab shop at six o'clock and was not sure which six it was for a while, trying both on and they both feel fine options.

When P. Harness came to do the Edinburgh Festival we all lived in a yellow submarine, I mean a very big flat in the Marchmont. Them four P. Harnesses, me, Brad Oakes and seven drummers and percussionists called Bad Boys Batucada. All from Australia with Brazilian connections; one of them was called Davide Drummonde and it turned out he was of Scottish extraction, hence he was really David Drummond. There were seven of them and they did capoeira and percussion. They drummed all the time. Smoked hash all the time, and drummed. The neighbour came up to complain, he banged on the door to get them to shut up, he had to bang in the spaces in their rhythms in order for them to hear him banging. He had to think. He had to listen to and understand the thing he was against. He started to get into it. They incorporated him into it, and went along with his rhythm, he'd joined the band now.

I'd asked comedian Brad Oakes to come over on a whim and do five minutes at the end of my hour. Like, say, I would do fifty minutes and then say "Well that's enough from me, now for the main act!" and bring him on. He wanted more, wanted to do more, I couldn't have it. He only did five nights. Or four?

At this show my act is doing the stuff about standing on an ironing-board with its legs supporting me in water at just the right height to make it look like I was surfing.

In the end he says he is not happy with just five minutes and is, quite rightly, a bit pissed off when I say we can't work together then. He becomes best friends with Brendan Burns, sleeps in a hall-cupboard, or my bed when I'm out.

When I first met Brendan he was nineteen, the air of a child of privilege, had a girlfriend like a jacket, took to smacking himself in the forehead with the mike and so had an ongoing, unhealed wound.

This was all in April 1992.

Cycled home early in the morning using the Canberra river, like the LA river: a concrete sluice although only twenty feet wide, and I hit some slime-green slidey water foliage and take a massive spill and end up laughing and wet and bruised; laughing my head off alone in the dawn.

Melbourne: well born. The greatest thing that ever happened happened here: One night I did a gig and brought on a wheelie bin and managed to get a German to do foreign puppetry or very big foreign R2D2 or something and I remember the next night there was a real buzz about this guy that does the thing with the bin. Remorselessly, I did the gig that night barefoot and post-coital and wearing a very tight lady's thermal top. Never works – pan-gender underwear and hippy feet. You know how tight those tops are – all that expectation bouncing around and me, far too fey about it. They wanted twenty minutes for the TV and I voluntarily left after about seven when someone spoke gently the dissent everyone felt, and the letting down by the bin guy – is this the bin guy, where's the bin? – dissent that I was kind-of feeling too for myself by not doing very well. There was a let-down and also a coping with the feeling of everyone else's embarrassment that I must surely be feeling these troubled feelings. Now the folks who are worried for your worry have to have an idea of what that is. So they must have experienced it. Often, when you die, it is hardest on others. Harder for them to deal with you for what they imagine you must be going through – "He went on last; he died" – as well as the thing that sometimes I just cannot go for it.

After ten minutes of hiding-lite and hanging out with Munnery who was having a nap I came out and they had pulled tables and chairs to the side for a dance floor. So I start dancing, took to it and started dancing on my own. Now at this point some of the smart folks were letting themselves see a long hustle, a sort of "That was so not-funny and now this here, him dancing all on his own looking at us all and at the ground, indicates maybe he chose to do badly; he has snapped through, like Andy Kaufman as Latka." No it was more like Cool Hand Luke when he was broken.

No, thankfully. Not a hoodwinking or Borat. It was more that I felt just like a member of the crowd there, and now I was dancing. In a way it was hard to sink any lower, except maybe looking at the folks at the bar and trying to motion someone to dance with me. I left the dance floor and walked over and asked a woman to dance and turned out she had a false hip, she whispered to me, and couldn't come dance. I returned and danced a bit more until it was almost going to be too much for everyone and then the best thing ever that could happen happened: Karen "Core Hen" Koren, my agent manager friend, came onto the dance floor and danced with me doing a few of those twirls and shimmies she's famous for. Then we held each other close and we danced that way, spinning around and talking into each other's ears and doing the lenient ballroom. A high percentage of available eyes could well have been on us and celebrated this lifeline tango.

When we had finished, Karen told me that she had slipped and peed herself during one of our opening shimmies. This was great, how amazing, how splendidly, serenly composed of her. All those folks watching, all the eyes. The dampness a growing patch. What a reward. Praise the dark trouser. Life-changing seepage. Residue.

Her fluid moves. Not strictly ballroom.

We have been incredibly close. There was that call today last year where she reminded me of that dance. There was that time we came back from Montreal we were the only ones in business class awake and pissed and still boozing – she had broken two chairs fiddling with the electric buttons and we had been asked to be quiet as we were the only ones witnessing the prolonged sunset and toasting it. The beautiful flat fireball of a sunset sky we were flying into making it last and last a bit longer. With those miniatures we felt large.

Mid '93.

Once sitting down on a plane to Hong Kong eighteen hours down the line right next to a woman five years older than me, we didn't have it. Right from the off, straight off the bat, we couldn't even begin to click. The feramoans bounced and repelled in this synthetic environment among this recycled air.

My usual way is to greet and make immediate contact on plane on bus en train and get at ease so the best long-haul conversation can happen or we can at least be at ease to not-chat . . . Shit being followed by the anti-humane black cloud of disenchantment, of fearful silence of sociality's demise . . . Aiee!

We buzzed with the so-not-happening of it all, touching elbows here and there and then we both took out books to get away into them, to not to have to talk for a bit then leave seventeen hours of sitting there, continuing or not, failing at thirty-five thousand feet, the opposite of the mile high club, nowhere to go to, nowhere to run to. In it together and the pan-global squirming that might be felt. We both took out books to avoid this, to avoid the having to relate. We both took out books that were meant to be roads heading away from each other. Separate directions, like Lurie and Waits at the end of Down By Law and we took them out and, by Fuck, we're reading the same book. Jesus with an extra E, then, that flew over us as now surely an obvious thing to be talking about yet it would only have served to heighten the fact that we had not-talked already. Plus, I didn't want to talk about bloody White Swans. That book was a duck to me, I could not love it, one of some big classics I tried and yet couldn't. Really. I have just reread one book over in the last twelve years: Infinite Jest by Foster Wallace – White Bloody Swans was the one I had at A&E that time I did my ankle in, doing a comedy fall during warm up for a Harry Hill pilot and went off on my own and they paid me only half because they thought I skived off and only Vyvian Claw believed me. And here I was with it at altitude; I daren't look and see where she is . . . What if we're on the same page and, and, and what if there's a love scene?

As humans our attempts to be separate seem daft. Here, up in the sky, enclosed and so close and random and free, we inhabited a solitary intimate apartness, though true distance was impossible.

After dinner the sky-staff came with a tray of brandies which never appeal to me, except now, and my lady took one too. Was it solidarity of the worst kind? Both doing things you imagine the other wants, both betraying oneself and the other's chance of real love. She drank it after her meal's wines then snoozed and woke up white and needing to hurl so just climbed over me desperately so at one point though we had not talked she was straddling me swiftly with no beforeplay. She went to the bog real fast to throw up and somehow she lost her contacts into the mess of vomit because the steward talked about it in a full Australian voice as he was helping her. Suppose she found them by looking out for tiny bits of magnified carrot.

We could not even talk now and at least that was obvious. Thing was, it was all too intimate and humans on planes, near each other, have to suppress a whole lot, just to keep back from an orgy of mania/where does one stop?

Injuries hardly ever involve blood on the stage. Mostly it has been sprains and bangs and scrapes to the hips, knees, shins, elbows, nose, forehead and top of skull. Once my big left toe got over-extensive onstage at the Old Atheneum in Glasgow the night I had two French friends of my brother staying and it was only after the jodhpurs came out that their casual racism became a lot better-dressed and rather smart actually and seriously rightly-winged. That toe has never been the same. Then it got fixed by an operation at Eastbourne Hosp., where I went under anaesthetic, stayed the night then left with a limp, coming down of strong drugs with a wee bracelet on my wrist – it was like it was the first festival of the summer.

Serious injury was luckily fully avoided that time in Australia the morning I was on the Michael Parkinson show and I had been at the cocktails till dawn and there, on the road by us, a very long flatbed truck moves away from the lights and I dive onto it and am rolling off the back like a log. The driver sees and hydraulic-brakes and I roll back up the other way. He is there and angry at me for how I could have bloody hurt myself. I thought he was about to undermine his concern by hurting me.

Then there was that guy twisting my thumb at that gig in Edinburgh, or the time I choked on a miniature harmonica that Larry Adler gave me that time he banged his car into ours . . .

July 2001.
No, occasionally there will be blood. The time there was most blood I went to A&E in Dublin for the injection right into the hand wound and the stitches. Blessedly I was behind a nun in the queue and filled with enthusiasm for speculation: What was she in for? Religious scuffle, bad knees from praying, genuflection chest wound? Holy smoking? Recently I saw a black nun on the internet in Glasgow airport. I was again very enthusiastic with wonder and tried to look over her shoulder at what she was up to. This was too good a moment to miss, like an albino unicorn fight-type moment. Bravely the screen's natural-angled shimmer hid her site.

Whereas the other night I was able to keep up with and read a woman's erotic novel on her Kindle, over her shoulder on the Overground. Pacey and racy it was and she looked about as it got steamier and she had it on big, big font so she was "turning pages" at a heady rate of knots and it was as thrilling as a sexy teleprompter, a stonkingly erotic romper-prompter.

My holy wound stigmatter was from the drive cog on a ruined wheel-less, stripped and abused bike I had brought onto the stage from the streets of Dublin where so many are being jumped on and bent by blarny boy-boozers on benders and then discovered, come back to a ruined, broken thing and then exiled and unloved and abandoned for rral, never taken home by folks who don't want them no more – damaged goods; unmovable now, unworkable, lifeless frames. A thing so strongly felt it's like the birth of a metaphor; these now so easy to leave that they are a thing other things are like. Yet not to me, I would find it hard to leave mine, would take it out of its chains, embrace it and restore it . . . – so, this one I rode it pissed and wheel-less down the steps off the front of the stage to give it one last lease of life. It didn't go well and as it banged its undercarriage main drive shaft directly on the top step's very edge's rim tripping us up. The leg's inside calf had nowhere to go to and so made like a gammon hough joint up against a mad rotary deli slicer with teeth that used to drive the chain. To be tied up and then attacked. To tie up. Gratefully, gratified that the bikes that I am on for a while, are not tied . . . Ee-oo. Sliced calf meat. It got blood on it the crank. Dark blood on the oil. Oil is thicker than blood. Blood is thicker than water and booze is the most viscose fluid of them all. This gig was a stunner of badness. I thought it was just me and they got support and I had to wait and watch the competent yet diametrically different I. Coppinger do fairly very well and set the mindset of comedy before I was starting . . . The worse the gig the more one can be willing to indure. Or immunity can be manifested. There is a cerebral haze that comes onstage. The stammer leaves. There are jokes I have had for years and meant to use and never did.

Wow, in August 1996 I did the biggest ever gig for me: fifteen hundred and three folks came to see me. Huge gigg, me on the poster, yet in the end it was just me compeering badly for four mates who agreed to do it with me.

Others are also at risk: I nearly killed Rich Hall as he lay flat like a flat star on a low piano-moving trolley and I span him near the edge of the Playhouse Theatre's high stage above the deep orchestra pit.

May have come close to death in Dublin once: Last thing I remember is drinking Jameson's onstage at about eleven thirty; finished at midnight oh five. Apparently the show I did was three hours and five minutes long, many people had left before I was dragged off by the considerate Eddie and Flee . . . My last memory of stuff said was twenty-nine minutes before the end.

So, I had blacked out during a show in front of 426 at the Vicar Street venue for all that time, lost that time and also I lost the same pair of trousers twice that night before waking up the next morning with a guitar broken from drops on the road and a feeling of amputation of life from the lost events. Who was the me doing all that stuff? The underling, the one who came from pure excess . . . Since those four years where I had blackouts, I have simply drunk less as a form of maturing.

If you wait long enough you will feel the booze, if you rush it your body can't take it. Like marijuana too – one ought to get a bit stoned and then let it be.

The trousers I lost were jeans worn over the top of performance trousers which were light grey linen.

I remember wearing wool flares and them being way-too-hot performing in the Nightclub venue in the Gilded Balloon. among the sweatiest of venues, where the slow dark ring of sweat's tidemark moves out and down evenly, in time a perfect semi-circle from the groin source.

At that show in my front row was Penny Arcade, the American performance artist. Her big show was called Bitch Dyke Fag-Hag Whore after the various names she had been called at one time or another. At the end she takes all her clothes off, turns all the lights down and walks among us round the auditorium. You can hear her approaching and want her to come your way, and eyes adjusting to find her. She wraps herself in an American flag, has the lights come up slowly and puts music on inviting everyone up onstage to dance. She says this amazing thing: "If you want to come up and dance, come up . . . If you don't wanna come up, don't come up . . . If you want to come up and don't, well folks that's what we're are on about."

I went up with my friend Tess and very-efficiently missed the foot-high stage with the front of my foot in the lights and scraped the very front of the skin away to the bone on the right leg's favourite shin. Dare not look; can feel the odd coldness of the warm sticky liquid's slow path inside the denim there, and then the sharp tightness around the sparkly congealing, and the haunting pain of just the cloth touching when the endorphins begin subsiding.

This pain was far greater than the slight bone strain of being held down by a Policeman with his knee on your back and handcuffs being applied.

Way more sore than bending a toe right back, getting a heal scraped, falling off bikes onto knuckle, splinters around the hip bone, breaking the scaphoid wrist bone, that tiny, unhitched navicular, boat shaped bone in the treasured wrist, the one that stays there as a pain, can never heal as it has no blood supply, that Betsy texted me to put the frozen peas on and Casey Stoner spent fifty thousand Australian dollars to not fix, playing charity football with Buddhists or popping both little toes out of their sockets, . . . way way more than the shoot from ankle twists that contain too much disappointment in that moment or breaking the big toe nail on the top step in Birkenstocks or the hernia from singing too much, the needle at the tattooings. One small toe came out when I was chasing Felix round a field in Suffolk and fast enough to stay up with him and chave my hand an inch or so from his back and make him laugh as he looks back angling his run, and my feet are close to his and pang out it clips his hard heel and is niced straight out to the side at right angles. In nature . . . a right angle . . . aiee . . . and I realize it has to be straightened up quickly before . . . before . . . and so sitting in the grass I grip and yank it and only a bit not enough and have to do it again this time for real and the eleven lane surge of knowing you're going and this time it cranked back in line. Oof, there's a run of nausea definitely at the release, it appears, of endorphins to cover the sever sharpness of pain anda total whitey almost pale blue against the gree. Actually it can't be that bed . . . seriously in comparison, and it's mad to live with comparisons for they will never and you can always find a further one to take you in the direction required, seriously it can't be that bad, so rising up I challenge Felix to run the swinging obstacle course over chain bridge, fixed beam and ladder runs and may well have won that race, got the colour in the cheeks.

Sitting here today I have a new scrape on that shin from trying to jump the wee wall near a war memorial in our village on a bike. It aches extra with the echo of the older wounded wound.

Mind you right now 17.01.13, 11:16 a.m., John Coltrane is on the high fidelity system, Live at Birdland on Impulse, 1964. At the time I first went to Australia listening to this album this is when I really got into John Coltrane, the absolute zenith, acme, pinnacle of musical possibility. Over and over and over I listened to this and other Coltrane albums and they are such good value, ideal Desert Island choice; they can never really be learnt, they are like watching fire and ocean, too much to hold and know yet reception is a form of processed understanding; they're too much in the good phrase, just too too much, too much proliferation and I am definitely a pro-liferator fan.

The other week I actually went to Ronnie Scott's jazz joint and hung outside in just a shirt and smoking the electric fag and mingling with the interval crowd from Ravi Coltrane and then just waltzed in, well six-eighted without a ticket and passed all the three levels of possible checks and into the room where leaning so very conspicuously, like a sore thumbs-up, like a pin number written on a wall, so obvious that I'm overlooked at the end of the bar I am seriously the only person in the whole room standing; everyone else in the whole room is seated at tables down the front or the glorious tiered bench booths . . . even the seven high stools at the bar are booked on t'innernet. Twenty-five quid in my pocket in case there was a ticket to buy. Now that money is spare so there's two massive Dalwhinnie malts and a portion of top-end fries for me eventually at a table. Fully undercover in full view, and buying. Next to me comes in late a definite mover and shaker from the world of music, don't know who he is, yet he sits down and starts reading a book. SuperCool shit, Iceberg Slim chilled guy letting the spiralling wonders of modal activity and coruscant showerstorms of notes be a backdrop to reading . . . waves and wavelengths of diaphanous tone holding, in the words of musician Simon Shannon – a meaning far greater in melody than in words. Sorry Slim.

Perhaps it's his newly discovered grandmother's memoir and he just can't put it down. More probably he is just able to best enjoy this untouchable shattering splendiferous, molten, sparkling, cascading deluge of sounds whilst doing something else . . . David Byrne said he wrote many Talking Heads songs writing them down while driving; keeping the right-hand side of his brain busy. Sorry Slim.

February 2002. The Police are very touched.

Me and street performer, musician and favourite friend of mine, David McSavage, were walking home from a gig in Dublin both with guitars and saw a car sitting by the road late at night with its engine running. David looked inside, closed the door and an off-duty Gardee came over and made a big deal about it being illegal – what David just did.

We had just giggles, we had been drinking, we were not too worried about the legality of something we had not really considered a crime. The guy was right in David's face. "Get out of my face," he kept saying. I stepped in between them: "Look, now he is out of your face. I am in your face."

It was only then he told up he was undercover. He threatened to arrest us. I ran at him with my guitar unsheathed raised like a baseball bat and said, "I am going to fucking smash your face in." He only winced as I approached and, getting close, I said, "See this is what we could have been like, because you are ootay-order, man." When I turned away he came for me and I resisted. It is harder than Wilde said it was to resist the temptation to resist resisting arrest. I tried to turn from his grasp and he implemented training techniques that I was not emotionally prepared for hugely. It was just moments until the sirens were visible. All the while David is asking them what on earth they're doing and telling them I am a comedian, for Christ's sake!

My hands are handcuffed behind my back, which feels a little daft so as soon as I am in the van I stand up and slip my legs through so they are around the front. Just as well because these guys drive fast like they are trying to shift snow from the back, or trying to make a prisoner fall about. At the station you help them fill in a form. I remember distinctly having to describe my tattoo which was just the letters "p h o n e j e l l y" on my left shoulder to remind me to call Angelica my goddaughter. Didn't really feel like a real prisoner. He asked me the colour of my eyes and as he looked up from the form I closed them and said, "An Astonishing Blue."

In a cell that was very hot and bright to make you uncomfortable, fall asleep, be pacified and wake up dehydrated and full of remorse, I chose to stand with my back close to the door and not go in, took my shirt off – tattoos out in prison at last – and stared at the tiles. Every now and then they would call at me from behind through a wee hatch in the door to sit down now and once the door opened and someone said it again and flicked a lit cigarette butt in on the wing of an expletive. All very exciting. All the while my man David is campaigning for my release. The Glasgow One. He moans at them for two hours until the duty officer can't take it any more and they let me out. Plus we still had the fact that David's Dad was in government and used to be the Minister for Justice as perhaps the largest ace ever up a sleeve unused.

The tattoos I have had done since are of fairies. My daughter Coco did a fantastic drawing of fairies at fairy school, all huddled together in a big cluster with overlapping wings and arms and legs, with one colourful fairy flying in late, her legs all bendy in the wind. The parlour made it into a laminate to press on the exact personal font and copy it from that and it is up on my shoulder forever.

In what little autobiography I've read it always amazes me how little space can be given over to friends' children and all other loving relationships. The ones that provide the reasons and support and foundation for the activities and happenstance, eventhood and journeys that fill the pages; that fill the life. That provide not just support for the activity and also the reason for them and the home to return too. They need their own personal book.

It's possible to oddly berate your situation and blame it on others and the world or you can happily describe the wonders and in the doing thereby thank everyone.

There is no such thing as luck or good fortune. They are phrases.

And serenity, tranquility, confusion, chaos are words.

The things and states in the universe which they are trying to relate to are also products of your own consciousness.

The meaning of life is to be conscious. Awake and responsive to stimuli and then attaching importance and through to an awareness of issues relating to this . . .

The words are a pack of hounds and all the things we just know everybody agrees on are expressed in words which really no one can ever truly agree on. Is hooray a word? Woohoo . . . ? Oi . . . ? They are certainly meaningful sounds.

Of course consciousness is still only a word and it also means the Set of opinions or feelings of a group. It seems to bring together the chicken and the egg: so, The word trys to says it is both the name for the state of being and the part of the mind that gets this.

How do you like them apples? With my conscious mind's awareness of stimuli. Broom-chee.

Consequently it is only our view and getting others to agree with it is mad. Hence religious war and difficult divorces and Terence Stamp's memory of sharing a flat with Michael Caine is apparently rather different from Michael Caine's memory of sharing a flat with Terence Stamp.

Or that which is expressed we assume is all the memory. Or the thing expressed is truly believed . . .

Shit here we go again. It can always end up here like by the sink in the kitchen at a party. The thing is that which we think it is. What else can it be, if no one else holds it for us except us?

Having the view that your view is only one view has got to be great . . . that all the cultures and practices of the people's of the world are just that a list of all the things they do rather than a list of also rans which are eliminated in the shadow of The Right One . . . The True Way. Do the Pentecostal guys really see the Latterday Saint guys as being way off and they way on?? Apparently they are saying that. Can they believe it? They can't.

If we affect the thing we watch then we are the thing – is a way to view it.

Who wants a drink?

Shoplifting Chapter

I usually put a scarf on these days when I hoover as it makes you get much hotter and so you tend to do it swifter and for not so long and when you're done the dwelling feels warmer too. And the dwelling in it: eccentric central heating. Yesterday there was a juicer out at the recycling bins and in our kitchen its motor seemed to work well. Then Felix my boy when he was 6 years point 3 told me he knew where we could get lots of apples. On his school-walk the boys found them. We went there and a tree had been blown down and all the fruits were all around on the ground as well as still on the branches and so we picked 'em like we was Giants . . . aarrr . . . look I can reach the top of this tree . . . Fee fi Felix bum. We filled our pockets and made pouches from jumpers and went back to the car. I was changing gear and talked out loud to myself in a humorous twist on downbeat, an inversion of subversion, a return to honesty. "How do you like them apples?" I spoke. Felix heard and, his ears virginal to North American-set sarcasm, phrasing and general human struth saying of opposites, replied before it had almost finished as a phrase, "They are great."

Really no reason for him to try and work anything out about how.

We spend time a lot together. Spend it like there's no tomorrow. Mostly from six to ten years old he was on the back of my bike standing on the trap with his hands on me shoulders, chatting. One time out of the blue he goes, ". . . my three favourite flowers are daffodils, orchids and thistles . . ." Couldn't be more proud, he had practicality, beauty fantasy and the natural heathery heritage that gets fashioned and polished to patriotism.

Sometimes folks are bamboozled by straightahead words, they kind of look like they are expecting to be not straightahead. As a comedian people can often think you are joking and often you are. They trust you quicker and it is much easier to borrow tenners from TV weathermen in bars and Scottish actors at railway stations and un-strangers this way.

It is easy to rectify the misinterpret-thing by repeating again.

Sometimes it doesn't work. I did the Laughter Lounge one Christmas where the bouncer warned me, after the first night, not to leave the stage and showed me a knife he carried as proof of how he felt the crowds were dangerous. I am always suspicious of a venue with a name that tries to ensure mirth, especially one with armed bouncers and large block-bookings from corporate mailing-lists.

Thankfully I could not give my best, could not play poker with the other male comedians and was released from having to perform on the last night. This meant that when I played another lounge of laughter down the south of Eire they had thoughts about me, were grumpy, didn't believe I was hurrying up another comedian because he was so late that I was about to have to go on and cover for him for an indefinite amount of time – floods and geographics. I think it was the way I was too calm, the venue man didn't believe me. This led me to be staying on at the end of my bit until the huge sponsorship banner pendulum came to hang completely still. It had become a symbol of symbolism and hanging there above it moved like a sharpened guilty guillotine pendulum severing my integral ability.

Onstage things are different, the adrenaline can numb feelings like in hooligan-activity and battle, and it numbs a bit of your conscience and morality can bend like a candle in a sauna: still all there, just liable to be in unusual shapes that will stay that way if taken out of the heat.

Some metaphors you want to stick with: Tried building a sauna once out of old telegraph poles with a surgeon and an architect, didn't finish it, built a bender out of tarp and branches once by South China freshwater lake in Maine with hot stones from the fire and that was the hottest sauna-heat I have ever experienced apart from the one in municipal leisure-centre in Elgin with all the bloody full-view glass that the kids had turned right up beyond the legal maximum. Course we had the sauna at my house when I was young and the pool and the foreign experts would roll in the snow after it then jump in the pool and give the body a trip round the world in under a minute. There was only one heart attack, as I remember, because of this. The Scandinavians, Finns and Russians use them to wash and there is always a beautiful community to sitting around nude and sweaty without any exertion to bring you closer to those you already know. I feel that now, where I used to live in Findhorn, because there were regularly three saunas a week available with cool dark still plunge pool. All Millennial Eve was spent up north in the sauna that Mr Webster, the innovative reconstructive consultant surgeon, built (after the poles were laid to rest) with all the artists: Perriton s, Deller j, Kane a, Wilkes j, Ogg k, Main d, Barclay c, Webster e, Starling s . . .

Sometimes it seems artists are just in search of a medium to be marvellous as humans through, that they believe in being amazing and communal and kind and immortally optimistic and faith-filled in themselves and are perfectly willing to exhibit these positive essentials willing to show and share this through their medium of work. This is the crossroads too; the best and the worst, for they can often be resistant to simple direct expression of this. Hang on though, they'll all have children and then it can really kick in: a true purpose other than tentative wish to exhibit a wish to inspire. Their work invigorates in others the way to be thus inspired of community? Mustn't it? Like they are a solo martyr to this urge that is visibly reborn by their next pieces.

This is why it is hard to pull off sometimes, stand-up or monologue, storytelling or troubadour tomfoolery; because there is just me and no make-up or outfit and the lights upon me are lower and the house lights are up and the medium is muslin-thin. The psychic-strong crowd get this and it is intolerable sometimes. Barracking and heckling have to happen. Even the last gig I have just done in London, last-on the Sunday evening at Up The Creek, I just used the energy in the room to sustain a thing and about six jokes and ended up getting the band to re-form next to the stage and do a couple of jazzy stripteases to build to a never-seen-before humorous, erotic climax. Even this was not enough for some folks who, amid the wildness called out "Say something funny!" Can't really argue with that for, in all its simplicity, it says what it wants to say: "Tell me things that are funny in a way I already know for at the moment you are doing things that are not sufficiently known to me to have a reaction to."

In some meantime reality I am still onstage in Ireland beneath the swinging symbol naming the club as a place of laughter with its sponsor's logo.

Like me turning slowly like the hand of a watery timepiece in the motel pool, the world exerted its power on the thing which was big enough to be affected, like a true Foucault's pendulum I turned, and it was a while after a p.m. hour in time that the pendulum show was meant to end, that it had ended and this meant paying staff overtime immediately, not over time. So now the manager had a concrete reason to dislike me. Thank goodness, for now he doesn't need to be a flustered, troubled tense guy for an invented reason. Shame really, he was doing well enough without one. If folks are upset at you and there is really nothing bad you have done then technically they will find a way to be against your goodness.

*

Okay listen to this one:

After all the years of shopping in Safeway on Byres Road I finally get caught shoplifting. I had introduced a very personal loyalty scheme a number of years ago whereby every now and then I get something for free as a reward without any registration. Much the same as this new Nectar points system though without the supermarket learning my patterns.

I go into Morrisons; although it was Somerfield the month before and Safeway just before that – Some-Morph-Field-Ways I call it. Obviously market pressure on this ideal spot has meant a battle of rivals over this store. Means, though, that the uniforms have been three different colours and surely some kids must be excited by this subliminally or just fascinated that the adults change their outfits so much.

I go in with a crumpled old fiver I got from a bag of fivers, payment from my mate Darrell who runs Just The Tonic in Nottingham. On the last-ever night of his club at the Old Vic in Notts, he ends up onstage with Daniel Kitson and Johnny Vegas, all in their pants and they pull down a chandelier causing a power-cut, whereupon the gig ends and most of his equipment is liberated by the crowd who are now nearly rioting-lite in the murky post-mirth coital dimness. Technically: a looting mob.

With this fiver I pick up, without a basket, a long baguette, a round tomato and a triangular English brie. The three primary shapes. At the checkout I hand over the money and the young woman scans and then hands the fiver back saying it is too old, out of date, not for use in circulation today. At that point I am holding the money and the beeped, barcode-red goods. At that point I feel a victory for the consumer, for the shopper, I feel an understanding through humour, I feel this is a representation of the Loyalty-Smoyalty the superstore owners can have to us, the not-so-humble billions. She says I will have to put the goods back and I admit I do nod. Yes, I would have to put the goods back to remain legal. They were not picked up, your honour, with malice; all I did not do, was replace them, milud. All I did was walk from a store I had bought from for seventeen Christmases with goods that I had handed over money for. As I left the store I saw the head of security and I walked around him three times pretending to make a call on my mobile phone, hid right under his nose, he was actually leaning a bit to look around me to keep an eye out for less-deft thefts. I was timber falling towards him in the woods he could not see for the trees. Walking out over the legal threshold I had my eyes closed and was waiting for the hand on the shoulder for leaving the premises.

Only just outside the store I sat down in the bright Saturday sun on the front step figuring either they are on to me or they aren't. Opened the baguette, chopped the tomato by hand and spread most of the brie in there too. I was eating the first bite when I heard fast footsteps and heavy breathing. I looked up and the head of security was next to me. He looked down and did a diagonal double-take, one of the first in this region, so I start to chew a bit faster.

"I have reason to believe those goods are unpaid for," he pronounced well.

"Oh yes, I have taken these things."

"No. Excuse me. I have been informed that you did not pay for these items."

"Yes, I have stolen these items," I countered.

He insists on holding the hot sandwich and escorts me back into the store. I am not sure if I want to go, so I sort of stand still just past the newspaper section with headlines I am not in.

He says come through the back because he is going to call the Police and it is going to get embarrassing. I say that I am actually quite proud of this theft-borne-out-of-circumstance and it is okay. Some taller strong shelf-stacking employees are summoned to come and stand by us. I ran over things with them then the two Policemen arrive and we go over it again; this time backstage in a wee interrogation room as they can have more authority.

When it becomes clear that I had tried to pay and the Policemen happened to know I lived in the West End near this store for all these years, he looked puzzled: "But why did you do it Phil?" he kept repeating, "It was only one pound seventy-two."

I told him I tried to pay, I handed him the fiver and they kept it as evidence. I said that now that you have my money what are the chances that I can have the sandwich back? One of the young employees was holding it at the time. The manager of the store was there and he had admitted he was a bit pissed off with me because of my attitude and he said that, although he could have refrained from calling the Police, he chose not to because of my way. He was a bit pissed off at the Police when they said they were not going to hand it on to the Procurator Fiscal and warned me against not going to exchange my fivers in future before consuming the goods. Again I asked if I could have the sandwich and the Police said it was evidence in a crime. I can understand bullets in the wall at homicides, we can't dig them out the wall and keep as a

souvenir – the sandwich though and I have already been acquitted . . .
"Please" I say, they decline . . . I ask them then if they want the bits that
are still in my mouth stuck between the teeth.

Then, one last try: "As a comedian my crowd often needs a decent
punch-line or a big finish or something. Please, you could give me the
sandwich back. You've already got the fiver. Think of the crowd, some
of them have spent hard-earned money to be there. Consider their
feelings." And I made a lunge, a laughter-lunge, at the sandwich, like
Hannibal, with my teeth. The Policeman holding the sandwich
involuntarily pulls sharply away Exhibit A, the said sandwich, away
from me with some force and a bit of tomato flies oot and sticks on the
wall and then proceeds to slowly work its way down the wall with all
eyes on it. For a while as it slid it was the only thing moving in the room
apart from hearts, it seemed.

Thank you, Orrificer.

Me and the Cops walk out of the store together and luckily my bike
is still there unlocked and waiting. Perhaps all the Police activity helped
keep it safe. I waved goodbye and then picked up my bike and cycled
away with them staring after me. I wait for the hand on the shoulder
and it, delightfully, is inappropriate here and absent.

January 2006.

Saw my bike getting nicked twice in ten minutes. In a café talking by
the big window with a friend and the precious outside on a busy street
where the accidental thief might come across it unlocked though not
unloved. So there is half my eye on it and then, during the minestrone,
there are the odd movements that inexperienced, not very good,
impulsive thieves do around a bike they are about to make off with: the
hesitancy, the looking around, the never-can-be-sure hover. Drawing
attention like water from the well. Then the hand is upon the saddle
approaching the nine-tenths that means possession. The door is a
"pull" and I am at it in just a few seconds and, marvellously, the only
security system I have, kicks in. Instead of a lock I left the bike in
twenty-first gear so that the kid is up out of the saddle in an effort to
get a little speed going in order to change down. First moment on the
bike trying to work the gears, you don't want to be investigating the
facilities of the stolen bike at this point in your guardianship. Up
behind him within a few seconds I place a hand on the saddle like the
coach at the start of the cat and mouse velodrome keirin, and the kid
performs a classy dismount. Out of my mouth come the words "go, go,
go, go!" – four times, like I definitely want him to be off out of here

rather than stay and possibly challenge me. Certainly I am very happy to retain custody of this bicycle and have no need for him to be punished or know I want him punished, although it wouyld be fumy to chase after him on the prize he failed to win . . . catch him up, ride next to him . . . ". . . here's what you could have won . . ."

Changing the gears back down I place it this time against the lamp-post secured by the advertising-board for the café, go in, sit down with the whole café applauding and barely has my breath and heart returned to a regular rate, honestly guys it was nothing, cheers, thanks, when I see yet another Reebok-clad suitor loitering with the same intent. This time I don't have to check the door to see if it is a "pull" or a "push" and am out standing in the threshold by the time he is just uprighting her from the leaning.

"That bike's with me!" I call out, with little need for anything save the truth.

Him neither. After a pause he said, "But it's no locked." He says it with a mournful tone, like he had to take it, was fated to steal it, how could he walk by it? Like how he could no take it? It would be a crime not to. There was also this helplessness in his voice – What am I supposed to do, just walk by, ignore it? What do you want from me?

Now I think this was a fabulous response, rather like a chess move acknowledging my position yet still offering solid truth. He's right: it is not locked. Splendidly, I think I've done enough and was able to go back into the café at this point and me and the whole café can watch him reposition the Puch bike back with the lamp-post.

Bikes don't really have owners. They surely have people who they are under more than others at this point. They are between your legs now and they will be between some other legs later.

May 2005.

I have a tandem that I often rode with a kid on the back or a mum and a kid and, a couple times, five people on it. Mostly just one person though. Then there were the times I went to pick someone up and they were surprised. Once it got nicked and then just left in a back garden of Glasgow tenement. In a bike shop nearby I happened to ask about it and they produced a wee note and said, "Maybe this has is to do with that?"

"Tandem Abandoned" it said with a phone number. I phoned and strolled round picked it up. You can't really ride a tandem around in very broad widescreen daylight and expect not to be noticed. I often got looks at me when I rode it of "Where's the other person?" I would eyebrow back the response that "You don't have to have someone on the back of your tandem." Many cars are travelling around with spare seats and we don't ask this question of them; really, it is the exciting nature of the possibility compared to normal bikes that you are pointing out in this fashion.

Like the brightly-painted Hippy Van parked by the road. Some say "It's too bright", some just say "Wow", some say they could paint it better. All are just saying it is brightly-painted.

On this tandem I rode one day to the service station. I had a rendezvous with an unknown person. Let me elaborate:

The day before I had been driving my daughter Coco to a birthday party off Shawlands Road in the South Side of Glasgow. I put her in the front and the bag on the wall and the boy in the back and the bag stayed on the wall and we drove off.

In the bag were my laptop and some wires.

Over halfway to the party I realized with the sound in my head of stallions being sucked into a jet engine that it was still there on the low wall: abandoned and very vulnerable.

I made a choice to go for the best of the best: drop Coco on time at the party and head back to find the green bag. Then I became one of those parents who just drop their kids at a party without staying and who don't want to: I practically didn't stop, zooming by drive-by style, she jumps out of the van's sliding door and me and the boy are on our way back.

Playing Bob Dylan very loud, driving back in the VW camper, who is listing the many uncompromising reasons why he almost certainly will not be going to work on Maggie's Farm ever again and I am über-ranting over the top of its full volume, my own personal thing about either it is there or it's not and my fear doesn't make any difference to the matter, the particles that make it up, and that simply heading back fairly briskly is the best thing to do. Pulling into the street there is the large absence of a green back on the low wall. Bag, wires, laptop: gone.

All I can feel is, again, the possibility of the best happening. I stay excited: win it back, get back to the party. Avoid a mad rage now, as it might be still-there. When I lose my keys I keep the eyes open, the eyebrows up.

The boy is asleep, all is peaceful. I have balloons that were never remembered to be dropped with the girl in the drive-by drop-off. I put up some posters with balloons that said: "A Loss. Oh, I would love to see that Green Bag again – Phil 07866453486." Why not involve aesthetics in recovery? No reason. People would read these and definitely see the message, perhaps more than one that just started another way – the note is definitely for the people who have found the bag – I do not care that it might be oddly or surreally perplexing to those who have not found the bag –

All those "LOST" posters one doesn't read if one hasn't recently found anything. So the balloons feel like the obvious answer – all those cats photographed when they never thought that they would one day be lost . . . May as well photograph your cat really well in advance on the odd chance.

I try all the buzzers at the front doors on the street two by two, leaving a not-a-big enough gap between each ring for someone to get out of bed and come to answer. It don't matter. I ring them all and just wait and say, "It's about the green bag I lost from that wall over there."

No bag comes from this and so a whim gets followed that night, suggested by my friend Pum, who says, "Call the radio station. Open it out, go chasing it, like Keanu jumping after Swayze out the plane." Amazingly enough they give a shit and it's out on the local FM shows and the net is tightening.

Can you believe it? That day I was getting my photo taken for the Glasgow Herald to publicise a show and told the interviewer about the laptop when I got the call.

". . . Aye, it's about the laptop. There was a man trying to sell it in the park last night . . . how much is it worth?" A reward enquiry, a loyalty-scheme update: UnFairMiles.

Now was not the time to question her story, cross-examine her and find a chink in her muslin armour of truth . . . She seems to be asking what its physical worth is rather than edging into ethereal fuzzy world of what it is worth to me, the writing, the sentimentality, a number on nostalghia. Id est, the bid test: "What will you pay for it?" A wise choice for me, just to get to getting it back.

She continues to evince her will for the bid to be accepted and granted there may be things beyond worth that are beloved and craved for and can never be got back if it is lost and yet we don't go there. At this time there was the messy fifty thousand words of an enormous novelette about optimism as the new realism.

"I would love to see it again and can meet you with a hundred quid cash."

Pause. Receiver covered by noisy hand for business conference. "Aye, whereabouts?"

"The big Shell garage here at Shawlands Road, near where the laptop was lost, I mean near the park where it was found, the petrol station on the next street. Five o'clock."

"How will I recognize you?"

I'm sure that's my line. I'll be the one wandering around saying have you got my laptop I think.

"I'm wearing all blue and I'll be peeling an orange." Just comes to me because I know it is a shop and has fruit; it just popped up and out and was accepted. Also too, plus petrol, plus oranges are napalm, and it just bubbles out; was wearing blue already. What I could have said, that might have nailed it like Jesus, was that I would be riding a tandem. Any number of folks likes fruit and denim yet how few would have the look of laptop-hope and be on a tandem? What a Venn-overlap, what a laptopia, this land of the overloop.

So, a few hours later and here I am, there I go, am approaching what will massively be all our most unusual handover for quite a while, or ever, or only one ever.

On the phone my man Zac, who lives nearby, hears the full story deal and when I ask him to come with a camera just to get some fabulous undercover shots that will never be used in reverse extortion, he is all into it.

Wildly, as I approach the forecourt of intrigue, I see Zac milling about all dressed in blue – what's he doing? And he's trying to signal me about something. He's carrying some orange juice, I kid you not. He is the worst undercoverer slash handover photographer I've ever used. Have to ignore him and inside the shop, after a quick scan I see there are no oranges – that is what he was doing, trying to warn me. Zac had tried to warn me so I wasn't Pacino coming out of that toilet with my dick in my hands.

Crumbs, ignoring him professionally and going in to see no oranges – gots to think fast . . . is it a risk to just hold a lemon . . . they're too hard to peel . . . it's yellow they'll tell . . . ? Maybe I could peel a tangerine and put the orange peel over the lemon, like a surrogate pelt to wean a kid back in. To fool a theft ring? They are a bit tricky, I might have to bite into it and then my face wincing might make them nervous . . . what about covering an apple in peel . . . could at least bite into it as I mime the peel.?

Ther's a small bag of tangerines that'll do and I come out of the electric door and quite clearly mill around a-peeling and looking expectant as a middle-aged lady in a filthy fleece comes towards me.

"Is that guy with the camera with you . . . ?"

"No (yes)."

We sit down on a low fence that neither denies entry nor exit, simply indicates the perimeter of the forecourt, the extent of the property. The laptop sat back in my lap and I pop eighty quid into hers. Off she popped and I went over to Zac to fire him from these secret services.

After that I was cycling up the road with the bag over my shoulder peeling a second tangerine and I nearly lost control of the tandem without hands and veered towards a group of folks by the phone box. It was them! The lap-nappers and, for a minute as I swerved towards them and they were trying to divide eighty between three, they all looked at me, frozen with the shame of deserved revenge; then I gathered the handlebars, tipped a non-existent hat and carried on up the road.

I had three crashes on the same bike. The first one was in the park over a ribbon of cobbles that laced the path at the park's edge, joining the drains together at its edge. I came along a route with my dog to come down a lovely swell in the concrete that was an incline down from the raised surface plateau of a playground. It gave more of a boost to the free-wheel that took me down the long low-gradient path at the pointy end. Free-wheeling has always felt good to me, especially when it is slowly over a long gentle hill. It feels more like a motor then; I can feel the pull of gravity through the inclination. The front end of the bike went as the front tyre went blind, pushed out by an invisible punch and went down listing like Liston to the left. 'Twas no longer there, gone, the moving balance, vamoosh and up comes the ground with a forward momentum and yet still tied up within the working of the bike, tore through my triple-thick brown canvas Carhartt inner-quilted snowboarding trousers and was instantly consumed with the whole idea of how unaware I was before of how slippy it all was. How the tyre went even when I was in a straight line, just the cobbles' smooth innocence. Placid deception. Mad dark soft ice. Obvious. So I became aware of how lucky I was to not have fallen already and aware of the emerging idea that it was massively slippy yet I had been okay till now. And how there is just one big fat Now. So, no real pain or distress, just a bit of partial undress and the invisible accidents that may have been avoided by having this one here. Like kids, letting them jump a too high jump off a sofa brings this idea into their mind. They may be less likely to try that really too high shed roof with friends watching later.

The second crash, what a beauty. Heavens! I was going down a big faster, longer slow hill in the full dark. Stoned and keen, I was free-wheelin' with my eyes closed and no hands on the handlebars and enjoying it as close to flight as I could afford at the time. Then I had an urge to go further, to be a star shape, to take my feet off the pedals; lovely pedals, not just a place to rest feet, more a platformed fulcrum of purchase, cliff nook, resting place for the delicate giant mass that was my possessed balance at this point.

It really was about being free to do it and so the conscious me didn't go into what might be experienced the moment the feet move off to extend a star shape, as my arms were already up. I was a flying star. I realized instantly I had no purchase, just the anus and small grip of the buttocks that was cataclysmically insufficient, no way to bring the legs back. I was like a star falling through space, was a tad gravity-less to my disadvantage. The demise began immediately the star was formed: a falling star was me, burst forth from an average nova, a shard of matter free-falling to Earth through the atmosphere and burning up; the birth and death of a star, the luminary crashes, the leading light fades.

The hands took it worst. The left one experienced a grazing fairly deep in, around the pinkie palm-bone up to its knuckle. The other hand took a sprain. In that curious quiet place in the fuzz-rush before the pains, in this space one thinks about getting up to stand fairly quickly, getting onto the feet as soon as they will: upright, dignified, erect, untroubled, civilized, evolved, invulnerable – fine, thanks.

Again I became aware of the oddness of falling when no one has seen and the thought that someone might think it silly that you are down there. The more one is injured the more one might need assistance and, in this case, there is the extra oddness of it being a silly thing, a daft reason that, for me, infused it all.

The bike had a cryless injury, its handle-horns twisted to one side, any hurt hard to spot as it lay there on the ground. Bikes are laid down all the time; humans are well obvious lying here in the park. Masses of lying-around goes on in parks on the grass in the sun, not here in an early a.m. chill, on the path. The hands' fingers were v. sore and it made braking very hard to do, making me be laughing and quite high from it all, having to brake in order to avoid more crashing, yet it was almost as sore to squeeze the brakes as it would be to have a little crash anyway – never considered walking. This situation's predicament's elements made me laugh more. As well as it being a reaction to pain, laughter comes in so many ways or comes in so many forms and comes from so many different sources and is almost a physical refles from the diaphragm, self-sustaining sometimes and itself a thing to cause laughter.

There is a hell of a lot written vainly about the definition of humour.

Reams of philosophy on what is funny and may constitute a joke. Much more could be said about laughter, the thing that all the humour is concerned with. And I include very loud smiles, with and without nose-puffings. There is an endless list of things that can cause laughter and going onstage has always been a chance to let laughter happen. Thinking to myself "What can I do? What can I be being on about up there?" as opposed to "What is funny? What do they want?" I know what they want: they want creativity, new concepts, flow, goofiness, intelligence illuminating points of understanding. People want to see you doing what you really want to do, they want to see you do what they would love to do; or think they would like to do or be seen to be doing; they want to be entertained by seeing someone being honest, swiftly deft, prepared and eloquent enough to get the offered meaning across. All these things are like what women want from men and men want from women . . . All these things are just part of the endless list and not exclusive to, or of, other examples. A list of words.

There was no real discomfort from the wounds, just hot agony, and the fierce awe all know as agony's realm, emotions as only reaction to pain. Twelve percent hysterical in light shock, chuckling and riding home wincing and slightly shaky, depleted yet invigorated, in pain, experiencing a lot. Vibrant and spurred on, I retreat to rest.

The third crash was hardly a crash and the best of all: Coming back from the video store, a mere two-minute ride around local backstreets to one of two member-rent clubs for which I have videoship. Cycling nearly home I have three videos right-hand bagged and follow the whim as it arises, to change gear on the busy right hand's right handlebar with the free left hand – this was early on and here, now, in the twenty-twelfth year it has been mastered a bit more. Back there, then, it was less evolved.

This is not something totally new to me, this courier bet-worthy skill; having spent quite a large number of intense minutes here and there on wild open tarmacs riding the bike in circles with one hand on the opposite handle-grip (right hand on the left handlebar is the easiest). It meant you had to use a different skill, had to over-ride the known manner. Use the hand to sway balance for real, re-learn a bit, feel hard, re-experience and also take it easy, not panic and rely on the balance that the rest of the body provides you from practice unless you wobble it. The easy, steady, bail-brother-bail nature of it was scary and tricky and yet great fun and something I would find myself doing to excellently fill time when I had time on a bike to fill . . .

There are lots of little things I practise by periodically trying over the years to do: stamping on fallen teaspoons in the kitchen or the tines of the white fastfood forks that litter the gutters and pavements and tuck under in a hedge, stamping on them to make them leap up and be caught at knee height . . . Bouncing pound coins on the shiny paving stones up into a breast pocket . . . The Tea Bag Thing: holding a tea bag and a cup in one hand and then throwing the cup up to do a single spin and in that time chucking up the bag, catching the cup and then the bag in the cup. From early on I would just allow myself one attempt because that way I knew it would take longer to accomplish, yet there would always be teas to be made so giving more enjoyment and be a purer thing and when it happened it could have a real one-off nature. Now, years on, I can get it almost every time. It is like a guitar move you become aware of, you get to a place where you can imagine a thing, a riff, a trick just beyond where you are and it gets tried every now and then and one day it is done and completed successfully in the moment of natural playing. And by that time there is a new horizon and a new thing just beyond you.

Changing gears this way is a little bit an extra thing, you know the gears need effort, purchase, leverage, twist and with the wrong hand doing it and this causes, obviously, the handlebar to steer the bike fairly efficiently because of the tricky nature of the manouvre using forces slightly untamed and also the extra bag-weight in centrifugal swing of the vids and your worry-weight mind that can steer a bike to the kerb like a dowsing.

Yet my body is in full relaxed forward-momentum expectation even as this gear-changing goes awfully wrong and, as the front wheel is caught and turns suddenly, whips to the right and the bicycle's pure, entire, seamless energy is all negated and the thing just folds up under me in the flip and disappears back between my legs; folds under me while I just carry on running off the front of it just like in a rodeo, the crazy steer crumpling below me. It felt like back in the days when they could still trip horses up in westerns; felt like it looked like that. Felt like it looked like it would feel like that – gone! It was gone, it was no longer under me and I just kept on running and was amazed, somehow composed, jogging off in front of the clattering, careering chassis carcass. I looked around and called to some huddled teenagers having public-secret fags behind the closed school's front-door columns: "Did you see that? See what just happened?"

They were trapped in an unreceptive area, a loophole: they couldn't really acknowledge me because they were meant to be hidden or, rather, resemble hiders when I think they looked like they quite like to be seen. Hoping people would not be generally as observant as they always are, they relied on being seen yet not having requests made of them. They rested in this accepted niche of apparent invisibility. One way to be invisible is to be surplus to the requirement of those with the eyes. Everyone accepts the concept of city kids hanging out having fags. It is what they do.

They answered without answers and I picked up the bike.

Although there was the silly hand-on-the-wrong-handlebar there was never a feeling with me that something was about to happen. In a way I don't think it was a daft thing to do as there are so many benefits in practising unusual things because, should something bonkers and similar be required sometime, your brain might let you be more able. Certainly to me these are the kind of thing that occurs to be to do in time's gathered eddies . . . enablers.

Wandering around Glasgow I never felt under the chilly shadow of imminent violent affairs. I generally don't imagine that anything is about to happen or that other people might be thinking something is going to happen or that people are considering fighting as a realistic option tonight.

A hundred yards and six months up the road from the laptop-exchange I am walking along this Southside road and I see two women on the other side of the road kissing and just have time to consider that it is still rare to see this open display, when a car pulls up full of lads. They too have spotted the two women and as they pull up right next to me on this side they start to call a few things out and a passenger door opens as one of them gets out.

Assuming that they are all getting out to maybe make things a bit unlovely for the lovers I say, leaning into the opening doors' quarter circumference, "Hey, let's keep their evening free of trouble, eh men?"

This guy getting out of the car unfolds himself into my world and he says, "What that about trouble?" and, quite literally, "I'll give you trouble."

He says, "Wait here. I am going for a piss and then when I come back I am going to smash you."

Admiring the simple intent contained in his primal diction: "I am going to smash you." The monkeys around the fire, no in-between, no recursion, simple statement and the knuckle-bone as weapon: "I am going to smash you."

So now I'm waiting while he has a pee in an alley. Should I stay or should I go? I don't want to leave and make him more angry and all upset him, like that bouncer in Prague. If they're that angry you don't want to piss them off any more. Yet, hang on, this is the bad thing. Would it be rude to leave? How long can he go for? Will he chase me while peeing if I run? How advanced is his PC-muscle to halt the flow. In a way it's lucky he has been drinking, I think. Then again all this maybe comes from drinking.

Around at the window now of the driver, the car packed with the boys and the driver goes for something tucked in his trousers. Luckily, it's just his shirt or a knife and he says to get going if I don't want any trouble. Now's not the time to quibble that technically I was in some already, so I walk away.

The tall man peeing in the alley says, "Where are you going?" Free to consider that statement as extremely rhetorical and picking up the pace then as I approached my doorway I began to run lest I got caught just here, so close. Would that not be awful: to run and then be caught anyway, right with your key out, which suddenly may have made me armed-in-the-eyes-of-the law and I might just have to "open him up with me Chubb".

As an adult the only aggressive physical situation I got into any kind of proactive stance was when I followed the bad sander to his car. He had done a terrible job sanding the floors of our little room upstairs in Glasgow in preparation for the birth in there of Felix in the year two thousand. He did the whole room with a rotating edger and so there were circle lines all across it like cats with claws out had been figure-skating in pairs. With claws out, against their will. That room was small and yet there had been room to swing a cat . . . hey maybe . . . .

We felt a bit sorry for him because he kept telling us it was a new business and so I agreed to pay his expenses for materials so long as he came back . . . he said that he would. He left with the house keys and that did not feel so right. "You must leave the keys" was my argument. He was at his car. He started it and I reached in and took his keys out of the ignition, swiftly – eye for an eye, key for a key. Then he moved quickly to exit yet had that same little trouble with the undoing the seat belt already-on and then came out kind of senseless and without actually making eye contact. He rushes after me as I skip around his car. Unfortunately I've got new Birkenstock sandals on that have not moulded to the foot to give good grip yet and so are un-ideal for the urban skirmish or indeed the tight-cornering around the car. I am pushed gently up against the very-temporary builder's fence which sways back like the loosened ropes Ali had in Kinshasa, and it makes enough noise to alert a neighbour who comes to both our aid. His elder Asian status brought us out of a beige mist and all keys were redistributed. Really I am not sure there is ever a need to hit anyone: there could always be quashing them in real close so neither can swing and subduing – stymying of the verve, a compression hold, a whole or part-Nelson, a monstrous drunken Christmas cuddle-hold. A push for tranquillity.

When trouble does, it must always come out of nowhere. You meet the bear in the woods you're best not to run. They can run down a horse on tough terrain. You raise a hand and dispel fear. Meet their eye, at least die with the massive endorphin-rush of a frontal attack to the face and throat and under into unconscious ways of pain-management at least. To run is to allow the worst.

So, I am walking down a road street after dark two nights later with my Swiss friend Mimi and we approach a guy shouting on the phone. From a distance it sounds like it sounds and that sounds like the sound of girlfriend rage. I get this feel that it is temporary mood stuff, not an actual considered point of view, and that he's not always like this – there is a tiny ingredient of desperation in his tone. Is there a good word for that? When you are angry at the one you love for you do not want them to leave yet you are being a thing they must leave. Efficiently turning your love inside out. Or more pushing the thing away that you want rather than risk saying it n losing it. Gulp.

At times he is holding the phone in front of him in order to hurl abuse and get greater aural purchase, aiming it at his hand, gaining momentum, it's aggression as an accretion. Holding a phone to your ear means you see only the pavement and that might not be enough to keep the tirade flowing. Maybe it could look as if the phone itself has pissed him off – not to me though. Certainly phones almost come to signify the emotions that they deliver to us. He has it out front, way past the orthodox frameworks of the logical "you fucking bitch, why can't you just fuck off?" etc. Definite shoutings at a woman who he certainly feels has wronged him . . .

Just as we pass he gets to the finale: a slurred escalation and ends the call on a big triple "bloody bitch, goodbye . . ." We're so close I can see phlegm refracting on the screensaver as tiny diamonds can do, and call out, "Press ONE if you wish to re-record your message . . ."

He came, he touched my chest. I was carrying a bag full of empty bottles for the bottle-bank, what a racket they would have made; what a selection of spinning bottles there might have been, an opposite to kids' random snoggings here, just a large killer collection with which we could bottle each other. I say, "Hey, I am your friend." And he doesn't believe me so I raise my bag and hand hand and say goodnight. He really is keen for me to get into it. "Go on, stay and fight," he earnestly suggests as some kind of solution. In fact he is almost asking a favour. Raise my hand and wave . . . "Goodnight, bear."

Some years later someone gave me a huge punch that didn't set things off in a tense mob situation outside the Forest Café in Edinburgh-forest – the Ryan±Chris-led haven of free-fun, pagan arts and European beauties and handsomes, roll-ups, sub-minimum wage enthusiasm, hand-drawn posters, poetry CDs and the constant newness of new-art exhibitions.

We are soft folks, numbering about a hundred, gathering for fags outside in an everyday occurrence here during the festival in August's mid-evening, and drumming along to the drums and their beats of our enthusiasms and around the corner come eleven sports-clad anything-but-casual gang brothers looking for a whole different kind of fun. They were aggressors and, though we were a we of about a fiftysixty, there was no gathering of eleven toughs all next to each other like these guys. As a whole they were far denser – like the Spartans, enough to render us. Here on our side were women and younger folks and they threw bottles horizontally and approached. On my wee white compact Raleigh bike of peace literally I cycled in front of their thin beige line of white-trackies and try and let it all be passed on, not chosen or taken up by being a whimsical distraction. Thing is, if someone wants to fight they will get extra pissed-off at you for being smoothly unruffled, especially if you're riding a smallish white bike. A young chap swings super-fast, connecting with my chin and I freewheel along a bit a little faster on the energy boost direct from his fisticuff to my head. At that point it might have been a good idea to jump on a car and rally our numbers with few rousing improvised chants: "Come on, us guys, let's bunch up together and run them out of here."

Instead, things never kicked off and a few more swings got no real response and as the approaching sirens began to fleetingly emerge, rebounding to bounce off Edinburgh granite, modulating to undulate, swell and surge to our ears through gaps in buildings and up streets, the youngish team dispersed.

Another year at the Edinburgh Festival, after Gilded Balloon's Late'n'Live had transferred to a highly-available room in a venue that had not burned down, I was on the bill at the end, with Daniel Kitson working his magic to make a room that might be ugly into a wondrous gathering . . . He had sent a guy to Barcelona on Ryanair with money collected at the gig previously and this night he had come back and paid to get in to tell Daniel about it. Momentous era-defining stuff. Daniel is doing not some crazed absurdist improvised-nonsense scheme. No, it is a soulful, wild, massively attractive new take on following your nose without meaninglessness. Hugely important, it is the sublimation of aggressive humour, jokes to love-filled actions. He is a true wonder, Kitson.

Onstage a comedian was not getting much laughs and he was going on a bit. Sometimes you just need to cut it all out, forget the routines, because it is you they do not find funny and either turn it on them or get out of there; don't keep on doing that which they have already signalled that they are not-into. Turn a corner. Lose them up an alley and jump over the wall to the roof-escape. It can be very handy to admit what is happening, though this often means that things are over. That space is a little scary. Anyway this guy starts on yet another routine and it is minutes over his allotted time anyway. Daniel says, "Go on naked behind him." So I sort of sneak on naked and go to the drum-kit and start waving the guy off, motioning him to leave the stage, when he has looked around to see what's making the laughs happen. Didn't pick me out at first, all flesh-coloured and seated on a stool surrounded by all them skins. He was very angry too and came towards me with that chesty-intent yet never came to much as Daniel caught his attention luckily and he seceded the limelight.

Excellently fortuitously, I bumped into the guy at about three fifty a.m. "Here we go," I form a thought as he left an ATM queue to come over to me, calling my name, whereupon arrival he starts hugging me and thanking me for what happened. That's the wonderful thing about the Edinburgh Festival: queues at the ATMs at four in the morning on a Tuesday, busy late-night activities softening the minds of comics. Some of their best work happens by mistake here in these hours.

Arthur Smith does a late-night walk that leaves the Top of the Royal Mile by the castle with the traditional Offering-Of-A-Joint to the soldier on duty in a wee army kiosk – except it's the Tattoo-approach; not real army-business because it is show-business – and then heads down the road by the statues of St Giles where people are encouraged to climb them and create on-the-spot artistic-achievements for cash. Most just drop their trousers and there is a great deal of refined milling around as a demi-mob while Arthur and his natural-wizardry of belief, or Simon Munnery or someone, addresses them.

The best thing I ever saw at large, at night was the time Malcolm Hardee climbed up onto the roof of the Police Portakabin. Ever on the look-out for crimes, the Polis had located a temporary field-headquarters here in the dead centre of the Midlothians, by the stonemade Heart mosaic in the pavement we all gob on for easy ritualized respect. Here in the centre of the world's largest arts festival, they have a wee bird-hide to study correlate and view the Crimes.

Funniest thing ever seen was Malcolm Hardee halfway up the ladder onto the top of the Police Portakabin and the Cop cars have arrived and a Policewoman was trying to grab him and get him down and magically pulled his trousers down by mistake. Yes his trousers her hands: a human illegal naughty rude lewdness in public perpetrated by the innocent long arm of the law pulling the leg – oh, it had everything – and this did impede Malcolm's progress up or down, whither way the legs would not let the feet move enough with the trousers there. He was in negotiation with her to try and come on up there with him and pull them back up when more back-up Polis cars arrived. Malcolm was loaded into the back of a Police Rover to the applause and cheers of a human revue. Some of his best work.

At Glastonbury I met Malcolm Hardee one fine morning with proud piss and shit stains around his person and we tried to hotwire a Police Land Rover, the ideal vehicle for this terrain. They do this trick, though, with the ignition's repositioning so it was right over by my side; he was at work on it and, alas, no joy. There was a whole field of tents there, and afterwards I did get the chill of "what if we had driven over a few tents and hurt folks?" As far as I know, Malcolm never really did things where anyone else died. He was a fiercely energetic and freewheelin' spirit, heavily undercover as a maniac and even buffoon. He was dynamically intelligent and rarely bothered being eloquent with me. You would have to live near him, I think, and be in his movements to get the more of him.

Malcolm definitely had the best actions most nights and one of the loveliest voices around when you heard him speak what he felt about something. Mostly those words I never heard. Everyone loved him because he did what he wanted to, and often what they wanted to too – did it for them. Sometimes his wildness was a safety-valve for others. They didn't have to when he did. Just needed to see it, be near it. We swam in a rooftop pool in Melbourne extremely high and he said he thought I had died onstage on purpose. He told me he thought I didn't give a fuck. Thing is I do; I did. We are completely opposite onstage: I am earnest and want to do well, and show it. I tucked the bottom of a very high red curtain into my collar and pretend to fly like Superman with a very big cape. Irreverent to one degree, yet not hiding from effort. Lovely visually. He said he liked it. Never would he do it.

He had a fiftieth birthday party on his boat-venue, moored at a vaguely Canary-zone London Dock that was not in Greenwich.

When I got there the coastguards were on it because it was sinking. Or lurching, rather definitely. Malcolm met me on deck and escorted me upstairs to drink a shot of rum with his Mum. He was right there, right behind those thick glasses. When he beat me at pool twice in a row he tried to give me the money we had bet back. You'll get a great read out of his own confessional I Stole Freddy Mercury's Birthday Cake. His is the best autobiography there has been so far.

Oh, Malcolm would have been thrown out of most of the comedy venues that are going on now and probably even a couple of the nights that were set up to honour him.

Chapter Ate

At one time my man Desmond was driving and looking after Tam, a BMW, with Nick Moran registered as the main keeper. Tonight it's me at the wheel driving to a gig in Greenock through the falling snow on the motorway that was beginning to lie. As you get to Greenock there are a series of roundabouts, each one giving me an easy way to turn back and get home before the blizzard blocks the roads. After the show, driving back up the motorway, it is real white and, going a bit slower than most people wanted to, I end up with a queue of ten cars behind me. With their fearless better-driving ability they were more confident than me in these conditions – perhaps they just didn't have that fear of the skid that I have. Perhaps because they were fully insured or at least have a chance of being insured. This car was lent to me by someone who had no right to, so he could not be culpable. The owner did not know that his car was being lent out so he was not be blameworthy.

Going along like this with all these cars occasionally flashing their lights and peeping, it felt like I was leading the big parade, so it seems fitting to open the moon roof and gave an ambiguous fist wave and carnival cry. Then next minute, hang on . . . what's this overtaking me? My own boot! The back of the car is ahead of me guiding us both rather efficiently towards the central reservation, backwards and to the side. Spin the car does until it looks like we are going to kiss the barrier with the arse – no, actually the mouth. Over-over-steering I nearly manage to contribute to our direction and at almost eleven miles an hour we stray directly into the low metal divide. The fear combined with the long drawn-out slowness of it forced my legs, pushed rigid straight out, to push down fully on the brakes and the accelerator at the same time, revving madly and gently snow-drifting toward the crash with all that noise and none of the effect. The slowest, snow-west, bestest entry level, basic crash one could ever be lucky enough to have and it was in a kind of pre-pardoned slow-snow-motion that stretched the time out long enough long for me to put on my seatbelt on during though, in this lengthy big fat moment of time. Time is time, yet the mind is the one that can really slow it up or speed it down. Clunk, click, bang, doing it just slowly enough so as not to get the inertia snag, here in this whiteout, Tibetan, the art of motorway zen collision . . . no barriers or central reservations deep inside . . .

"This is, just had, my first crash" were some of the words that went around a few times. Got out stood next to the car that had been through it with me and watched as all the mean drivers, all hurrying from behind, were now skulking past like they had willed me to crash like it was their fault for peeping and egging me on and forcing me off the road. None of them looked my way or stopped. It was too much for them.

They may have felt ashamed to see the manifestation of their darker wishes in a roundabout way. Bypassed kindness . . . Overtaken with guilt . . . Cat's eye tears . . . No hard shoulder to cry on.

Anyway – and I'll try and use that word only this once in the book – N. Moran, the main keeper, was away in Barbados, how could he ever find out? Not a chance in a million, two million; how could he ever find out; fucksake, what are the odds? Jeeeessus, what the fuck? No way, unless: he was on a beach on Barbados with a Scottish guy reading a three-day-old imported Daily Record with a review of my gig in Greenock that mentioned that I had mentioned having driven there in Tam, a BeeMW, belonging to him . . .

So then, this gig review is of course pre-crash yet enough to make Nick phone Des pissed-off, shouting from the beach. Des is sleepy and thinks this must mean that he knows it was crashed. He owns up by mistake with a "well the damage isn't that bad" and Nick twigs whatthefuck! Des twigs the twigging – a further insult, betrayal and theft – shouts and hangs up. Nine days later Des receives a postcard with the ownership papers stapled to it just saying:

"Cunts."

This reminds me as to when I ran on that railway platform in Warsaw. Incredible tour logistics gave me an extra night for free in the Warsaw Marriott, then the gig there before flying back to Colchester and then on to Budapest for the third leg of the three-day European tour. With my extra day I decided to go to Lodz where Krzysztof Kieslowski had been to Film School. With me was my Camera so I could make a ShortFilm about FilmSchool. Ambling slowly to the information desk of the Warsaw Marriott or equivalent, and asking about trains the ladies said there was one in eleven minutes. The lifts are plated in imitation cheap chromium goldplate and swift and I am uptomaroom packed and back down past them again in under three, and over to the other side of the road by the station in five and a half, and then searching on a classic giant standard flickering mechanical departures-and-platform sign, the absolute paradigm of paradigms of a thing looking exactly like the best version of it in myour mind's eye to try and locate a town I have to reconstruct the phonetic spelling of in a different alphabet before then reminding myself how it is then probably not spelt, to then look and find that. Fonetik. Just how it doesn't sound. There is one at the time I need about to leave that looks like it could be a spelling of the town which is sounded as annunciated in a secular way as "Wooch". This one is spelt "L-U-D-Z". Yet I am familiar enough with being unfamiliar with a language's physical rendering, its rubric, no, its typeface, so I just have to work out which probably is unfamiliar in the right way . . . being familiar with things and can guess that, were I to not know I did not know this one, it would look like this still. El You Dee Zed spells my best bet.

One minute to go and late enough chase platform three late enough to validate and require a wee run down an up-escalator. In the middle of that I look over and, with all my running and haste, I am only going down the up escalators the same speed as the man opposite me is going down the down one while standing still. Our eyes meet to form one huge eye, meet to form an opinion about this. He looks at me forming an appropriate response face. As I come off it onto the stationary platform my train is there just gently moving very slowly, pulling out of the station – aaiee, so close! Lots of folks look at me when I scream "Noooooooo!" fairly loudly. Then the train slows and stops because it was, in fact, pulling in. There were some strange looks from those who perhaps thought I had the great psychic power to bring back two hundred tons with my will.

I chose a cabin by walking along the aisle, European style, by the window looking in and auditioning cabins with folks in.

Every now and then there is the whole idea of "what if?" a lot closer to the surface. What if I had chosen those folks; would it have been different?

Opening the door and drawing the looks of everyone in the compartment; the simple brushed metal handles operate easily and close the door behind me. My Sony camera and the cheap Chinese cashmere safely above my seat. The individual seats are not a long shared-bench-type thing and these seats have wooden sidings, wings, like the sides of a leather chair. Compartmentalisers looking for the thinnest of antimacassars, so I could not see anyone unless I leaned far forward round and surprised them. It reminded me of that game a bit, where you have your mystery-celebrity written in Rizla stuck to your forehead to guess and everyone else can see it yet the big thing is that everyone is seeing what you cannot. This is like your own face, your own identity. You wear it, you have it and you are the only one who cannot look at it. The only one who can never know it.

There were four on either side. The man opposite me was reading a Caribbean travel brochure and flicking through it, smiling, like it was a work of fiction. All of them can see all of us on this side and know that none of them can see anyone else on their own side. It is rather lateral-anti-lateral even though we are going forwards. All this is training through my brain when a man comes in with a trolley selling chocolate. He asks everyone and I am still puffing from the running and it sounds great: hot chocolate. And then a bar of cold chocolate in a v.plain graphic-less blue, municipal, tirelessly plain communist manifesto bar-wrapper. After I give him the money he stands for a bit and then simply holds out another bar for me to buy. Sensational tactics, refreshing – how brazen, how internationally audacious. So I buy a second bar. With all thoughts still eminent in my mind, I am sat right-forward on the edge of my seat so, now, if I want to, I can see the people next to me. Opening the bar in my lap I see there are no decadent, easy western groves in there to help one apportion it, no snapping rut or furrow, no weakening. So I just start elbowing it in the lap of my knees and breaking it up crazy-paving style. It's cold and hard and it's a geometric wonder, the solution to Mensa sliding triangle shapes visual puzzles. All long-sided acutes and overlapping obtuses.

Now, spread out on the paper displaying it and offering it around my compartment, at this point no one accepts. no one takes a bite apart from me. It was not all for nothing. I mean if the train went off the rails now and we survived, it would be at least somewhere to start from. The taste was paste and not to waste so I offered it around again and a young woman in school uniform took a bite. We sat, the only ones chewing, though, surely, not the only ones salivating. The birch forests flew by, sometimes in a milky looking lake, the closer trees moving very fast, the further ones coaxed out of the view. The people left and I helped the schoolgirl close a window and then, practising English, she told me a dream she had of marrying Al Pacino while I corrected a few blatant mis-translated words in the glossary-type limited dictionary at the back of her English textbook.

The battery ran out for my camera the minute I arrived at Lodz so it was a very short ShortFilm about FilmSchool. What I would have filmed would have been done on the basketball court. It only had one hoop and I came up with the idea of some drunk director coming back to his old alma mater and seeing this then tracking down a hoop late at night from an irate Polish sports-retailer then having to find stepladders and fitting the new hoop and then sitting there under it without the net attached in the late night light like it was a halo, like he was an angel and as the Polish Poleesh come by they are distracted by the momentary tail of a rocket flying up across and back through the skys.

Momentary is another great word for it means both lasting for a short time and/or happening at every moment, though maybe not both at the same time; so either and or or, or and/or, yet not in action. The word can hold two meanings yet not be both. Love.

Sometimes in a dictionary they can only give usage as meaning. Yahoo.

Back in Warsaw I met the other comedian for this European Tour. Over the next three days he made me laugh as much as anyone ever has even after we both got lightly kicked in by the Russian doorman of the Club Barbados dancing-establishment. Rob Rouse, Robert Rouser was his name. They advise you not to even make eye contact with these Rafia guys, who are mostly armed and in power. They don't mention what they might do if you bare your arse and press it up against the glass of the door they are not allowing you through.

Already they must have been tough because we guys had already hung around the door after being denied entry. They know they are feared so, when we mistook their "You will never enter here" for a "Do you mind waiting for a few minutes please we are rather full", they must be quite brave to come out here without a pause when I press the arse up against the magnifying lens of the plate glass. Poor Rob is punched first and, in a terrible moment, I run away, out of the circular courtyard and have a moment to feel weak before I feel I must return. Running back in the gateway I pass Rob running out after me. The doorman can't believe his luck: here he is again, how you say more biting at the cherry . . . He winds up for one of those round-the-corner kung-fu kicks which starts with his body turning away. For a moment I thought he had reconsidered and was away, until the foot came round on the end of the leg and managed to lean back just enough so the flying foot made only slender contact.You don't want to make him miss completely or he might get mad. A quick punch and a stumble has me down. Then the bouncer runs at me to give me a big kick and as he does the most beautiful thing happened then: as he was coming at me like a rugby guy to kick a conversion, he did a little jink-like skip just to get his footwork right, to make sure he didn't arrive with the wrong foot. It's an instinctive thing and I appreciated it. If you've decided to do something, if you are in the flow of reaction, moving with the river-strength on the momentum of choice, that is a lovely thing. I remember getting a little solace from that as he powered in and I was half prone half getting up offering him one last chance to reconsider with the raising of a shoulder and hand and taking no evasive actions and he kind of kicked me back up onto my feet to run away again. This time with a free cracked rib.

In a proving show of justice Rob's injuries were thankfully the lesser, bruisy whereas mine were totally debilitating with the cracked rib. Next day my movement was very slow as all the muscles and other bones would push and pull somehow against and around it. Aw Warsaw, awe, s so sore. Only moreso.

This was funny because I would wince and then that would make me chuckle slightly at the wince, then that chuckle would hurt, so I would wince a bit more and that would make me laugh – picking up all the items, one by one, and taking them to my bag. This was packing: delivering each item without any stress on my ribcage. It took me forty minutes to pack. Then Rob was just so funny in that way that the jokes are not jokes, they are loveable bits of essence of him, just the sound of his voice let me laugh and I was near hysterical and laughing and wincing. Does it hurt? "No, only when I'm pissing myself," we said.

All this went on for hours and I was internationally giddy.

The greatest moment was yet to come, when we got back to Gatwick, went to the gig in Colchester, ended up naked on chairs like Christine Keeler: One of us, in agony, befriended the British Olympic Judo Squad and went back with them to their soft-floored practice-dojo that had a bar, where the adrenaline of fancying one of the Olympians, combined with the therapeutic nature of alcohol, meant I actually went through a few throws with her without feeling too much pain then.

Amazingly this moment is captured beautifully, on the free accompanying not HD, 2D DVD footage, of the ribaldry n ribcage ribbing.

The greater greatest monu-moment was still to come as we returned to Gatwick to fly to Budapest and we were caught forty minutes short while waiting for "Three Harry Specials please" at Ramsden's Fish restaurant. Suddenly our flight was called on time and our three giant fish-like child canoes sympathetically come at the same time and we have the options: (a) eat like mad and choke a bit and leave fairly heavily unsatisfied. Or, (b) take them through customs. We decided to take the meals with us through customs. A gallant choice and, this being well before Twin Towers, may well have been the one thing allowing our

supper's passage. We held them and ate them in the queue right up to
the X-ray security machine. Into a tray they went and I popped round
the side to have a look over the attendant's shoulder. Just as my supper
passed through his monitor he stopped the belt feeling my presence. He
looked up at me . . . "I'm just checking for bones . . ."

Would the X-rays bring the fish back to life . . . will these this be the
only fish doing posthumous last wiggles entombed in batter . . .
shoulda got stingray and chips . . .

Folks are just carrying Ferrero Rocher and Toblerone and other dried
or colder foodstuffs; oh, and perfumed gifts. Our moist food's aroma
filled the air on the queue through passport control, the pungent
amorous familiarity of vinegar through warm paper packaging rising
on thermals of fish-reek, and folks are licking their lips all over the
place. Eventually we managed to finish them on the bus that takes you
from the waiting gate to the plane. As we scrunched up our wrapping
we were content and walking down the aisle of the plane Rob and I kept
sniffing and saying, "Excuse me, does it smell of Fish and Chips in here
to you?" "Yeh." Self-camouflaged subterfuge, public invisibility . . .
Have you ever written your own pin number in chalk up above a cash-
machine before you go on holiday so that when you come back and
have forgotten it, it is all okay? . . . Just me then.

The better best was yet to come: By the time we got the bus out back
to the very distant long-stay Car Park Number Nine at and on this the
second last day ever, of Concorde's scheduled international flights.
There were lots of spotters gathered at the end of Gatwick here with
lenses large and paparazzi-sized as big as little stools. They told us
about the pointy one. When we knew this, we kept our ears peeled for
Concorde as she did indeed come back in to land and Rob had the
groovy idea of getting a picture of it flying in the sky behind him like
it was going into his head while I lie in the road. My chest and pressing
full weight on the ribs in a new kind of pain, to get the angle, and
laughing at the wincing and more than wincing, lying on my belly and
ribs, holding a camera as Concorde came in, and suddenly realizing
we were actually in the road as a car came and peeped and then, at the
moment the great jet entered Rob's left ear, the phinger pressing
down on the gentle release that doesn't come fuckfuck I've not wound
on . . . I hurt my chin on the road from laughing, That was a first.
Unable to self-raise erect, to complete a resurgent resurrection up
I had to roll to the kerbside to get out of the way of the oncoming car
park traffic.

Adrian the promoter paid me in grass from the boot of this car in

Car Park Nine. It's okay to say this because he has subsequently got a conviction for growing and so become a non-show-business tree surgeon in Bath.

Like the French lady said at the Castle: the fact that it is happening is unusual-risky, partly sublime, rare, enough, intuitive, trusting, dorky and kind harmony. Human interaction. Getting fresh objects is a thing I normally leave to the venue as opposed to trawling around charity shops to find things.

Once me and Ross Noble were fiddling around before a show and went to the Scout Shop and bought lots of badges for the modern categories of achievement. They had a badge for computer skills; fair enough, though it was sponsored by Compaq the computer maker, with the logo sewn in gold. Their achievement: getting sponsorship where no one dreamed of it, in-between personal ability and culpable-responsibility. That ain't right. Anyway we both had some onstage that night and were able to flex our minds around it in our own both different ways and in both our own different ways – both in our own both different ways. Ross added new skills and talked about sewing designs for the new achievements of joy-riding and stuff. I stuck to validation, authority of power, no one can stop you buying these things, if you want to be held in the realms of other's defined parameters then dib dib dibIn truth we can all be happier as ourselves with everything folks do . . . the white ribbon . . . you can buy those huge mirrors for people who live in the country wherever you live . . . travel-iron wherever you're going, children's plasters on a wound of any age . . .

Last year the doctor said my ringworm was Textbook and could he take a Photograph.

"Have you ridden a bike with a wet bike seat . . . ?"

"Every day . . ."

He gave me a cream that did that and also my minor piles. An hygienist not, there are very few showers in my life and baths seem to come in clusters, quasi-periodic, with no immediately apparent visible pattern . . . bit like the periodical cicada coming out every seventeen years. Google it and that is the only time I'll say that. Saving that.

Gil Scott Heron's Dad played football for Celtic. Another great fact.

I shaved for the first time since nineteen ninety-two, when Phil Nichol did me and cut my hair in the mountains of Spain. The ones I had already hitchhiked to with the un-fluent thumb.

I bought a new toothbrush in Ullapool, here the venue for the kids' show with the long, long window-cleaner doing the man's glasses. Two for fifty-eight pence and some basic teethpaste and brushed them in the rain by the gutter outside Boots. In truth I was marvellously happy at this moment because the suddenly-found umbrella came from the back of the car and that is where the kids' show came from and I realized this when I was camping and taking stuff out emptying for a re-clean/organize and there seemed to be so much available for kid fun.

At this kids' show all the props were laid out and they had some very, very, very extendable window-cleaner and so, let's call him Callum, got to clean a man's glasses in the back row. Ziggy got to draw me with his left foot. Two Freyas, next to each other and one played Sledge Me Gaily on we go as she was dragged to the piano. Lots of kids utilized plastic bags for balancing and post-it notes as false eyelashes. One kid was winking as fast as she could as I urged her on ridiculously; everyone was laughing and she was losing rhythm and having a sort of eye-fit for fun. Looking around there is just the smiling-ness of people enjoying something that's a bit nonsense and yet is not about nonsense.

Also there was time before the gig, no lateness-compressed timescale. There was time to have a bottle of Old Peculiar with an overcooked pastie pastry from the glass case in a corner store with the closed post-office window . . . Roundly, this is a lovely feeling, doing shows that are joyous and altruistic so the shows are one end of the entertainment spectrum as a stand-up comedian.

The other end of the spectrum of being a human is attending live television-awards for comedy. The British Comedy Awards nineteen ninety-two. With me friends and agent and our table collapsed just moments before the broadcast. We got all fresh bottles. Poor Paul Whitehouse was put at our table and he was kind of not-happy there and turned his chair round and watched it all kind of breaking loose. I felt puffed up, great and yet giving in, wanting it too much and yet not liking it. Feeling it was not real what was real was saying what you wanted to say and the gig and it going well after are separate entities. Guaranteeing something enough to be eligible for the consistency one would usually need to win an award was not what I was good at. Is good at. Not something that I wanted to be good at. SO it feels like you would appear to be there to seek validation and to enjoy that and to be around others who are doing this too and then either you are comfortable with this or you are not. Made me a bit wanky. Paddy Ashdown handed me the award and in the acceptance speech I got everyone to sing happy birthday to my friend Toby; told them I knew what they were thinking "who's that?"; ruminated on how the two joker cards got inside the deep laminate of the award. On the way to the stage I passed a big-wig table at the front and patted Steve Coogan on the left shoulder and kept walking as he turned round the wrong way. A funny thing happened on the way here. That night me, Al and Morag ended up at Jonathan Ross's house playing Perudo. When we left, went right over town and the driver said it was all paid for. That's when we sent Jonathan some sellotape and some Endorphine-Rush Chili sauce. Who doesn't need sellotape sometime soon? Next time I was there two years later after my TV show and I was up for Best Newcomer and they announced Graham Norton as the winner and I jumped up and shouted, "No . . . it can't be!"

This year at Edinburgh I was just standing on a wall with McSavage, and a purple people-carrier with unique access right routes came right up to the Gilded Balloon and Coogan gets out with Brian De Palma and some of his friends from his new job as an actor – I cover my face with my hands and shout, "Yes, you're Coogan. Who am I, though, who am I?"

He peers a bit and is kind to give, comes over, My hands come down: "It's only me Phil from-years-ago Kay." He is in a chat with us all and goes with his friends into the inner sanctuary of the Star Bar, a celebrity-stuffed gilded rooftops exclusive entry-only meeting place for beers, spirits. This bar is very quiet during the day and ideal for naps on the big huge sofas.

Naturally you get weird gaps between some people and others. Celebrity is a velvet-lining to the barrier. If you wish it, it can keep you far away. Nicely though, you get an awareness of when you are bypassing that shit, both as the one who is well-known and the one who is less-known. The reason Josh Homme and Nick Oliveri give me a wave is daft and cherished. The reason I could not get Alanis Morrisette to buy a round of drinks is because she was attaching the velvet to the barrier herself; kept saying I was only asking her because she was her. "True," I kept saying, "and I am skint."

Queens Of The Stone Age were playing two gigs at the Barrowlands, perhaps the finest-sized and loveliest room for rock in the world that I have seen: upstairs, feint air of decreptitude just the right size for two thousand to go for it, with a quaint purple-starred roof all a nice height way above the sprung ballroom dance-floor. Managing to wangle guest-list tickets, I take my friends Lawrence and Joel, whose Dad from Viz gets us all backstage-passes. We head down in the Jag and get all the lights green till we are parked out the side, shedding a few outer layers that will not be required. All the way down, all the way in to the guest-book and collecting our tickets and running up the stairs and in to the room opening the door just as the band walk onstage. Everyone cheers it feels like it is for us, like making love at Glastonbury, there is always some cheering from some direction as you are doing what you are doing.

Onstage they play the hits and the not-knowns and the young crowd leap at the rhythms and, every now and then, are thrown off by the exciting alternative time signatures from these gifted rhythmists and if you leapt up and down then you were the only heads. At the front of the stage there were eleven men in yellow T-shirts as security and looking out from the pit at us and sometimes spraying folks up the front with plant-sprayers – so nourishing and tending the blooming generation. Suddenly it occurred to me that someone had to go up onstage from this side just to kind of say, "Hey you guys in yellow, really we are here to love the music, we are here to watch and enjoy, if we wanted to get up there we would. It is with expectant concern you keep an eye, how about a friendly infection?" Someone had to go up and gently reflect this truth. My plan was to go to the very edge and ask a young bouncer at the edge for a water and when he turned, jump up past him over the barrier. This went well till I slipped and he turned back with the water and so I took a sip. Then I simply went to the other side and did exactly the same with the young tender newcomer they put at the edge. This time it went well I had a foot up on the barrier and leapt the meter moat and was on. I walked towards the bassist who stepped back from his mike and left it clear for me to speak a very inaudible "wooyeh" as I went past. Now, Josh the singer was looking at me with the eyes to see if I was to be mad or no. A few of the crowd now up the middle are cheering and pointing in a way that leads the experienced crowd-watching senior security men that something is unusually occurring just behind them. As they turn this is my moment to fly from the stage. There was not nearly enough velocity or altitude at my departure and so only half my body made it into the grateful hands of the kids down the front. They pulled me and their faces were all there wild and cheery . . . The rear-portion of me was firmly in the grip of the men in yellow; I was being twisted and pulled by them in

glorious harmony of a practice. I was getting twisted to snap, wring-out
full body Chinese burn: so I screamed at the crowd to let go of me and
pulled my hands back from their grip and extricated myself to
surrender into the yellow sunflower. One enormous pair of arms took
me down and began to squeeze me tight. All sweaty, so slightly
slippery like a big fish I kind of slipped up in his embrace and then I
felt him re-fasten the hands for more and then it all went slack.
Opening my eyes I saw Nick, the bassist, reaching his hand down to me
and grabbing it to help back up onstage.

"Take a run up from the back, there's more room," he advises.

By this time the gig had temporarily stopped and as I go to the back
the eyes of the show are on me and I run to the front of the stage and
launch myself considerable more eagle-like off the front and soar way
up and over the men in yellow. Startlingly, this extra time to see me
coming triggered a unique response in the crowd and they parted
exactly where I was going and I landed flat on the ground. Keen to not
be a wounded wash-out I immediately jumped up, bounced up onto my
feet and called out, "I'm fine!"

Nick the bassist was looking at me with a hand over his eyes that
could, at a stretch, have seemed like a salute to the successful stage-
diver. My ribs were perplexed and gig continued.

Finding my friends, some of them recognized me as the fellow off
the stage.

After we went with our passes backstage to the dressing-room do
and, as I entered the doors, a guy came up and patted me on the arm:
"Are you the guy who dived off the stage?" And he was right up at the
back of the hall. "Man, I heard you land."

There's not going to be many times you hear this phrase so I was
very glad. There were canapés available and I remember building
deluxe crackers canapé triplestack wonders as something to do as
opposed to sitting down which can be a curse. Then Josh Homme
asked if anyone had any drugs, there's my pot I say and he means
could someone get some cocaine and I said I could, so he gave me his
laminate and out I went to phone a woman who was snoozing in bed
with her half-sister and she gave me a number and I met a guy in a
Vauxhall round the corner. When I came back, the most prestigious
laminate worked against me because the guy knew for sure this was
not him, me no he, Josh Hommes . . . not Josh hommeself . . . himself
. . . you josh you're not him . . . anyway The Pass was too good. Fail
Pass. Re-Access Denied. Passage Blocked. Overqualified me . . . vilifie+-d
me, philifide. Forced exemption, laminated cavitation. The cheese was

too rich, the handmade chocolates you made for Granny had her throwing up . . . Blowback hurricane, feedback-backdraught-backlash horrorstorm: . . . Tie him up by the lanyards. So I unpeeled out my lesser stuck-on-the-thigh pass and convinced him with a combination of charm n chutzpah, feeling that he might recognize me from my fame: ". . . perhaps you heard me land tonight . . . or got kicked in the face a bit by me last night . . ."

". . . ??!? . . ."

At the end of the evening for us non-members we were all ushered out in a big bunch from the backstage at the same time and as we were all jammed at the door Josh calls out my name and passes me over a fifty. Everyone knows/doesn't know what might have just happened aas it passes from hand to hand.

". . . ever so slightly girl on girl half-sister classy class As . . ." may well have covered it, yet as we all know sometimes the answer does not solve it . . . Explanation gives no clarification . . . the illumination no resolution . . .

Driving a few folks home, the fifty is placed under the windscreen wiper as our totem and ticket, our reward and our reminder, our ritualistic sticker promising to pay the bearers on demand and swiftly shift-flickering in the drive's wind as seemingly the only thing ever to rival a hummingbird. Excited and moving I forget and leave the fifty overnight on a Glasgow street in full view right there and it is still there in the mid-morning flapping like a leaflet nobody wants. Right under their noses. How is that possible . . . well no one actually looked at it and connected is the answer . . .

Next evening me and Norman Macleod are at The List party, a magazine I wrote an ever-diminishing column for for two years. It started as a whole back-page then became a half-page at the front then, eventually, had to fit in a box at the beginning of the Comedy listings section. The mag was TimeOot for Scotland. As the column got smaller my sentences stayed longer. Overestimating or, rather, estimating more highly the concentration span of readerships is a fabulous aim and guide. There were ever increasing pieces to write as I got more and more journalism jobs and at one point a senior editor of a Sunday paper wanted to meet me out in my world and we had a drink at King Tut's Wah-Wah Hut in Glasgow and, in his ironed weekend jeans, he commissioned me to go to Newfoundland. The mission was send exciting man to the most boring place on earth so on the internet I found a mining equipment convention in St Johns, Northern Canada, where there are no beards allowed; so, go to a remote industrial town and not even be able to go to the one event. Really this was about finding IT wherever you are. Wherever you are you are alive, and alive is the excitement. In the end they flew me to the wrong St Johns and it was on the tip of the North East where Cabot landed, the new found land, and for two days there were locals' foot-tracks to follow, a kid to befriend at a silent auction . . . there was Screeching in a Pub where you kiss a furry penguin . . . there was the strip club where I only had the exact nine dollars in change for a dance and it all fell out of my pocket onto the floor and down on my knees, it's hard to find in the dull pink strobe beneath the tables, by the workboots.

In the end then Sunday Herald travel supplement folks too cut out the best bits and shortened sentences too. Imagining what others want is a tricky thing yet many folks make their living at it. Fine these slippers. Wine these hipsters. Chinease whispers.

Often I have stood in empty auditoriums and gazed at the stage wondering what people might want to see and hear. This only lasts about six seconds or three breaths and then I go back to the hours of summoning-up what it is I would love to present.

However much I make up in the show there are always lots of jokes, bits, nuggets, one-liners, two-liners I cherish and would love to remember to tell folks. I get into a rhythm sometimes and tell a big story at every gig for a while or let old ones emerge when they are appropriate. Sometimes I find myself telling one and have to really think about what the hell it is as I am telling and, often, leave out crucial chunks. There are splendid little one-liners that I have had for ten years in a wee notebook that have only ever popped out twice or never.

Last gig I did, Sunday 02.06.13, there was forty-two minutes for me to tell the story of going up north for a Handfasting party, staying up all night keeping my passport close and mocking it and toasting it on the fire a bit here and there and then leaving without it in a wee white 924 dart at dawn and spending all day at the airport like it was a festival, getting free milk and reading all the papers, seeing people come and go, watching inappropriate videos in the bar and meeting an old bass player, until they took me on the evening plane.

Norman heard the story of the previous QOTSA barrowlands, flicky fifty night and said, "Let's go again tonight." I said I have no guest tickets and he said, "Let's go again tonight."

That, there, was a huge moment for me, because we got on a train in Edinburgh and headed towards the venue. It all was so clear: if you want to get in, you have to go to the venue. No matter what, going towards it is the first thing. Impossible to succeed; absolutely impossible to get into the room unless you go to the building. Allow the best. Allay the beast. We get off the train and share the well-pumped, thin-tyred Puch bike all the way until we see the grand Barrowlands sign neon dancing itself loose to fill all the puddles on our way with an impossible sizzling puzzle . . . We have this great thing going: "So far so good. Nothing has gone wrong yet . . . Here we go . . . so far so good . . ."

Stowing the Puch bike under the rear eighth overhang of the serious purple tour bus behind the wheels we stroll into the venue. We are late, it's quiet and before the door has shut behind us a big In-Charge security guy in his fifties eyes me up and says, "You're not going to be landing on any of my men tonight are you?"

I kind of smile and stroll past him to the lady with the big guest-list. In a way, him talking to us sternly just there must have helped, because she had noticed it we were known to him, so we stood in front of the guest list-lady and said our names and she looked very hard. Now it is very hard to find something that is not there. She really looked hard again some more and could not see them, it looked like she must have really wanted to find them names, so she kept searching. Then again how can you be sure something is not there??: is v.hard to be certain something is not there when there cannot be any sure proof of that. Absence is only a guide. Dodgy guides.com . . . be a miffed Sherpa . . .

"Well . . . Thanks very much then . . . ," I say fairly loudly for all to hear and Norman and I just jog up the stairs; right through all the foyer security, like the end of Leon in reverse; back up and in right through under their noses. Norman's wearing corduroy and it made a light veet-veet sound, loud enough to hear in this v. conscious moment as we were reaching the top of the stairs . . .

Inside the room Queens Of The Stone Age were into the alternative rhythm-ings and Norm and I moved deep into the crowd's midst and proceeded to tremendously enjoy our more-mature leapings. The younger folks who we came and stood by were friendly and good at space sharing. They were certainly slightly aroused beyond amusement when one of these bouncing corduroy type latecomers was suddenly surrounded by fourmen in yellow and lifted from the room with no need to use his own feet. Imagine one minute these two olders come in, start a'leaping and then, without any reason, are suddenly surrounded and one of them whisked away. Why not both? Was his dancing really that bad . . . Mystery is a basis for legend . . .

Foolishly, and thank goodness, our unusually-high rhythmic

jumping put us heads and shoulders above anyone else so when the guest-list lady told them we were stowaways on this voyage they must have been spurred enough to come up to find us with a smidgen of thinking we would be hard to find – jackets off, up the front, in the mess. What are the chances? Two in two thousand. Yet there we were, though happily, simple to locate. Bouncing up, sometimes on the off-beat, giving them many chances, eye-catching sudden movements, to occasionally, momentarily the only ones head and shoulders above the rest. One good thing was this that we were easy to find so they were in a relatively good mood when they threw me out. It was the fourth song for me that night as I was quite gently propelled from the venue.

They were watching me through the glass front-door as I extracted the unlocked Puch bike from under back within the purple cantilevered cave. I was going to keep warm and have a wee ride around. Then Norman came out – said it felt a bit daft without me.

Next day, I was cycling through town aboard the tandem and got a glimpse of the big purple tour bus doing a noon-depart from the downtown Show-biz Radisson. As I got near I saw Josh and Nick with ambling in hoods carrying fast foodstuffs and as they caught sight of me they both gave a little automatic wave as I did a fairly brave U-turn through traffic and went over.

Months later I read an interview with the QOTSA, and Josh mentioned they love touring Britain and Scotland was great and things happen and they had had a guy onstage and helped him jump into the crowd an' all. Yes, I was a mystery anonymous guy from a gig mentioned in the music press.

Sometimes I love folks way more than they love me. Like Vic Reeves, we just couldn't hit it off with me wanting it too much. Years ago we were all in a loose bunch after a show in Edinburgh and Vic goes, "Do you take drugs . . ."

For some reason it seemed best to answer and say no not really, when of course I'd've taken anything with him. Takes years of not-knowing him and coming back with a decent old tweed jacket that I have sewed up around the cuffs to get us together over a pint in the afternoon. Finally did one of those crappy comedian-interview based shows with a tenuous reason to get comics to speak about a subject in a funny way . . . usually with shoe-horned material, and one of those foot-long long shoe-horns, dipped in goose fat with huge purchase and leverage, where they list-prepared things about God's Best and God's Worst things. That was the concept: Best Sandwich . . . Car . . . Worst

Film . . . Did it just to be in a room with Vic and it was delightful. They didn't want to pay me because I find it hard to follow that format and, deeper, and plus too I find it hard to think of things as either good or bad. Sometimes that is what is shit about comedy: all agreeing that a thing is shit and why we don't like it. It seems easier to rip the piss that anything else. Certainly a lot of folks look like they are finding it hard to be positive and get a laugh.

This is why Vic and Bob were so beautiful and best for me: they saw another route through and made the positive so mind-blowing and daft and deft and superbly eloquent. Their choices of lunacy were like a new hope. I first was told about them swimming across a freshwater lake with Richard the Cadbury heir and was laughing with the mouth right there at water level.

The tweed is still the new tweed and it is getting holey and I have devised a plan where I go back to Harris and locate more of this particular tweed cloth by using the number on the Orb label inside and wearing the jacket and asking around, and this could be a little docu-com-reality TV and Vic said he'd do an afternoon watching footage and getting recorded narrating, impro-citing dialogue.

Channel 4, Thursday night, eleven p.m.

Plus there's another televisual idea blooming in me: SuperKidDiary. There is so much fun to be had when you go to a huge Sainsbury with a boy of four and his mates when you have no real deadline and are free to follow them and answer questions about the huge amount of broccoli or the wide selection of hovering machines . . . Or imagine in a B&Q with all loo seats on the wall or all the door handles to try . . . large things to explain . . .

On QI with Stephen Fry I was teamed with Clive Anderson and could not get into it at all. Almost the best in rehearsals, I was show-stoppingly rubbish and outwith it all during the recording. At one point they actually did stop recording and asked me to do better. Just couldn't get into actually doing it . . . Could not love it . . . Lovely Alan Davies said, "Come on, let's have some of that old Phil Kay magic." Bless him. Perhaps he had an image of me sliding on the turf down the mountain or filling in for him as he was half an hour late at Screaming Blue Murder in nineteen ninety, or us all chasing that convertible that had zoomed past our early-morning hitching thumbs in Montreal off the mountain and then had to stop at the traffic lights so we all rushed it in a bunch and started to climb in . . .

That show was an ideal place for me to be rubbish because in the end I do not want to do that kind of thing on-call torso comedy, sitting and humorising from the waist up, seated so all the blood available for the head, the head, the head. It's just too contrived for me, only me, and so go twelve percent autistic to the convention of agreeinga and doing it, yet everyone on it now seems to be utterly loose and superbly creative.

On lots of occasions part of the reason I look forward to gigs is the way that people let you into their life. If they have come to the gig there is the working possibility they can trust you and welcome an evening of adventure and revelry. That gig I nearly missed in Lewis because of setting off late in a hire car from Glasgow and racing two hundred miles until one of those moments where it is make-or-break in life: Do I do it and overtake here on this road to the Ullapool ferry, for the money, for the tickets sold, for the people on their way home to get ready for going out . . . ?

Do I go for it? Yes.

And when you overtake on a road with others' cars coming toward you it is so emblematic for you have to speed up because they are approaching and they are using the other lane and yet you have to speed up and yet speeding up brings them closer quicker. Brings it on. They are a perfect guide as to the position of their own threat. The fine thing is that they can make a point, hold their line, hold their speed and cause a crash, or they can see your definite purpose and be happy with where they are at and pull over a bit and ease off the gas. That's what I do if I see a madman overtaking and driving with the indicator really on: I think, "Where's the nearest maternity ward he is off to?" . . . Is that orphanage-smoke I smell . . . ?

That gig was got to partly by phoning Nevis FM and asking them to get the ferry held and they contacted it and I parked randomly and ran on the big gaping whale's-mouth entrance for cars with my guitar and my laptop, unplugging a fruit machine and plugging in the laptop to write a column about that day. The best thing was I went out to a big house party afterwards for Melanie's fortieth and ended up standing in a speedboat on a trailer in the garden getting sprayed by sparkling wine and garden hose to simulate the surf – and there is definitely a photo of this somewhere with, shit, the highly appropriate photonic splash of the flash among the moisture's lashings.

Sawn-off shotgun wedding ring.

Another party, one time in Kyle, I remember chasing a puppy around the rockery to retrieve it because I was the most-able at that late hour, shortly after Bongo left to walk the three miles home to rest before his prawn-shift started and we filled his wellies up with water. The joke backfired as he was too pissed to notice and walked off with water firing up out the back in an arch vaguely reminiscent arc . . . rooster or small Parisian fountain . . .

At that point I had a ring on my finger.

I had driven to Kyle by the Skye Bridge to do one of those gigs in a small room in a small town to about sixty percent of the available humans there over eighteen. They rang the bell and shouted "Time for The Comedy" and everyone went through from the So'Wester bar into the function lounge. It was good and all, yet there was a togetherness of folks that I did not really get greater than. We all sat and drank and I got given some hash by a guy I had given some hash to when he was begging in Glasgow a few years before – Hash Karma. Out all night among rockery and pipes and in the morning I was taken to a walk-in shrimp refrigerator and got a case in the back of the Jag. Back at the pub by eleven for the change of shifts and there was always four folks in overalls at the table. Some would go off to work on the prawns and some would be replaced.

Two days earlier playing football with Jake, aged eight, here at Findhorn and had had to play a little under best which is a skill in itself: not looking like you are too good to therefore be patronizing them in a visible way, mocking and playing with them and yet not looking too shit to them or when people walk past. He had a nil and I had a few. I kept moving my jumper and jacket posts further apart and devised a missing dive over the ball to let it in a goal that went wonky and sprained my finger to a swell.

This swollen finger now here still had a ring on it, in the bar in Kyle at 11 a..m. the morning after the night-still-going a man looked down and said, "You are going to lose that finger."

Not like a threat, not mean, just radically honest. I laughed it off for a few moments then asked how I could get it off. They all agreed in their blue overalls: saw it off.

"Where am I going to get a saw?"

"At the ironmonger's at the top of the road."

Inside they had a lovely display, a pyramid of saws and there on the very sacrificial peak was a wee saw for one pound seventy-two. They asked if I would like it wrapped and I said, "No, open. To go." Walking down the road you have to choose whether you have the saw hidden or the saw out and open. If you hide it, it can be discovered and you'll look darkly motivated and cause fear. If it is out and open and showed then it is enough to cause fears as to why you are walking down the road brandishing a saw, revealing this implement. This is exactly the predicament when I rescued a family heirloom stroke treasured cheese knife from my love this year when it could not be taken on EasyJet, and walked out of Edinburgh Airport carrying a knife too precious and treasured to be put in the see-though cube-of-armistice.

Oh Christ what a laugh, me and the wonderful Miss Janice Fayre were coming back from Jersey Island and there they had a beautiful display of elephant foot, eagle wing and rhino blood, knuckle-dusters, half-opened bottles of milk and furs . . . We were wetting ourselves cos it looked like it was an evil display case in a shop offering these things . . . like a normal South African grocer's . . . like it is v. funny when they advertise things bad to be good. You'll've seen those posters of children smoking et cetera, fully illustrating the thing they do not want to happen. Yet there it is the image up there. The best ever was a big bill poster in Adelaide of a child smoking a cigarette with a huge puff of dry-ice smoke coming out of her mouth every thirty seconds . . . huge giant child smoker right there to be witnessed by all kids that age who cannot read and just witness this in their gaze. It's daft and fails cubed and costs a lot and it is ad space to be sold and is as bent as Jesus Army pick-up trucks.

Right anyhow . . .

Back at the table I now have to choose someone most-able to saw through the ring as I try to do it myself and can hold no purchase. Alan to my left is a graduate and is chosen. He starts in a blitz of speed, trying to get a groove and stay in it. Everyone else, as wasted as him, is looking down at the blur of steel and teeth and the little spray of fairy-confetti flying off. After a while I notice that they all have the same expression on their face: A neat wee smile and alighted eyebrow. Of course! Because any minute now under the serrated teeth of the speeding saw there will be no more metal. At some point, imminent and fast-approaching, there will be suddenly no more metal: just flesh. If even for one or two strokes only it will stop screeping across silver and flay into skin. There is not much anyone can do about this so I am able to not resent these smiles and just seek personal distraction from the unavoidable moment of agony by looking around. By art: on the wall is a superb example of the silver-elasticated thread around-nails to form a Viking longboat all-on-black-velvet-background genre. It amazed me and yet my eye drifted to Alan's yellow wellington boot. To stop them from being nicked in the workplace there was "ALAN'S" written on the side in pen. Excited, I gained a little more distraction from this through enjoyment of a more-acute personal manner. This is the first time I have seen punctuation on a workboot. Just then the ring pinged open and there was no pain. Down to the last, very last stroke Alan had been with it and saved me.

One pound seventy-two: good price for a finger. Could get a nice baguette and brie for that too.

The silver pieces were put back on the dashboard of the Jag and then they got nicked from the unbnlocked Jag by the next morning. Really I am the luckiest man because the only thing I have ever lost in a robbery from cars of mine that have rarely been locked is one broken sawed-off ring and somethings not known. It would have lingered there waiting for its sentimental value to sink low enough for it to get thrown or melted.

Lucky is the nearest word to the feeling I get from many things. Many adventures and many situations, fortunately flukey . . . Being alive is so auspicious . . .

Apart from Shetland and Orkney and Wick the most northern comedic work was way up on the profile forehead of Scotland at Dornock, if Britain is shaped like a jaunty young man with a tiny waist. There are several petrol-crises on the way up as my fuel gauge is greatly overestimating how full my tank is, like it is trying to make me feel good, and in the end that never works. I am writing ideas down on the atlas, matching ideas with wiggly arrows to the corresponding point on the drive. They are large and easy to write on with your left hand while driving. Many of the words I do not see until they are finished, and they have a curious natural arch to them. There are no hitchers.

At my Castle Inn it's a nice fire in the bar and immediately there's a chat with a man at the table by the bar, planning his wedding next year, now, with his wife to-be, then. A year away, I say "How are you going to maintain it?" the chap talks to me and leaves his fiancée to plan, there is a slice of their actual-recipe wedding cake; we try it, Chris from Essex and me. We quarter it, but we end up getting two bits each. "It tastes of brandy," I say. He burps – what amazing karma you are having methinks, your wedding cake is already coming back to you a year before you have even got it yet, already. Tasting fate, tempting cake.

I did a show in the Village Hall, Clashmore, the audience surrounded by huge orange bar-heaters high up on the wall, like grills grilling the crowd. They were like those highly energy-expensive other-era un-ecological-logic red ones that heated the bathrooms back in seventies, pointed down the way because they are so hot; fat single bars glowing red-orangey-red in elliptical cases like the half-opening eyes of devils. They force heat down against its will, unblinking, fighting the trend of the universe, monsters of inefficiency before eco-fuel saving ideas had ever had to be born into consciousness. And also the ways that birthed them.

It's like people are always saying, "Let it out, let it out, man!" Well, you have got to let it in then. Have to burn up the oil to get to the present wave, wind and solar resolution.

It felt exactly as it would be in the Church of the Tanning Christ. Rows of mahogany-Miami-toned pilgrims. People laughed as I ripped down a shiny curtain to wrap myself in five metres of wipe-clean Spar Tartan. Me the patterned-cape crusader vs the evil-eyed villain of fossil fuel.

Four teenage girls with similar scarves called themselves The Spinsters and it seemed an extremely wise and shrewd way of expressing their position just outside the areas of matrimony and just the similar mode of non-choice as a real spinster, yet with the humour that this time at one of life's stations was ending for them.

That night I met Ian in the pub full of Dornock's young folk. The pool table with just reds or yellows – Ian is a champion hammer-thrower and I tell him I wish to Hammer-Throw.

Ian keeps not-believing me, that I am interested in throwing hammers. I am absolutely into it and want to do it primarily on the beach so that our marks will be easier to judge as it's mostly dark now at fast-approaching two in the morning. I get him together with a neighbour who lives "35 metres" from Ian and who he has never talked to. He's a good judge of distances. He drives.

Ian has boots in the boot with huge flattened spikes coming out of the front of them like clumpy prototypes of the Rosa Klebb's nearly in James Bond's shins. They mean Ian can stick them in the ground and then never fall over when he hammers or when he is mighty pissed – and and/or both. In a playing field my first hammer-throw is about nine metres with those quickening spins learned off the telly that feel so different to do as they do to watch. We are on grass near a playground and one of my throws goes and bangs some children's climbing equipment rather loudly in that way only a climbing frame smashed by a giant hammer at night near council housing can be.

After, me and Ian walk the mile and a half to get freshly-baked bakery stuffs. We walk through the countryside which is lit by street lights and I was loving the look of them enormously and we got to the bakers and inside they are as meek as early tomb-builders or people doing the cleaning for some monks and they are all delicately-iced with flour.

Macaroni pie, steak pie and a buttery, all warm and dusty with the soft flour. It was when I was ordering my steak and kidney pie that I heard one of the world's truly great short phrases: "I'm sorry, we have no kidney." Hurray, I embody, say goodnight to Ian chewing and walk home and my key will not unlock the hotel front door. There is no working it so I give chase back and, there he is, ahead of me well lit in the amber fields.

Even now among the front-room trophies he still will not say that he accepts I am genuinely interested that he is a champion hammerer.

Ian points out his daughter's room: "Go in there and I'll kill you."

". . . I only want to stand over her bed reeking of booze, Ian."

A friend once told me about a guy leaning over a cot thinking he was leaning over a balcony and was smoking and flicking his ash . . .

At seven it is quiet to leave, and the right hour to get some reception. Or at least . . .

It is an amazing two-hour drive to Wick up a road set back evenly from the cliff edge. All I can think is how the sun is such a simple sun. It is bright and unbothered by clouds and not too bright on the eye, and bright as possible on the sea ahead around far corners.

I park in Wick and immediately meet the Town Madman, David. He takes me into a fish and chip shop. He talks of fighting for his missus and keeps asking me if I know he is a street fighter and what do I think his hands can do? "Eh? What about these hands? . . . I've got Kung Fu hands."

Not many people last more than ten seconds with him, or ten minutes so that is all the chat he has to have, like a busker that can survive with technically the amount of music for the time it takes people to walk by. It is a great way to do a song part over and over. Thing is, he is all I have at this point and there's a windy peninsula day to fill without getting too sore feet, so as I'm happy to be around him for a while longer, and so get all the chat all the way around twice. The human nickelodeon . . . second time around I leave with the very effective sudden leaving leave technique calling out, ". . . this is where I came in . . ." My motive is honesty, so leaving before feeling bad, so he is not around another person who does not want to be around him . . . its like being a love surrogate . . . yet my motive maya ill-appears a bit swift, borderline incompassionate and somehow a tad unfair; and then this may reflect on him to him like a trace dose, like a bit of his own medicine, ouch, like the venom refined to cure the bite . . .

At that point some too, solace – not much, perhaps a quantum, the smallest discrete quantity possible, no a bit more than that, an iota . . . no bigger, Hedron collider-full . . . still more that the infinite possibility of succor is fractal and atomic and a wee bit it is all, is enough, is ample, is sufficient, . . . a prosperous bounty, adequate, stacks . . .

Mean what I know.

Jesus didn't magic up so much fucking bread so there was twelve baskets of crumbs left over. That's a good one . . . honestly John there was so much scran we had a dozen binbags of leftover scraps . . .

No, that story resonates, reminds people they can be happy with whatever they have or what bread they are given.

". . . Right so that's five thousand people all totally full that maybe twenty-three hundred baguettes . . . gosh the crumbs from that alone . . . would be about what, Geoff! A couple or three carrier bags, eight, ten . . . better safe than sorry . . . a dozen . . . . . ."

Tenth Chapter

My advice to you if you are going to Glastonbury with a daughter and a borrowed tent is just have a quick look to check that there are enough pegs – just a quick check.

Me and Coco head off on a great route: easy-flight to Bristol and then an easy-bus to the bus station then the special festival double-decker, leaving every thirty. And we're in Bristol Airport, that's where there is a golf course running right up to the fence of Runway Five. As we are taxiing in, Coco notices that there are no eyes and noses or mouths on the people in the safety brochure, like they didn't even bother to give them features.

"How are they going to find their way out, Daddy?"

Good point love. Out the window there are men pulling golf bags and this is them golfing right by the runway. You could hook one right over here and 'twould be like the little white roulette ball whizzing around trying to avoid the jet engines' turbines' flimsy ruinable suction . . . In court you just blame your bad grip rather than fundamentalism.

The bus has us right in, in no time.

Poncho, tent and wearing all our clothes, we pitch up in the Family Field. All that talk about sharing and love and relaxed hippy ways and the first thing I have to do is nick tent pegs from surrounding tents so that three of them around us do a wee slow lean as they get one important anchor slowly taken out. We have a laugh and invent The Yellow T-Shirt Game. 'Tis very simple, with only one rule, which is the objective, and no scoring and no losers. Simply put: when you see a yellow T-shirt you simply say "yellow T-shirt". Now you can yellow T-shirt someone else's yellow T-shirt or do your own twice; it was more a mantra thing, a thing about looking and a thing about seeing. You would just find yourself spotting them all over the place, then none for ages then the subconscious periphery would kick in and you would realize you had still been playing. An excellent game. Non-competitive, co-operative and faintly philosophical. Something about seeing them everywhere once you began to relate them to you. Like kids in prams or litter and landmines.

All the way down our thing had been to find out if Snow Patrol were playing, and if they were playing when I was on, and if they would play our favourite song. Every day we sang it in the Saab and I would look at Coco in the eyes as we freewheeled through morning traffic to school. "Would they play it?" we thought. We found out they were on in the afternoon and, hurrah, we are walking towards them, playing Yellow T-Shirt, and we go up, approaching the stage from the side, and we can see the band milling about out on the edge having a fag. Garry the singer is wearing a yellow T-shirt. Coco and I spot him and point shouting, "Yellow T-shirt!" People think we are a bit mad so we go in closer and I shout, "Hey Garry, it's Phil." He is an full fifty-five metres away, though I am sure in my memory he looked up and waved.

Our yahoo gets even bigger as we are there bouncing together, Coco on my shoulders, when our song does indeed, it comes on. They do play it, the favourite. Out of habit I try to look at her in the eyes as I always do, yet she is on my shoulders and I throw a disc out of the spine as I do this. It really gets me, it is sore, I am troubled, kung fu handstabbed in the indefinate lower spine. I am in, though, one of the best moments ever for my daughter, as she is up above everyone, seeing humanity at its best, watching a band and floating raised out of an ocean of happiness, an ocean of people being what they truly want to be – a cheering swilling fluid bunch. So I just reverse the motion and throw my hips the other way and look up at an imaginary daughter on the other side and presto, hey presto, it works! I slip the disc back in and we carry on bouncing and turning and rodeo-ing unstoppably.

When she was in bed at night I would nip out for strolls around and, at dawn, I saw a lone fire twirler twirling her poi until her flames faded to smoke trails as the flying fires died out and she twirled glowing smoulder trails with a huge appeal.

Next year we were back and with friends and more kids and they all came into the great Cabaret tent when I was doing my half hour. At that time I was in among the audience getting together an improvised Kid Orchestra with one kid on didgeridoo, another singing, one dancing and me on guitar. Then all the kids I knew came in and was able to tell the yellow story of the previous year with Coco there.

A thing about Glastonbury is that there is room for wonder. There is a chance that the two thousand or two hundred people in the tent will listen and they are open to more gently groovy stuff. They are not a comedy-club crowd. They have momentum and can go with you to more fabulous places. This gig has the opportunity to be the greatest show ever done like this.

The following year Coco and I had befriended a group who were near us at the KT Tunstall gig and a few in she calls out is there anyone in the tent whooo's young . . . anyone fourteen . . . or something like that and all the friends round us knew Coco's name and age by now and they were calling out yes over here . . . and then Tunstall the funster got her name and dedicated her favopurite song to her. Chances of that. Random. Marv.

After that Glastonbury there was the G8 meeting in Scotland and I remember a moment when it all seemed to be a big mess. A big mess of how to understand it and how to see oneself in it.

There emerged an amazing set of details that laid it all clear for me. For I had actually been at the anti-G8 camp near Stirling with my kids and lots of people from Findhorn who had helped set up the infrastructure. There were loos to be built and dug and roads to be laid and kitchens to run. There were folks from all over Britain and Europe and there were secret meetings of strategy happening all over. The field was very bumpy and kids ran about and Spanish women's dreads and flags moved around and Yorkshire cake-makers set up their ovens. There was a hell of a lot of boots and solar-powered computing, mattresses in horseboxes. There were Council Permits: people were serious and, as you entered, there was registration and the Police were keeping their distance for the Clown Army was strongly represented.

The day before the mass-march towards Gleneagles I made a salad for a woman, with watermelon all spread about to look like sushi, in a piece of rare field-cuisine. Watched her eat it and played my guitar.

It was like being on the same side as someone yet not at all. Here we were, inside a fence, all supporting each other, all on the same side and yet I suddenly felt that there was only one side. There were people wearing Glastonbury wristbands where we had been. The G8 meeting was being held at five-star Hotel Gleneagles, where I have paid for a room and stayed the nights of T In The Park once, and in paradigm style was truly straddling worlds as our Rizlas blew off the roof of our suite's balcony and were falling like massive deluxe confetti over the main entrance and landed on the shoulder of an Italian in tweeds, too straddling like a bad straddle over a strange someone in a plane and they wake up, when I was five-star busted and almost caught nicking a bathrobe checking out because the long white belt tie was trailing behind me as I left reception like a massive mousey tale from the bag I'd stuffed it in. What a year there is definitely the memory of driving away extremely slowly from Gleneagles in the Reliant Scimitar wearing the robe and posting it to my sister Deb for her birthday who said years later that it was kind but it had shit on it . . .

Am I undercover then, or now? No.

Was that time I stayed there accidental twenty-four hour research for this life now? Yes.

I have been to ten T In The Parks, it is on land owned by a branch of my family and it is on the farm next to that of my childhood best-friend and only a mile and a half from where my Mum still lives. Cycled there one year on the white bikes with BennyRamone and we were cowboys of mirth. I was born near here, know Gleneagles and Glastonbury, I watch the riots on TV from the house of the guy who plays the opening chords for the Proclaimers to launch the whole Live 8 Gig. Played rugby at Fettes a few years after Blair had left. Am "in" here.

Around this time we got the Nicklaus on the banknote from St Andrews, where my Grandfather had won playing for Scotland against England in the Calcutta Cup, and we got London getting the-Olympics-after-the-next-one at the time, and the bombings all in one week.

The bill to host the Games may well be six billion pounds which may well be the amount Bono wants to get the World Bank to drop in debt from "Third World" countries.

I do not know where my T-shirt is made, by whom, how old they are and how poor the conditions. All I know is that we allow it. We, us, allow Fettes to continue, support Gleneagles, Tesco and Westminster, continue the voting system we have endorsed. They aren't the problem, their misuse is. Seems to be that all of us will make a mistake of taking sides in an effort to end the abuse of the planet yet that would appear to be the only thing that contributes to it. An only-solution would be free to be able to enjoy the flavours others already taste and be happy with less: second-hand cotton and used cars and new voting systems and cycle paths and a hundred Glastonburys up the coast in place of motorways which increase car-jams replaced with the old solar-powered electromagnetic monorails or milkfloats, golf carts, who knows, and cycle paths. Simply skip an Olympics or two, cancel debt, be an austere bunch and spread it all around. AutarKy.

Up at Fettes, the posh Edinburgh fee-paying independent public school for boys and girls where I played rugby, there is a monument in giant stone material of a full kit First World Warrior/Second World War British soldier down on his side and below etched in stone are the words: "Carry On." As schoolboys we had to laugh and snigger and see the overview and lament the hypocrisy. Oh, oh oh what a lovely class war! Honouring the footsoldiers that must die here where they surely aim to train officers.

"Oh, Matron . . . will you set up extra medical facilities and save as many as you can?"

"Oh, General, they're getting slaughtered out there."

That M77 road to Prestwick is bloody handy yet I do remember going to visit the Camp and doing a gig to support the blockade and the tree-dwellers living there to stop the bypass cutting through sacred land. What a coincidence because Me and Des were accidentally the first to use that sacred road. The synchroni-city bypass. Can you offset your own goodness?

When we all left the G8 summit there in an untaxed Volvo, we left early and alone and attracted interest the Police were there in numbers to check all vehicles and we were the only one and they pulled us over and checked everything. Even taking out a golf club seven iron I had and gave it a good inspection on full terrorist alert, and heightened realms of concern, so much so they missed the missing tax-disc. Aaah, thems was the good old days back in the day before computerized vehicular registration. Shit, maybe there had been a golf ball golf shot terrorism act finally.

Mmm, oh for the perfect three-month marriage . . .

Went through a Marriage Ceremony in two thousand and four.

We met on the street. Nelson the saxophonist and I were busking with a harmonica and enthusiasm. Her friend knew my friend so they talked and that left us together. I asked if she would like to wrestle and she said yes – turns out that if someone accepts this invite they will marry. Not your usual wrestling though, no, Eskimo wrestling – which involves standing in a forward sportstance with one's right foot big toe-to-toe with theirs and then one right hand holding the other's and seeing who can get the other off balance by pulling pushing, feints and force. Despite large amounts of bling, necklace, blouse and make-up and a shiny dress, she beat me four-three. That was my first defeat in this game ever. Our friends were now waiting for us.

She was Betsy. She got in a taxi and after the door closed I managed to drag down the window from the outside with two flat hands and ask her to stay and not go. The meter was running and the friend close up to her, yet who doesn't want to hear those words if they are meant?

Slightly less homed at the time I was charging my phone in the hoover-socket in pubs. Have a drink, stand over it and hey presto. This time in Groucho's Glasgow she was there again and when I came back for the forgotten phone, she asked if I remembered her. A yes. We made a date for the next morning, met at eleven and then, after a short walk in the park, took her dog and her ex-boyfriend's Volvo and went skinny-dipping. It was rather lovely to sit on a rock naked together and swim in the fresh warm infinity pond outside town. "There'll be no kissing," she said and she was right. Even though we hung out all night, lying in the back of the Volvo, with a good view, listening to Will Oldham through tears of joy and discovery.

Courtship, lovemaking and nights out drinking followed until suddenly it became a thing-to-fear-the-loss-of and she was gone. We both sat at the back of different buses leaving Edinburgh Bus Station and she decided not to see me again. Mad and ideal.

We did though and then she really meant it, later, again.

I spent six or eight months longing for her, accepting she was away, staying in and learning the different sounds made by different trees in the wind and leaving the house that I stayed in at dawn because the builders came early and going to snooze in the Mini Clubman . . . yeh then.

Then one day I passed a café and she was there in with a friend. I walked around and came back to the window to meet her eye and write the words "I Love You" backwards in a heart shape to her through the window on the glass steamed up with my breath. How could that fail? Inside, kneeling at her sofa, I said more of what I wanted to say. Then some people at the next table had their order of nachos arrive and I spoke to them, explained the situation, begged a little and they gave us them.

That night we met up with four other friends in a pub, at a good table, where a pub quiz started to grow around us. We entered under the name "The Victors". We won cash and wine and it was I who got to throw the winning dart in the Activity round to claim full glory. Coincidentally my car boot was full of kindling so I suggested we drink our winnings on some wasteground nearby with a fire and cook some sausages. The local Snack Van that I had been going to for fern cakes and bacon rolls for years, and where I talked the son out of joining the Police Force, they lent me a pot of already-boiling water to make mashed potatoes. We sang songs and the harmonica was out and everyone left me there with some discovered pot-plants around me as a gift so it really felt like a home.

Next day I met Elizabeth at the supermarket and convinced her I still loved her.

Moving into her house, we made a crazy dash towards everything. One night we were drinking champagne at a piano-bar and she said, "Shall we get married?"

We set it up and the night before I was making heart-shaped confetti by hand cutting it out of coloured crepe paper and yellow wanted ads newsprint with curly-edged nail scissors; after an hour there were thirty two pieces. We took the early slot and were married at ten in the morning. In this ceremony at a Registry Office they don't do vows like in the churches on television, no one gets to repeat the romantic coda. No, here it is a negative in primary aspect: "I know of no legal impediment by which we may not be married." No vows, just this harsh Scottish truth: It's Legal. The moment we arrived at the Registry Office there was an old style security guard in peaked hat and diagonal white sashy plastic belt affair and he opens his mouth and the first thing he says is: "There's No Confetti Here . . ." It's pure genius and "he's wrong" because I have some . . . Guess they can't be bothered to hoover . . . well they've gotta hoover so I suppose when they hoover they don't want it to be teeny light wee scraps of . . . no no . . . when they hoover it clogs up the machine . . . no they'd have a wide-nozzle attachment . . . it must be just the obviously accidentally most likely wrong thing you can do, whoops, which tends to lend itself to resemble petty mean-spirited awfulness.

Then we went and bought the Chocolate Labrador Puppy from the ads in the yellow newspaper and I did a gig that night in Falkirk. We had Krug champagne and Bobby shat all over the foyer of the theatre. Fucking double-booked myself on me own wedding.

When the confetti was thrown in, just two handfuls, some of it flew so well it was caught and thrown again.

The fact that I already had kids became a thing that ultimately grew into something that could end it all, and it did. One day I said I was going; she smashed up my guitar, cut her hands on the sharply pruned strings at the top and I wrenched the car keys from her to leave and to drive to a gig in Hamilton. There the staff lent me a guitar and the gig was an unbelievable relief. Sadly her hands healed without my help.

Recently up north in Elgin at the Johnstons Cashmere Sale in December there were a few Italian and French voices heard. They come to buy a great deal of cashmere at mere fractions of the other prices they are marketed at. Their flights must consist of less cost than the difference because of Ryanair from near Naples for example. There is this lovely image in my mind of a conscientious Italian millionairess planting trees to offset her so-many flights that she is mulching her paper tickets and cashmere garment receipts and tags in an offset olive grove or offset orange-tree orchard, pulling the wool pullover over their own eyes. There were also lots of Scottish mature ladies who pull out their own larger size from the bottom of the cardigan pile causing the odd cashmere avalanche. Get back, cardigan landslide! . . . Buried under a lambswool-rug pile . . . Death by Angora . . . you can just hear the sounds of quality buttons clacking together.

Everyone queues outside and are given black bin liners, classy, so there are no hidden woven thefts, woolknit nicked in handbags. Inside my job is not to buy, my job is to saunter around watching others and talking about the new synthetic Plasmere and letting people feel it a bit: the neatly folded bin bag worn as a shawl, the plasmina . . . go on have a feel . . .

There is an Real offset-plantation and billboard a mile from Stansted. Clever ideas yet surely not the best place to plant trees with all the fumes. Offset Trees Upset By Fumes In High-Flying Irony – RyanAir IronyAir, British Air Ways – they could print the tickets on the leaves that have fallen prematurely.

It is all so mixed up. In Manchester last night at the Lowry we are opposite MediaCity, all one word. It doesn't want to be all one word and it fucking is and it sounds a bit too much like mediocrity, and the head of the beebc still has not taken up residency here, and is maybe sad and afraid of salford's medium shitty.

Last week me and three-fifths of my brothers all heard a radionews man saying, "And prostitutes will be rejoicing tonight as the Suffolk Killer has been caught."

Rejoicing, let's see it as they dance in the filthy park and have a badly lit dark street party with prophylactic bunting; as they sell their bodies in the night along cold wet streets, partially dressed sometimes, to feed dangerous drug-habits; rejoicing that now, at least, they don't have to fear being killed as well. We had to we laughed and it nearly did our nuts in with its mix. We care for people yet we do not save them.

All we can do is believe the truth that there is one race of humans, there is no "them" only "us", and try and require less material stuff.

I gave away a hat once on a night out after a gig at the Alhambra in Brighton, by the sea. We were all being threatened for our annoying bohemianism by the pool-table in a pub. The hat went to someone as a mirror of the camaraderie-bonds developed in conflict.

A year and months later I drank all day with the Orb by mistake and the beautiful dancer Shelley Love outside the Spiegel Tent before doing a gig inside, where the hat came back. It was at the end and I was putting on a grey tweed jacket and talked about the hat and then there came the call that it had been brought back. It went on the head like crown; I was milking it, knowing that those that know and believe knew and believed and some would not be able to now. It was another karmic tweed hat, a long-haul boomerang of what-goes-around headwear. Lowering it slowly, trying to out-do all them false kings who take their crowns.

Outside afterwards a brand new set of youths asked if they could have the hat and it seemed it like to move on this hat so it went off again.

For two thousand and six's August Festival accommodation I took a tent out the back of some luxury flats in the most beautiful of Edinburgh's internal city gardens. Looked out upon by the hundred kitchen windows of two amazing concave Marchmont Crescents; there were trees and little lawns and a stunning lack of fence. The branches would caress the canvas. My upstairs neighbour was Tim Minchin expecting a child very reasonably soon with his partner. He was the new-form protegé discovered by my agent and doing as well as he could for her. The show I saw was inspiring as hell, being retrieved from the back of it at ten eleven p.m. to be on my own stage at ten fifteen. For me it was useful and possible and helpful to carry straight on with his energy and the remainder reminder of a jolt from one of his songs to go for it. He had sung directly, pitch imperfectly out of key, with his accordion as an emotional statement, I seem to remember; singing in one key playing in another.

Each morning in the gardens among all the kitchen windows there would be acoustically-enhanced coffee-cup tinklings and conversation, a multitude of different radio stations and, no doubt, a few eyes checking out the commune-of-one. A neighbour was worried there would be more than me of us and when he found out it was to be just a single-tent-city he was happy to let me be. There was a room rented for me in the ground-floor flat yet it just seemed better out here in the air with my non-office hours and long battery-life of the mobile. It definitely seemed like if people could be happy with one tent spread out in a garden like this there could be a lot less homelessness. The kids though might be worried about and that is a sound reason for the objections that would be raised yet the system is still intact, or the principle. We have space for homes unused. You could audition them as old time wise storyteller types, and this might create a cooler vibe about it all.

The "backs" is where it's at. All this not out the front, in the traffic and the commerce. The rowdy kids can define the class. There is another truth. Here was a quiet double-oasis because this is not the Sahara, this is Marchmont. It was delightful and informed the geometry of my show that year. Also there was economic streamlining at work here and so hey, if the cheapest jacket in the charity shop is the one you like then, double bingo bonus ball plus rollover . . .

Chapter Six

Like the time I was on the way to visit my Desmond. We lived together for a while. I said, "You never have to do the dishes." We did not explain too much. I would buy him an aeroplane ticket. He would give me forty-two quid if I was in trouble. I love him. Excellent flatmates in a summer of love. This time I am off round to visit him he says to bring him a fish supper and a can of Coke. Buzz him on the phone to let him know I am outside the crescent flat he is borrowing. He comes to the window singing on the phone and up opens a big sash window and chucks the keys and carries on dancing the rest of the song. I'm dancing too. We dance together. There's another man along the curve at another window sees me dancing. He has more chance on a crescent than any other road of seeing Desmond dancing, though I think he can't. Me, I know Desmond is there so I dance with abandon. Of course, it would be a great way to have a dance on your own if you wanted one; if there was no friend at a window still no one would know that there was nobody so as long as you gave it considerable laldy you could dance without worry.

Thrilling are these little areas like this. That, if you see a man watching you do something from his window, and he cannot be sure there is no one there or someone there then you give him the gift of your confidence.

Des opens the window and, leaning low-to-knee height, chucks the keys out and down to me. I am still in a dancestep quietly as I hear them do the involved "scchhing" with themselves on the way to spreading out that keys do in the air. The beginning of their trajectory is noticed and I decide in that moment to catch them falling in the pocket of my jacket. They fall as a trajectory known to me in the seeing of it and – "floot" – they are zoomed right in there to slot into the jackpot jacket-pocket where they pierce the can of cola which then, so upset, starts spraying cola out of my pocket up into my face – handy travel Cola fountainhead, personal sasparilla pocket-bedee. The man who saw my dancing may have been excited to see a pocket fountain like this especially if he had not picked my movement as the catching of keys.

Desmond is laughing at the window into his dancing. The keys are with me now and yet, for all the sticky excitement, I somehow go into a place of having forgotten that and, overcome with my own champagne reception, I go over, up the steps and stand at the front door having slipped into a wrong pattern to be waiting for Desmond to come down and let me in as he usually has to do. It was like flashing, resetting, wiping the situational slate clean with the soda face-wash, a mental sorbet. Standing there almost impatient until Desmond realized there must be something up. He comes down and just as he is about to open the letterbox to speak, for he is now effectively locked in, it dawns to me. When he looks out I am retrieving the sugary keys and moving to the door.

"Coca-Cola amnesia," he says.

Aye.

Chapter 23

All its own: the un-squareable lone Fibonacci high prime, pi cubed chapter.

An unexpected drink: It all began round the back of the same Marks & Spencer's building; twice, round at the staff entrance. And some of the staff do entrance. The wee group of boys were on their way to a club, I admired their Jack Daniels bottle-drinking on the street, took an interest, watched them look for a place to drop the bag with the ones they couldn't manage – handy. Saw one of them take the white plastic bag and stash it by a bin. "There's three bottles," was what one of them called out and there were a few other people about to be passing that it was also heard by. Though it was me who had just come out of the film and it was me who was counting my money and wanting to go for a beer. It was me who didn't have enough for a pint. It was me who had just passed a couple on the date that was going nowhere. It was me who wished them my happiness and it was me who had held this staff door open for the sales-assistant right here, late on Christmas Eve, just here, out the back of Marks & Spencer, ten paces from where the heavy clinking of full bottles is happening and am aware that all the luck, that meant I delayed here and there to get, just in time, to the boys and their bag; now is a lifetime of chance turned to all this time. This life is the million other-ones that could have been. Either that, or you don't look at it like that – I don't. It's only one theory of worry . . . It never enters my mind that there is an absent parallel life. There's a nothing spooky-mama and I know this because you'd have to work out what all the other things that could have happened are and one can't. So there is no chance of holding this proposal and knowing you are right. You can never be true to say it's right. Yet saying it might be is not enough for doctrine writing. So you have to ask then: is doing that not merely another way to not have to get into this life, here now contained in this moment, to talk of possible others? It's a kind of an infinitely vain state; will never end, can be kept going. Well aye, I think there is a thing being shown in the state and it is a statement, and that statement is "that we do not know how we can even exist" and, all after that, until that is answered, is the elephant in our front chambers. That good-thing-happening is not the opposite of good-thing-not-happening or lost chance – it is all, to me, about open eyes and not squinting. Squinting is for a good aim. Nothing in my actions made it happen, just open to it when it did.

Everything in my mind let me enjoy these salvaged ales.

Opened a beer by bashing its lid off on a flat metal edge with my arm in a plaster, the untethered bone breakable by sending out a rigidity that is not suitable. We are meant to roll and bend, not hold back the world with a frigid wrist.

Really it had all begun exactly as I got onto the train. There are a hundred billion points it could start at and it has always begun by existing and it started here: As I was just about to get on a train that I was not absolutely sure I was going to go on determination as the lack of the need for anything other than that choice to happen. It's either all starts or no starts.

The best thing to do by far when leaping off a waterfall is to keep your hands high above your head, lengthen yourself like an arrow, straighten your flight and avoid flapping your hands in a dodo's attempt to break your fall, slapping them on the surface in a terrible twin twists position.

I got on the train with a tiny last mouthful of mulled wine, received from Fiona who was opening up as she closed the stand selling the last of the last batch and telling me of her honeymoon in Vegas and getting up at six in the morning to go clubbing. Before the first day of Christmas Fiona gave to me two cups for free and I stood by the ice-rink watching the skaters skate and the hoodlums hoodle until some kids I know from my street came up to talk to me. One of my mulled wines had been the perfect thing to leave with them; one step up from shandy and with a culinary essence like brandy-snaps or sherry trifle. It's Christmas time, it's spontaneous, it's around an alpine activity where a mild stimulant is helpy.

The other was small and swishing around in my hand on the platform as the forty-year-old lady came up, the very long snowboard bag which she was technically dragging and was in fact designed like that with wee hidden wheels at the end. She looked unusual in that instant veil of framed intuition: like, where were her other bags? And, if she was ski-lady, why wasn't her wardrobe seemingly in line with this at a first glance?

Of course it was her daughter's bag and, as I stood in a phase unknown, I heard her call for "Hazel" and offered to go and look for her . . . No, she is here, coming up the platform running, shouting about having lost her and it all seems to make such sense. Her Mum was the kind that worries enough to go ahead and leave the one she worries about behind at the ticket office, and they only left Balloch forty minutes ago – the chain and the link – I step on the train with the daughter and help her with her long long-bag.

Still standing up, she says she met me last night and I say "Eh?" then I ask if she was the water-girl.

So, in fact, it had all begun during the dancing at Club Optimo which I was lucky to get into because I was a bit late and had gone to the wrong club first and when I did come to the clubmouth inside the curl of queue my friend Pum was not in sight. I was all ready for the ultimate moment of standing looking, alone inside the curl waiting and just definitely being all unwith my friend. She is Pum, she is six feet in her stockings in platform shoes and with bleached hair still is not visible; maybe she's inside. Think it's all over and my name is called out loud. Pum is one person back from going in the entrance so I run over, vaulting a small marble vaultable thing and cheer an inner-city close echo cheer and join her in the queue, noticing the bouncers look on almost poignantly.

Inside we dance a lot and at one point my dancing is just to consider the water I could nick, and I pick up a lidded-bottle and a wee lady in the dark says with an arm and a hand that "hey do you mind?" a second, then, with a calm kindness, looks at my face and waves me on – "Okay, seeing as it's you." We never say any more although she pops into view here and there.

Now I am sitted right by her on this train and she is Hazel and flushed and lucky to be on this train and phewth.

We talk thickly with few gaps and get so much from each other that we get onto even personal things that are part of the pillars and Hazel tells me about the monkeys she loves that are so agile and so unbelievably believably good at climbing that they are unable to walk on the ground with their bendy legs and so they skip, have to skip, can only skip.

On a bridge now, it seems to be the one that you cross after Perth . . . Now Perth is where we both have to change, where we are both looking out for and being aware of. The kind of thing her Mum would say is "Don't miss your stop." . . . We have missed it and Hazel has to get to Aviemore to start a new life and job and residency.

The ticket conductor moves by and we are clearly expressing Christmas Eve horror at the fact we have missed Perth and ultimately there is no thing he can do. We are startled and I decide after a while to run after him up the train, bang on the driver's door and put forward the idea that there existed an option to pull the emergency stop button if there was a valid reason and could we please, just imagine, and accept our need now as being valid.

We'd've had to've run back up the roof of the train fast 'er than it was going, with the big bag to get a bit back in time to cover the distance, with only ten minutes to get our connection anyway and that is hardly enough time to stop a train and drag the bag over miles of Scottish fields to get back to Perth over a bridge we have lamented being on at high-ish speeds three minutes track-time ago.

All night now, from now on, Hazel and I would follow this objective, we would have this marvellous thing to achieve. The Objective: To-Get-To-Aviemore. And, if we ever faded, we could cling back on to it and we would try everything and anything and all would be acceptable as we had each other's belief and each other to be on it with. On the continuing journey to Dundee, city of the Discovery, I worked out that I would certainly borrow a car through my good club-running friend Joon Broon and would drive Hazel up to Aviemore and then myself on to Findhorn to see my friend at her party.

It could have been so easy and we were so relaxed as we got our stuff out to the front and I went back in to use the phone all prepared to achieve and come back with good news. I stood below the unusually reminiscent grill-heating of the station concourse, and so recent, it was just the other month they were at the Carnegie Hall, Clashmore, and just a chapter away for you. On the payphone calling my agent to get the number of Joon whose address I had mantracised yet was not sure of her real name. Karen reminded me of the Stand Club and I called them. Of course Karen is Norwegian and December Twenty-Fourth is their real Christmas Night, they decorate the tree, and when I phone they are all dancing around it and opening some special Scandinavian delicacies.

'Tis perfect timing to share with her a happiness and then, of course, they are right in the middle of opening the kransekake and I wish them well. Then I track down Joon's number from the bar I did a gig at with her, from the boss Ian. They say she is in Amsterdam, which I remember I did already know from the time we watched her son come on after half-time playing rugby in the sub-minus winds here in Dundee against my hometown of Kinross that Sunday last month when I was last here.

I explain I am off-route and need to take a car to Aviemore then on, and will return it later. Her brother cannot lend me her car and of course I am at ease with that and decide never to press and only suggest, in order to be sweet, and also because if you do not put too much pressure there is not that far for folk to come back from if they have said no.

Luckily there is a long van-cab at the head of the queue at the train station, capable of fitting the board-bag all the way in and we slide the doors shut and head off, calling on the man to stop at the Repertory Theatre as there seems to be activity visible through the handy glass-sided architecture. In a way it is fortunate that that design was chosen for this theatre.

I nip in and ask for Hamish the man who runs it and there he is not; and I ask a lady if she can lend me a car and she is close to agreeing. She said, "If I had had one."

This is encouraging, and actually it feels wholly plausible as a viable option, and an optional vibe, like everything can be encouraging to you if it is, and because it existed and anything that didn't open up, well there was always the chance it could have, and would do also, in my mind. Which in itself is a good thing – like getting to where we wanted to go.

The big thing is that getting there is the thing. The fun is here not solely arranged for later. Earning is as good as spending the time. The glory of earning is as strong as spending time or money.

There was a fierce realism to my optimism. Soon we would be working the floor of the big rock-bar near here with a common aim – Hamish, who has booked me and known me for nineteen big live shows in his venue can be called later and this is referred to as Option B, should we need it. We take the long bag into the depressurizing zone between doors of this rock venue where the bouncers are keeping warm.

We get straight in and ask them if they can get us a car. We cannot afford the price of being downhearted, so when they say they cannot think of a car we could borrow, we think, "Well, surely there will be one. It's Christmas after all."

Two drunk women come through, they have their own mistletoe and "Have they any generous brothers?" we ask and "Any brothers with a car?" . . . Just gawps.

Ian welcomes us and we move through-and-in with the bag.

At the bar Hazel sensibly has a half Guinness and gets me in a pineapple juice for to borrow a car.

I start casually asking everyone if they are from here and if they feel they can lend a car or if they are aware of anyone who might be into it. We are trapped at this special time. This is crowdfunding old school. I ask a young man who gets down on his knees to praise our request. Together on our knees, we hug. He has no car and looks like he is thinking about it though too.

The two drunken ladies with their own mistletoe try to call me over and I go to talk to the man who they are with.

Sometimes people hear us and don't believe it; sometimes they don't really hear; sometimes it is too much of a seemingly-jokey thing for them to accept. All this and it is our objective . . . It is perhaps ten thirty-five by now.

Hazel and I now start to have fun with it all, starting to have a laugh talking to all the folk about The Objective we have and working the room.

One guy I ask suggests the radio stations as with the laptop-loss and me and Ian go up to his office to try them and they are all pre-recorded with no one on the phones and even the rental companies are unavailable. Besides, as I tell Hazel, we need to keep some options back because we would prefer to borrow than hire and we can always hire.

We start to develop not only the language of this situation, also the bank of options, I start to call it. Option A: Joon's house, and B: H. Glen @the theatre, and then C: being here, and D: the radio stations, and then the rentals, E.

So when a man offers to start a fund with three quid to buy a car I jump half the alphabet and refer to it as option S. Kickstarter at 3 percent . . .

Option T is the fact that there is a rock-covers Tribute to Tribute Acts on the stage and perhaps I can go on there and appeal to the bar in a more-good widespread way. In the meanwhile I take my first break and ask the fund-starter's lady companion to dance. We dance to You Really Got Me and she is perhaps the finest rock-dancer in the room. The table of eight women at the front watch on and I am aware that, even though I am on a break, I am still forwarding The Objective by being highly visible as we are the only people dancing.

The band, Option S, asks me onstage and I say I will go on later when they are on their break.

One young man thinks about letting me borrow his one-o-six for cash and then changes his mind – offering us a lift to Pitlochry. Option U.

I go for a pee and up the backstairs meet Aaron, who will turn events enormously for us in two distinctly different ways.

He is on the stairs, it's him! We have already been on our knees together and here in the quiet he gets quickly around to the fact that he is glad to be seeing his daughter tomorrow. He is not with his partner and they are still fighting, he looks around in that way people who are about to cry can often do rather that just look at you and cry.

I pee and ask for a car in the loos and a chuckling man says he has a Porsche we can have outside and I knock it back saying that we need something bigger for the large bag, and I remember the Porsche that did pick me up the other day because it was a highly visible one with a spoiler, seen around my area for a while, and he recognized me and it was a quick hitch and he ran a massage mansion yet said he was a mechanic . . .

He accelerated so fast my spine cracked in the fine leather-backed wing-tip seats. Osteoporsche.

All night me and Hazel just had our story that we told over and over, it was all we had and it was all we needed. Terrifically so: all that we were was The Objective. We decided to go outside for a spliff and, after a brief conversation and me going inside against the wind to roll and coming out and going back in for a lighter that I borrowed off a guy who saw me at a gig at Reading and it had a leather thong to keep it safe we achieved this little objective quite well and rolled a large one and were sitting finishing it up when the two girls without-their-own-mistletoe came out and passed us and wanted to say goodbye and the less-drunk one with long hair said that she had been out with a footballer and had abandoned a wee Ford Fiesta a couple of months ago and it was just down the road. Option V. Pretty soon we would have to start an alternative system like the number plates.

Hazel and I had many options and this was the first actual car we might touch. "Where are the keys?" I ask, as the less-drunk one is describing it to me as white and registration plate un-memorised – they should still be in it.

She starts to show us where it is and suddenly realizes and mentions that it is now behind a fence in some sort of yard. Yes, so we have to relegate it in the bank of options.

Inside we walk and Ian is saying, "You are on now. Where have you been?" Wow, late for a gig!

I walk to the stage as I have not done in the hundreds of times I have walked to the stage. I mount the steps casually with The Objective on my mind.

I talk in a way I have been waiting to do for years, to simply be telling of our situation and appealing for help.

Here, en masse, the lads are shouting; not hearing or finding me too preposterous for their fun night.

Fixing on Hazel and telling our story of long bags, water bottles, mulled wine and missed stops and it could have been hilarious too and a man is shouting and I threaten him with The Objective threatened. Then he makes a move for the stage and I move on him as Bruce Lee would and, as he comes up with one foot onto the steps leading to the stage, I simply push his forehead with enough force to send him back down and am away from the mike for perhaps just under three seconds.

It occurs to me that I don't need a room full of cars. I just need one and, from being onstage here now for The Objective, I need just one person to be inspired to be committed and to give it to us . . . There has been a thing learned from the laptop balloon-poster.

Using that approach seems to work and leaving the stage, Aaron comes forward and says, "Yes, yes." He will help us and he punches the air to prove it.

We all go outside, passing the man with the car for sale that he has talked down to get out of lending it to us and then decided to sell it and is asking, "Two hundred too much?"

Outside it goes to a new place: Aaron is tripping and, as much as life is a trip and a game and something you can play and get really into, he can't seem to get with it.

He started to skip about and twice I apologized as twice I had to ask him if he was really into helping us.

"Right, what shall we do?" he said. "Well, you live here who do you know?" "Ma brother George." "How do we call him?" And Aaron takes out his mobile – this is it, the business – it comes out and he says he has it. I laugh and am happy and, as a group pass by I shout happily "Aaron has a mobile!" and reach into my pocket where my mobile is resting dead. Already dead and nevertheless do what I have been waiting years to do: I chuck it and fuck it . . . A huge throw right over the dual carriageway, orphaning it in an arch with a happy turn-away before it lands.

Aaron says then that he has no talk time. "Talk Time" is what me and Hazel have tons of, so we look for a phone box and there is one right across the road there.

At it Aaron starts to dither a bit and kind-of makes out that he can't get his brother's number off his phone and I state quite clearly in a rhetorical way that "You do not need to have Talk Time to access the memory on your phone." He is right here with us and he appears to be kind of stalling and I check with Hazel and, to my lack of shame, ask him once more, so thrice if he is with us and he says yes and phones George from the call box.

He talks, then I talk to George and I sense that George is together and believes us and I ask him about a car and he says "Do I know what kind of car he has? He has a BMW!" in a way that I take to mean that I will never drive it.

He says to leave it with him and we are to call back. Aaron calls back in two or three minutes and it doesn't happen.

At this point it becomes clear to me with the vision of The Objective that Aaron can't be helping us, and we ask him to "Right now, start now and tell us exactly where we all are at and what we are doing" or we can't be with him.

"Aye. Well, erm, thing is . . . so, first I would have to say . . ." It's Over. He knew it. He did the look-away again. Then we stood still until he walked away across the road.

It was like he wanted to be into a thing, a real friendship-achievement of some sort. Yet that's not enough for us: we want a car.

We are in a sheltered moment now and Hazel says she is losing faith and I say some things along those lines you would to inspire someone and say, "Well, we could always just get a cab."

We go round the corner back into the wind and she really is a smashing person – others would have snapped or bent or been lifted up and blown away by now. Aaron has left, so I press re-dial in the phone box and George answers and has got a Mercedes taxi he can get for us.

Well, that's something. So we take it and here it is: outside The Doghouse, the Mercedes with the driver. We get in and again, from scratch, tell our story with the front passenger door open to the kerb; I sit in on the lintel, the threshold and am in a bit and, as I am telling him the story, I look up at Hazel and she is here as I am. Charlie, wonderful Charlie-the-driver says that he loves the job. In a way he was the first just to listen to our story and say "yes".

Ian had helped, Joon would have, Aaron did and all the others: the boy who offered the lift and the mistletoe-girls and the lighter-man and the fund-man and the table-of-eight.

Aaron is there and asks to come with us. So I do stress that he is not to be daft and stay here to see his daughter and we'd way prefer to leave with his full kerbside wave-off for us.

We got helped, he got kid, kid got dad.

Hazel is here now and the long bag is beautifully in.

Hazel chooses the back seat and Charlie slides us away from the stop and we are in a sense beginning again and I wave at Aaron out the window until we are out of sight up a hill and around the roundabout that must have some remnant of my phone in it.

Charlie is a magnificent driver with over forty thousand miles of driving and, as we smooth into the night at a constant temperature, it really is a pleasure to be travelling in this style of way.

So quiet and lovely and with no need, no overriding compulsion, without The Objective or a need to convince anyone of anything, we were free to express other things. Off the hook to shoot the breeze and have fun story, and find stuff out and recreate. War-stop, make-art.

The feature of all this story is how amazingly helpful it was to be positive. Now it was so true too of Hazel – she had understanding of things in forms expressible that are usually results of more years in a sense. She had this beautiful way of expressing her optimism, that some people see a million ways to fail and one way to succeed and how it is best to see things just as occurrences and therefore all is equally possible and so too the idea that toast always falls on the marmalade side is really not true, it is just that we care. We, selfishly, care so much more about the marmalade side, the side of human-interest that we make it feel like it happens more. Plus there might also be something in it – maybe the toast falls like an arrow, weighted to be led by the mass of the condiment.

Charlie tells us of his great passion for golf and he tells of playing at dusk at Carnoustie with a flask of Drambuie and whisky and about how he thinks he will play on Boxing Day on what he thinks is the most beautiful course in the world.

Charlie pulls over at a lay-by and says by the way, Happy Christmas! – and it is twelve o one and he has to get a present out of the boot and Hazel says how, if she might need a pee in half an hour she doesn't want to pee by the side of the road. Charlie says he knows a good toilet in Pitlochry.

Then Charlie opens the gift and it is a miniature of whisky and some chocolate breasts.

Actual chocolate bosoms.

Here and now. Hazel says, "You boys have the tits" – and we all have a near-hysterical fit involving, for me, looking around as I lay on the long bag.

"Mmm. Lovely tits," me and Charlie say occasionally and we all have two tastes from the whisky and I pretend a sip so Hazel will still have a little bit more. Charlie tells us of the Moto Guzzi in the Garage and the son in Golf Academy.

We are three now and the snow is coming in very much like the engagement of light-speed or hyper-speed in spaceships on television or vomit off a bedsheet . . .

In Pitlochry there was a U-turn by high street Chrissy-lit knitwear and back to the hotel for to pee. It is far easier to get out of a car than wait in it when someone has got out so, as sure as I am of anything, I have to make use of this and I open the door looking at a ten-year-old boy at a first-floor room window, backed by four aunties and a fifth auntie or his mum and I threw a snowball up at him and got him to open his window and his name was Josh and he was up late and I got him to shout "Clear off!" and "Humbug!" while his aunties and mum perhaps beamed all lovingly of their love. They were English. This may make their concept of Scotland tainted/embellished forever. I am able to throw snowballs well enough to miss humorously and circle the window like it's Bugsy Malone cream-pie massacre.

Then a moving snowball-fight group comes by and I challenge a lady to leave the snow alone on our Mercedes and slight hell breaks loose and there is snow and there are flakes falling as big as flowers. It is lying and yet we are using it up as fast as it comes, as it comes so slow. And Hazel is newly-out and she is caught in the crossfire and Charlie starts the car and gets us the Hell out of MacDodge and he takes off smoothly and the windows are going up slowly compared to how fast the snowballs approach.

We all enjoy that immensely, and the snow on our clothes turns to water.

Charlie knows roads and he knows weather and yet I think perhaps he is going too far for us into this weather, driving into a storm towards a town that is where it is in order to catch the snow. He keeps saying "It's not our business to make sure he gets back" with a warmth that means we can relax.

There is a pass that we get ten miles of the worst of, then it is all looking better and we are into Aviemore and the snow is beautiful and Hazel is working a bit from memory as she takes us to the nightclub, following a semi-intuitive going-back-there process.

The night club is The Crofters with its own car parking and Charlie is in and comes out with us and the bag.

There is the curfew and Hazel mentions it in a way that seems to indicate that there might be trouble getting past them and in. Both Charlie and I know that our quest would not end on a stoop. As Charlie and I come through a corridor outdoors of very-full trellising, up towards the mouth of the club through which I can see and hear Hazel talking to the bouncers, telling our little story in its smallest form and still the bare-keen-bones-y bit got her past and in. Me with Charlie was almost ushered in and then Charlie says "goodbye". We are sufficiently close now for me to ask Charlie if he wants to come in and say goodbye to Hazel and he says he'd better be going.

I walk in and come to find Hazel by the bar and she is holding a drink and can't find Gill yet. We are by a group of folks and a wee woman comes through them and says hello. The wee woman with short, short hair and the happiest of lovely faces puts some glitter on my lips and says she want to give me a kiss and I say yes and she puts a big smacker on me just like the most-rewarding reward of all times and glitter on my lips with her lips, and recently melted snow transferred from my eyelashes to hers. After all the talking it is a great pleasure simply to give her a real wee kiss and do it honestly with the taste of chocolate and Drambuie in my mouth for her.

What an evening, it had everything: adventure, chase, chance, cheer, options, direction, objective, resolution, snowballs, charity and oven-glove humour.

She is clearer now and coming up on a nightclub drug and that is so fine and I believe in the wanting to do this kiss as a real thing. Can't not relate to her openness now as falseness, compared with daytime's ways.

Think of it as the other way round.

Her name is Natalie and the barman is called Jack and he says to me that he can't serve as the bar is shut and I say "Well, so you can't sell after the tills are shut?" and Jack says "No" and I say that we don't want you to sell them, we want you to give them to us and he kind of just does this semi-surreptitiously: A pair of Budweisers. Wise buddy. We leave.

I see a Police car lurking adjacently and wonder if they are not better advised to park right outside the club and prevent exit-fights rather than be murky and lurky and look to be wanting to pounce on trouble once it has started.

Then Hazel sees Avril and Avril can hardly walk and we have to walk her down the slippiest compacted slope by two elbows and she is a tall thin banshee of swaying emotional leans, some with the internal thoughts let out in batches.

She nearly has us a few times as we do the three-man curling shuffle of care.

At the all-night garage there is a queue and there is a doorman limiting entry. I went up and said that I was on the Guest List.

He didn't nearly fall for it so there was nothing to fall for. He just said "Aye, no" and shut the glass door.

We walk to the party, and in there I am mostly making drinks and remembering everyone's name.

I made a dance floor and heated up an oven-glove in a microwave in order to slip on and warm up the feet of a woman who had come through the horse-field with open-toe sandal-heels to this party and had got awful fucking freezing cold feet.

Dave told a joke: what do you call a Russian vasectomy guy? – "Ivan Inchov" or something, one of those; and Chantel, who sat down, said, "A smooth-willied post-communist." It just came out of her, and so was better than the actual joke for its invention, for its subversion and off-the-markness; for daring just to answer.

The dance-floor needs better lighting, so one light gets switched off and I wrap a red Chicago basketball-team vest around the wicker shade and disco-fy it. Then I attempted to make a homemade Baileys with whisky and cream and maple flavoured syrup that curdles a bit, so it was me who got to drink it. Recently we tried to make homemade twiglets rolling spelt doughsticks in marmite.

Joey tells me that I caused a riot at an Oasis gig that started a bottle-fight and his friend lost an eye and was on the front page of The Sun newspaper. I remember this well and it was one of a few times in my life when I was conscious of all that I did yet I am told I definitely did things that I cannot remember. These things were: goad a huge crowd into hurling all their bottles at the VIP exclosure at the front, for Oasis used to have their guests and friends cordoned right up the front at their gigs.

This is the best time to be homeless, when fridges are fullest . . . Then a lift is offered by Wopper exactly where I'm going.

We are all saying goodbye in the quiet snow just as barman Jack, of the free Buds, drives into our grouping.

It is happy Christmas morning: cars drive absolutely slowly and sure-not-to-run-folk-over. New sleds are in use. The quiet hum of sanctity is in the air with muffled audio as we make our way up white roads.

It is quite a moment to say goodbye to Hazel and I do and hug her off the ground and, even as I walk away, I remember her words on occurrence and Sod's Law and caring and her rolling spliffs and sitting hoarse on the bed at half six and how we met through sharing water.

She was the story of the story; the incredible chance that was brilliant of the wonder that you can find in the random presentation that is.

And plus as well I had actually taken a tiny wee sixth of an LSD tab dose there with the mulled wine and ice and was working all those last hours to finally a phone-free zone with an extra fuzz.

On the way to Findhorn we passed a blacksmith's house with an enormous pile of horseshoes outside. You could lie on them and roll around in good luck.

Arriving at my friend Lesley's wee house I got brought my Christmas dinner.

Another time I had to make it north to Findhorn before living there was when Lesley was off to Thailand with her boy and had burnt her arms in a freak cafetiere incident Whilst plunging, the plunger twisted and all boiling water and coffee particles holding the heat leapt up her right sleeve mostly and worked mostly on the skin there. Having talked to her, there was one definite bus I could get to go there that night and I cycled towards it rather swiftly. At Buchanan Bus Station Depot I have no lock and have to leave the bike. They would not let me stick it in the belly of the bus, could not allow it have for it was to them a rival transport method and they would have no two-wheeled Trojan treachery, no harbouring and helping the enemy. Right by the bus I tried my best to get him to admit it was okay because of my grand purpose and the skin on her forearms and please, this once we'll tie it up and stop it damaging other things in there.

"No."

So I hopped on and cycled across the concourse and zoomed straight to Lost Property buzzed the buzzer and when the man came I said: "THIS is lost property." Propped it up by the stand I was able to kick out with ease, and more or less left it at that and ran back to the bus.

If you look, often at train stations the guy that runs the Lost Property is also the guy running the Left Luggage. Usually there is just a different end of the counter separating them and One is free, the Other is not. Left properly, lost properly . . . lost luggage, lugged lostage

One time, before going to Venezuela, I left some boots I knew would not be needed by just leaving them on the unattended lost property counter. They hold them there for three weeks then store them for free in an obtainable department somewhere else. For me this really is an empress moment of free stowing away: Queen Of The Store-Ages.

Once I used the free cloakroom at the Tate for overnight-storage of a guitar and bag and was free to enjoy London's London sights without them. Once there was a massive art show at the Tramway in Glasgow of lost items on British Rail and there were canoes and watches, umbrellas and false legs. You could claim them too.

Often the best way to obtain swimming-costumes for free is from lost-and-then-found boxes at sporting facilities: They ask when you lost them, you say, ". . . yeh see what you mean . . . some weeks ago." They say, "What colour?" You say, "A sort of bluey-grey with a lighter patch across." And they bring the box out and you select a pair. Certainly Hotels and Resorts have better quality than Municipal Baths; the fit at Public Baths is a bit wide and floppy yet the selection wider in a good way. You can always just shake your head and imagine somewhere else they might be.

The best ones were five-star hotel trunks from the Balmoral Hotel in Edinburgh.

Once in Montreal I bought some trunks from the hotel that were made of jay cloth; the lady said they would last three to four swims. How did she know? What if I swim gentle?

Me and Jimeoin and Ardal O'Hanlon went to a Water Fun Park and the first slide I went down the trunks split open; my trunks, so I walked around like Tarzan in the side-less jungle-brief.

Jimeoin was sponsored by Oakley Sunglasses at the time and, while we were chatting, I managed to form a perfect imitation pair by bending two shiny teaspoons around the side of my head with their concaves out. They were very impressive with a fabulous chrome effect and no light at all got to my eyes.

That time returning four days later to Buchanan Street Bus Station for my bike, after doing most of the tasks that Lesley's arm would likely be involved in, I approached the Left Properly department and said to the man, "It's about the small foldable lady's Raleigh compact-bike . . ." and just kind of left it hanging; neither saying it was mine nor it was left.

He looked a bit miffed and agreed. I then told him exactly what had been executed: the drop, the run, the bus, the burns, the tropical heat, the boy and my Jeeves-duties.

He was tutting with his shoulders and took out a small book and there was three pounds-something to pay. Out of curiosity I asked how much it would have cost to store it and it turns out that it would have cost twenty-one pounds more to store for that period.

"It would cost that, yes, though we actually don't have room though to store a bike."

Unless it is lost . . . contextualized and re-categorized as a necessity, it seems to manufacture space.

Getting things back is one way of putting it. Seeing them again is another. Them being in your possession at this time is one too . . . ooh, like, for instance, cycling up a city street towards a silver Volvo and sweeping a mobile phone off of the roof as you go by because it is yours and you left it there an hour earlier . . . That felt good.

Once got a new shock-proof Nokia phone and on its first day with me it got dropped out of the open door in the car, parking by a taxi-rank to feed myself fish and chips from The Bronx Café at the top of Leith Walk. Came back half an hour and a half later because it was the only place to start retracing the footsteps and tyretreads, and there it was: luminous and crushed from being driven over by a taxi on the wet black road, holding its own among the amber streetlight puddles; a little show of psychedelics emanating from its very small screen. Swooping by, I reach it from the open door without having to stop; pick it up and cradle its wee mad screen all shattered and colours everywhere. It wouldn't sleep, couldn't turn it off . . . Got a new shock-proof Nokia the next day like I was taking the piss . . . What a coincidence . . . Well, that it was still there.

Right, now today 19.03.13, 18:43 p.m., the seventh big loss of a phone has just occurred on the sledge slopes of Forest Row . . . three times back there sloping around looking for it phoning it and hearing that it is alive somewhere . . . it's not lost it's in England. The second youngest daughter Delilah was asleep on the jacket in a toboggan . . . the thing is, there had been a false alarm, a pretend loss the week before, so I had had mislaid it and got a wee free practice at the loss, a wee phoney homeopathy taster to let me, get me less upset this time. A few breaths then thinking . . . well all the numbers, they were all friends that ill find again.

Chapter of Coincidences

Most enjoyable coincidence category:

I had been sitting in a pub in Bath eating a three-meat Sunday Dinner the Sunday Morning after a real big gig in town and a woman called Helen who was at the gig chats and then says goodbye and that she always goes to play frisbee out the front of Royal Terrace on a Sunday and so she nearly came with me because I was walking that way to get picked-up for my flight.

It's lucky she didn't. I went there and played frisbee with these incredible men who could all do the extra throws: the forehand throws and the reverse-slingshot and were warming up for that game of frisbee played as moving as soccer and gathered like netball and scored like rugby.

I played and walked off, they said, "Where do you mostly play, the beach?" and I said, "The park." When I went for my key at the hotel I saw my bum-bag was open and thought, "Phew; that was lucky that nothing fell out."

Well, my wallet had and, luckily, Helen did go to play frisbee a while later and was there when a guy found it and saw it and looked at the name and said it out loud. She heard it and said she knew me. Even luckier was that I was at the airport walking past the information desk, when the desk clerk said my name to write it down because Helen was telling him who the wallet belonged to, on the phone, right at that moment. She heard me call out to my own name while not even on the phone because he said my name and then I said, "Flying to Glasgow" as he asked where.

I had only walked there to the desk because I had walked past my check-out desk, missing it by mistake.

This was on the fifteenth of December and the wallet took until I returned from London on the twenty-third to plough through the postal sea.

I had come up from London with no possessions because I had done a gig in the Soho Theatre theatre in London and nipped out for a meal and come back to a locked-up-until-after-Chrimbo-on-the-twenty-seventh-type theatre doors. This was cool as it meant that I was unaffected by the enormous conveyer-belt breakdown at Heathrow and walked through with just my pockets slightly full and then got my phone in my hand in the morning.

As I approached the house on this Christmas Day after the epic Dundee car quest, my friend Lesley came to the door open with her arms and said, "I knew you were coming." I fairly soon was at the table and me and Lesley and Clancy and Bridge and Paul were delivered a huge turkey-dinner with all the broccoli and potatoes and carrots you could wish for and I ate my first sprout from Brussels happily ever because all my life they were taste/texture culinary anathema to me. Greatest was the gravy: a fluid rich made good-stuff of all forms of food that there was plenty of and more too; ate everything and had fourths and all with gravy and all unprepared by me. First time in nine Christmases that I had not basted and prepared, diced and drunk, bought and delivered all the sundries and berries and nuts and ham, champagnes and brazil nuts, ginger ale, cheeses, drinks, chocolates, sundry treats, birds, veg, biscuits, leeks, onions, spuds and warmth, warmth, warmth . . .

Chapter and a Half

The School Years:

My sister Deborah Jane Margaret and I went to a wee fee-paying day preparatory school called Craigclowan that sat at the edge of the original Perth. We would get on the bus in Milnathort village, three miles away from our house, for half an hour through Mawcarse, the Glen and along the Baigley Straights from school. The girls in gray berets and us boys in caps; the caps had a solid cardboard brim which could really crack of the back of a hand if utilized properly. The main building was a fine high stately home with classes going up as you got older. There was one tennis court with a loose net and one cupboard with some broken equipment. The climbing-frame was a modern decahedron shape of metal tubes and that was the only new item around.

Old Mister Spence the headmaster ran it fairly invisibly with his moustache and we were about to all slip through the net and fade away until the Dynamic new English Head took over with his wife and two daughters and catapulted us into fast-track Preparatory School progress – Mike Beale a regular master from the famous Downside School. Within a term and a half we had some structure, an Upside, some overall concept fitting onto us, we even started to play rugby against other schools. We had no school strip so we played in whatever we had. I was Captain and fly-half and wore a 1978 Scotland football strip. The year was 1979 and Naeim Noori came from Iran and he could run fast and was five foot two and fully mature. His Dad was Persian-posh and part of the hated ruling aristocracy in what would become Iran and he fled here to run a sweet-shop right outside Perth Prison. Frae Persi tae Perth.

Once when I was in the Royal Lyceum Theatre I heard a rich business man from Glasgow say, ". . . Frae Ibrox tae Ibsen in one week . . ."

Our rugby team was Bruce, David, John, Ian, Christopher, Mathew: back row. Front row: the twins Chris and Robbie, their brother Nicholas, Alan Graeme, Peter and wee Andrew. One time the girls' tennis team was one short so I partnered up with Henrietta Dewar, the whisky heiress, and played in white shorts that were so tight the zip would not go up. You were allowed to serve underarm if you needed to.

New buildings were built, new strips did come. The feeling of playing rugby when you were always getting beat then started to have a glimmer that we might score, coming together on the pitch just ourselves, then achieving that among all the effort and physical heat is still with me. Naeim came to school each day with sweets. The best was a box of Cola Fizz – Jesus they made you wince.

Now the School is World Debating Champion and has its own ski-slope. From chopped-up rags in potato-sacks as our high-jump crash mats to a car park the size of a playing field.

All the while my Mum was living with Jim, the best stepdad possible. He was wealthy, huge like Orson Welles, kind, erudite, with grace and he built us an indoor swimming pool and sauna with his own construction company and never put shit on us emotionally. I was hugely fond of him and this house called Huntly Hall. Jim refused to watch ITV and we'd all watch Mastermind and he'd give us five pence for every answer we got right. Mum had the first of her St Bernards here. We had Brumas and there was Dino the basset Hound, Lindy the black lab and her pups Chad and Jip. There was Oliver the Welsh mountain pony, Sabre the Dartmoor and PhilBor the Shetland. Surrounded by fields with our three ponies, and streams and conker-trees and, just one huge field away, the best next-door neighbour friend you could get, named Tom. He wasn't at my school; he had a big brother we could fight and team-up against and he had a very pretty little sister, Alison. His Mum Lily made pancakes a lot. His Dad worked for Thomas Salter, the toy manufacturers at the time, and would come home with prototype toys for us to test out. Beat that.

It was idyllic: streams and fun; rocky outcrops to climb; the woods and bikes to get to the farms nearby. Tom would come to mine, we would sneak into the utility room underneath the pool and turn the temperature up and snorkel all day with flippers on going around the edge of the pool. Then Geordie would come and his sister Nicola and maybe Francesca Fairbairn, Nicholas Brayden or Caroline, Iona and Cosmo Spence from Cleish Castle. Their mum Caroline let us ride on her car roof when we were on the grounds of the castle.

There was an opera house nearby in a giant country home that had been inherited by the fabulous man John Calder of the brewing Calders who named his daughter Jamie in order to be able to introduce her to the dying grandfather with a boy's name because Ledlanet was only to be left to him if he had a male heir. He was a literary genius and editor for Samuel Beckett, had his own publishing house, fought the obscenity trial for publishing Hubert Selby's Last Exit To Brooklyn in Britain. Together with Jim Haynes they had the first Happening at the Edinburgh Fringe. Haynes had opened the first paperback bookshop and founded the Traverse Theatre Club.

The Opera House was close and stepfather-Jim and John were friends, so lots of folks came down from art-infused opera parties to hang out in our pool, barbecue garden and music room. I remember coming back over the fields with minnows in a jar and hearing that aria from The Pearl Fishers being played loud and sung along to and folks all lounging around in the sun scantily-clad . . . French voices.

Those summers my Mum was having a great time, always sunbathing and gardening topless and those were the summers up to the end of Borg and the matches of Connors and McEnroe and fresh tomatoes picked from the conservatory on the way through to the pool and chewing them so sweet as we jumped in the water. My bike was a Raleigh Chico that was gold and there were Action Man dens hidden in among the trees. There were walls to climb on and sweet routes to the roof and noisy, grippy acousticky slates to climb across. There were mud bombs all over the pebble dash walls.

Most of my holidays were spent, if not at next-door friend Tom's, in the large music room playing one-man cricket, football and tennis against the wall, against myself. There were two grand pianos, one at either end, and the foot-pedals and support made perfect stumps to bowl at. Hours I spent commentating on myself, feeling really happy, achieving long rallies and being fouled as Pelé in front of a girl I fancied. Julie was her name and just as I began to feel the first-feelings for her she got taken away and put up a year for being so clever.

Being able to make fun on my own was a marvellous bonus. Not being down about it. Being able to follow my nose and decide everything.

Then I started cycling to the golf club and, from eleven to fifteen, played masses of golf. One time all my clubs spilled out as I was cycling down Church Brae cos the trolley my golf-bag was on overturned and all my golf balls bounced down into the village gathering speed. All random and unfollowable like mass roulette mania.

All the while my sister and I would also go and spend every other weekend with my Dad and his new family. He had met the only exotic woman for miles around who had taken a tiny flat opposite his house. Catherine, she was French and Italian and had three boys. They all soon moved to Edinburgh to set up home and so I had an instant brand-new adventurous life mucking about by rivers instead of streams, playing football and coming up with scams to raise cash. Three boys: Timothy, Francis and Christopher. Then Catherine and my Dad made two more boys Sam and Jools.

Over the last few years we have all been hyper-involved with each other, going to Franky's gigs when he plays in The Darkness; going to Sheffield in a limo that got lost and had to do a seven-point turn in the middle of nowhere. We went to Reading when they headlined; we went to The Barfly and King Tut's in the beginning when brother Sam's band Easy Tiger supported them. I even went on in a cat-suit at The Barrowlands while Justin did a long outfit-change. Brother Chris would come over from Venezuela for fun and he and the biggest-brother Tim would work on events for the Russian billionaires that Chris had hooked up with.

They ran it together and Tim, an accountant, helped with finance when it needed to expand. Then one time it all came together when Tim and Chris were brokering and handling the deal-of-a-lifetime: four billionaires wanted a New Year Extravaganza in Ecuador and Frankie and me were hired to come.

The billionaire who runs the Bank of Moscow and his friends wanted fun at a high altitude and here they could see Cotopaxi, an active volcano smouldering moodily twenty miles away.

I was there to role-play. Had to pretend I was a wealthy South American speaking drug-lord who owned this lovely High Chaparral. It was hard to pull off and even though it was acting, it felt like lying. I only lasted a day and a half. The morning I came into the courtyard with the llamas it all fell through. We brought them in because the Russians had finished breakfast and we had to arrange things for them to do and see. They stood on a balcony-bit and were told the llamas would come in now. Then they said not now. We had to bring them out and keep them waiting with a basket of carrots.

Suddenly, "Now . . . NOW . . . Now. He wants them brought in again. They Are Ready For The Llamas."

In we came, me trying to be nonchalant surrounded by these mean looking nibblers with my ill-fitting blue blazer and basket of carrots. A bit hungrier now, they became slightly unruly trying to get close to the veg, and I must have looked a bit daft getting slightly bumped about by these massive furry things who are exactly the same height as me and I've heard they spit and is that camels . . . dunno . . . I talked with a pretend South American Españo-Uraguyan accent about how I loved them all and knew them all and got a bit carried away, saying it was I who named each one and they were all known since birth. The Russians asked their names and this is it, the moment in my life when I have to name a herd of llamas, in character, in Spanish and at altitude. There were three Marias and two Jesuses before I was even halfway . . . "Emilio . . . erm where are you? . . . Yes . . . Manuel . . . Julio . . . Gonzalez Bias . . . There you are, my beauty." It was hard to carry off and I didn't.

Mercifully my services were no-longer required and I owned up on the Hacienda balcony overlooking the Russian New Year, which was three in the afternoon. Billionaires are easier to confess-to when they are stoned and drinking ice-cold vodka surrounded by Brazilian soap-stars and models and they have eaten the flower of a special plant.

New Year's Eve I nearly died on a motorbike when a lorry came around the dirt-track corner on the right/the wrong/the right side and my feet and hands did the brakes/the throttle/the scrape on the ground. Frankie had his Warner Brothers' record executive over for the fun and the free cocaine. We all got high yet appetites were lost and no one wanted their lobster except me. That night I ate four, had too much, was sick of lobster, watched my man Jonathan Gent do paintings on a giant canvas of the naked dancers and saw a DJ do the highest-paid gig of his life. There was even an ex-Formula One racing driver on stand-by there in case anyone wanted driving someplace.

Our digs were far away that night and, after staying up all night playing pool, getting high every nine minutes in that desperate, chasing it way, everyone went off to their rooms and I pretended to kip in there with the pool-table. I opened my eyes to a man with an automatic weapon in his hands pointing at me asking if I was "residenta". My Spanish/Castilian/Ecuadorian did not stretch to "Well no, though I was here all night with those who are." I agreed to leave and caught a local bus along the road to then walk up the miles to the billionaire's Hacienda San Angelico. In order to look smarter, brother Chris had got me some new black boots of the smart male-style variety. The cat was out of the bag now so on the way back I passed some folks tilling the land and I went over and offered my new shoes to an old lady who took them without a whisper. "Felicidad Nuevo Año," I probably said.

I left a millionaire landowner and returned a shoeless drifter.

After the Junior School I went to Glenalmond, an almost-all boys' boarding school near Crieff. My Stepfather died and Mum moved to a smaller place which she did up and sold on for great profit. Made a fortune, lost it. There was a small bursary to help with my fees and Mum befriended the accountant at the school. Without another childhood to compare it to I found it great. Many found school harder and I was lucky. We slept in dorms, you could make good friends. Sport was big and I liked sport and was pretty capable. To play rugby felt brave and yet I knew it was not the way for me. Cricket was far more the vibe, with my friend Alex at first slip next to me, wicket-keeping, there was time for our growing adult humour to flourish. That was what it was all about: friendship builds so many avenues for humour and laughs because so many things are established to then to relate to or call on. Plus we had a bit of the old Colditz in us and the teachers-and-boys thing to define us. A framework. The school definitely promoted it and this was its biggest failing for me.

One day out playing rugby for training, Chris Parks scraped his studs down the back of my Achilles heel and my boot came off and I was lying on the ground writhing slightly and rubbing the back of my heel. The coach came over and stood by me and, in a less-than-just-inquisitive tone, asked, "What's the matter with you then?"

He never expected "I've got earache, what does it look like?"

He sort of lifted me up and pushed me down a tiny embankment (nothing serious) and called me something that related to me being at this posh school. Hang on a minute, I am just from the country and our fees are always late.

On the first day I met Alastair Mackenzie who became my best friend. He loved Monty Python and I learned to. He had had a brother at schools like this and knew a few things.

Alastair and Toby and Gus and Alex and I became a bunch and definitely had three or four of the most advanced hairstyles in our year. Toby cut the hair I had over my ears for me to enter adulthood. Alex played me Jimmy Hendrix. Gus played guitar. Al had records by the Doors, John Lee Hooker and the Triffids . . .

We all smoked fags smuggled in as the tuck shop didn't sell them. My Mum smoked Craven "A" and I always came back from home with a pack to distribute: meeting up in Alastair's room, lighting joss-sticks, stuffing towels around the bottom of the door for the smell and playing Velvet Underground on vinyl. This progressed and so escalated to Saturday nights on magic mushrooms by our third summer there. Hours of running and laughing until you're sick; picking fifty fresh and strong off the ground and retching and stuffing them in and retching some more and gagging; the dry heave, the moist heave and the wet-boke. The full gamut. Crawling around at night; nicking booze from the

Army store; drinking whisky with orange-concentrate and stream water. Once the whole school was away watching a rugby match in Edinburgh and we four or five were all tripping around the grounds when we ran into the headmaster Mr Musson. We automatically stood in a row and became superbly serious and, in a mythological interface, Toby, our least rugby-orientated, enquired as to Scotland's progress against England at Murrayfield. This was it an ultimate moment of them-and-us that stayed at the forefront of our psyche as the most amazing thing for ages. And yet that is it that is where this school survives, flourishes and fails miserably. It had to have the big authoritarian Them-and-Us stuff. You had to mindlessly obey folks and then rise up the school system until you accepted being mindlessly obeyed.

Even then this seemed like a big joke.

One time someone set a Braun clock-alarm to go off in Chapel and the Headmaster cancelled the whole of the school's home-weekend because of this. It was probably Mathew Hovel because he was quite good at that sort of thing. Every Wednesday there was CCF (the Combined Cadet Force), where real Army soldiers were allowed to come in and pull our ears and teach us to strip and fire guns. Once a year there was a big parade in front of the school where everyone stood still for half an hour. Mathew set up a hi-fi in a high quadrangle window on timer to come on and play the theme from Spaghetti Westerns. There was beautiful outrage.

There was a quadrangle with cloisters and on the last night of school a few of us ran around the whole quad before the twelfth chime struck, exactly as they do in Chariots On Fire . . . yet we were imitating a tradition that we knew because of film and did those films in ancient times do it because of oxford, and did oxford do it because of another older quad-trad ritual. And is that is what they all are . . . something to catch on, and be followed, something that can have a power and then that power can be claimed. Aiee, the cruel basis of posh schools feeding the Empire. We ate in a high gothic dining hall just like Harry Potter, long and with four long sets off tables for our four Houses and massive portraits on the wall and headboys' names painted in gold around the high skirting in a fiddly gothic gold-leaf olde golde paint font.

Mathesons, Goodacres, Patchells and Skrines were the Houses. Occasional mass food-fights did occur and if they got big enough, with enough people involved, then nobody got punished. It was within our grasp, if a few started it, to back them up and include the entire population and get mass exemption. The teachers sat at the boys' tables at lunch and there was a wee stage at the top with the school prefects learning to converse with visitors and the odd wife.

There were some attractive wives around that had the attention and amorous night-thoughts of us boys. They would walk around and now, as an adult, I really know it may well have been as exciting for them as we then naively lusted after it, to be. There were boys who had flings with masters' wives and one or two daughters around the place that would hang out with the handsome or the daring at the squash courts on Back Avenue.

Every day, after lunch, and every evening, after supper, the smokers would gather either down at the top of Jacobs Ladder or out the back of the Science Block. It wouldn't do for the school to keep expelling boys for smoking or there'd be none left so they rationed their entrapments – I'm sure. This meant hiding the sound of matches, carrying single fags in crushable positions, the sharing of polo mints and furtive complicity.

There was grass you could not walk on unless you were of a certain rank and there were doors you could not go through that boys a year older could. There was hardly any bullying and hardly. There were theatre plays to be in and cross-country running against tough local schools, porn-mags folded in half that lasted a year or so going around. We lived in our own rooms for the last two years. Hung drapes on the walls and posters and peed in the sinks. Made homebrew in four days, once.

The word for the kitchen staff was "skoyt". No idea what it was derived from, yet it had this awful appropriate distaste that was hard to like. If one of them dropped a tray or anything while out among us at lunch the whole place would erupt into a screaming "Skoyt, skoyt, skoyt!"

We were told that we were being groomed to run the Empire. This made us laugh. First: what Empire? Second: had they not seen Star Wars? "Empire" is used as a word for a reason because it is the equivalent, the standard of international badness . . . You take over others' land then you have to manage them in an Empire.

My terrible flat-top hairstyle evolved with a lopsided nature and is in the North Cloister, photographed with the rugby team.

Some of the teachers were great. Mr Macdonald brought in a box of novels and chucked them at us. We got early Ian McEwan in our lives early. What made teachers great was when they got on with a love of their subject and left the whole nature of this kind of school out of it.

One teacher smacked me on the head then the true culprit owned up and he said, "Oh well. I've had enough of you anyway." Bless him, old Mr Willington with his sideburns and his Double First in Classics, his deerstalker and his Boxing Blue from Cambridge. The head of Maths came from Perth and, amazingly, got his daughter Gillian into our school. She wore a uniform from her last school. One young woman, all these boys. Was it just me looking at her in Chapel?

We all wore black trousers and white shirts and ties and nifty sports jackets.

"Grant us, we beseech Thee, O Lord, that in praising these, Thy gifts, for Thy glory in this present world, we may in the world to come have life everlasting. Amen" was the prayer the head boy would say after he ceremoniously slammed the big dining hall doors shut to get our attention before lunch. Actually it ought to be ceremonially.

Torquil, the Marquess of Lorne, heir to Argyll, was our first common-room Captain, our first entitled power figure, and he would have everlasting nosebleeds and accept being superior. Now he is the Duke and runs international elephant polo. The first Walkman I saw came back with Scott Wylie from Saudi in 1983. Kenneth MaCaw got alcohol poisoning, hospital stomach pump, then promoted to junior house captain in that classic old school tie, old boy world network of rewarding the troubled guy to envelope him in authority – straighten him out, harness his girth.

Me and Gus and Toby and Al performed in a band called The Karate Killers. We did a school-music gig then arranged one ourselves at the cricket pavilion for everyone to come in casual clothing.

We made a film called The Life And Time Of Phil KayRisma with Kevin who nearly won his second Oscar for directing Last King Of Scotland. Alastair became the Monarch of the Glen on television's BBC One. Toby runs the Modern Institute Art Gallery and handles Turner Prize winners. Gus works in TV in London. Alex was editor of Prospect Magazine . . . we all have kids. We do not all have each other that way now though.

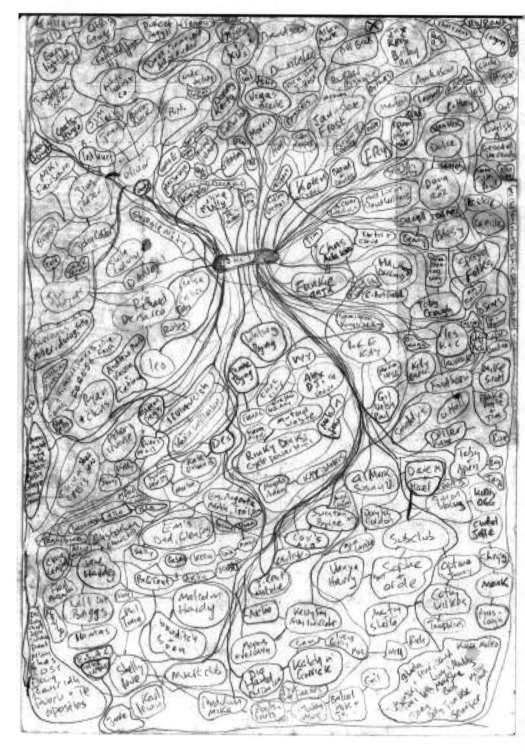

. . . all the names of everyone I knew in showbiz . . .

Chapter: It Just Is

Coming back from Glastonbury one year through Bristol Airport I had a little extra time and decided to put my little hash-pipe in the tray to go through the security X-ray machine just to see what would happen. A lady with a very big skirt on asked me as I went through, "Just back from Glastonbury Festival?"

"Oh yes."

"Just back from Glastonbury this one," she called out as the electric doorframe of metal detection, the threshold of truth remained silent. Only half the truth. Another lady looked through my tray and held up the pipe and asked me what it was and then called her security who then asked me to wait in the departure lounge for the Police to arrive.

Twenty minutes later my name was called over the Tannoy system while I read newspapers and continued Ronnie O'Sullivan's memoirs which I had been reading in various airports.

Back at the security they were keeping their eyes peeled and when I came up close they came towards me: the security boss and a nice Policeman. They took me back through the electric detecting doorframe and into a small room airside.

"Just back from Pilton Farm, are we?" the nice Policeman asked. "And how many times have you been to Glastonbury Fair?"

"About six or seven times," I answered.

"Oh, I've been nine times."

"For fun?"

"No, on duty there."

Soon he was telling about him and his and his wife's plan to retire. Another Policeman came in at this point and my nice Policeman was telling me he was not that happy in the force and he and Mary were going to get a caravan and head to Spain. The senior officer requested him to "cease" at this point; my friend kept on talking and the senior officer repeated the word "Cease", this time with a capital-punishment "C". Too much intimacy reduces the power, for the personal politics of this human interaction. The uniform is extremely dark blue, not purple.

The un pc PC was v. kind and kept stating that he was trying to hurry this up so I wouldn't miss my flight – to protect and serve . . . And save me hassle. To punish yet not delay. He did me a DNA scrape of the underside of my tongue with see-through gloves on and fingerprints and put it into zip-lock. Talk about multi-task force. All done; minor caution, minimum fuss. Cool Fuzz.

"Have you any more cannabis?"

"Oh yes, thanks – one always makes sure there's a bit left for travelling with."

"No. I mean can you hand it over."

"Oh, you've none?"

One time I was driving just past the big Glasgow Police station on Peel Street (no relation) with a bicycle in a bike rack on the back of my car that was partially obscuring the number plate. As I passed the Police headquarters two officers were getting into their saloon car to start their shift and just put their siren and light-set straight on and pulled me over.

"Did you realize that the straps falling down from the rack are partially obscuring your registration plate?"

"What registration plate?"

"??"

"Isn't that why there is one on the front too, Officer?"

"You could go through a speed camera and we would not be able to identify you."

"Good info, thanks for the tip . . . nice idea."

"That's not what I meant."

"You can't control the meanings of the things to me."

He then asked me if I had any comment and out came this little piece about how it seemed ridiculous to be on about such a tiny thing . . . :

"Have you ever been to Shanghai where the people cycle together in swarms with a togetherness and the city functions because of the mass goodwill and harmony of consenting humans pushed together in their thousands; not because they obey laws, because they choose to get on with it . . ." . . . and they're trying it now in London, on Exhibition Street . . . where there are no curbs and no street markings, just a slower more groovy flow . . . and there's possibly a whole town like that in Belgium or Holland where it's like it was when they invented cars, mingling with horse and cart and big skirted bicyclist.

Somewhere there will be a record of it. Like there will be a record in Manchester of when I was interviewed by a head of the Vice Squad because he was forced to arrest me when he just came across me sitting on a low wall in a pedestrian precinct having a relaxed smoke while he was doing a tour visit for seven members of the Liverpool Vice Squad around his precinct. Once he heard my story he said, ". . . oh well I've called the van now . . . gotto go through with it now." All I had with me was my Iceberg Slim novel which was a comforting read in the back of the White Mariah. In the interview room my reply was something I tried to make rhyme: "I had the weed. You had to do the deed."

That's all that can be recalled now. You were allowed to acquire a copy of the tapes for three pounds fifty. Perhaps now you can download them straight to MP3. That night several members of the Squad came to the gig and had their own table and were a bit rowdy and authoritarian; jeering and whooping during the telling of the story. Bad cop, bad cop. Un-easy pc PCs; no empathy. Wild though, to be heckled by the Police.

Three years ago in Edinburgh when they were putting the finishing touches to the new Scottish Parliament me and three friends were driving gently around it at two o nine a.m. having a good look. It really is a tremendous building, we all agreed. A Police car suddenly swooped gently out of a hiding place and with lights flashing came behind me. We slowed down as slowly as we could, dragging it out, pretending to pull in, going on a bit so that at one point both me and the patrol car were doing two miles an hour together just to be doing the slowest chase of all time. I kind of pulled up at one point and in the wing mirror saw the leg of the Law come out then go back in again.

I am sober and feel good.

At rest now, with my window wound down in advance, the long torso and arms of the Law fill the space.

At that point my life was well ordered and all my documents were in order and rolled up in the glove-compartment tied up with yellow ribbon. There were even some gloves in there. Just couldn't wait for him to ask for them and he did and I smiled handing them over like a royal love letter. It could only have been better if they were all presented on a small velvet cushion with gold trim . . .

"You were driving rather slowly," he alleged.

"Yes, it is a tremendous building isn't it . . . we all agree . . . ?"

This low speeding was enough to arouse suspicion so he led the way to his car for a breathalyzation. Yes, going fifteen miles an hour way down by the grass of Arthur's Seat is enough to get you slowly pulled over. My friends were scared as they were all pissed and imagined I must have been too. Small pale faces turned back to watch me from the rear window getting into the thing.

Sitting behind them in the back seat it was hard not to ask, "Are we there yet?" So I just pushed my knees a tiny little bit for my own enthusement into the backs of both seats at once.

Breathing in confidently the machine was explained again. Green: Clean. Amber Ya-Bamba: Had A Drink. And Red: You're Dead. I passed with an Amber that hovered for a while.

The great thing about this is now they might rethink how they saw slow driving. Nah, the great thing is that now I was proved sober, totally exonerated and free to be me.

An enthymeme is an argument that supposes the truth of more than one premise in order to go through a sequence of elimination to omit them from the logical sequence. The Police don't have the time to do this.

Fairly normal driving arouses suspicion, yet now crazy daftness arouses none. Often I meet people that have bumped into me at a festival or some night out and they tell me that I was mad-out-of-it and will not remember; but often I do. Turns out the wasted-ness of me is hugely in their minds .

So getting out of their car I literally skipped back to mine and jumped up to land my full weight on the bumper and make the whole car sink and rise and wobble all the turning heads in the car. The pale faces went less pale. Then, as the Police pulled away I ran at the car yelling for the back window to be rolled down quick and dived into the back seat into the bobbing laps of my back-seat friends . . .

This is what sober folks get up to . . . abstemious mayhem . . . tee-totalled it . . .

One day I was in a bath in a flat in Glasgow, a lovely summer day, with the front door open to the street at the end of the hall, and there comes the familiar squeaky creak of our front gate. In fact I'd oiled every other gate either side of us on the road so that ours would be the only squeaker and then it could be a very subtle advanced warning system of visitors . . . sometimes it worked so supra-subliminally when the doorbell went and you kind of knew it would and maybe the plaintive whine squeal had squeezed through ultrasonically . . . : so, this time in the bath I slosh and turn to see coming up to the door are a Police of each available gender and I watch them as they close the gate . . . nice . . . and come up peering into an extended dullness they can not pierce with mere squinting. They can't quite pick me out at the end of the hall until their eyes adjust, so it's up to me to splash about a bit to curious-ize them.

"Hello, hello?"

"Hello."

They can't quite come in, I realize, without premises and due warrant, like a vampire they need to be invited so they are left with naught save to be asking what I am doing.

"Having a bath."

"The front door is wide open."

". . . !"

"Why are you having a bath with the door open?"

"Because I like it."

They didn't seem like they were asking a trick question yet I was not certain at that point whether they were worried about me exposing myself or myself being exposed to criminal possibilities. Then it became clear.

"Someone could come in here and take that cassette player and be off with it. What would you do then?"

"Chase him or her down the road naked, Officer. If that's not a crime."

"It would be, yes."

" . . . "

Then they would have to choose which of us was the most in need of arrest. Perhaps they would overtake the naked chaser, have a few words, and then on in hot pursuit of the hotter target . . . . Perhaps, like pacemakers, from behind, they would help the naked man run faster to catch up with the thief.

It was tempting to stand up at this time and do a little extra sponging. It was fascinating the way I was almost to blame for allowing crime to be drawn here by the opening of a door. Like the lady in the short skirt being responsible in some way for her attack by the old judge, and that felt daft. Either way they were happy to leave after our chat. Leaving me cleansed, untainted, uncorrupted, innocent.

At that point I was still wanted by the East Sussex Police from the last time I had been in Brighton because I had been out cycling with Helen the promoter of the gig sitting on the bar of my bike when the Police drew up next to us going down a hill for a bit of synchronized justice. They lowered their window and said to me, "Will you pull over?"

"Certainly, we must . . . ," I replied. Trying to be as honest as possible for, as well as having no lights and no rights, we had no brakes really either so pulling over on this long incline would take a while. It cost sixty quid to do this and sadly they only pick only one offence so the ticket was issued for the "unlawful carriage". Never forget the aim of the Police is for your rehabilitation and cessation of activities, never forget they have a five-second instant cognitive trust judgement thing and if you can apologise, admit your mistake, voice responsibility and promise not to do it again there is a chance they will not proceed. Of course it's difficult in the US where Police can get substantial overtime pay cheque bonuses for proceeding and processing their case and doing court time.

There was the VW before it got nicked. I was transporting it from one side of Glasgow to another and I ran out of petrol on the Kingston Bridge. This brought the Police to help who would normally tow one off the bridge and simply be helping you on your way. Not this time: there was a tricky to remove old school, tubular steel children's seat, so for swiftness the Policeman said he would steer the van and for me to jump in the back of their Mercedes ahead. Now it was my pale face that watched from the rear window. It was a lovely touching, highly unique sight looking back out the rear to see a Policeman in my hippy van with the dashboard littered with personal memorabilia; a man of uniform in my awfully unlawful mobile home, who had more than the usual time to take a look at the photos, dried vegetation and lack of even this year's this year's tax disc. At that point I was hoping for purple discs to come around again soon and, at least, be in the right colour. As it happened the fine in the end was a lot less than actually buying tax. Foolishly they did themselves out of a bit of revenue.

I still believe that being uninsured does not make it any more painful if you were to run into someone.

I have only done four gigs in China. All in one year. Second time I went I got a bicycle from a Shanghai supermarket near midnight on my first evening. They are lined up with their handlebars loosened sideways and so I took one for a test drive around the store. It did cross my mind it would be an incredible theft to just cycle around the food-aisles for a moment, grab a stack of tuna fish tins, then just keep going towards the automatic doors, hope they would be super-responsive and ride out of the shop and off into criminal history books . . . a folklore outlaw . . . Shanghaied 'Em . . . 'Twould not've taken them long to find me as there are only about a fifteen hundred guy low white folks in this city and they'd've probably been at my hotel room before me.

One time I remember travelling to a Dublin hotel and then just unlocking the door, throwing a bag in, then leaving . . . and returning the next day in time to pick the bag up, and not actually use the facilities.

Cycling with the commuters in the morning in China is fantastic; all of us together in massive swarms like birds; all quite quiet and seeing and harmonious. There were never any Westerners on bike – Gwai Lo, Western whites, Greengoes – only me – rare enough to hardly even be looked for. Sometimes someone looked at me with the expression just before amazement: straightforward receiving, the pre-interpretive gaze.

That was the time I had stayed up all night boozing at the Karaoke Palace and ended up ballroom dancing in the park with the older generations as the morning began to move. I kept standing on a much older very muscley lady's feet as I was laughed at openly for five minutes as we danced. Laughed at yet with an honest unworried way . . . so it's a big smile laugh of cultural appreciation. We are so intellectually positioned that laughing openly at a chinease guy is hard to well. It's much worse. There were fifty-sixty of us and one amazing cheap cassette player turned full volume to play music that somehow the quality and tone of which was not really affected by the distortion.

All around, folks brought their birds to be near other birds in little one-bird ironic cages that they hung in trees. Little strangely un-cruel closeness-es to being free as a real bird in the trees, they hung there individually barred from life; cared for . . . Everyone was smoking . . . There were many variations on tai-chi and definitely individual interpretations. I saw an old man jogging backwards around the park clapping – beautiful. This could be an age-old tradition-laced accepted standard, or it could be a pretty bonkers one-off whim. I don't need to know.

Even the most solid textual proofs, religions and laws are just whim plus time mixed with practice and popularity.

The other time I was in China was Guangzhou in South China, the place where, if it says "Made-in-China", it is made here. It's not like tennis shoes, water-pistols, Star Wars figures and plastic apples are made all over China in villages as part of a tradition where the techniques are passed on and down from generation to generation. This is economics. It is just one area the folks come to from all over. The reverse of staying: Family, heritage and sharing – Leaving and doing stuff with no meaning or ritual: No legacy . . .

At my gig my trousers came down and stayed down for a while until the prominent uniformed Police with the video cameras ordered them back up or the Show Must Not Go On. Is Communism the opposite of Showbiz? Nope. They made me laugh. They were a double act, full uniform and thise slightly large hats. Luckily just as their shameful intolerant powerful disgust reached a zenith, and they began to move to the stage in twos, I did my belt up. Timing . . .

*

Next time I was breathalyzed was in Glasgow and I had been drinking, although I have no proof. Stopping outside the King's Café for chips on a Saturday night and putting the whisky bottle in the child's seat and strapping it in – Safety First – I bound in and do not have enough money because it is one-seventy on weekends so I zoom out, open the passenger's side door and lean in to grab a handful of the change that collects between the seats under the hand-brake. Back in, one-seventy for chips, it can't be, and stepping out into footstep-synch with two walking Policemen. As we all get five paces nearer to the vehicle they see that it is partially obscuring the alley entrance at the rear of the establishment. They are tutting and objecting to it. I tut as well, then quickly, as they are looking, I offer them chips and they decline then watch me go around and get in to drive. Now the keys are actually still in the passenger side door lock where I left them and my efforts to locate keys in pocket in a sitting position make the car move slightly and the dangling keys begin to dance ever so like her ladyship's earring when she is being serviced by the gamekeeper and this attracts the keen eyes of Justice.

They come around driver's side and one announces that due to the forgetting of where my keys are he has sufficient grounds to be suspicious enough to warrant a breathalyzing. Now, he had to call for the kit to come because they don't carry them and in the six minutes I eat my chips while they watch me and I start to breathe very heavily.

"It's not a crime to breathe very deeply," my eyes must seem to say to them. In the end a machine has no prejudice and lives in the moment and reacts blindly, only working with actual input, so it seemed okay to set up the lungs with the best chance. Hyper-ventilated, all the fresh air surely must re-boot my lungs and lower the al-content. I am sure to cruise through the test.

Green: Good Boy. Amber: Dodgy. Red: We Have You. Again, it hovered on Amber and after it was done and I had passed, they were about to leave and I had to ask them for my keys.

"Oops," he said and fished them out of his pocket.

"Ah, showing neglect and forgetting where the keys are arouses my suspicions with sufficiency . . . ."

This only comes out half-heartedly and doesn't really get a laugh from him. Fair enough.

As with most of these types of leverage-based twangs you never wuite know what kind of torque your gonna get so I aimed with what had a chance of being just enough to fire it over my shoulder and I opened out a reverse palm to catch it on the sly fly. I stamped down with the fist and there was no other sound the screw vanished into thin air. Or gone so far as to be quiet landing . . . no . . . was it on an eeyore toy a fluffy cushioning sound bed . . . no . . . was it . . . wow . . . on me? Had I shot it into my hair line . . . no I shook myself it never fell out . . . then standing back where my feet were I brushed my sides

Confession is un proven words that you choose to believe.

It matters not if you know they are lying, it matters that you know when they speak the truth.

There are no lies. Only perceived limits to release.

The most fortunate interaction with the forces of policing – apart from the customs man who reached down into my wee ticket-pocket in my jeans, touched my wee silver pipe by the nozzle and said, "Oh, it's a whistle" – was this: Approaching some traffic lights that were red in the red-light area of Glasgow well after midnight and about to go through them I saw the Police car. Normally I would have stuck my tongue out and ridden on because I believe it is OK. Tonight I waited until they had gone by, kind of like an act of deference and being kind, saving them the bother of having to ignore it.

They went through, past me, so I moved on through straightaway tailgating and they pulled in, turned round, me caught up and they called at me to pull over.

There is no point denying it, so when the older Cop in the driving seat said, "You went through a red light back there." I said, "Yes I know. Why are you telling me that?"

The young Cop looked at me, as I declined the invite to chat and said, "What if I just ride off, you would have to chase me wouldn't you . . . ?" I cycled off and around the front of the car and the young Cop had trouble leaping out of the car because he still had his seatbelt on. He undoes it then sharpish, and comes around the back of their vehicle as I worked my way back towards him. Acquiesce, I guess. Renounce, abandon, forfeit, conform, submit and offer. He grabbed the frame and I dismounted with no hands leaving him standing there holding it like the coach again. Then take it to the kerb and park it for me.

The larger dark-haired Cop comes around the front of the Police's estate vehicle, approaching me from a westerly direction, carrying a small travel clipboard arrest-book and asks me my name. We are both still in motion.

I say that "I am not really into this . . ." and "we all have to make decisions in life all the time and red lights like that one are to stop midday collisions and unhelpful biases in morning's rush-hour traffic distribution and that at midnight times like these it is not quite the same . . . How can you flex them muscles of Justice if you don't know when to rest them? How can we use the laws properly and how can you enforce them if you forget what they are trying to protect from happening: can you not see that what they are trying to prevent has not happened yet? . . . They are to protect me . . . And look, I am fine."

The big Cop opened the back door of the car and invited me to take a seat and again I said I was not really into that and that they were being a bit silly looking in their rear-view with a dim view and, in a sense, inventing the crime. Then it occurs to me to remember the statistics that an officer on the beat will come across an actual crime happening once every six years or so. Maybe this night is more important to them than I realize.

As my Gran used to say, "There's only one kind of adrenaline in the body Phil and rutting and strutting, fighting or running away all produce it . . . ."

So then it happens the miracle moment . . . the door open, the older Cop telling me to get in, the younger one standing by my bike and . . . a man in a purple shirt approaches running from a northerly direction and says, "Quick, quick! There are three cars in a pile-up around the corner."

Terrific timing. "You guys are going to have to go . . . ," I said, loving the precedence of this event over my crime like finally the hierarchy of poker hands in my favour.

All smiles now and the good big Cop kind of packs away his clipboard and says I am lucky.

It's true. And then he says I have a terrible attitude.

Meanwhile they're burning.

Big Cop opens a small book and asks me my name and I say Phil, surname K-A-Y. Home? I say I am not sure tonight. He writes NFA and tells me, "Without lights, it is an offence to ride the bike." I tell him it is light enough and that I will be riding it. They overtake me as I am making my way up the road with sirens that are not for me . . . sirens is golden . . .

Once Jimeoin told me that he was asked if he had any comments whilst getting arrested and he said, "Stop kissing me, Officer."

Now fabulously, listen to this, I was arrested recently on trumped-up charges and fibs from someone and the Officers took me to Eastbourne

Custody Centre an hour away and so there was time for me to muck about with words in handcuffs and at one point I am saying, "Stop winking at me . . . she winked at the female officer in the back seat with me.

Christmas 2006.

Out in the wind in Forrestown, Moray – "Whisky Country" it says on the road signs – and am putting up posters for a local show in Forres, my town, in my love's borrowed car and during one of the sellotape-huggings that gets a poster on a lamp-post, there they go, the Police, cruising by, I am lucky and kind of hug in closer to hide my naughty activity a bit better and they pass. Turning around I must've left the hand brake off and notice the car running slowly back down the hill, without any lights on, luckily, otherwise they might have spotted it and me and again had to have chosen which crime to go with. I ran back and generously Radio Three was on and an uplifting piece of choral symphony inspired the rolling mount, running to jump in before anyone drove round the corner.

Last year but one at the Kilkenny Festival some folks came back to my hotel room for wines and a late supper. We phoned down for wine and were told that it was not possible. Me and Gerry went down to see the man at the desk with large denomination euro notes, and found the front desk abandoned. As we wait, the phone rings and, after six, I pick it up and chat to a man in the room next to ours as he complains about the noise and tell him, "Not to worry, Sir. It will definitely be attended to", "Rest assured, Sir" and "All that can be done, will be done." He says he has kids in there.

The front man arrives back, we pay double in cash for reds and return to await our sandwiches which come eventually quite cold and yet are marvellously warmed up, in the Corby Trouser Press laid horizontal, in a matter of moments.

It is very hard to keep quiet and even harder to keep a person happy who had called that quickly. A knock at the door delivers two new men in uniform who inform us everyone who is not a resider has to go and so folks dribble out.

By this time Gerry is comatose, napping face-down, even resistant to the hairdryer on him and the flash of digital cameras. Everyone else has passed them and I say to the men, "This fellow is definitely not a resident and he must be removed or I will make a complaint."

This loophole does amuse them and they depart happy/un-happy with Gerry in their arms. This hotel supplies free apples at reception and you can always get half a dozen Walkers Shortbread Fingers in two-pacs as you pass a service trolley in the hall and, this festival weekend, this is all I eat for Friday and Saturday until the cash comes on Sunday before I leave.

It, surely as day never ends, can't be the best thing for me to revolve my life around authority figures and break as many laws as possible, like the boys at Public Schools and men at Colditz with a duty to. It is just so many things happen, so many tangles of fuzzy interaction with those who hold the rule-books closer. Certainly, for me, all that can happen can happen without official guidance; it is just that it really works for some.

Once I drove thirteen hours to go to a party at Annie Nightingale's house in Brighton with my love and young Urph the puppy dog and when we got there Primal Scream were very unkind to us, calling our accents insufficiently Scottish and their manager kept saying, "I'm not calling you a cunt, but . . ." In the end the large guitarist sat on a chair surrounded by girls, threatened to throw a bottle of Jack Daniels at me because I had answered back to B. Gillespie when he told me not to touch Annie's records. When we went to bed early to get away, they really livened up and had more fun. We just intimadated them in a topsy-turvy way. They threw stuff at the door and we had our puppy with us and they were making plans to hurt it. Then, all of a sudden, they were singing about a big box of chocolates: "Get your chocs out, get your chocs out, baby." Yeh, I kid you not. Fabulous!

Next day we were all sneaking in the back way to the Oasis gig and Bobby APOLOGISED in capitals. No therapy, no practice, no nothing, just be awful then be forgiven.

Playing the guitar outside the venue in Paris before the show and lots of people do not know what I look like so, naturally, they could be a little sniffy about the busker hassling them for euros in bad French as they go in. It's easy-peasy to forgive n forget. Punched in the face while being escorted out of The Tunnel nightclub through a dark backroom one evening by a bouncer; would you believe, I bump into him a day later planting trees in my local park and we chat about his plantings and general good works of re-forestation. Surrounded by three security men and asked to leave Harvey Nichols in Edinburgh because I was eating from a punnet of strawberries. They're bound to have their reasons. No point questioning it, maybe they had fruity terrorist last week, throwing bluebarries, ruining white blouses, nows not the time to process it through . . . They never came close, just stood back, ushered and herded me out in case the whole punnet went off and got seeds on their suits.

New York City has a bunch of comedy clubs and I spent one evening going to a few of them. Sporting my nice new second-hand zip-up cardigan that I bought in a store where Elizabeth LeCompte was searching too. She founded the Wooster Group and said they were doing a show that night. I went. Willem Defoe was in it and it was amazing. Leaving in a cab and looking over at the lights to see an actor still in make-up from the show. We traded cigarettes between the windows and chatted at the next two sets of lights.

With my cardigan I went to The Improv with a fifth of whisky secretly inside. You pay a cover, get a few drinks and watch seven comics. They all do a bit for ten minutes and mostly zoom on to the next gig. Most of them have not watched the other acts. Each one that came on commented on my cardigan's stripes and asked me a couple questions, which I began to answer differently to give the crowd a laugh. At one point I got up to pee and somebody went: "No, don't go."

Great gig.

There was a big "IMPROV" sign on the wall. There was very little improvising, very little of seeing what could be made there and then. Sometimes improvising is just re-arranging everything in the moment of presentation and being the thing the crowd reacts best to at that instant. I wished I had a large "E" with me to add to improve the improv. Being open, making up the structure. Often that too involves going for it with things they would and could never see any other night.

Then the terrible timing error of opening the whisky bottle at a quiet moment and everyone hearing the familiar metal screw-top's noise. It was the first time I have actually been physically thrown out of anywhere in the classic style: by a hand on the seat of me pants and a hand on the collar.

Next night I see that Irvine Welsh is giving a reading at the biggest Barnes & Noble bookstore in the world, along with James Kelman. My idea is to go and watch and hover at the back; you never know, he might for some reason see me and whatever. As it happens that is exactly what happens: I am loitering at the back by the escalator and Irvine comes by with entourage catches an eye with me, passes and then comes back.

Our eyes had nearly met once before when I had a whitey and actually swooned at a play he had written that was on at The Tramway venue in Glasgow. Someone was shooting up and the tie around the arm always makes me go a bit weasy. In the bar after, it looked like he was looking over and smiling, and I had looked behind me to see who he was looking at.

Here by the escalator he raises this moment and I was amazed because his smile had been so generous and bright I had just assumed it could not be for me.

All of us went out and were provided for and drank at Max's Fish Bar and ended up the three of us in an Hispanic coke and crack house where, at one point, I stood up quickly, laughing, to make a point and two guys nearby perked up and turned our way with their hands going inside their bloody jackets for their guns.

The joke I will never forget is Irvine saying over and over, all night, a thing the Americans could never get: an impersonation of Tommy Burns, manager of Celtic: "On behalf of myself and Celtic Football Club F.C." Over and over and it was funny every time until it was funny going down Fifth Avenue in a cab with him, after the sun came up and pissing myself and slipping down low in the backseat and feeling the mormning sun which is always so hot . . .

The amazing thing is the next time I saw Irvine was a June the eleventh, my birthday, and I'm playing in the Charity Football Match of Trainspotting versus Charlton Athletic. Tommy Burns was there and Irvine was doing the impression again, near him, then he nutmegged Tommy on the pitch. Remarkable events.

I was nothing to do with Trainspotting, apart from the fact that the producer lived in my flat for a while and the Volcano nightclub where Renton meets Diane is where my teeth were knocked out. And lots of my friends were in it as extras. Oh, and the wrap party:

It was lucky that I was at the wrap party because it meant that it was not daft to invite me to the producer's wedding party where I was able to cling to Cameron Diaz's ankle when she came out of the loo and beg her to let me drink champagne from her shoe – an ordinary life is no less than an amazing thing – she declined.

The night of the wrap-party there was a party up at Kelly Macdonald's – J. Lee Miller and E. McGregor wearing a Darth Vader mask – which like with all these strange laughs about it and Trainspotting a year old, I reckon he knew about the Star Wars Trilogy of Tunisian and blue-screen filmings to come – Andrew Macdonald, D. Boyle and Irvine all smoking the leaf I'd got a bin-bag load of from Ian the artist who sliced tramlines in the back of his legs with a razor.

You've got to try it. You've got to fly at chance, take a running leap over the odd hedge that might have a large drop on the other side. You have to remind yourself what it is you have actually been protecting yourself from in order to keep from real big trouble later. This is especially true with kids. So letting them hold an old ceramic jug in the garden and break it on a rockery rock is okay if then they actually get the untroubled event of this in their life of something going; being broken to be gone.

Fragility is a myth. The best armour is not needing to control. Perhaps love is that, amour not armour. The greatest protection is in your mind, coupled with the sensuality of the flesh. The greatest worries a wobbly reflection of love. Football fans scream at the other side as if they are against them, as if they hate them and want them gone away yet, if they did, there would be no game and so no game to win, no team to support . . . Apart from all of us. You could always support the game too. That's what I feel when watching Scotland play at rugby; there's not the feeling they must win for me to be happy, there's just the wish to see a great game.

Once I did a gig at the Centre for Contemporary Arts in Glasgow and it was not going too well. At one point the woman who booked me was trying to get me off and I ran through some glass doors which I held shut and continued talking into the mike while she tried to open the doors. Can't have been that bad . . . Must have been.

Sometimes it is just there in people's faces that they are really very, very definitely not into what you are about, about what you embody and are saying to them. The terrible look of disdain in the eyes of the CR Smith boss as I battled with a short mike-cord and a bingo-caller unit to defame their Christmas party. The terrible Oil Barons near Aberdeen I offended by asking if they made all the gulls sticky and poisoned with their sick slicks. That corporate gig was my best ever pay: four grand. What about the man who wouldn't stop talking at the bar so I unloaded a cartooned-extreme aural personal offensive of the highest degree about his granny so that he had to be restrained by his friends and members of the crowd as he came at speed towards me through the seating, trying to hoist a chair up as a weapon.

Man, there have been gigs where you are just somehow representing and being the opposite of what they are and want.

Like, if one makes fun of the genre form of comedy presentation in stand-up form, sometimes it is too much.

One gig it was ill-advised to book me for was a kind of half warm-up half opening-slot at the Scottish BAFTAs: As guests from film and tv were gently filling the room there was me doing whatever seemed appropriate and most of this revolved around the vol-au-vents and the lectern. All the Trainspotting folks were there and their film was eleven and a half months previously and may even have been shoehorned in to make this affair more glittery. I ended up hiding a wee canapé on the underside of the lectern which Ewan McGregor pointed out when he collected his award for best actor in that film.

Years ago I was badly-booked to host an awards ceremony to celebrate youths on a government-sponsored volunteer initiative. The hard thing was saying stuff like that there official four-worded title over and over again and not being allowed to go with the new form from a flow of mistakes. It had to be right. i.e. there was a right for it to be. Usually the best part of the amazing freedom of stand-up is that there is actually no certain right. If folks love it, you have done well and so you can chose your own right route. At the end of the government gig when government leader Jack McConnell had left the lectern I offered to sell his handwritten notes on eBay and the special aides were on me in a second to retrieve them.

There are days when it all it's so marvellously together. A fabulous exciting day will have occurred which, in the telling of, will remind me of all the other things in life that would be handy and useful to say in this gig and up they pop. Some shows then settle into a long low-key personal affair with the last half hour like the last bit of a disaster movie where the actors have all come through something together and learned about each other and and their clothes are messy . . . the bonds, James.

You can get whole rows of an audience to shift their chairs sideways along so a woman can hold hands with her fiancé across the aisle. You can turn the whole six hundred-strong audience in the Queen's Hall into the two sides at a wedding and find some marvellous flower arrangements at a good time and use the actual bride-to-be from the hen night to go through a trial run with me as the fairly erotic, innuendo-led reverend priest-type. In Dundee you can lead fifty folks out of the venue to stalk a couple who have left early and cheekily creep up on them quietly spying round street corners then run loudly as a mob and catch them as they enter a pub just down the road.

In Ireland during a gig there was a window behind me at the back of the stage and opening the curtains to the street was a man sweeping. Suddenly I was a magician. I closed them and said them magic words, flung them apart again and he was gone. Inspired, like on a roll, I did it again more magic words flung the curtains open and he was there again.

Morecambe is a troubled town, sorry, tourable town outside the season that was the Fifties and Sixties and Seventies. On the bill were Daniel Kitson and myself and the first half was a Newcomers competition.

During my late slot Daniel actually had to come on and tell them to stop being so unresponsive:

"This is what Phil does. This IS his act," he said, beautifully, to try and help. At the time my joke was about convertible Porsche Police cars and lady PCs with the wind in their long hair . . . stockings . . . a loud laugh . . .

Many folks had to leave early because they had to catch buses to Lancaster or could not abide my rubbish-drivel; either way, by the end, I was leaning on the mike over the edge of the stage and even Daniel was leaving, there were cleaners sweeping up, there were and I fell off the stage onto the ground and sat there with the sixteen remaining audience members. We took stroke stole wine from the backstage area and went over to break into the old art deco Midland Hotel across the road and run around its rooms in the dark along crescent corridors until we found the door to the roof and we were all up there swigging away making howling noises among the rooftops white stucco icing shaped shapes.

The night before the penultimate night of my last comedic tarriance in Australia had been a beautiful evening spouting a v.loud stream of Revolutionary-Spanish Incitement diatribe from one of the big stone balconies of the Melbourne Town Hall until my voice was hoarse, and racing a taxi full of friends back up to the Burlesque Venue. At four a.m. Hung Le, a/the Vietnamese Comedic/Violinist, looked like he didn't know what four it was. Next morning Hung came to my kids-show, as did Daniel Kitson and David O'Doherty together.

There were also The Amazing Johnathan's assistant and her pals that I had met in the comfortable recesses of the Gin Palace at four the night before. There were two friends, Jenny and Elka, who brought their kids: Nuie, Oscar and Natalie.

It was not like some night-time adult shows; this was all comfortable for friends to be around and okay to do well in the show and all altruistic. The best thing is to have a bit of this and a bit of that, the lucky thing is to see we appeal to not a narrow slice and have the wasted Vietnamese violinist comedian who hasn't been to bed and the mums who certainly have been up for ages, the magic assisters and the new wave thinkers. The brand-new friends, only just met, and the comedy folks I have known for quite a while.

The definite highlight of this day's show was getting a kid to put something in the flip-top pedal-bin whilst wearing a pair of flippers. Scuba-diver clearing-up.

This was a rare venue, this Umbrella Revolution Big Top, and when I turned up the morning after the big last-night party to help de-rig it into its container, it meant I got invited to the staff dinner and ate the best food I have ever tasted at the Lemongrass restaurant. Everyone who ran the Strut and Fret Theatre Company was there and me. Very posh highly advanced fusion of Indonesian back through Australian markets: Red Champagne, Chocolate Chicken and Rice Ice-Cream Cappuccino, to name but a few.

Massive solid marble lazy-susans span the foods around as time and globe had brought them to us, as shifting cultural tectonics. I moved in between two empty tables and spun them around with a hand on my ear like huge Stone Age DJ-ing spinning the Technics techtonic panasonic phonics . . . king of the stone age . . . lazy susie q . . .

This is being mentioned because sometimes for me it's like the endless variety of new dishes of experience are coming round the whole time. There is no centre, no end and all is beyond compartment. Cuddly toy, hair straighteners, set of Tupperware; they were all on a conveyer . . . a test, yet things coming round that just keeps a-coming that's the truth, that's free to enjoy.

Also it has been my secret idea to write the words "anyway" and "but" as few times as possible in the book. Check out G. Perec who wrote a novel without the letter "e" in it. In French . . .

For me it works to avoid "but" because it seems to negate the thing said before and that does not make sense, it stifles it. Replace it with "and" and have a wee look. Things are and other things are. He had been up all night and he came to the show. I would love to come out and stay up late and I have work in the morning. Try it.

When this book got started it was Up Here in Findhorn Village on the Moray Peninsula where there is everything: municipal unbreakable binoculars, two piers, a post office and two pubs; a sandy bay, a massive pebble beach, dunes and forest, boatshed, boat-taxi, tennis courts, hostel, ice-house, rentable flats. The established and flourishing Community of the Findhorn Foundation sharing a fence with RAF Kinloss, until it closed recently, one of the biggest Air Force Bases in Europe. Right next to each other and both here because of the weather: the airforce loves the lack of cloud cover and the commune began and really took off because of the gardening, which is all about tutelage and going with the weather. There are geese hunters and a Candlelit Vigil held together on the Bird Sanctuary boundary. There's a bird hide sharing a bench with the planespotters. There's a wee road down to the beach with a sign for each house: "Heathsands" and "Inyanga". Right there the two worlds are really one world. There is a Steiner School on the Hill near the Standing Stones, there's a Fire Station, Railway Station, Health Centre, Whisky Distilleries, the "OrganicPicnic" Sandwich Shop and The Eagle Nightclub. One pile of sand plus another pile of sand is still one pile of sand.

When I was young my local Chinese restaurant was two miles away in Kinross. Now it is two miles away in Kinloss. I love Chopin and Slint; and childminding. There's only an ever-expanding list. Douglas Gordon has an artwork in the MoMA in Edinburgh that he has added to each year and it is just a list of everyone he can ever remember meeting. The idea that this life is a list of events, there is no definition other than that, is a strong one for me.

Just last once I was with Clancy when he was ten while his Mum goes to be a professional Clown Dr. in the intensive care wards of Children's Hospitals. He always goes to bed at eight, right, and at ten to nine after D&D (-ungeons, -ragons) we are there and I bring the clock off the wall and shake, listen to it and put his toothbrush on his D&D notes and open the door to the hall and stuff. I will not say it; I don't have to. It is time for bed and both of us know it.

"How are you going with this slightly later time? . . . It appears to be . . ."

Clancy is hanging about trying to get another Samurai-battle going with the draught excluders and I am like the smart parent-figure who knows he's got to go . . . And he hasn't.

"What, have you got an alarm to get you up or what?"

No response.

"So, you're up at seven fifteen. What are you going to do till then?"

"Sleep," he says . . . Aha! . . . Still he loiters around the open door.

"You're going to make me say it, aren't you?"

He smiles.

"You know it's . . . , . . . , . . ." I leave three mysterious gaps in there with head nods. He laughs.

He's at the door saying goodnight: "Well I'm off now. It must be . . . , . . . , . . ."

I am alone laughing in the living room, the door is shut and Clancy is laughing in the hall with just a big space that hung there without spoken words. Heard they were though.

Finding a thing that is a goofy play on something you both understand. And you can milk it. You have to milk it until udders are sore; you have to.

That is when adult stand-up gigs get good for me: When there is fabulous understanding shared through a goofy milking. That is why I have done some gigs that go well and yet I do not feel that good about it because I did other things rather than share the shake – just pre-arranged safety ideas in a row. That is what nerves are really about: Concern given in to or exploited for the goof. No point in crying over unmilking though, just get the wee three-legged stool ready.

This is also why gigs have gone awful, apparently on the surface, for ages and then suddenly all come together like a white sauce. Because I have stuck to what I want to do and the sour-then-sweet consensus has come around like it's on a big rotating centrepiece. This is why really good shows are similar to really hard ones: and they don't determine what the next one will be like.

It's best to be as positive as you can because all the next hundred and six people who have worked their way through their life to that day and through that day to get ready and see a poster and buy a ticket and then remember to come along, well, they were not the audience at the last show. Often comedians will say something like "Oh you have done a gig in Aberdeen, I am going there, what are they like?" I always assume they are joking and might say something about their hair being a bit long yet rather stylish and them being overbearingly affectionate and a lot more with tiled bathrooms than you would imagine . . . until they tell me to stop being ridiculous. Well you started it.

Once I came through customs into the US and the lady official said: "You have long hair . . . are you in a band . . . ?"

"You need more than that to be in a band, love . . . ," was my response.

"No need to be cheeky with me . . ."

". . . you started it . . ."

On a radio show that last time a while back in Melbourne I had some rubber bands with me, nicked from stationery pots on people's desks on the way round the open-plan offices on our way to the studio. Experimentary, my dear Watson. There was a plan though, for You can get quite a good tune out of pulling various bands' widths to different tensions and pinging. This music-making accompanied most of my answers and was accompanied by a fair amount of bemusement from the hosts, of whom one was standing. Just before the show a man had told me not to do too much local reference stuff because the show was being beamed over the whole of Asia now. He's right: how unfathomable might my hunour be to folks learning English as a foreign language listening to this? He is right and he is wrong.

At the gig the next day, a lady told me she had heard me playing the elastic band on the radio and that was the reason she had brought her son along.

"There was more than one band," I said.

Things happen and affect butterflies everywhere.

A Russian café-owner let me take my porridge with me when I realized I was late to be on radio one day in Dublin. This became the feature of the feature, Live Oats, and by the time we got back there with the plate, he said lots of folks were coming in for porridge saying they heard about it on the radio . . . OatFm . . . Pinchofsalt.com . . . soak it up and absorb . . .

At Billy's Bonker's Cosy Comedy Club a gig went a certain way that things began to be important to us, me and the crowd, so that I unscrewed a low roof vent with a penknife and we put our own Time Capsule in there, of things that meant much to us from the show and might explain the gig to anyone who found it in the future. This wee club I have done with Billy for years, just me and an hour and a half standing on the ground by the bar getting my dribnks direct, sometimes full with eighty-six folks; sometimes I meet a stag-night of sixteen and bring them in, doubling the numbers. Shows have been fabulous there and intimate and there's times I have done exactly what I want to do and reach all the stories that are there and needed and, one time, I have come back from my agent's fiftieth birthday party at the Tennent's Mansion and only need to talk about what happened there to remind me into all that the gig requires.

There have been times when shouting boys take my wind and I battle on a bit, realizing there is no entertaining here and die the death of a thousand deaths when you find yourself trying again, responding to a bigger laugh yet still sliding off the roof – looking desperate in the true sense: deplorable and beyond redemption.

Starting gigs sometimes is odd, it's mad, it's fun because it can define the trajectory of the whole show, yet it is a new moment, it's up to you, it always going to be easier to add your own individual touch. Like I am not ready to go in the starter-cage like horses that race.

Usually it is fine and I can arrive cool, do the things that need to be done and stroll on, run on, get on before the crowd, or as they are coming in, create a disturbance behind the curtain, be last in the bar ushering folks out to the show. Rarely do I have to be in a dressing room if it doesn't feel right. Soundchecks can often be done in reality by any voice and soundmen have just learnt to offer it to people so that they cannot be rightfully upset later. And instruments and sound queues and lighting requirements – bands and groups obviously need to check levels. Me though, it can all be incorporated into the show. In fact a few gigs have started well because there was no sound or a faulty sound and then you have something to work with. A thing to be doing; something to avoid the reality of it only being a comedy show.

These are shows off course that are bigger and at theatres or art centres and are just me. On the whole the gigs in London there is a compere and you kind of have to come on and regular, yet there is still your own style of words and sometimes these beginnings are alike a mad rowdy fourteen minutes, then a wee song and you're done. Sometimes coming on and hand-shaking the compere is so formal and its just tag-wrestling and you've come on to have your go at them.

The hardest show to start was the Edinburgh after my television series for Channel 4. The show was called Phil Kay Feels Like Playing With His Friends and was at the enormous Playhouse Theatre. With me were Rich Hall, Bill Bailey, Dylan Moran and Phil Nichol and, accidentally, I fell into being like a shy compere. What a bill though – the Mount Rushmore of modern comedy, four stellar conspicuous, building, unique talents. Dylan Moran is definitely the only comedian to ever come to my hotel room and disturb a nap by an open window in a Manchester Hotel and then tell me I was his favourite stand-up. Save my life and compliment me.

Just before it began, Nina Simone was singing "Birds flying high you know how I feel . . . I'm feeling good." The song started playing and folks were clapping and whooping, the atmosphere was huge, with the fifteen hundred and three people, and it just didn't feel right. Waiting far too long as Nina sang, held back by the lights and myself and didn't know how to hit it, so all I did was to just kept doing a few minutes and bringing on a guest. Shitty. Like I couldn't see it as a real human event, it was a big cash in cop out. All my friends the acts did brilliantly, with nothing to lose.

Rich Hall was especially fun and mucked about with me: that was the time he got on the low piano-shifting trolley and I zoom-span him lying low down on this in the Da Vinci star-man position to nearly skydive off the edge of the stage into the very deep orchestra pit.

Genuinely, people I talked to were very sad as they could sense I had been hiding. Hiding is mad yet comes along as a kind of sane option when the context of actually "being on" and doing it in front of everyone don't seem to click and the here-and-now is too strong. That gig was a disastrous let-down debacle.

S'not easy and its not going well, this is me trying to tie it all together when one of the things I'm expressing is that it can't be all tied together. The random element is not an element. All is random in the kingdom of the uncontrollable, unruly and uncontainable in the world. At least this means I am never let down by things going a different way than expected. Shit show, fair enough. Best show ever, fair enough.

Sounds a bit daft yet it is true to me that I try and let the shows be primarily a human event, their own occurrence, like a real simple affair of a person talking and wanting it to grow and be an natural growth and not be a controlled thing, because that is a myth to me.

What I want to do is what I do: a wild random selection of mostly one-off venues and shows and crowds and moments and the chance of the best show ever a real contender all the time.

That is why I was so shite on QI: I did not want to do it.

The subconscious – the sub conscious – my back brain knows that and so could not release the genius selections.

If you are borderline-skint most of the time then this can really improve the taste of pistachios.

It really works. This is a choice.

It is the best to fully appreciate things by a rationing rationale.

Finishing gigs is hard. Maybe it is impossible. They are abandoned; at some point one leaves. If it is possible I like to leave without climax and segue gently from the warm ocean to the warm air, walking out slowly.

Once it worked the best at a show in Auckland, where things had gone well enough for there to be an atmosphere of normality. The lights were up and people had had a long show yet the point that maybe it is all closer than it appears to just a person talking like we all talk and I simply edged my way off the stage through them gently saying "hang on a minute, watch this" and slowly getting to the bar. At this point they are watching someone who has finished yet they are still rapt; this is the draughty barn in the storm, it feels great. I made it to the bar and ordered my drink quietly and turning back gave a wink and said, "Well, that's it."

A comedian said to me afterwards that that was the funniest show that had ever been done in New Zealand. Like it was possible to measure it like a sprinter's hundred metre-time.

Honestly the last gig I did at the Lowry in Manchesty was a St Patrick's Day-themed Celtic Cabaret with burlesque and my ending somehow managed to involve mentioning the Troubles and bloodshed and a plea not to limit goodwill to predetermined dates like March the Fifteenth . . . totally serious, and at the heart of my accidental, occidental views, yet still it went comedically well as it could.

Often the crowd is asked to leave first, so I don't have to. Often they have nowhere to go and I have to leave, to go to be at the bar for pineapple juice or whisky or beer. I went through a phase of getting mightily pissed onstage after the interval because I would stay on and ask for drinks to be brought. And they came. In England they think it is a joke and don't bring them.

Just recently I realized my Mum used to play a Billy Connolly tape in the car all the time and have his records at home, so there had, therefore, been a strong influence surely in the example of hearing a storyteller doing well and seeing the Mum you love loving it. It always sounded so good: Connolly, saying real things in an exciting way and singing songs.

That daft BAFTA warm-up gig with the milking of the heroin canapés, where no one would speak to Daniela Nardini in the dressing room because she was so hot at the time, was the year they honoured Mrs Brown and, while I was struggling to get any attention to keep, as old friends took their seats and saw each other for the first time, all eyes and ears were on Billy and Judy Dench who had become like their characters in the film: loving friends across an apparent divide. There was a kind of hush now and the lack of laughs for me and what I was doing in the room became a concern and almost tangibly audible, or audibly tangible and then as the room hushed to listen in on them Judy said something and she and Billy laughed together, friends, and he looked around and saw what was happening and looked towards me and said, "Don't let the bastards get you down!"

. . . Did I ever tell you about the time I was doing a short moving house and got in a police chase with a sofa on the roof of me car? A smallish move, not the smallest house move ever though. No that one was in Glasgown and I moved over the road once, and actually threw some of my stuff to the next house. Hurled it across the road. Anyway this move is only around the corner two hundred and eighty yards, up our street, slight incline, fifty-degree corner to the left along past the desirable Hymer body camper van, all bulbous, and not an inch wasted, on past the police garage, right well before the miniature chemist where you can reach the shelves from the queue. Right there through the lights and sharp left around the garage that fixes cars on to St Ann's Crescent with the fresh air view along to the Downs. Yes the Police garage . . . That's the issue. I used to pass it every day and ha ha stick my tongue out for a laugh. ". . . ner ner . . . you can't chase me . . . you are up on a ramp . . ." . . . it's a fact the Policemen's cars break down too, the Queen's got an arsehole, wake up and smell the roasted grounds I've shot up your nose. Anyway I'm moving house really slowly one load at a time, going to take four days and one of the boxes has a tweed hat I can't remember being there. Loading stuff on the old classic E30 and you can strap anything up there. Fridge, prams, cupboards and now last of all final item the big blue sofa. Neighbour Nathan says he'll help though he's late and I'm walking it past his window where he's on the phone and gives me one of those neutral mime-signs you don't know if he is saying that he will come off the phone or that he can't.

So. It's up and on and I strap it up there yet a bit loosely. Like a cowboy will tie up his horse, not really with a knot, just a double wind and the horse is like "well I could have that and be off . . ." and the cowboy is saying "well where are you gonna goa . . . ?" and the horse thinks "see your point . . ." and makes the huffy noise with the lip flaps and all. So it's up there and I chuck a strap across and tie a single granny placebo knot and off we go taking the incline easy as you come on the the left-hander then ha ha raspberry as we pass the Police oh no here's a guy coming out all fixed, all revved up and ready for Justice and here's we are, fresh chicken meat in town. The Sheriff is out and right behind me and the best thing is to pull over and get out of their vision before they feel the need. The sofa is wobbling and I'm driving it easy so as not to rock it and I remember driving without brake lights with the Cops behind me and having to just keep going straight and not look like I need brakes until they're gone. Gulp. And so they pull in too game's a bogey I'm up and out and telling him it's cool and he's telling me that it's inadequately strapped and I'm telling him ". . . it's okay man I'm forty I'm just popping round the corner, it's fine . . ." the clipboard is out and fair enough if I just go straight on here there's the motorway and the sofa would be danger there . . . I could get up to seventy it could break free like Kong and rise up there and fly back and fuck a Smart car into the road like a rivet.

". . . honestly mate it's fine . . . I'm just going round the corner . . . you do what you have to do . . ."

And I drive off and up to the lights by which time he's got the sirens on and the chase is on and stupidly I stop at the lights which have gone red. Silly because I'm already in a Police chase, it's a bit late to be legal Phil. They screech in from the Sofa Squad and in so close he can't get his door open and we're giggling a bit and when I'm out and in handcuffs he says, "I suppose you think this is funny?"

"No, no, I'm absolutely certain," I say.

It would have been much better to have just gone through the lights, much better way to arrive on the new street with the new neighbours wondering who these guys are what are they like the new folks and there could have been me: zooming in and skidding to a halt and the sofa flies off and lands on the pavement and I've got my feet up with an electric fag on when the Police scream in, lights dashing off the full Georgian croissant facade . . . the full boona.

As it is they pull in the old MW and me in the backseat and handcuffs, they pull in on the closest place to pull in out of the traffic and that is the our new street. Ha. Here's where are I tell them. This is it. 'Twas not a figure of speech, "round the corner".

There is an argument put forward that they have over-reacted, they say not from the visits they have made to parents of dead teenagers. A bit harsh, yet I do feel for them and yet I'm like "well man I hear you yet look it was a rational move, just so close, and one strap was enough . . . look it's just survived a Police chase." They had to smile. Of course by now I've learned my lesson from Dublin and got the cuffs round the front so I can send a text to Melina. "Hey it's me . . . parked on the street." It's a lovely moment when I see her come out of the new house and look around, do a few scans and then she sees the Police car and kind of does the head lean and starts to proceed towards us. That was our submarine moment of Mr and Mrs.

In the very end I wrote a marvellous long letter outlining my various points of order and admitting mostly how I understood why the men had to act and that that would affect my behaviur in the future. They let me off, no court worries and no points.

The letter of appeal was written on stationery from the Hotel California in Zurich that I got a huge stash off from three years ago when gigging there with the tremendously sunny and funny Stuart Goldsmith, when we got the free bikes and made a funny film commentating on the Segway riders doing slalom in a beginner's class . . .

Chapter Ate

Ultimately it is not as easy as you think to prepare and administer your own cleansing eyebath whilst driving and having a spot of bother . . . Reminds me of eating a Marks & Spencer fully prepared half-lobster on my knee with no cutlery, at the wheel, for the first time, and meeting the Police on a corner near Troon and almost veering into them in the VWan with the shock and a nice lemon dressing all sliding my hands around the steering wheel. Definitely the medics would have been trying to find an explanation for the sharp crustacean claws embedded in me flesh, in my belly . . . Points of entry: from the window, as we're near the sea; Atlantic mid-drift wound; CSI Troon; Sea-SI; looking for claws; on the net; lured with bait; hook, line, stock, sinker and too, smoking fish in barrels; trawling through the evidence; Goddamn bottom-feeders! . . . "Lobster Lap-Dance Of Death" Says Crusty Old Ocean Coroner Of Old Crustacean Corner . . .

This time I was even trying to be safe and methodical and had already performed faultlessly the relatively-simpler vault: the Jacket Put-On . . . zipped up around the seatbelt without taking eyes off the road. Picked it up from behind me in the blind fruitful sweep that knows it has a thirty miles to find the thing-on-the-backseat and bring it forward. At this point something minute changes in my focus on the road as I have to give a small part of consciousness to deciphering what my hand is running-into back there with the twisty heat in the shoulder – I put my right arm through the sleeve and, as it comes out, the hand is straight onto the steering and the left takes the majority of the rest of the jacket and helps it up and around in a full salsa hand-move, incorporating a slight shimmy to get round the belt, to get the left inside-chest stretched to cling over the corner of the left shoulder ltight ike sofa-cover failing and all it needs is a readjusting of the right-hand grip to allow the left shoulder to sink and tuck and a little twist and roll-through from the left wrist and we're there.

The eye-bathing was simple: just eighteen to twenty mils of Strathmore pure Scottish "You Cannae Bottle It" water poured into the cap and the bottle gripped intra-thighly and the millilitres applied to an eye tricked into staying open in a backward flip to look briefly out of the executive sky-roof . . .

If you ever want to make friends with a water-waiter, just ask as they pass, "Is this water still sparkling . . . ?"

We all love the sun and, in truth, it is always there. What we really crave is cloudlessness. Yet in the end that's the only complaint about LA, the constant samey old sun . . . so all types of sky can be seen through a "sunroof" and if you have it open and drive in the rain the aero-dynamique of the sincere French stylings of this Citroën allows no rain down in – I had my hand up out of it and I could feel raindrops hitting, going up. Once I was going along in autumn in the winds and blusterings and caught a leaf. Not really trying to yet there it was the hand was available. In it to win it, or out there to pluck it from fat air. The point is it is not the weather that determines the mood. The weather determines the rainfall and that determines the health of soil and plant, that is serious and fairly traceable, checkable and linear . . . To place your mood at the whim of globally changing patterns is a cover-up, a façade, a smokescreen that you is operating with little buttons and squirts from behind the scenery. Check out that farmer crying in the rain, adding his tears to be hidden in the wetness after a drought. Whether the weather affects you is the climate. The conditions are your conditions.

Sorry. Otherwise you could have your entire life controlled by, what? – the externals you chose. Even at the heart of it is the camouflaged truth: that still it was your choice about the weather.

Even when they quote the bible they choose which bit they want and in what way they want it. Secondary to the will. A bit like kids underlining the parts of The Great Gatsby that they consider better than the other bits. Aiee. When I studied it at A-level I just highlighted the whole book for a laugh. Probably around the same time A. Kaufman was reading it out aloud onstage and he was the oddest addition to Taxi. Once two departments in the same Glasgow newspaper asked me for a review of Man On The Moon, the biography of Andy Kaufman, so I wrote two different reviews from different perspectives: one open and loving and gushing of his ability and the other weirded out and suspicious of the book, its style and motives. One of the only times I have ever hidden my true feelings as a mischevious deception. It didn't feel right it was just the unique opportunity to earn an extra hundred quid and too adopt two personalities up against a comic who famously played with the public perception of his good and his bad. Everyone knows about his wrestling matches against women and everyone knows when a director took him as a surprise to a whorehouse they all knew him there already.

The only thing to do is be brilliant and so funny they can't resist watching. Concentrate on the ones that are hearing, and not let the ones that are not affect the reality of what is being watched. Honestly it's like the electron thing, or the fucking traffic thing, harnessing this . . . so let the ones that are not interested see someone being interested, the example, the possibility, rather than telling them to get it . . . let it be worth it.

First Rule of Comedy: Be Funny.
First Rule of Being Funny: Share.

So . . . The way this bigly relates to gigs is very strong for me: Be so fabulous they must laugh. No other possible scenario. And believe me I have done by far the shittest, cataclysmic, calamitous, disaster-zone meltdown gigs of anyone I've ever seen. Once I watched Simon Day's face in a canteen when he had to sit next to me at lunch when he had seen me die at Late'n'Live and he was so uncomfortable. Later we toured and he saw another thing and was loosened. It is huge.

Go on the line and surf upon the world wide web and there is a thing from a gig in Aberdeen.

Here's the story: Friday night the wee promotion company Breakneck Comedy have me on in Stonehaven whereby there is much hilarity from me after some other good comics . . . I press my bum up against a steamy window and get the Arse of Turin imprint and start the gig with an impressive song all about the history of the town and local famous open air pool . . . all of which I was able to garner from B&W photos with captions in the short corridor as I was waiting to come on. Very typical to be thrilled by the facts and so immediately inspired with some fresh ingredients like a harmless, wise-ass Kaiser Söze utilizing my surroundings, with the usual inspection.

It goes well and they pay me.

The gig is run usually by Naz in Aberdeen and him and me smoke the pipe of peace and muck about before the four other gigs we have already done together at the beautiful Blue Lamp bar in Aberdeen.

Naz is my man and a laugh and yet he is not here the next night when I arrive at the venue. For the first time ever it is being run by a lass for her first time. So it sparks an interest when she tells me for a second time when to be at the venue then asks me how I am going to get there.

. . . Same way I get to all me gigs, I tell her, bus, train, rail or bike . . . what's your point? The point is it's her first time running a gig.

So, I stay over in Stonehaven and end up winning a guy a bet by going back to a party twice after the nightclub dancing when someone bet him I wouldn't show up. That was the party with the hilariously cramped pool table in the kitchen with so many things to knock off shelves with the cue . . . and of course my exercise-bike embellishment evolution, is that my cue ends up under the toasting grill while I really deliberate over a shot and all eyes are on the ball and what's that burning rubber smellllll????

Anyhow, next morning I hitch with some christians in the raining rain into Aberdeen and have a smashing day and end up in the coin-op massage chair in the poshest Union Square shop mall with a can of Tennent's Super brew foamed up in disguise in a Costa coffee mug like a real loutish latte, smoking an e-fag getting a back rub. It's more like knobbly like Felix's knees in the car, yet when a security guard comes by I just start wriggling and moaning and she thinks I've put a pound in.

Arriving at the gig on time, the lass tells me that there are other comedians on, I'll be on in an hour and a half. It's boogie nights time . . . I'm ready to rock . . . let's go . . .

No, it's not boogie nights time . . . even though I could be, I'm actually pretty forgiving because me and Naz have arranged this and she is clearly oot da loop, and it's not her fault that she doesn't know that its only meant to be just me, without any other comedians . . . I chill out after letting her know that it's meant to be solely me-o and then I check if the deal is known to her the sixty percent . . . because what are they going to pay the other comedians with . . . aiee . . . there's a whiff o' trouble in the air . . .

She's caught in t'middle and thinks I'm a bit out of order and when the comedians are done she comes through to tell me she has asked them to leave straightaway after they have done their slot. Eh, wrong end of the wrong stick.

Truth is now I'm miffed and so when they say you're on in four minutes I sit waiting in the gents leatherette lounge with a new pal till exactly three minutes fifty then head through and of course they say "Where have you been . . . ?"

Anyway now I don't like the gig and it's mad though it is busy . . . and I start the show with a beautiful appraisal of the features of Union Square massage chairs and faux-foam and the Asian family who all sat and giggled next to me as Granny got the massage chair to wobble her shoulders. At that point only Granny knows what I know: that there is a hefty slice of up-force fisty movements massaging the old buttocks and she hides it well. Counting the folks in the room I get up to over a hundred and five before stopping . . . and trying to do the math . . .

hundred and five times a tenner . . . thousand fifty times point six equals six eighty five . . . some sum like that.

Antyway I do well for about eleven minutes and then people at the back all began to chat and get restless giving it the old "this is too weak and not enough jokes and if we wanted an on-the-spot Spalding Gray imaginative thoughts-based monologue we'd go to the Edinburgh Fringe thanks . . ." and then I flip out of doing a gig and ask out loud if they were given freebies because they seem to not know what I do and I am out of order and certainly not hilarious no more and of course really ought to just Be Funny and Irresistibly Brilliant.

Then after not doing well I try to implement a break so the people that don't like it can fuck off to another room or get a drink and chill out. Yet this is a break where I don't want to leave the stage, so up there ploughing on in a tractor with a wheel missing it goes pear-shape, devil's avocado pear-shape then crushed and mulched pear . . . the lass turns the power off, her boyfriend says they are not going to pay me and, hang on . . . if I don't do my time . . . then the smell of the burn of non-payment has grown around me so much that at first it was a whiff now it is definite and, in sensing this, action must be taken.

My family is on holiday at this point in France in a rented house that I am to arrive at on a flight the next morning with this Aberdeen money and pay for. So this is looking a bit unfun . . . the actions that must be taken are me going back onstage and doing my time and begging her to pay me . . . holding onto her leg onstage to let her see how serious it is for me as she makes an announcement that the gig is over. Can you imagine watching this shit, when normally a bad gig is a few of your jokes not going that well?

Here it's like fucking a mad brawling earthquake crack to the foundations of entertainment.

Seems like it would never be the right thing to do, to beg for myself and yet it's the kids' baguette money and house rent is what it seems to me, so there's no issue . . .

No no, it's got worse to go. The lass offers me a hundred quid and foolheartedly I do not accept for it appears there is still another route to pass Go and collect what's really owed. By this time we're all going down the road and I have nothing left save the plea to consider my kids stranded in France. They probably don't believe me and the boyfriend lunges at me with his fists and changes my mind about asking anymore.

I send a few texts from the bus station where cleverly I have a ticket for the four a.m. bus which will take me directly to fly from Stansted.

Most of the journey was sat in an upright stunned position and this
was rather cool – the injustice, the lack of fun and funds, the fiduciary
breakdown and financial perfidy, the running over it in the mind really
limited all that fidgeting and moving to get comfortable.

So the deal with this gig is that it is payback for the three gigs I have
done for him for just two fifty. This gig it is just me, and sixty percent
of the door price taken is mine all mine. Next week me and Naz are on
the phone sorting it out, he remembers that we had arranged no other
comics and the maths and all and he sends me some cash . . . and then
books me again. Meanwhile the lass has put something definite up on
the web making it sound a way better worse than it was, adding the
nudity from Friday's steamy window and adding a few more things you
would . . . stealing drinks . . . tears . . .

NOW, seriously folks, this is where it really philkays, where the bomb
is, where it is definitely me in a unique situation: He's rebooked me . . .
who gets a chance to come back like this? Who? Who can come back to
a town after this kind of disaster couple months with the same
promoters from before and do a gig with such a heavy, superb extra
context? Nobody . . . it's mad and superb and rather grand.

Will he go mad? . . . Will he strip off? . . . What will go down? . . . Will
there be violins? . . .

In the end I am able to do what is really my kind of show because the
lay-out and the set-up are as they were agreed and we know what time
I am on and two mates drive me over from Forres so the drinking can
have good timing and as well the J. Savile story waves were just
breaking on the beach of conciousness enough to surf the point a
while. The best best thing about it all was telling at the very end the
whole story like I have just typed it and the best icing on top of that
was the lass who ran it was there laughing and she passed me her
iPhone up onstage which keeps all texts and there were all mine from
the bus station explaining how my children are going to be stranded
and THINK ABOUT THE WEE ONES . . .they will go hungry . . . and stuff
like that.

Wow, forgiveness, time travel, a new dawn . . . and the audience are
laughing at it.

Fucksake, that was one of the top nineteen achievement gigs of all
my times.

Like:

An hour-show on a Sunday all about my agent's fiftieth birthday
gathering weekend telling how we all laughed more than we ever had

before as she opened her presents in front of everyone at tea on the Sunday and took the piss out of a yellow teapot someone who had left had given her.

The one early on in the British Airways staff lounge at Prestwick where a lady vomited with laughter and had to leave.

The half hour I did with the Thighmaster to three hundred and thirty people at the Dundee Rep after they had seen me do compering week after week there.

The Queen's Hall wedding gig.

The hour and a half instead of forty minutes gig ending up nakedish with an audience member's phone wedged between my buttocks singing with the band.

The kids' orchestra at Glastonbury.

The entirely Django Unchained-infused sociologically-infused show at Up The Creek seven Sundays ago where I'm dropping the H-bomb and "we don't got no nigger pope . . ." and whipping the all-Scandinavian Aryan looking front-row boys with a long stripey sock half-donated by second-row lady from her own leg with revengeful post-ironic backlashes . . . Me and Simon, my new best man, my accordion and piano player, had just seen Django Unchained and were all saturated with the feelings of watching a slave wreak retribution set to great music . . . settling old scores to a fab score . . . oh the payback playback . . .

The car is going like a dream flying over Scotland and is very much a big grey wedge. It's the XM. It is an early-nineties family estate and it has that feeling of a heavily-beaten guard dog learning to love and trust and exert itself for a new owner. Something is sad for the abusive-revving and chortled clutch-ridings he invisibly bore.

Or suffered. This word really interests me – "suffer". It relates in meaning to the act of putting up with, abiding, enduring something yet the big deal meaning today is just of the bad feeling that must come because of the enduring, the abiding, the putting up with.

They are different because one cannot define the other to definitely happen. I feel this car will, with strokings on the dash and doing the soft long nudge that lets gears find their own way, especially into third, will keep it going forever and maybe die under me on an uphill, like the horse in the original True Grit.

It has some of those fading glorious semi-executive car features like central-unlocking and electric chairs that you can have going forward as you accelerate which puts an added zoom on it somewhat. If your braking seems like it isn't going to be enough you could always reverse away from the crash, inside on your seat, and delay it slightly.

I have the seat quite upright and feel like a rally-position and I muse on how lucky rally drivers are, their insouciance to insurance and parking or the triumvirate set to irritate. The three horsepowers of the apocalypse, the three main driving problem-feature things: "Who's paying for petrol? Where are we going? I wonder if anyone is coming the other way?"

Having kids has saved my life, given me something to put my energy into and something worthwhile.

Sex once you are pregnant is like rally-driving compared to regular driving.

Safe sex is really dangerous – trying to make love yet not babies. High I love you, look we're making love yet no all that it is it can't be yet, here look in the throes of lust and lost to logic we must be logical. Safe sex is all worry like normal driving: "Where shall we park? Which way is it? Am I even insured? . . . Shall we fill up now? . . . Is there anything coming the other way? . . . Is it okay to back out . . . "

Once you are pregnant it becomes like rally-driving because you are allowed to drive this car like it was designed to be driven. You are in the driving seat and the fireproof suit because you are a great driver.

Who's paying for the petrol? The sponsors.

Where are we going? The wee man with the map on his knees knows exactly where we are going to the metre and to the angle and already the upcoming corner is announced.

Is there anything coming the other way? No, it's a rally . . .

Put your foot down; care no more, operate at ultimate levels; get the rev needle and the m.p.h. needle to both be pointing up at high noon; doing sixty in second.

Tell you something: Being in a place to dig someone else's insouciant ways, their carefree attitude, their free happily unconcerned ways, their big car, their larger fridge, their great hair, jumpers, oven-baked vegetables . . . Being able to be into others' stuff like this is magic.

That is the way I am and I treasure it in myself. Looking at the way my life is lived – around kids and their mum, with work slotted around and me eligible for almost all breakfasts with personal interests catered-to and an attainable, at hand, feasible, gettable heaven in a decent ale while I cook – well, it seems these must be constituents and causes, results and determiners.

The omlette is from the chicken is from the egg.

The daffodil shares DNA with the ape.

Is that glass half full or three quarters . . . and isn't it a fine design?

I once shared a flat for a while with Johnny Cooper Clark. Went in one morning and he was actually sleeping with his sunglasses on. He had a great joke: "What's the fastest car in the world? . . . A hire car."

I've been to get a tattoo three times: First in Strasbourg where I had gone to see a solar eclipse. At Glasgow Airport with a poncho and a list of cities the eclipse would be visible from I asked for the first flight to one of them. In Strasbourg I hung out with the locals in the square and ate cheeses of the area and avoided buying the protective glasses and joined in solo in the whoops. It was all in the main square and all over were signs warning of pickpockets. Obviously they were new up and obviously too there was not a precedent for this. It is not like there are always pickpockets at these bloody eclipse things because they happen once every century and a half in the same city. It is just that the conscientiousness of the city council comes through. They think of all those folk standing there looking in one direction, blinded and wearing light-resistant specs and they think of all the chance that provides for pockets to be picked. It would have to be an illuminating experience, though, for a criminal . . . To be there, in amongst it all, forsaking the whole marvellous sight, the panoply of flaming circus-whirls around the sun's edge, the spiralling speedy darkness articulated from behind the source of all life, excluded for a minute or two. Surely he might get it, then surely he might see that his energy might be best going into proactive stuff. Surely he might see he was Missing Out on stuff here and he would be better to be poor and watching the sunworks in the sky? Yes, oui, ja.

Anyway it was all happening at ten-ish in the morning and a rich old man who lived in an apartment on the square came out on to his balcony under where the sun might be and everyone was cheering him. The cheers they did were of a short nature. The nature of a joke. Later people would cheer the sun being blocked out and it would be a longer higher cheer. Would generate itself, regenerate itself and be of unexpected return.

I felt free to shout unusual things in English that may or may not be understood and may or may not draw British faces around. "Come on, my Sun!" I call. That night I wander the streets unsuccessfully doing my biggest ever, try-to-get-lost method, taking any left or whatever in a big arc.

And it leads me after an hour back to the same place so I set off again waiting to discover the encampment of traveller revellerers and they weren't. Then after a while I was brought back again. So it was a massive fail.

And end up curling up under the tables of a restaurant's outside patio area. There was a moment at three fifteen a.m. when walking along a Strasbourg street when I flick up the head and look up at a fourth-floor bedroom window and, on a beat later, the light is switched off as I pass. Lovely. There is nothing more to be made from this than one's enjoyment of it and the noticing of the noticing I feel. A human excited and thinking on it is as high a reaction as this mind can expect. Awareness of one's own observational-aptitude faculty is security.

Like the coincidence of the moon covering the sun. On thinking one can realize that there is an eclipse all the time somewhere justly not from our position. There is a possible mapped shaded curve of where the eclipse falls and a plottable route when it is next back with us as important as the comets. As the knees of the Italian Granny are as important as Micky Mantle.

We give it a name when it affects us, when the shadow falls on us, when it brushes with our life. I find it better to imagine it as good and on all the time, not just when it appears to be beneficial in our own life.

The next morning, coming back towards something, I pass a tattoo-parlour and pop in with the view to having a design of my daughter Coco's name on my arm, the idea is that the Co-Co can overlap like a moon going on and coming off the sun. On giving the lady my design she draws it out badly and looks a bit too worried by her own stoned stone to trust, like she don't trust herself. Then there is a wait for almost an hour before realizing my flight is in only one more. Seems all wrong to be sitting there anxious about a flight getting a tattoo that means a lot; so I walk away.

A year later I walk into another tattoo-parlour in Glasgow.

It has seating around the edge of the room with numbers between each set of knees. People move around towards the tattooists, as each person who is next stands up and picks up their coat and goes in, everybody else stands up and moves one seat closer to the needle. Generally there are two types: the Those who are having more tattoos, and the Those who are having their first. These are the ones mostly with their coats.

Ahead of me are two naval Americans stationed at Faslane, talking very loudly. All their excitement turned to blood sugar, all their nerves incorporated bypassing fear of pain. They talk loudly and are very, very keen to exhibit manliness. One of them tries my guitar without really having to make eye contact with me and brushes off a couple of intimate questions I ask him. Across the room comes another marine and they talk real loud to him about supergluing some guy's locker shut and hiding his boots and, because he could not remember simple English, he was a dickhead. They muse onto things and end up talking about the sniper recently shooting from a motorway bridge. They ask what could make an asshole do this. I am reminded of the interview between Michael Moore and the executive at the Lockheed Missile Factory, downtown Columbine, where he muses over the fact that he cannot imagine what would make a teenager go shooting while he is standing under actual missiles. Perhaps psychologically these weapons of mass destruction have an effect on the consciousness of the children here: fathers and uncles and friends' mums, the adult humans here are concerned with instruments of death. I ask them if they have seen Bowling For Columbine and they say no. They wonder again what could make someone go crazy like that with a gun.

Right there and then it would have been the right time and place to stand up and say, "Assholes like you are the reason. That you are mean and short of well-missed praise yourself and aggressive from the midst of an all-boy group." That it is these weirdos that are turning around and saying, eventually, "Well, fuck you and here's how it can be done."

Here it would be the perfect jump up and for all the common folks give-'em-hell truth: "It's You! You foolish men, you have to see that the stupidity of your disregard can no longer be your excuse."

I could swear at them and spray words over everyone in this room. They couldn't attack me; not here with so many witnesses and their Americanism and naval status so announced. Plus the evidence of their tattoo-singular-identity, so brazenly spoken of, would identify them to Military Police.

By this time I was after the word "p h o n e j e l l y" to be tattooed on my upper inner shoulder facing me. It is to remind me to call my goddaughter Angelica.

In the end I didn't rant at these men and I didn't get a tattoo because it was Saturday, the queue was too long, and again I had to travel within the ninety minutes I'd started with.

Third time was good: Had visualized my sitting there all upright and strong and chatting sentences whose ends had lost some of their filling. I do know that talking would alleviate the warming waters of dissipation around the middle in contractions.

As it is, I lie down and there is all the periphery activities that I fail to consider hovering around the ink-filled needle. The tattooing is over soon and the tattooist was good enough to end each ten-second phase just as I was beginning to find the scratch on the same spot to be too much. There is an element of squeem bigger than simply the pain. The eerie feeling of the needle being on the same spot for just almost that moment too long.

"p h o n e j e l l y" was cheaper all as one word so there is no space and it is at an angle on my shoulder so I can read it and looks a bit Chinese from straight ahead.

Having it put on meant it was red and ridged there to see when I visited Angelica four days later.

The tattoo man gave a list of intricate creaming procedures, washing and tending-to instructions which I laughed at a bit.

Got in a bit of a pickled loophole the once, when I rejoined the AA again for the second time. I called them up an hour later and asked for roadside assistance.

They said that I could not call them with a vehicle already broken down.

I remember the warning: "Calls may be recorded for 'training purposes'" – sinister *moo-ha-ha* laugh in my head, or do I do it out loud? – and I decided to speak clearly realizing that calls may also be recorded in order to be played back in crisp Nicam truth from the courtroom's surprisingly state-of-the-minute 5.1 quadrophonic surround-sound system that envelopes your peers, the jury, in a crunchy resplendent exactly digital soundscape of your actual words and oracy with dry tongue clicks and swallows. Turning the Dolby-tables on them and using their system to get them, much like a celebrity camouflaging up and refusing to get out of the jungle and picking off the producers on by one with spring-loaded bamboo traps.

Like getting the CCTV footage and doing a felon's cut.

The best thing is to remember their business is broken-down cars, it's alright, and belt it out.

"The car was not broken down when I joined . . . It broke down subsequently . . . Surely," I continued, "there must be the member somewhere who has broken down the quickest of all times after joining . . . for real actually, and there must be someone somewhere who is that, technically there has to be one . . . Can I just be that one . . . the one?

"You are not allowed to call us for twenty-four hours. "

Next day. Twenty three hours later.

"Hi, I require roadside assistance . . . . . . My very recently acquired memberhood club-ship number-code is . . ."

"Sir, you called yesterday with a car that was broken down . . . You cannot call us with a vehicle broken down."

"Well, shall I call you when my car is fine and get you to hang out for a few weeks on the off-chance?"

I pleaded, "When can I ever call you out now because you will always think it already broken down?"

"Sir, simply prove that you have fixed the car."

"Then I shall not need you . . ."

". . . *(moo-ha-ha)* . . ."

"So if I can prove that the car is fixed then I can call you?"

"Yes, sir."

"And which car is this?"

"Erm . . . You have not told us that sir."

". . . *moo-ha-ha* . . ."

So to recap: AA have got themselves into a bit of a pickle-dicament as an org. who wants to come out and help me: They cannot come out until I have proved that I don't need them whereupon they have to verify that it was indeed a car they have no idea as to the identity of that is indeed the one which they are now not allowed to come to some more now because it is (a) fixed and (b) not provable that it was the one that wasn't originally fine anyway. I cannot un-join because to rejoin will open up old files and take us here to this point again and staying a member means they can never come. How can I prove all cars on the mainland Britain were not the one I was calling about? Eh? Eh eh, AA?

Absolutely Awful . . . Awesomely Awkward . . . . Alliteratively Anathema . . . Absent Automobilia . . . Anti-Associative.

I was illegal to them and yet I just wanted them to do what they do all the time: come and assist a motorist at the roadside.

Over the years cars with me in them have spent a fair while driving on long roads across Scotland. My Heaven's the A82 out of Glasgow; has you out by Duck Bay Marina on Loch Lomond and up by Luss before you can say "Jeesusfuck, look at them hills!"

Although you could just sneak out of the centre of town to The Carbeth Inn on the A809 through Mingavie (pronounced).

Really two days is long enough to get a set of views. Head up the A814/816 by Helensburgh and Garelochhead and Kintraw to Oban on the Low Road and, after the wee port of Oban – with the massive Folly on the Hill where they filmed Morvern Callar because that is where it was written and we got the taxi there on the film company's budget cos we were all extras in the party scene and my friend got a hundred and fifty quid to take her top off spontaneously and run around the fire in the fire scene. After this, head way up to Fort William and then on the way over at Invergarry, you can either go left and up to the Kyle of Lochalsh and right onto the Isle of Skye, or take a right and right up Loch Ness to Inverness. See how you feel. From there it's a choice between forging on north around the lovely Cromarty bend and up to the links beaches of Dornoch and then Skibo Castle where Madonna married a guy less richy, then pressing on to the Sutherlands and less-and-less trees on to Bonar Bridge he he and the wolder winds of Wick and/or scooting along the top of Moray on the well-named A Ninety-Six past Findhorn Bay, Forres Elgin of Johnsons, or Johnsons of Elgin to make your big life-choice at Fochabers – go in to see the massive, old school and have some chips and ice cream, or belt it round smoothly on the brand new heartless bypass towards Buckie, Portsoy, Macduff and Banff, the correct Keith, there's Battledykes, Affleck, Fogwatt, Meikle Wartle, Methlick, Slacks of Cairnbanno . . . All beautiful and on the coast in different ways. Sometimes as a tiny, scruffy council-town brown with dreams all pebbledashed and the way out, right here; houses of grim design with the play-park – an astonishingly good one with the double long slide embedded into a grassy slope – of course! And a hundred coloured beach-huts by those craggy smuggling coves.

Rock Pools Rock: wee worlds to study and redesign. Yes I do not like video-games or SIMS and yes, I like to re-pebble the rock pools and fetch additional shells and crab legs . . . Grand Theft Auto . . . no thanks, I'd prefer to whiz about on a bicycle steering between all the pine cones on the ground . . . What is it about twigs of dried seaweed that make them crinkly yet bendy? Well, it's the extreme saturations and desiccations they go through on the tide-line and, eventually a thing, designed to be in the sea without the sea being in it, succumbs its form, to do to its material form-self what "to subsume" does with the self . . . For soul is just a word, and soul is funky-rock.

And so then the seaweed becomes a brilliant material to work with for arts upon the beach-bendy: stick it in; arch it over; lay 'em like tentograms and corridors. Man, the kids love a two-dimensional house map . . . Tell them, they are always playing houses; to play hotels instead – And the dried wood without bark and the starfish that get swept up from a big storm with twenty legs.

*

Aha! So now you are either at Wick or at Huntly, on the way down to Aberdeen.

And We Have Not Even Touched The West Coast: Ullapool and up, the hidden worlds, inaccessible peninsulae, beaches of miniature coral, Stac Pollaidh and the Caribbean Hebrides, Uibhist . . .

The A Car Chapter

CHAPTALIZE – *to increase the alcohol content of wines by adding*
Sugar.

CAPITALIZE – *to treat expenditure as an asset in a business account*
instead of an expense.

As Granny used to say, "Fuck Nietsche . . . go and cuddle a horse . . .
you were only ever writing about yourself . . . nice coat, now Friederich
we were busy as women while you fought how only to see yourself as
a man . . ."

And here are some things that have occurred to me whilst driving:
David Byrne will often write while he is driving for the specific purpose
of occupying the right lobe, frontal gatherings, eyes moving around,
hearing shifting gears, the beautiful short term, present moment,
heart-hub focus on avoiding other moving metals, and staying alive . . .
all this to free up the creative quarters.

That packet of nuts that may never end, and be always a lunch was
part of an illegal consignment of walnuts that spilt in the footwell and
there I got most of them and there are still some, way in there in the
Merc three hundred TE from 1991.

People that you pass at speed in a car are in a relationship with you
however short it seems to be. Proximity, no matter how brief and thin,
is a truth. Memories from brief interactions have led to investigations
based on one letter remembered from a licence-plate. Sometimes
someone will overtake you and you can speed up a bit and be with
them.

Buying the supermarket items gives you a relationship with the
check-out girl. A point is: How much are you giving?

The twelve hours on an aeroplane gives you a relationship to and
with the flight-attendants . . . One-night's-standing is a relationship . . .
Short three-month marriages . . .

When someone tells you "You don't know me", well technically they
are wrong because you are there with them at that point to hear that
and that is something enough to know. They of course mean "not long
enough", or "not like my sister and other friends", yet it is that fuzzy

impossibility of naming the exact moment someone has known you long enough for them then to believe you know them, and that fuzzy area that is not known. Plus if it's you who decides, just decide it sooner.

When you hitch-hike up to Col du Somport to cross the border fae France tae Spain . . . you have to walk about one point six miles before it is Spain you're on and there is this fuzzy inbetween borders bit . . . and it is massive enough to reside in.

I know it's pedantic, the thing is, why say a thing that is so immediately disprovable in seconds?

"I'll never leave you."

"Cheers. "

"I'm just off to the shops."

". . . what! . . . You said . . ."

Driving made me think after a while:

1. I am in here with all my thoughts and all my songs and all my stuff, all my personal ideas and recollections and memories, rushes of love and clenchings of other and so are all the other drivers that pass so fast.

2. Ever sat in traffic and got delayed by busy roads and ended up saying "Fucking traffic" and then just realized that you are traffic?

3. If you drop something in when driving you can relax because it can't be lost, it is still in the car somewhere.

4. That we only see what is by the roads, what is relatively near to them.

5. That roads are nowhere near as thick on the ground as they are in the atlas.

6. That atlas sounds very like "at last". Are we there . . . oh Atlas. Driving is good time, all in good time, a good time and with all good time. There is always enough time on a good drive, to do it all in time, to get stuff out of bags and write notes and cease texting; to then resume later. Nothing need be a hurry.

7. All the delays can work for you. Delays are not true. You are only delayed by being advanced enough to even be here. When you get to roadworks it's cos you weren't delayed.

8. It's easy to be incredibly so relaxed travelling at safe speeds of eighty. Insurance doesn't help make it any less painful on the child you bump into or on any less painful on your ankles yourself compressed in the crash.

9. Insurance doesn't make you safer; it can make you less careful and more unsafe. It makes you safe only really from prosecution for not having it. This is definitely modern folks' simulacrum, a shadowy resemblance trouble, secondary replacement. It invents a danger it can then save you from.

This replaces real danger with avoidable bureaucratic danger.

Insurance ensures nothing. Except payment.

Did I tell you about driving to Nozstock festival last summer in Herefordshire and the gridlock and the greatest achievement of my life when leaving the big main stream of the clogged M23 intuitively with a big vague head-compass feeling and then drove the wee lanes of England, judging its old medieval market routes, divining the next town three miles away and, AND, and using a five-year-old atlas where the bit I needed was down in the crevice in the bend between the pages in by the staple and and one page had come loose and so I was having to line it up as well right down there in the dim cleavage . . . and there the car and me went through Iver Heath, Stoke Poges, Egypt, and then hitting the A4094.

Too:

10. Often when you hurry you are already late so you needn't bother overtaking yet it seems all completely worthwhile at the time to the psyche. Meanwhile to strive is to live, to crave benigns the grave.

How many cars have you seen right up behind you filling the r-view and then they're ahead by less than a second miles after?

When you are late try to remember that the invention of the car to move has not been delayed.

See how much ground you cover when you are free of the jam . . . open the door and see how fast twelve miles an hour feels when it is after sitting still.

11. Driving, see how it aches when you know you are going the wrong way and cannot turn around and know you will have to come back this bit again and so how lovely it is when you turn around again. In the mean old meany meantime you may as well sing.

12. How it feels it was when you didn't yet know you were going the wrong way . . . and so how far a car gets you . . . how your feeling defines it . . .

13. Tyres, breaks, exhausts, batteries, suspension . . . sounds violent. The idea of driving as fast as you want legally fills everyone with the glee of an orgy. It is safety from blame that is wanted.

14. Engines have got safer for the environment and quieter and then so quiet you don't hear one coming, just the crunch of the gravel, like from an invisible car. Prius: The Silent Killer. Solar silent, laser distance monitoring, reflecting the environment around it and emitting oxygen Car born free footprint . . . perfect for the organic hitman, the hemp hoodlum, running organic moonshine, wicker racketeer . . . They are so sleek and over-designed like big silver teardrops and it is hard to tell if they are going forward or backwards; coming towards you or moving away . . . tears of joy or relief or agony or wretched desolation. As my Granny used to say, ". . . there's only one tear duct . . . whether it's head-out-the-window wind-tears . . . or bereaving grievement . . ."

15. Pick-up trucks are so that grammar don't matter no more. In cars we sail along . . . go cruising . . . go flying along . . . we use the obvious other modes' descriptions because we are the ones moving . . . not travelling . . . Being in a car is being in life . . . you cannot just step out of it when it starts to go badly . . . you can step out of a car once you do not need to be in the driving seat . . . it is hard to transfer drivers while in motion and is rarely attempted.

16. There are roadworks so roads work. There can only be roadworks because there are roads.

17. . . . The driver in the Bentley can be pissed off in traffic. There he is with all he wants. Fucked. The material things can heavily suggest happiness is possible and realizing it is still your job.

Driving is a place, like cycling, you are somewhere. Yeh moving yet as we know the fuzzy logic of the French border . . . All the world and all our molecules are moving the whole time yet it just seems amplified as to be sacrosanct to me at the new speeds of the car.

Now . . .

18. Passing things is a matter for discussion . . . they pass over in your mind as you espy them on the road ahead . . . they are forgotten sometimes on their way to you for a minute then they are seen again as they re-approach the mind's cognition . . . then they zoom by . . . and all the while they might never have moved . . . might have been parked.

You can pass things that are moving . . . then you pass what is passing others and all is up in the air then you pass cars that you remember passing you; lorries that you passed in the past then had a pee and have to pass again; making it all seem daft then you remember that lorry drivers have to piss in bottles then throw these previously mysterious bottles-with-the-lids-back-on out the window at round-abouts and such. Then you overtake at high speeds that are just a bit higher than the high-speed car you are overtaking and it all seems like it is all so small and sitting in the middle lane doing seventy with, all around, fast-moving congestion, all hangin' together, all seeming a bit sullen and unmoving, hovering there in direct opposition to the truth that we are all blasting along at breakneck speed. All is moving, all is unpassable and passed all the time . . . You can turn around on the spot 360 and pass the whole universe.

19. Cars bring you to a truth of Scotland: TheActualBeautyOfGlens.

20. Park in a passing place on a single-lane backroute for lunch and just receive those mouthed thanks, finger waves and be bathed in simple love for an hour . . .

21. The rear-view mirror, which has to be just in front of you, shows you what is behind you at the moment and what has, most likely, just been ahead of you a while ago. Remember the past, as now, what was once, for a while the future is visible behind you along with things that are presently behind you yet looked-forward-to in the rear-view. Cars whiz away into their presented future and your past. They have their own rersr view that you are in. Cars that were far ahead in the present anr soon to be presently sat in the past behind you yet about to come ahead. It goes on forever. You try . . .

Yet from a different angle, so it never was too. There are cars coming up in it behind you that will one day be ahead and then you may get ahead of after and have them present in the rear . . .

Synaloepha is the word for joining the sound of adjacent vowels together when one word ends in a vowel and another up ahead in front starts with one.

Like us in the cars . . . joinable . . . sharey . . .

So, Dear e-Reader, you try and define the rear-view mirror's aspects in how it affects the language used about it and if effects it too . . . Please send your RearViewSynapticSynopses, your own freeform thing as well as a version, an ultimate version of the rear behind ahead future present riff . . . and have it in the next book to _ HYPERLINK " me @t__philk8@hotmail.com . . . close_ brackets]

Pee aitch aye ell kay ate at hot male dot com . . . Fonetikally speekin.

22. It works like a memory, looking back to a point then running the story forward. And in it there can be bits of road that were ahead and are now receding; passed cars that are coming forward yet have never been ahead of this. Looking at it, it is the past as the future once was to be now that which has presently gone; the moment of now all together.

23. If people wanted to die and did not care if the others died too there would be many more head-on collisions all the time. While on one journey you can plan another and realize it is all one road . . . And all roads lead to Simon Munnery's house. Unless he has moved to live on a disused airfield and the runway is his driveway.

24. Things can only be said to be boring – it's like arrogant and audacious, just responses, things can't ever be boring or look boring; you can never get used to anything. Nothing can be known because you are always looking at things while moving fairly fast so you are never really looking at anything from the same place.

Especially a mountain or a glen.

Come drive with me and we'll slowly rotate a mountain and see it afresh all the time.

It is an excuse to say that a drive is dull.

Are we there yet? Yes we are.

Are we there yet? I see your point.

Are we there yet? Yes Granny lives here on that soft verge by this little river.

No she doesn't . .

Moo-ha-ha. Aha, are you sure we are not there then . . . yet now soon ahead . .

24b. Sometimes they put a sign up to remind you this is a "dual-carriageway". Sometimes for a few minutes therefore you do not know if it is; if everything is going your way they could be mad reckless overtakers or comfortable insured drivers in their fifties with no-claims bonuses stacked up back longer than I have been hot dinnered . . . or cold buffet-ed . . .

Sometimes you are told that it is not a dual-carriageway and are reminded that at-that-point that (a) you were thinking that it was . . . (b) were not, and (c) that they are saying you might have been, that it's understandable, and we don't want perfection, that would be a foolish vain quest, so on you go . .

And versa vice . . . Things may be and you may not know . . . . They might not be going your way and you don't know.

25. Neil Young sings the song the same way every time from within on the cassette player. He travels with you whenever you chose. You get him singing over and over the same and he never got from himself that version again. I have seen people moan towards Oasis and Bob Dylan when the song was not what they knew it to be or had heard it as before. Drive-time is great – all this fleeting and moving is as fire or ocean, never the same.

26. The hands-free is good. Hands-free can look like you are mad, talking to yourself. Bluetooth or blue teeth. Are you haywire or hardwired. Mp3 or empathy? . . . .Cyclepath or psychopath?

You don't have to buy an iPod; just get ten Silk Cut and some Tippex and paint some earphones on coming out your ears down the neck that never fall out.

27. The make-up mirror may have come about when women were driven statistically to suburban parties by men and has stayed and now cars have them mirrors on both sides or neither. Again it's either either or neither. Once apona time the rear-view mirror used to be made the same as a make-up mirror, was just they covered up the size of it in the make-up mirror . . . then one day it was a new piece entirely and they fell in love. The rear-view fell for the make-up mirror and the wing was jealous. Poor wing mirror out in the cold . . . poor, mirror of specific function . . . poor wee thing, born in to servitude of such a definite thing. Oh for the odd moment a duchess straightened her pearls in you or a rollerscating six foot dutch girl in rainbow tights rolls by . . .

28. The cigarette-lighter is too useful, it's like a portal to power, an other universe, a true alternative, like alternation of generation, the existence of two types of reproduction in the life cycle of an organism, . . . like the car now giving after all the taking. Cigars are hardly ever lit for it, the surrogate plug-in stand-in . . . a nexus that connects us to the possibilities beyond. This is a moving car, it is a heavy object with momentum and power and weight and huge amounts of potential power and potency as in for growth in the future. Plug in a toastie-machine or a dust-buster . . . record player, aye-pad or dip-and-boil coiled water element . . . Chess machine, home baked potatoe with the shop-based-taste machine . . . They bring on the cup-holders every fucking where . . . mini slow-falling sunglasses shelvestash hidden drawers that let you stuff stuff in there and the steering-wheel-volume – crappy extra-extras not required, yet they are part of a thinking that has finally led us to electric cars that charge themselves with their own braking. The problem is the keeper of the solution. Well I'm pro-Fusion as in the combining of elements to release energy. I'm into looking at the thing as another thing that it also is. The Lateral . . . The Tangental . . . The Divergent . . . radiating lines of thoughts and ideas growing from and creating more than before. The release, the freedom from the grip of a debt self made. Thus this could save us. Every Car(riage system) . . . every roof, every drain . . . every waste product every tide rise, every beat of the sun will save us. Humanity has come up with graphene, way more effective than plasmere, graphene is an atom-thick and the best conductor in the universe. Carbon-based life form comes up with carbon-based form, which apparently can make lighter and better things and reduce the planet's carbon bootprint on its own face.

So drive old automatics and hold your cider between your legs and adjust volume with thumb and first finger or step into the laser car fuelled by the kung-fu unity of need. Cook the flapjacks jack and hit the road one way or another. The lighter power source is a diamond king lense. They iMarket rear-guidance and the statutory navigation system – fuck that, go for the subscription-free communal bank of knowledge in the folks with ChatNav and just ask people . . . The all-see-through roof and yet where is the lighter-socket-friendly mini-travel-animal-brander? The whole of the engine's internal combustion and momentum energy of this two-ton RR Phantom becomes a power-socket to plug in the inflator pump to pump up a double mattress. Glamour used to mean magic spell.

The term "apparent wind" is used to refer to the combination of natural wind and the wind produced by a ship's motion.

29. Getting philosophical with driving seems to actually mean finding a way to be cool with it so I never get road rage . . . when someone cuts me up it just seems like good use of the road as less time he will be out there using fuel, plus I'm only here to get cut up because I was not delayed.

The speed limits only came in to reduce fuel use in the shortage crisis of the nineteen seventies and apparently the immediate effect was the increase in accidents because there were more hours spent driving.

30. Follow your loved-one in a car . . . You look at their shapeless head-rest head with tender affection. People overtake because they can have no idea you want to remain just one car behind your love, gifting you the ability to understand more easily the burning orphanage. Empathy on the M3.

30b. Every registration plate is individual like a snowflake. Oh aye.

31. Little smiley-face thirty-mile-an-hour signs in wee towns that flash an angry face that your kids can see and tell Daddy to slow down when you are doing above thirty. Well, you can be so busy looking at them, keeping them happy, slightly obsessed enough you could miss the young child stepping into the road, way down right in front of you at the previous eye-level.

"Your Honour . . . Your Honour, I have CCTV proof I was within the speed limits, so intent was I on being legal and safe I became too closely an observer of what the Crown has seen fit to hang there to attract attention . . . albeit to get kids in on it to let them see when you could kill one . . . a danger." You could probably get away with running over the judge's triplets for he has to follow the law and acquit yourselves well.

Imagine a courtroom romance where the judge and the defence lawyer are in love with the defendant and the acquittal looks imminent and the judge is a woman and she wants the accused sent down rather than lose him to her, the lawyer, who he's bound to love soon, and so feeds the prosecution bits and and then the defence lawyer manages to convince the man, the prosecutor who maybe loves her a bit too, yeh he loves her enough to help her get her man . . . and they conspire to fool the judge and get the guy off and into love . . .

32. Most prefer the wave to the rear-hazards-flash to give thanks.

The Citroën Picasso: Is nothing sacred? No, everything is.

"Guidada a la sinistra . . ." is how I phonetically remember "Drive On The Left" on road signs by airports in Spanish in Scotland.

There are road signs in Australia that say "Consider Drivers Following". Yeh consider for a while what it might be like to be them. Consider their view of you that you are, in turn, behind someone and ahead to be looked at, mate . . . g'day . . . All forever chained and linked together as ones . . . good life.

There was another: "Buses Merge Right." They Sure Do. Happens all the time, can't argue with that, don't deny the immense weight of the machinery. "Cyclists Dismount." They surely do. One more: "Pedestrians Give Way To Trams." Bet they do; it's a given, they are silly not to.

33. No philosophy of driving would question the surety of pain in collision. The tree falls it makes a crunching, ripping acoustic, swish, clatter, hum and thud loosening itself enough from its own shorn base and moving through the upper branches of its neighbours even as it begins to fall . . . there is no end to the noise of a tree ever, no point in saying there is a point when the noise begins as it hits the ground . . . the question is not a question, Your Honour. The other drivers are real folks whistling tunes with a sensitivity we share. Look how we drive: To miss each other.

34. Whenever there was the word SLOW written on the road I am usually doing that . . . and SLOW upside-down is MO7S, almost . . .

A bus driver toots with the horn at a cyclist who came in front of him at the lights, then a jogger holds up the cyclist and he tuts just as the jogger is blocked by a lady with a pram who is waiting for a really old doddery man who has been halted by a crawling infant that has pulled over to pick up a feather that reminds the old man of something he knows he loved once in the war with the mud and the death.

All of life is an inordinately coincidental meeting of amazing chance. Every car you pass is this. Whether we feel that at the time or not, whether it has someone we know in it or not in it.

When a jet stops a hippy's conversation, because they share a fence that is just the amazing nature of juxtaposition in everything, made more clear, above the parapet and, once known, means less amazement is wasted for me on that and freed up for . . . the uncluttered hunch of the sparrowhawk on a fence post seen way down at eye-level from the low riding position in a Mini Clubman passing the massive satellite Golf Balls on the way to me Mum's.

We put a boat in a moat. Put a car on a moat of tar-macadam and that's 200,000 watching Indian-a-polis.

Formula One is just one formula.

There is a thermometer in many modern cars . . . to help with . . . erm . . . knowing if it is icy to slip.

Some have a remote-control for an in-car DVD. How far do you plan to go from it?

When was the first car radio put in? When was driving along faster than a running man not enough? When did it run out for mankind that he needed to listen to music? When, when was enough not enough?

1932?? maybe . . . very nice Friedrick . . . nice jacket . . . so . . . well . . . what a journey . . . yes marvellous . . . so uh huh . . . what shall we do . . . have you any tunes?

The evolution of the car is the evolution of our evolution.

The petrol gauge can show you how much you have left, can approximate for you a point you mostly will never know and if you stop then you might have made it, Captain Scott . . . keep going.

It can do this, it is up to you what you do. The gauge can be wrong or early or stuck or four miles is a long walk at night when you do not know it is four miles.

You have to put the next twenty pounds in your petrol tank. There is no point ignoring it; you can get money in your hand, you may as well put it in for that it where it is going to go. Also too, as well, however you can save money by putting less in as, if you know that there is little in there, you may drive less.

So, holding back may be daft because you have that extra fiver in your pocket that you then spend it on pork pie. Savings, cut-backs, reinings-in.

Tightening the belt is not a proactive thing, the phrase must mean what we have to do to accept where we are?, yeh: tightening the belt to keep the trousers up on a body thinner now due to less food.

And Finally . . .

So, I am driving down the motorway – down because it is south and I am rotating the whole universe to suit my sense of direction – trying to force a description of the cosmos simply from where I am located, like astrology. A car overtakes me and I see for the first time in action in-car entertainment family DVD-viewing-ing. Both the rear headsets are in use. This seems to me, all at once, to be both good and bad:

Good, like it is a fun thing. Movies, hurrah! What a treat; the kids smile and then get to watch a film in an unusual environment and it is a thrill. Perhaps they have to drive to a sick grandmother three hours every weekend and that repetition is too much and how long can they die for? A long time. Look at the pope and all those unrefunded Ryanair flights to Rome booked with a return based on the faith in the pontiff's decline. And it keeps kids in the back happy.

Bad though now, because it keeps coming back to keeping-them-happy. Like there are no sabre-toothed tigers anymore and it is the wrath of the pissed-off offspring that adult humans now fear most . . . What if they can develop something else? Maybe one-parent-in-the-back rotational seating without rotating the seats, a quick change at service stations . . . Your turn to play I-Spy with dad . . . My turn to watch with mother. The car they have is fast enough for the journey to be short as it can be.

Imagine they put on a good film and Dad can hear it perhaps though he cannot hear his wife speak so they get bored and she drifts off while he might drift off into imagining and re-imagining the movie from the sound he is hearing right here, right behind his skull, the mad phonic stereo-terrerro right there in conciousness surrounding doubley dolby loudness, a clammer-blast din, a headrest with no rest for the head . . . and he might just go mad and tip over into whiplash backdraught, neckbrace backlash, and start to visualize scenes on his windscreen and see the reality rushing towards him as secondary, less real, without stereo sound. Maybe it's Ben Hur and the thirty-nine minute chariot scene with a tiny Fiat500 on a hillside in the background and the pace is mounting and the crashing and veering and the real stunt-man snuff pile-ups. Then maybe, every now and then, he is curious to see and can't bear it any more and starts to try and look behind, flip his head round, and he might get it edged as his wife has drifted off and the kids sense the danger and warn him off like he would warn them off things that look dangerous: "Stop it Dad, you'll lose the road . . . Someone could break ahead of you, Dad and you'll kill us all, plunging into the back of a lorry or something . . . DAD!"

This makes him feel a bit shit and all the effort he has done. The training for the job to maintain the job to raise them to keep working to have money to have them and the house and keep working still and attain this fabulous car to then listen to their demands and balance the love he feels for his own dying Mum and responding to her need when she wasn't able really to respond to things and, all the more, travelling now at ninety to get there quicker and the upgraded headrests and they are reprimanding him . . . Perhaps then it is better to show really too-young age-group films so as to be less interesting for the safety of the family. Then the kids get bored with this . . .

Imagine the very high quality movies you either buy or rent. if rented, then there is the possibility of Gran deteriorating and you having to stay down there and not getting back in time for the 7:30 return DVD deadline and the double fees; or trying to end your holidays early in order to get back to ball-breaker blockbuster . . .

Or it could be a teen-race driver on the inside lane might want to keep it in view just for a while to watch this good bit . . .

"What's this joker up to?" asks Dad of the pimped-Nova, full of four thin-shouldered boys, three of them rolling joints and so they move like large skittles on the back seat in the lane-changing and the swaying flowers on the verge rocking forward and back in their apparent wind, looking like they are all laughing at them as they zoom by . . . they're right here and just for ten seconds stay up on his rear hip for a laugh and it is, in fact, the chariot-racing re-enactment scene from Gladiator with Crowe Maximus, father of a dead wife avenging everything and the children and stroking corn and there is the action's noise-of-battle-and-clash and souped-up smashing and it, the car racing behind him, and all the built-up pressure of Mum ill and the failure of the DVD to solve the travelling-issues, results in a strained massive burst of speed that frightens everyone as they, all as one, see the compound irony in Dad's situation: Where he'd rather have a golden-breasted lady with a bow and arrow to fight, rather than this invisible foe of brood and plague of torment, apathy, apparent boredom and vexation from those that ought to be somehow happy enough in this safe carriage, this hero's chariot-racing along.

Not safe, not to sixty.

All this ends up with Mum asleep, Dad pissed-off, the kids kneeing the back of the seats and Dad upset while Grandma's breathing is steady down at Nine Wells that he says "Fuckit" and throws his head around the back to finally can't help it just get a decent look at it and he flips it round and gets his head stuck in there . . . anatomically the neck just jammed in there from the side under the raised headrest . . . so he brakes pretty suddenly and is the only one with throatlash. .

Miracle whiplash passed and, after Mum had woken up because of the knees and the shouting and the horses and C. Heston's snarl and the swerve and the screams and her own pain in the neck now . . . the reprimand and the ripping out of the adaptor from the lighter socket and the quiet, quiet screens. Into focus comes the view slowly and the lovely valleys, horses they might have missed and the roller-coastlines . . . "It looks like Harry Potter Mum . . . or the mountains in The Hobbit . . . "

Good and bad, filled with possibles: They pass with their films on and it is dangerous because I want to speed up to watch the action . . .

Nought safe . . .

Noumenon.

Though the engine is untroubled, its advanced computerized engine is able to deal with a stroppy foot-to-the-floor kick down in-fifth, and the automatic rev-monitoring onboard computer system keeps it all safe.

Favourite Films: . . . . Nostalghia, Tarkovsky, . . . HisGirlFriday, Hawks, BlackCatWhiteCat, Kusturika . . . Chinatown, Polanski, . . . threeColoursBlue, Dekalog, Kyslowski . . . HardressersHusband? . . . Miller'sCrossing, Coens . . . Magnolia, PTAnderson . . . Network, Chayasky? . . . Nashville, ThePlayer, ShortCuts, TheWedding, TheLongGoodbye, Altman . . . Magnolia, PTAnderson . . . MulhollandDrive, BlueVelvet, Lynch . . . NightOfTheHunter, Laughton . . . Kes, Loach . . . SomeLikeIteHot, TheApartment, Wilder . . . CoolHandLuke . . . Naked, Leigh . . . BladeRunner, Scott . . . ApocalypseNow, Rumblefish, Coppolla . . . PrinceAndThePauper, ? . . . MaryPoppins, ? . . . HorsemanOnTheRoof . . . . Ridicule . . . TheShining . . . Spartacus . . . GreenForDanger . . . DoubleIndemnity . . . AndreRublev . . . FiveEasyPieces . . . Ran . . . InTheMoodForLove . . . Hanna-b, Sonatine, KidsReturn, TakeshiKitano . . . Jaws . . . TheSting . . . SilentRunning . . . Alien(s) . . . BrotherhoodOfTheWolf . . . PulpFiction . . . Leon . . . Frenzy . . .

Final Chunk

Most recent "most recent" top twenty eventy on the mind:

Took a pen out my jacket pocket a tiny bit then just dropped the jacket off it . . .

Lit a pipe, cycling.

Did the best physical thing ever on a bike . . . moving my bodyweight one way to force the bicycle the other way and take then the body out of the path of another cyclist on a pavement . . . or was it a wing-mirror . . . or just the edge of the curb?

Was cycling with two bikes recently and a fellow called out of the passenger wind eye window of the car overtaking me on a roundabout: ". . . cycling on a bike . . ." it sounded like, although that was bound to be just a fillet . . . escorting a spare one home, steering it by the front handle horns and some three days after seeing Django twice and still high from slaves get revenge to rap soundtrack culture smashup concept . . . and I'm primed and ready and imagine someone shouting fucking hippy . . . I'm older and fully bearded on a bike – with another one . . . fair enough if you are going to shout something . . . so I'm ready and when it comes I immediately draw two imaginary superfast guns from a holster each side of me and flip the finger from each hand . . . like fuck you all you do is show your kids The Lord Of The Rings shit with that old master wizard cunt with the beard and the non-vehicular scruffy travel roaming . . . fuck you like a slave taking the main house and fuck you for not seeing, being forgiven, having the solution offered, ignoring it, ignoring when you are told about it and lashing out the lash.

Lamb lash.

Next: Going to the sink in the morning and reaching out the long dong of the kitchen monotap slides up my sleeve as I push down the raiser paddle and water is released up the sleeve and the appropriate noise for this was made.

Did two gigs that were well filmed and have some worth:
Goldsmithscollege//slash slash link.
Lowry Theatre comedy song mayhemisphere . . .

*

Some ideas for short films to be made:

93minutes . . . Join our hero as he sees a rich couple leave the key to their car dangling in the lock as they run into the movies and he has 93minutes to reek the opposite of havoc . . . "Pandaminimum" . . .

Bedtime Not Bedlam . . . so bedlamb . . . bedside lamp . . . Feeding sheep on farms, driving conscientiously . . . helping a lady with her shopping and getting it back on time . . .

– OtherWayRound –

Grannies grow dope on old oilrig platforms to end the control of violence in the North East of Scotland in the surreal anti-gangster film about life from the female perspective . . . Our woman holding the whole of a room late at night with a story about her idiotic stepfather . . . swimming with whisky . . . replacing a lost basketball hoop in your old primary school at night . . . Virtuoso camera swoop following our friends through the bar as they go all the way in to see if someone is there and all the way out when they are not . . . We never see the violence only the fall-out . . . the broken cakes . . . the single dads living in empty flats with just stolen camping equipment . . . inflatable beds gas . . . titanium cups . . . and the older lady cleaners interrupting the old men as they have a top level meeting and threaten them with having to make their own supper . . . . – TheOtherWayRound – . . .

And:

The one where lots make from the same script: KilledByATennisBall . . . a tennis ball falls off a shelf as a family are preparing to leave for the country and somehow ends up behind the brake pedal in the footwell . . . You decide how it ends . . .

There's lots of wee filmic stories written waiting to come out . . .

The phone currently being charged by this human is an old-school Nokia with full options on graph and acute and dipthongs.

Recently I stood on a small camouflaged army toy probably because it was hard to see . . . the green van has on the side "Army Force – Mobile Commancentre" . . . and hang on, it's actually a bloody ice-cream van they've sequestrated; the manufacturers in China have clearly got a few extra vans from the catering sector and fobbed them off ON THE KIDS WHO CAN NEVER KNOW THE AUTHENTICITY BEYOND THE GREEN ARMY PAINT . . . which may result in either a natural fear of snack vans and a reduction in heart disease or . . . yeh the opposite . . .

Phasebook . . . it's just a phase you're going through don't worry when you are fifty-eight fifty-nine it'll pass . . .

I can't find the Discovery Channel . . . . . .

Cover album, album cover . . . what am I going to put as the cover art on an album of covers called Art Of The Cover . . .

Dear artist, what are you actually proposing? The title of your shows and works are revealing of how much you want to reveal . . .

Repubrocrat/Demublican . . . it would appear to be worth millions to spend a campaign's energy on appealing to the people who are not going to vote for you . . . i.e. mostly peoples in the states'states have taken sides already which is why they have . . . The California Decider . . . or the Let's Take Florida It's Decisive . . . Democrats appeal to the righter-winged aspects of possible proposals you can later simply not act on . . .

Hotel spa . . . HospaTel . . . hospitel . . . hospice . . . hospitable . . . hospitality

Nice rack thank you knife rack . . . fank you . . . nick knife rack . . .

The other day a kid asked me something and I said, right well, leave it with us and we'll see what we can do . . . May I also suggest: The cimmitee meets every other Tuesday and it IS definite they will address your concerns . . . and my favourites: 1. All complaints must be put through the appropriate channels . . . and 2. (the only one I actually use) You are aware of my position on the matter . . .

I wrote a song: ". . . There's a feeling that the old man putting up the Winkworth's estate agent sign isn't Mister Winkworth . . . and the Tesco delvery man in his fifties isn't Mister Tesco . . ."

Tesco Burlesqueo . . . some say there are two too many burlesque shows playing at provincial theatres and are watering down the superb aspect by presenting in proscenium, not in the intimate surrounds of nightclub . . . some say it is a good and strong thing and will always be welcome and can stand on its own two high-heeled feet in Manchester at the Lowry . . . or Eden Court in Inverness . . . and that it's better that it's out there're . . . some others say it waters it down and it's like the Woolworth hippy wig paradigm . . . others still say naught about it . . .

The loneliest Monk: who is he and shit he must be lonely . . .

And who is the least sexual Nun . . . there must be one to touch herself the least time . . .

The Last Leaf To Fall . . . Another song: somewhere when any leaf falls it is at that point the last leaf to fall in England . . . no one can check it it just has to be true for an instant, like passing someone in a car, like how long someone was No. 1, like a reign, an empire, a civilization, an ocean . . . some suns are really just a spark in the longer scheme o' ting.

In terms of the Sandwich? . . . I'd rather have half a fava bean from the favela than have half an alfalfa after a father figure fella . . . rather favour the favela fellas hearty flavours than the faux false half-hearted hearty wholesome . . . Trust is something you give.

Now, so do unto others as you would have them do unto you . . . it is not to me just a phrase about avoid doing bad to others, it's also about do the big expansive good . . . borrow without asking . . . love freely . . . endow with trust . . . what you may love all could.

Get the cream off the crop – get it off the saddles too . . . Sure I'm into bondage yet I am tolerance lax . . . get the double cream owf that bridle . . . close to a lax lactose intolerance – whereas you are intolerant of why I chose lax . . . those lax intolerant relaxed toes . . . lax atonement . . . tax those intolerant . . .

Relax zone tolerance . . . zero tax tolerance . . . real lax lost instants . . . lack zone tone atonement . . . lactose dominant . . . fucksake dominate . . . fructose absorbant . . .

There's snow business, like, snow business . . . it's like no business I now . . . everything about it is exciting like when you're steeling that extra plough . . .

I say I say I say . . . Why are there so many mountains in England? . . . Because they keep making them out of molehills.

"This is not a logomachy . . . this is not about the meaning of the words: it's about useage and how useage affects meaning." "No it's not, it's how useage affects meaning not whether . . ." "It is whether . . ." "It isn't, it's whether it's whether . . ." "Actually it is not it, it is this."

If the driver in the Bentley Continental ever gets upset in traffic then the whole notion of happiness given by circumstance is false. Happiness is a word humans have come up with to name a feeling.

Cleanliness is actually next to "cleanlimbed" – "having a well proportioned and youthful looking body" . . . so about as unholy as you can get . . . or . . . hang on there is nothing to be ashamed of . . .

The godwit is a wading bird related to the curlew . . .

50 Cent the rapper is bringing out a perfume . . . it's called Fifty $cent . . . and his own independent letter and package postal service . . . Fifty Sent . . . and he's patenting a certain way of feeling, the Fifty Sense . . .

Sometimes the closest you can get to someone in England is to piss their shit off the toilet bowl on the train . . . or press your hand to theirs on the glass on the tube . . . or make unbroken, gently intense eye-contact as you pass them going the other way on the escalator . . .

then start walking backwards down with them for a second or two . . .

Genuinely real genuflections . . . can you have them? . . . like a pretend mirage?

Finally I stood outside the tremendous old classic garage of great classics in our village and brushed up against a 265 GTB and said out loud: "When will it be ready . . . ? It is my Ferrari . . . it is my Ferrarri . . ." with a man there . . . just to see if I could do it . . . just to see if I could act and no . . . I cannot act, it is lying with permission.

LowGo Ltd.

What Am Go Need.

Worth buying a Diary for: Taking down some bunk beds I was buying in Bedford with a completely Muslim woman . . . and following her instructions . . . and seriously she had no problem helping me help her . . . no issue telling me what to do . . . and none for me following her and getting behind there and finding a long lost pen calling out "here it is" for her kids and getting it to a light fun place dear artists . . .

I have had a drink with five Oscar winners.

JonJon's Hat: Nicked it from fro' the church, because they forgive you immediately . . . It got recognised by his Mum. Passed him on a bike and threw it at him, left-handed. He caught it.

Joined an autistic rock group . . . OC/DC.

Britney Houston . . . Whitney Spears . . . Denzel Whitaker . . .

The special Winter ±Paralympics.

Who Loves The Sun?

Since she won gold I do want to kiss J. Ennis.

Assad's wife is gorgeous. So is Ryan Giggs's wronged rich wife . . . England are in trouble . . . the footballers' wives are not able to get away from it because the Maldives are having a revolution.

Teesh Hurts.

Titantric.

Wanktrick sex

Out of might, out of sound.

Follow Up: The Prequel . . . From the Producers of The People That Brought You, and the Director of That Other One That Did Well . . . Starring Juan That Didwell . . . Academi Ward . . . and Oscar.

Bill Ding . . . and his brothers Stan and Ben . . .

People ask how many miles I get to the gallon . . . I say about fifteen . . . it's a very old engine. . . boom boom.

Noodle doodle.

. . . excuse me on the bike it may look like me talking to myself . . .

in fact I am honing the act . . . you know, sharpening the blade . . . musing on, doing the mull over out louder . . . increasing the intensity . . . and coming up with a thing as brilliant as it will be hard to remember unless I do a gig that night . . .

There's a nice word for it: 'metathesis' is the word and it means the changing position of two letters or sounds in a word due to mispronouonciation or historical development . . .

To enthrall: to claim legal ownership of someone, and make them a prisoner.

My home is near Gatwick so every now and then there is more chance of seeing a grown man walking around with a pillow.

GoogAll . . . why not just googallthings . . . google it all . . . goog all the time . . .

In Scotland the seven-inch tablet is the biggest confectionary of all.

Which came first the chicken or the rabbit?

Dickens . . . Darwin . . . Diamond Jubilee . . . Olympics . . . Newton . . . Beckinham Palace . . . It Is A Big Year England . . . Quick get Ennis seen from space . . . crash a plane into her shorts . . .

Turns out the Police are racist . . . well I never . . . whatever next? The Army . . . well they've got to be to be effective . . . they is exempt, Uncle Jessie . . . where will we be then if no institution can protect us from the acts of men when they are run by men?

Beatroot.

The traffic-calming narrow bit on our road just seems to speed people up so they zoom in to assert their right to the right of way . . . racing towards each other, neither sure if the other has seen it is who's right of way . . . like a mad gambling game of chicken . . . come on come on Calm the Fuck Oot the way . . . KEEP COMING . . . FUCK CALM and THIS CARRY-ON . . . the write-off way . . . its okay if it's a pun you stumble over . . .

High We're The Stumblepuns . . .

On the London Tubular Train ride there was a woman one side o' me with a Kindle and a woman the other side doing Crochet. . .

Upload {0, H<>?: "|}{ =Applaud . . .

Downcast is how you feel when you can't get something down off the internet. Internot. The ethernot . . . either knit hornet nets or not.

The Olympics = The Hunger Games.

The Gherkin, The Cucumber, The Shard . . . InnerCity Sir Fry.

Prince Andrew: Absail down The Chard . . . Prince Harry Abyssmal charade . . .

Kate Middletits.

Heath Ledger up the garden path . . . he's led yer on a wild goose chase . . .

Everything's going to be alright, everything fits, now John Terry's been to Auschwitz.

And Sinn Fein have a merchandise shop . . .

Piracy: liquidation, flotation, bail-outs . . . wave of recovery, in an ocean of debt . . . a fiscal fisting, jolly rogering . . . bluebeard with a blackberry, I mean blackbeard with a blueberry . . . high and dry up on a sandbank . . . treasuretrove treasury . . . the rigging . . . safe harbour . . . safe from the storm . . . . all washed up . . . the seven Cs . . . soiled the Seven seas . . . stalled the Severn cease . . . Barbary coast/Burberry coats . . . swash buckling/posh buckles . . . message in a minibar bottle . . .

Walk round a kids' party with the chocolate-covered raisins calling out, does anyone like olives?

The Savile row. Your letter was only the start of it . . .

Did the Mayans invent mayonnaise or salad cream? . . . Or did they predict the end of the salad days? . . .

I predicted the Mayans were full of shit . . . Have you seen the new David Beckham Mayan Calendar, cor he's gorgeous . . . his prophetic limbs . . . yet it only goes up to March . . .

Fifty shaves . . . filthy shames . . .

What have Ronnie O'Sullivan, J. J. Cale, Eddie the Eagle Edwards and Little Richard got in common? They are all born on the same day . . .

So sorry Astrology.

Women: The Eggs Factor.

Travel log. Kindle.

Peggy Babcop . . . Peggy Babcop, Peggy Bacpop . . .

Gnome genome . . . trace your DNA . . . G-Nome the rapper . . .

Some young twisted tongan tongue twisting sisters twice twisted a twisty tongan tongue twister, now if twice the right twisty sisters twisted a tight tonguan tongue twister what is that tightly taut tongue twisting tautology the twisted tongan tongue twisting sisters tongue twisted twice . . . well . . . they totally taught it to their sisters . . .

Oon taka aktak a tarkarakatuk tak . . . oot oon too toor karat, oo takarakarat a aratakarakarat . . .

However . . . this is more synonymous with sinuous moaning samoan motormouth summery summaries, whose sinister illustrious sinistrous singular sinusoidal sing-song's samoan samosa summertime samplings, supposedly summoning something of someone's sumbitch lip blistering sisters' sumptuous sump-pump sing-song sum-up . . .

　　　　　The Habbit. An expected journey.

　　　　　"I am The King of Poundland . . ." Good Song by caravanband.

Is it wrong to make love in a disabled toilet? . . . If so then one may as well use the special handles in there for extra grip and really athletic positions . . . and the emergency chord as a kind of sexy garrott . . .

Everyone was very upset at that Italian cruise ship captain for smashing into the island . . . yet who did they want to be driving it? . .
.

There's two kinds of people: those who cross out the number of the clues they have done as they go through a crossword, and those who know that getting an answer familiarizes them enough with the clues to know they have done it and that even if they do read a clue again that's cool and there's hardly a massive gap in time that this is saving you, the scoring out, and it takes time to do and in certain areas damage limitation is entirely how you relate to it . . . like swearing: if you don't give a fuck, then it is not bad.

You can sit on a train doing soduku really quickly and no one will challenge you, just lick a pencil and write a six . . . then a three . . . they all fit . . . you can zoom the pen about a bit . . . .you'd have to be unlucky to sit opposite someone who could do them upside down well enough and then also be outspoken enougjh to spot it and call you on it . . . and then what . . . what move would be made then?/and what answer to this solution? . . . none the same in the same line . . . never repeated that line . . . . . . or is it sokudu, or sodoku, or suduko . . . just try them all till it fits.

Dragons' Den idea: Scottish voice recognition service on defibrillator machine . . . after D. Bannatyne's tremendous men's heart tremor . . .

The Tremolites – great name for a band, and a decent natural alternative to asbestos found in metamorphic rock.

　　　　　Great genre for a band – Metamorphic Rock.

　　　　　The American Idle.

Pop-up pop-up book bookshop,

Ho-bo wi-fi . . . . Hy-Phen . . . Hi, Low, Hello.

I went to see Looper in the cinema and watched the second half first and then I went to the next showing and came in at the beginning and watched up till the point I started at . . . and I watched Memento on a laptop walking backwards up a plane as it went over the international date line at the very end of a leap February full blue moon cusp . . .

Semibold is darker than ordinary type yet not as dark as **bold** . . .

Wow I surely feel that it is thoughtful of me to consider my intuition that she can really compassionately relate to my empathy.

Wow I surely feel that it is thoughtful of me to consider my intuition that she can really compassionately relate to my empathy.

I fixed my ripped trouser crotch with gaffer tape and it gets you a little revenge waxing for about a week.

Every time I see a leaf falling to the ground I think myself, "Without doubt, for an instant, at some point this leaf heads the list, and indeed is for a moment The Last Leaf To Fall In England . . ."

Repeated myself to see if it got any better. Was it?

At the chemist in a special no-frills stand they have walking-stick rubber tips . . . tweezers with a light . . . illuminated magnifying glass too . . . a grabber, obvs . . .

My favourite chemist is in Lewes, and it is so small that you can join the queue and yet still be browsing at the same time . . .

Bottle bank . . . throttle thanks . . . mottled manx . . . shottle shanks . . . tottled tanks.

Riskysessment.

Tortuosity the act of being twisted.

Car Key and Clutch.

Plankton is cod.

The name's Bourne, James Bourne . . .

The name's Bond Names Bond . . .

And as you drive down the A303 through Cornwall you'll pass de duchy on the left hand side . . .

Totipalmate – the pelican, the gannet . . . all four toes webbed . . .

The aura – "a distinctive sensation or visual disturbance that may signal the beginning of an epileptic episode or migraine headache."

The crisis – the point in the course of a disease when a patient can suddenly get much better . . .

Right now, three a.m., a Wednesday in March and there is a garage glove sitting upright above on my wee lamp filled with the warm thermals from the bulb . . . a permanent tiny moving wave . . .

Wordy Argument
Knock knock
Ah it's you . . .
Ah it's you who?
. . . that you have the audacity to say that . . .

Well it's interesting because, sure me saying that can mean I have it, the hard copy manifestation in an action, the audacity to say it and the audacity needed the audacious thing to be said to be alive . . . you would not credit someone with being audacious if they had not said the thing or done the thing that you deem that; yet audacious the adjective doesn't lend itself so easily to anything save the boldness . . . as if you could never be audacious without the occurrence . . .

Ahem . . .

. . .

I meant audible.

Pardon.

I said: Imagism is a move in the early twentieth century to improve poetry through a modernization with ordinary language and precise everyday imagery . . .

Well actually imagism itself the word refers to the name the movement developed once it had started using the new ordinary words et cetera . . . it wasn't like a football club name these artists applied for . . . e. e. cummings

Okay don't be pedantic . . . so nitpicky.

Well pedantic just means too concerned with what are thought to be the correct rules of language . . .

I never meant that . . . One can be a certain kind of pedantic that doesn't have all the finicky, carping overtones.

See what you mean . . . overtones are where it's at . . .

Well as my Granny used to say, "Better blow over the rim of an empty milk bottle generating tone than to spend an eternity on even the new Nord keyboard."

Wouldn't go that far.

She did.

Mp3.

None at all.

. . . so you say we're arguing about the use of words and I say we are arguing about individual meanings within . . . . . .

Well you are using words to argue about words.

Nicely put.

I agree.

Then it's a discussion.

Discuss the discus cousin: "Aerobie is better than Frisbee." Discuss.

Eh?

Bee cee.

A cavil is what you consider this . . . a tiny thing . . . well it is not to me . . . it is indeed the pivot, man, the crux, look at that hinge, we are fulcrum . . . whatever it is is made by both . . .

Whatever . . .

Whomsoever . . . that's what the posh kids say . . .

Pitting your wits . . . hollowing out, husking, weakening from the middle . . .

The thing I purport is constructive and greater than the sum of its parts . . .

Fusion?

The part of semantics I like is the concept of how meaning in language comes from the interrelationship of words like the effect of musical notes on each other . . . the bumping of waves if you like and the un-independence, the co-dependence and hence the Overtones . . . combination harmonies . . . all these words come into their own when barking at the heels of music.

That's not what you said before.

Don't be semantic . . .

I'm anti-semantic.

No you mean "semantic" for it's an adjective and which noun or pronoun is it qualifying? . . . I'm serious, I'm not getting at you . . .

. . . it's deeper . . .

You make very little sense.

Thanks.

I'm anti-thesis.

I'm the opposite to that, it's antithesis, a theorist.

Bollocks.

Fairy nuff.

No I don't mean to be mean: The semanteme is the smallest known unit of meaning in the language . . . that's what you have still to aim for.

You mean I have not even begun to aim.

You know what I mean

Super.

That's the morpheme . . .

No the morpheme would be the actual meaning of the semanteme. To me the holders of meaning are like the holders of the meaning of the word "god" and every other word . . . They number the same as the population of earth . . .

There are two types of people: those who have been born yet, and those who have not . . .

My latest Dragons idea is little things that fly, hover on your dashboard when you switch on your heating fans . . . tiny rainbows and little helicopters . . . and it's all given away for free for Dragons, what's on offer here is the mind . . . Dashboard flyers.

Tom Tits, Sweden is an amazing place of reinventions . . . check it out on the line.

Audacity.

Better than you could ever dream of . . . that's where I live . . . in a totally self-contained luxury lofthouse penthouse stroke music studio apartment where my bed is in the music studio, right in there even though it's all one room big as a barge boat. And one flight up so more of a skyhigh snow goose ark . . . and it's an informal arrangement and we're all mowing here so I don't need to hide the smell of grass, and there is a table wide and deep and low enough to be my lowdown maproom strategy table . . . possible options . . . and on it the Police threats and the battery-powered little portable record-player . . . with A Love Supreme Live on there . . . live . . . Jesus, Mary, Jose, Gonzales, Gustavo Dudamel . . . Henri . . . Terry . . .

Some really full-on Afghani kebab guys used to real pissed folks around town make fun of me just for a minute then come around the counter and feel my jacket . . . ah the tweed . . . every country has its woollen garments . . .

You've got to stop sometime. The best thing about an unchronological, non sequential autobiography is that you can finish it by starting it.

. . . so, today, the last day of writing I have just saved a burger . . . it's
getting grilled in the pan with the handle out and at the last minute
throw in a date and some seeds. The dates turns to the tightest
sticky tough toffee of sweet taste and best of all there was
an oldold plate that had brown sauce on from a
week ago in the fridge and it comes
back to life as a lizard
might under the
soft red heat
of the ele-
ments.

    *   *   *   *

Kickstarter Heroes

Bob Slayer	Tessa Mitchell
Tim Mouncer	Anna Robertson
Conor O'Neill	Elliot Mather
Ben Sansum	Gail
Charles Ballard	Paul Freeman
Nathaniel Metcalfe	Rhodri Thomas
Guy Stevens	Anita Squires
Gregor McKinlay	Simon Willcocks
Alasdair Beckett-King	Mark Rampling
Geoff Rowe	Ems Coombes
Gerry Millar	Julian Benton
David Hall	Nick Jenkins
Ben Walters	Natalie Thoren
Alexis Dubus	Al Napp
Pat Cahill	Mark Saltmarsh
Alex Petty	Stu Coates
Alastair Smith	Tory Gillespie
Eddie French	Stuart Bourke
Annabelle Holland	Paul Bulmer
Ryan Van Winkle	Roger Langridge
Laura Hill	Andy Candler
Stephen Corrall	Norman Lovett
Graeme Armstrong	Murray Robertson
Steven	Paul Ledingham
Stuart McNicol	Whyteleafe Comedy
Stephanie	Gary Phelps
Ben Golding	Luke Tickner
Sarah Sutherland	Darrell Martin
Girvan Burnside	Stuart Orford
David Ephgrave	Lorcan Lyons
Leanne Mckie	Christy Allen
Hamish Drummond	Tracy Hickman
Christopher McEwan	Henry Cottam
Matt Kane	Thom Chesser
Dale Wilson	Justin

Paul Marks	David Munro
Laura Barton	Lee
Russell Howard	Dougie Thomson
Alan Davies	Sian Morgan
John Steel	Mike Facherty
Anna Szabo	David Robert
Andy Hunter	Sean J Ruttledge
Finlay Christie	Paul Oldfield
Lucy Gardner	Arthur Smith
David Baker	Hilary
Nicholas Troop	Russell Dalgleish
Mathew John Wardle	Kieran Brocklebank
Alexander Head	Brian Cooper
James Christopher	Greg Searby
Findlay Maciver	Tahlullah Sweetshop
Isy Suttie	Sarah Falk
Sophie Watt	Geoff Weate
David Gillen	Wendy Jane Ivers
Joe Hardy	Amy Saunders
Andrew Cassells	Simon Jones
Alistair Vale	David Paterson
Melina Clark	Sally Western
David Rule	Chris Patterson
Rahul Joshi	Richard Davidson
Matthew Harpham	Tom Dalziel
Iain McNicol	Robert Wells
Richard Davison	Rob Keelan
Mark Fisher	Carl Day
Stuart Wilson	Glenn Wool
Pete	Paul
Susy Campanale	Niall McLean
Julie-ann Laidlaw	Steven Chisholm
Billy Morris	Chris Evans
James Spencern	Jules Poullain
Tommy Mackay	Sam Poullain
Alan McNicol	Frankie Poullain
Jeff Clark	Jason Manly
Andi Woodward	Mairi Dana Ksemirdera
Nicky Hamilton-Smith	Nick Steel
Karyn Dickie	Joga Bains
Ann-Margaret Campbell	Davey Byrne

David Charles Holton	*Nick Reed*
James Richard Woroniecki	*Farah Cleret*
Craig Gillespie	*Garry Platt*
Steven Lalley	*Jason Law*
Lyle Russell	*Robert Clements*
Steve Hewitt	*David Harry*
Danny maines	*Nick Awde*
Beth Hollins	*Aidan Killian*
Jelly Green	*JonHarris*
Craig Cattell	*David Jesudason*
John Robins	*Iain Smith*
Mike Grenville	*David Chapple*
Steve Griffin	*Callum Whiteley*
Jonathan Mears	*Andrew John Hayward*
Gordon Moar	*Bernard O'Leary*
Patrick Myers	*Shirley Cheungn*
Dave Atherton	*Paul 'Dacky' Davies*
Tom Hensby	*Daphna Baram*
Alex Finch	*David Allison*